Muslims' Place in the American Public Square

Muslims' Place in the American Public Square

Hope, Fears, and Aspirations

Edited by
Zahid H. Bukhari
Sulayman S. Nyang
Mumtaz Ahmad
John L. Esposito

ALTAMIRA
PRESS

A Division of
ROWMAN & LITTLEFIELD PUBLISHERS, INC.
Walnut Creek • Lanham • New York • Toronto • Oxford

ALTAMIRA PRESS

A division of Rowman & Littlefield Publishers, Inc.
1630 North Main Street, #367
Walnut Creek, CA 94596
www.altamirapress.com

Rowman & Littlefield Publishers, Inc.
A wholly owned subsidiary of The Rowman & Littlefield Publishing Group, Inc.
4501 Forbes Boulevard, Suite 200
Lanham, MD 20706

PO Box 317
Oxford
OX2 9RU, UK

British Library Cataloguing in Publication Information Available

Library of Congress Cataloging-in-Publication Data

Muslims' place in the American public square : hope, fears, and aspirations / edited by Zahid H. Bukhari . . . [et al.].
    p. cm.
    Includes index.
    ISBN: 978-0-7591-0613-0   —ISBN 0-7591-0613-4 (pbk. : alk. paper)
    1. Muslims—United States—Social conditions. 2. United States—Ethnic rela-
tions. 3. United States—Race relations. 4. Islam—United States. 5. United States—
Religious life and customs. I. Bukhari, Zahid Hussain.
    E184.M88M87 2004
    305.6'97'0973—dc22   2003021528

Printed in the United States of America

⊗™ The paper used in this publication meets the minimum requirements of
American National Standard for Information Sciences—Permanence of Paper
for Printed Library Materials, ANSI/NISO Z39.48–1992.

Contents

Glossary of Foreign Terms

adl. Justice.

ahkam. Prescription directly taken from the Quran and Sunn.

Ahl-Dhimmah. Protected people who adhere to their faith; the people with whom a compact or covenant has been made, and particularly People of the Book; an individual of this class—namely, a free non-Muslim subject of a Muslim state.

al-aql. Reason.

al-din. Quranic term for faith in God.

alim (pl. *alims* or *ulema*). Islamic scholar; literally, "one who knows, a scholar, a scientist." Commonly used for someone who has a thorough knowledge of Islam and its sources—the Quran and the Sunnah. An important characteristic of an alim is that he or she is deeply conscious of God and stands in awe of him.

aliwa. A wooden slate used by Muslim students in West Africa.

al-munafiqun. Quranic term for hypocrites.

al-qist. A Quranic term meaning "equity"; a synonym for *adil*. It is used in the Quran, surah An-Nisa, verse 135, to underscore Allah's demand for Muslims to stand for justice.

al-wahi. Divine power of communication granted to prophets.

attieke. Food made out of seeds of manioc.

bayah. A pledge of loyalty.

boubou. A flowing gown worn by West African Muslims.

dar al-ahd. *See* dar al-Islam.

dar al-dawah. The land where Islam is propagated.

dar al-harb. The land of war.

dar al-ijabah. The land of compliance.

dar al-Islam. The land of Islam.

dar al-muahadah. The land of trade. Some writers have used this term to describe Arab Muslim presence in Brazil.

dawah. Muslim propagation of their religion.

dhan (azzan). Call to prayer.

esusu (osusu). An originally Yoruba term for community savings/credit group.

fahm. Understanding.

faqih (pl. *faqihs* or *fuqaha*). A specialist in Islamic jurisprudence (*fiqh*). A faqih can be a synonym for *alim*, meaning an Islamic scholar.

fatwa (pl. *fatwas* or *fatawa*). A juristic opinion given by an alim, mufti, mujathid, or faqih on any matter pertinent to Islamic law.

fiqh. Literally, understanding; knowledge of Islam through its laws; science of the law of Islam. The term *fiqh* is to a large extent the product of human endeavor; the Shariah is closely related to divine Revelation and knowledge that is only obtained from the Quran and the Sunnah.

hadith (pl. *hadiths* or *ahadith*). This is the oral form of the Prophetic tradition that combined with his actions in life to form the Sunnah. When the term is capitalized, it applies to the sciences dealing with the Prophet's tradition in all its aspects.

hajj. A pilgrimage to Mecca.

halal. That which is lawful (legal and allowed), as distinguished from *haram,* that which is unlawful.

halaqas. A study group or circle among Muslims in a given community.

haram. That which is forbidden and illegal under Islamic law.

hijra. Migration of Prophet Muhammad from Mecca to Medina.

hudud. Islamic penal code regarding criminal matters.

hukm. The rationale behind the legal reasoning for fatwa issued by a faqih.

ibadat. All matters relating to Muslim belief in and worship of Allah.

iddah. The term of probation incumbent upon women in consequence of a dissolution of marriage, by either divorce or death of her husband. After a divorce, the period is three months; after the death of her husband, four months and ten days—both periods being enjoined by the Quran.

ijma. The Islamic jurisprudential term relating to consensus of the Muslim community on matters relating to the teachings and practice of their faith.

ijtihad. Considering that the accepted juridical sources of Islam are valid for all time and space, ijtihad may be described as a creative but disciplined intellectual effort to derive legal rulings from those sources while taking into consideration the variables imposed by the fluctuating circumstances of Muslim society.

ijtimas. A gathering of believers.

istihsan. Juristic preference. *Istihsan* literally means "to deem something preferable." As a concept, it is close to equity in Western law.

jihad. A Quranic term that means struggle for spiritual development, on the one hand, and resistance to injustice through armed struggle, on the other. Unfortunately, *jihad* is now commonly reduced to the single meaning of "holy war," losing the concept's spiritual, intellectual, and social components.

Juma. Friday community prayer that Muslims offer weekly.

khatib. Any Muslim who is sufficiently knowledgeable to deliver a Friday sermon.

khutbah. A sermon delivered by an imam or khatib during Friday prayers.

kufir (kafir). An Islamic term for "unbeliever."

madhabs. The schools of Islamic jurisprudence.

madrasa. Muslim schools where young people are trained in Islamic sciences.

maqasid. The ultimate aims, objectives, and intents of the Shariah.

masjid. Mosque.

maslaha. A term in Islamic jurisprudence that deals with the principles of social harmony.

mizan. Balance.

muamalat. The praxis that reflects the actualization of the beliefs and teachings of the faith.

mudejares. A term used in medieval Spain to describe those Muslims who remained in Spain as vassals of the Christians, adapting themselves to their new situations but maintaining their Islamic culture and religion. In 1499, Ferdinand and Isabel decreed the forcible baptism into Christianity of all Muslims and Jews and the conversion of mosques and synagogues into churches.

muhaditthun (muhaditt). Those Muslim scholars who specialize in the study of the Hadiths.

muhajirun. The Muslim refugees who fled to Medina to join the ranks of Prophet Muhammad.

mujtahid. The Muslim scholar who is sufficiently knowledgeable in Islamic law to issue a fatwa (ruling) after going through the process of ijtihad.

musallahs (pl. of *musalaah*). A place of worship for Muslims.

qadi. A Muslim judge who arbitrates on civil cases involving marriage, inheritance, and other domestic matters. The role of the qadi was limited by the colonial experience, which curtailed the role and place of Islamic law in most Muslim societies.

qiyas. A Muslim legal term that denotes the use of analogical reasoning in arriving at a fatwa.

salat. Muslim prayer that is performed five times daily.

sati (also written as *suttee*). The traditional Hindu practice of self-immolation by women on the funeral pyre of their deceased husband.

sawa. An Arabic word meaning "coming together."

shahadah. An affirmation of belief in God and in the mission of Prophet Muhammad. Anyone who makes such a declaration in the presence of Muslim witnesses is a Muslim.

Shariah. The collective name for all the laws of Islam. It includes all the religious, liturgical, ethical, and jurisprudential systems.

shura. A Quranic term that denotes the application of the principles of consultation in decision making among Muslims.

Sunnah. Literally, "a clear path or beaten path." Referred to whatever the Prophet said, did, agreed to, or condemned. The Sunnah is the second source of the Shariah after the Quran.

talfiq. A concoction or piecing together.

taqlid. Uncritical adoption or imitation and following of a particular scholar or school of thought.

tawhid. The act of affirming that Allah is the One and only God, the absolute, transcendent, Creator, the Lord, and Master of the worlds.

tazkiyah. Purification.

tijani. A follower of a Sufi order named after its Algerian-born founder Shaykh Ahmad Tijani, who spent most of his life in Morocco.

tontine. A French term used in West Africa for a community savings and credit group.

ulama (pl. of *alim*). The collective name for the members of the learned class in Muslim society.

ummah. A Quranic term that describes the community of Muslims.

umran. Taken to mean the cultivation and development of the world as the arena harnessed for discharging humans' mission and the crucible for their trials, accountability, and development.

uqubat. An Islamic legal term used in connection with the penal code of hadd. The knowledge of fiqh is divided into four divisions: ibadad, munakahat, muamalat, and uqubat.

usul (sing. *asl*). Principles, sources, origins.

usul al-fiqh. The science of Islamic jurisprudence, philosophy of law; the methodology of deriving laws from the sources of Islam and of establishing their juristic and constitutional validity.

zakah. A Quranic term that describes the obligatory charity, one of the Five Pillars of Islam, enjoined upon Muslims.

Foreword

Within a matter of decades, the demographic landscape of the West, Europe, as well as North America has changed significantly. Though for some time the second largest of the world's religions, Islam had remained invisible on the cognitive maps of most Americans, whose first major encounters with the Muslim world were the Arab oil embargo of 1973 and the Iranian revolution of 1978–1979. However, by the beginning of the twenty-first century, Islam and Muslims represent the second largest religion in Europe and the third in North America.

Islam in America is a mosaic of many ethnic, racial, and national groups. The majority of Muslims are immigrants or their descendents from various parts of the world and African Americans. Many immigrants came to the United States in pursuit of political, religious, and economic freedom or educational and professional opportunities. African American Muslims, like many African Americans in general, seek greater political, social, and economic equality and justice.

Muslims today are part of the religious and demographic mosaic of the United States: neighbors, colleagues, and fellow citizens in America's multireligious and multicultural society. Despite this reality, knowledge and information about Muslims in America and, in particular, Muslims in the American public square are minimal as compared to that regarding Judaism and Christianity and their many organizations and institutions. Indeed, some of the most basic information readily available in libraries and on the Internet, such as directories or lists of major religious institutions (mosques, Islamic centers, and schools), religious leaders, and scholars and demographic data, so abundant for other Abrahamic faiths, has been nonexistent or woefully inadequate.

The Center for Muslim-Christian Understanding (CMCU) was founded in 1993 to address relations between Islam and the West. However, within our first years of existence, we quickly moved to an emphasis on two foci, Islam and the West and Islam in the West, for major Muslim communities were no longer restricted to Muslim countries but could now be found in New York, Detroit, Los Angeles, and Washington as in Marseilles, Paris, London, and Berlin. We were delighted when the opportunity arose to include Project MAPS, Muslims in the American Public Square, as one of the center's major programs, and thus CMCU could contribute to a better understanding of and the development of the Muslim community(ies) in America. The project, funded by The Pew Charitable Trusts and based at the CMCU, Georgetown University, has been a major attempt to correct this problem.

From the beginning, I knew that the critical ingredient would be the leadership of MAPS. Sulayman Nyang and Zahid Bukhari proved to be ideal directors, working closely with a distinguished advisory board. Sulayman and Zahid were tireless in traveling across the United States, talking with Muslim religious and community leaders as well as meeting with intellectuals and professionals to assure maximum input and participation in the project. Their focus group meetings in selected cities attracted participants from a cross section of the community. As I witnessed firsthand, discussions were open, frank (sometimes very frank!), and productive, producing the data and insights so important to this project. At the same time, Zahid and his assistants, Ayub Alam and Faisal Islam, worked long hours, often well into the evening, out of their offices at the center, the "command post" for the MAPS project. As word spread regarding the project, the MAPS program was swamped with inquiries from Muslims across the country to scholars and the media. MAPS quickly set up a first-class website and within a short period of time began to produce newsletter reports on MAPS and its many activities and projects.

The vision, commitment, and success of MAPS are reflected in the significant number of projects and products produced, from directories of leaders and institutions to a major poll of American Muslims and two major books, including *Muslims' Place in the American Public Square: Hope, Fears, and Aspirations*, the first of two MAPS volumes. In addition to studies that deal with demographic realities, the volume addresses a series of issues that have been integral to the experience of Muslims in America, questions of faith and identity, religious pluralism, political participation, religious institutions, and organizational leadership.

Muslims struggle with the nature of their identity, the relationship of faith to national identity and American culture. The identity of the community and, more specifically, the formation of a new identity in the United States have posed many questions: the relationship of faith to culture, Muslim life as a minority in a non-Muslim secular state, religious pluralism, political participation, the role of the Shari'ah in Muslim life, responses to American foreign policies that negatively impact on Muslim countries and societies, and participation as American citizens in wars against Muslim countries or populations.

At the dawn of the twenty-first century, the American Muslim community seemed well along on the path to mainstreaming in American society and institution building. The aftermath of September 11, 2001, has challenged many of these successes and once again raised fundamental questions about Islam, the faith, and identity of American Muslims and their place in American society. *Muslims' Place in the American Public Square: Hope, Fears, and Aspirations* provides a much-needed perspective on American Muslims and their experiences and place in American religious history and in the public square.

John L. Esposito

Introduction

Hope, Fears, and Aspirations: Muslims in the American Public Square

This volume presents the findings of the Muslims in the American Public Square (MAPS) research project funded by The Pew Charitable Trusts based in Philadelphia, Pennsylvania. It provides new theoretical perspectives and empirical data on the American Muslim community, based on the research findings of commissioned scholars working with the MAPS project. This research project was based for three years at the Center for Muslim-Christian Understanding at the School of Foreign Service of Georgetown University as part of a larger grant that funded seven ethnoreligious projects to study religion in the "American Public Square." Among the religious communities studied through these major grants were mainline Protestant churches, Catholics, Evangelical Christians, Jews, Black Christian churches, Hispanic churches, and Muslims.

In organizing this research project, we decided to focus on five areas of interest that could help us understand the hopes, fears, and aspirations of the American Muslims. For this and other related reasons, each author was asked to address some aspect of the following issues: theoretical perspectives on the Muslim experience in the United States, the historical and sociological understanding of the mainstreaming of Muslims, the question of Islam and the Black experience, and the demographic and behavioral aspects in our quest to locate Muslims in the American landscape. Four chapters deal with the theoretical issues relating to the Muslim experience in America. Three take on the task of understanding the mainstreaming of the American Muslims. And three other chapters look at the issue of race and Islam as part of the American dilemma.

We believe that the issues raised here could help policymakers and the leaders of the Muslim communities around the country to focus on the needs of this minority at a critical moment in its history. Even though the authors of this volume and their editors embarked on this project without any idea that their work would be greatly affected by international events, the tragedy of September 11, 2001, has magnified the significance of our study. Indeed, both U.S. policymakers and Muslim leaders around the country are likely to gain better understanding of the diversity and complexities of this young religious community—what is now called the new kid on the religious block of America.

Before we introduce the research findings of the commissioned scholars in this volume, let us provide the historical background to the rise and development of Islam as a religion and a community in the United States. Such a recounting of the history of Muslims in this country would help us understand the nature, diversity, and complexity of this third branch of the Abrahamic tree of faiths in the United States. It will also give us the opportunity to assess the state of research before we undertook this task and the contributions of this volume to the field of American Muslim studies, a disciplinary field that is still at an embryonic stage of development.

American Muslims have become an integral part of the cultural landscape of this part of the Western Hemisphere. Their history is now inseparable from that of their new homeland. At least 6.5 million Muslims live in the United States, drawn from almost all the countries with a Muslim majority or minority around the world. Such ethnic and regional representation is more evident in big cities than in small-town America. Specifically, more Arabs are living on the eastern seaboard of continental North America than in any non-Arab country of the Islamic world. One can also say that there are more Hyderabadis living in the United States than anywhere else outside South Asia. We can further illustrate this Muslim diversity by saying that it is only in the North American Muslim experience that one finds a white American Muslim standing in prayer next to an Indonesian Muslim, a Palestinian Muslim next to a Pakistani, an African American next to a Senegambian or a Syrian, a Lebanese next to a Bosnian Muslim, a Trinidadian Muslim next to an Indian or Egyptian Muslim. These are, in Muslim parlance, *ayatullah* (signs of Allah) that North American Muslims must learn to appreciate as part of their historical experience in this part of the world.

Since 1999, the Muslims in the American Public Square project has undertaken the task of documenting the Muslim community in an unprecedented manner. Building on what has been done by scholars in the field and drawing upon the resources of the Muslim communities around the country, Project MAPS has succeeded in accomplishing the following: the collection of scholarly pieces from leading students of Islam in America in two volumes, the creation of a new directory of mosques and Islamic centers around the United States, the publication of a *Who's Who among Amer-*

ican Muslims, and a website that provides the findings of this research to the vast body of Internet surfers around the world. Before we discuss the content of the present volume, let us give a brief history of Islam in the United States and show how this project benefited from the research efforts of those before us and also how it can contribute to the further development of the literature on Islam in the United States.

FIVE STAGES IN THE HISTORY OF ISLAM IN THE UNITED STATES

The history of Islam in the United States can be divided into five distinct phases: the pre-Columbian, the antebellum, the postbellum up to World War II, the postwar period up to September 11, 2001, and the post-9/11 periods. In writing about the American Muslim, scholars must consider the varying degrees of documentation of the Muslim experience during these different periods.

The data available about the pre-Columbian Muslim presence in the Americas are limited to a few sources cited repeatedly in the literature. No one knows when the first Muslim landed in the United States. There is, however, the story about Mansa Abubakar II, of Mali, who traveled across the Atlantic Ocean to reach what would later be called the New World. According to Muslim medieval writer al-Umari, Mansa Musa of Mali, on his way to Mecca to perform the *hajj* (religious pilgrimage), told Egyptian emir Abul Hassan Ali Ibn Amir Hajib that his predecessor had "equipped 200 ships filled with men and the same number equipped with gold, water and provisions enough to last them for years, and he said to the men not to return until they reach the end of the Atlantic Ocean or their provisions and water give out." When one ship returned and its captain reported that the other vessels disappeared after having entered a river with a powerful current, Mansa Abubakar decided to undertake the journey himself. He, Mansa Abubakar, "got ready 2,000 ships, 1,000 for himself and the men he took with him and 1,000 for water and provisions. He left me, Mansa Musa, to deputize for him and embarked on the Atlantic Ocean with his men."[1]

Apart from this Arabic source, we have no other evidence from the African and Arabic sources to support this claim about any Muslim presence in the New World. The only other source that comes from a linguistic analysis of the languages of native Americans living in what is now Mexico is that provided by Leo Wiener, a Harvard University professor of linguistics who studied the languages of the native peoples of that part of the Americas. In his *Africa and the Discovery of America,*[2] he argues for the possible cultural interaction between the native people of Mexico and the Muslims of northwest Africa.

In the Columbian period, some evidence indicates Muslim involvement in that exploration of the Americas. Some scholars have speculated that

Columbus's voyage itself may have been influenced by the Arab scholar Al-Idrissi, an adviser to Sicily's King Roger in the thirteenth century. According to one historian, Columbus had aboard his ship a copy of Al-Idrissi's work that told of the discovery of the new continent by eight Muslim explorers. Also on board was an interpreter to read the document, an Arab "renegade" converted to Catholicism named Louis Torres. Muslim tradition holds that Moors came to the New World before Columbus, but there seems to have been few in the United States before the 1850s except for the thousands of West African slaves who came through the Middle Passage.[3]

The arrival of Muslims in the United States in the later periods is more documented than that of the earlier periods. In *African Muslims in Antebellum America: A Source Book,* Allan D. Austin provides an excellent documentation of this period by bringing together literary fragments written by contemporaries of the slave trade.[4] Michael Gomez's *Exchanging Our Country Marks: The Transformation of African Identities in Colonial and Anti-bellum South* and Bryan Turner's *Islam in the Black Experience* add immeasurably to our understanding of the Islamic experience in the United States.[5] Gomez addresses an important issue of identity change in the peculiar case of the American slaves from Africa. Not only does his research shed ample light on the de-Africanization processes in the southern plantations, but he also documents historically the development and solidification of a new African American identity without any significant Islamic content. Turner's contribution to our understanding of the relationship between Islam and the Black experience has made it clear that there are many historical, intellectual, and moral threads linking Islam and Muslims to the larger American drama in the nineteenth and twentieth centuries. Even some Marxist scholars and intellectuals, such as Cedric Robinson,[6] are now arguing for a historical connection among Islam, the rise of the Portuguese state, and the origins of the "Negro" in the New World. We now know from the writings of Philip D. Curtin,[7] Allan D. Austin, and others that many American contemporaries of Muslim slaves recorded their experiences before the end of the slave trade.

Documentation for the third stage, the postbellum period up to the end of World War II, is provided in the literature on various ethnic and national groups that immigrated to the United States. Materials on Arab immigration have become plentiful because of the research done by Arab Muslims and Christians. One of the best collections of writings related to the different ethnic and national groups that settled in the United States is found in *American Immigrant Cultures: Builders of A Nation,* edited by David Levinson and Melvin Ember.[8] Those who are interested in the history of almost all the groups that came to America as immigrants since the founding of the Republic will find this encyclopedic work most useful.

Since the vast majority of Arabs who came here were Christians, much of what was written before the end of World War II centered on the Christian Arab experience.[9] The advent of the Cold War added a Muslim presence to the Arab American experience. *Islam in North America: A Source Book,* edited by Michael A. Koszegi and J. Gordon Melton, provides valuable bibliographic data for researchers interested in tracing the history of the Muslim and Arab presence in the United States.[10] With respect to the coming of Arab Muslims to the United States, the pioneering work of Abdo A. El-Kholy[11] offers a sociological analysis of the state of affairs among the first, second, and third generation of Arab Americans. These contributions would be multiplied manyfold by Arab and non-Arab Americans who went on to write their master's theses and doctoral dissertations on some aspects of the Arab/Muslim experience in the United States.

Building on the work of others before her and collecting and editing several volumes on the Islamic experience in the United States, the pioneering research of Yvonne Y. Haddad and her collaborators has also added to our understanding of the Muslim/Arab experience.[12] Much has appeared, yet much remains to be unveiled and discussed. Three significant things happen during the fourth period (the end of World War II to the start of the Cold War): (1) the opening of America to third world countries; (2) the decision of American leaders to host the newly created United Nations in Manhattan, New York; and (3) the granting of scholarships and financial support to a large number of students from Africa, Asia, and Latin America to study in American centers of learning, a part of the larger Cold War–based cultural rivalry with the then–Soviet Union.

The events of this moment in U.S. history were unprecedented. It was indeed a radical departure from previous U.S. immigration laws and regulations. Because of the two world wars, American cosmopolitanism developed to higher levels, and American willingness to engage the wider world broke with the tradition of isolationism that had brought a sad end to the League of Nations. With the Allied triumph in both the Atlantic and the Pacific theaters of World War II, American self-confidence created the conditions for greater entanglement with the rest of the world. Muslim peoples would soon become beneficiaries of this change of attitude. Because of this turn of events, best exemplified by the change of immigration laws under the Johnson administration, thousands of Muslim men and women entered American universities. Many studies deal with this period. Sulayman S. Nyang's *Islam in the United States of America* (1999), Jane I. Smith's *Islam in America* (1999), Robert Dannin's *Black Pilgrimage to Islam* (2002), Yvonne Haddad and Jane I. Smith's edited volume *Muslim Minorities in the West* (2002), Baha Abu-Laban and Michael W. Suleiman's *Arab Americans: Continuity and Change* (1989), and Sameer Y. Abraham and Nabeel Abraham's edited volume *Arabs in the New World: Studies on Arab-American*

Communities (1983) are just a few of the growing number of books on the Muslim experience in the United States.[13] Although these and other works have covered much ground in our understanding of American Muslims, there are still many gaps in the literature. Project MAPS was undertaken to address some of the burning issues about this period in U.S. Muslim history. There is a growing feeling among scholars that the much-needed synthesis of the ever-growing literature published by Muslims and non-Muslims about the Muslim presence in the United States is still begging for attention.

The fifth phase in the development of Islam in the United States begins with the events of 9/11. This day will never be forgotten by Americans and Muslims around the world. If the preceding period was the beginning of Muslim engagement with American society, the tragic events of 9/11 have distinctively separated this period from all other times in the history of America's relations with the Muslim world. Although some scholars have suggested that America's hostile encounter with certain Muslims goes back to the days when the U.S. Navy was deployed along the north African coast to deal effectively with the challenges from the Barbary pirates of the early postindependence era in the United States, evidence suggests that this new era in America's relations with the Muslim World is unique and unprecedented. For the first time in U.S. history, this country was attacked by a band of terrorists who ruled no state and whose activities fall outside the pale of international law and convention. The guilt by association that the perpetrators of 9/11 would like the American people to make against their fellow Americans who believe in Islam has created tensions on both sides. Also, the events of 9/11 have revised the patterns of assimilation of immigrants into American culture and society. This change has made life difficult for many Muslims who are caught in the cross fire between the terrorist acts of men like Osama bin Laden and his followers, on the one hand, and the new restrictions on civil liberties purported to combat these dangerous elements in society, on the other. Although the immigrants of the generation of Adams and Jefferson faced the stringent laws identified with the Alien and Sedition Act of that period, the effects of globalization have made this new state of affairs more complex, dangerous, and untidy. Yet, American Muslims are working with the authorities to deal effectively with such challenges. A search through the *Bell and Howell's Index* would reveal hundreds if not thousands of articles published in the major national newspapers detailing these crises and capturing the domestic and international ramifications of this American tragedy.

In concluding this brief review of the five stages in the history of Islam in the United States, we can make the following points about the events of the past and the challenges of the present in as far as they influence the lives and times of the ordinary American Muslims who have chosen to live permanently in this country. First, Islam has a long historical connection with this land, but it was only until the last century that it took roots here. Slavery and the toll of the Middle Passage apparently conspired to deracinate African Muslims through the Kunta Kinte destiny. Second, the literature shows that African American Muslims generally see the religion of Islam as a spiritual and moral force that could enhance their ability to deal effectively and meaningfully with challenges facing them in a society. Third, there is compelling evidence to say that the Cold War changed American society profoundly, to the point of changing the ethnic and racial mix of the society forever. This radical alteration of the ethnic landscape in America was one of the unintended consequences of the Cold War. Muslims and members of non-European religions have now graduated from being the "Children of the Cold War" to new partners in the construction of the emerging global American civilization. Fourth, American leadership of the world, which dates back to the end of World War I but became most evident to all Americans after World War II, has come to a crossroads after 9/11. There is presently a moral and political challenge facing our leaders. We must either mobilize the moral and physical resources of the planet with diplomatic aplomb and political sagacity to contain the havoc of the global terrorists, or we must grope clumsily for a way out of this present predicament. The manner in which our leaders face the present crisis in domestic homeland security and international politics will eventually decide the fate of American Muslims in the United States and the pattern of relationship between the United States and the Muslim world.

THEORETICAL PERSPECTIVES ON THE MUSLIM EXPERIENCE IN THE UNITED STATES

The first chapter of Part I is the work of Taha Jabir Al-Alwani, a distinguished Islamic jurist known for his attempts to develop in North America a new understanding of Shariah, the jurisprudential body of knowledge that has guided Muslim behavior since the days of early Islam. According to Al-Alwani, the American Muslims and their counterparts elsewhere in the Western world have found themselves under conditions and circumstances that are radically different from what existed at the time of the Prophet and even in Muslim societies of the contemporary era.

Al-Alwani's objective here is not to formulate some specific legal injunctions that the Muslim minorities are required to follow but to provide a methodology for the development of a new approach that combines theology, ethics, and law into a coherent structure capable of meeting the demands of modern times. Being chairman of the Fiqh Council of North America, he is well aware of the challenges faced by Muslims in the New

World, especially when it comes to the application of traditional Islamic juristic formulations in a non-Islamic environment. The five recognized schools of Islamic laws were developed in a context of Muslim political power, when Muslims lived in societies where they constituted majorities and could call upon the coercive power of the state to enforce Islamic laws pertaining to marriage, divorce, inheritance, contracts, trade and commerce, and the penal code. In the contemporary globalized world, however, when citizenship has become "mobile" and "flexible," large number of Muslim populations have moved from their traditional abode of Muslim majority areas and have settled in countries of Western Europe and North America. Given these new developments, a theology and law developed by classical Islamic theologians and jurists for a "sovereign *ummah*" (Muslim community) cannot answer the needs, requirements, and questions of Muslims living as a minority in Western societies. This new situation calls for a systematic formulation of a new *fiqh* (knowledge of the practical rules of the Shari'ah), what Al-Alwani calls "the fiqh of minority." He calls for a "new *ijtihad*" (independent and intellectual reasoning) to resolve the issues that arise from the current divergence between the inadequacy of the traditional formulations of Islamic theology and law, on the one hand, and the special circumstances of Muslim communities living as minorities in Western societies, on the other.

The second chapter is written by Omar Khalidi, an Indian American Muslim who hailed from Hyderabad and has lived and worked on the MIT campus in Cambridge, Massachusetts, for many years. He addresses the question of the Muslim identity in a society where Muslims are a minority yet would not like to dissolve in the American ocean of names and faces. Drawing from historical and legal materials about the history of Islamic minorities in Muslim Spain, British and postcolonial India, the Balkans, and the former Soviet Union, Khalidi provides a historical tour of the Islamic past by discussing the intellectual origins of the ideas of *dar al-Islam* (the land of Islam) and *dar al-harb* (the land of war). Pointing to the fact that the dichotomization of the world of humans into these two categories has not always been true, and that there have been moments in Islamic history when Muslims found themselves living beyond the pale of Islam, Khalidi presents a number of arguments made by Islamic jurists from the Sunni and Shia traditions who opined that living in dar al-harb is not allowed. However, his research has also brought to his attention the varying opinions of different Shia and Sunni *fuqaha* (jurists) who maintain that whenever and wherever it occurs, those believers who find themselves in such a moral quandary must accept the limitations to their Islamicity and to their eligibility of protection from Islamic authority. Among the Sunni jurists, it appears that the Hanafi school of thought has been most accommodating on this issue of Muslims living as a minority in a non-Islamic territory.

Besides this point concerning the different fiqhi positions of the leaders of the Islamic *madhabs* (schools of legal thought), Khalidi looks at the manner in which Muslim legal minds grapple with the challenges posed to Muslims by the loss of Mughal power and the primacy of British law in colonial India. According to his findings, a body of Muslim legal opinion developed during this time that said to Indian Muslims that it was acceptable to live under the British Crown while their rights to worship their God was not threatened. Yet, in pointing to this fact, Khalidi shows clearly that there were other opinions among the Muslims in India who simply could not accept the hegemony of British power, and the persons so disturbed opted to immigrate to Afghanistan. The author also looks at the situation in postindependence India and found that Muslims could not secure their rights as a religious minority because the constitution of 1950, like almost all liberal democracies, confers citizenship to individuals and not to groups, except the scheduled castes and indigenous peoples. He argues that the Muslim minority in India must accept the secular foundations of the society and negotiate for their rights within the framework of the politics of bargaining and compromise rooted in Indian secularism. He discusses the Shah Bano Begum case and the Adoption of Children Bill (1972) in India that created a political and religious crisis in the Indian body politic. After a careful examination of the evidence, Khalidi concludes that the Indian liberal democratic system does provide some constitutional guarantees to Muslims. However, he, like many other writers on India, expresses some doubt about the politics of the Bharatiya Janata Party (BJP) and its implication for the freedom and rights of religious minorities such as the Muslims.

Aminah Beverly McCloud's chapter addresses yet another theoretical question about the American Muslim community. Her focus is on the nature of the Muslim community and the issue of intergroup relations between the native-born Americans who converted or reverted to Islam and the immigrant Muslims who, self-selecting, opted for American citizenship or permanent home in the country. She finds that until the end of World War II when American immigration laws changed to allow more non-Whites into the country, the United States was basically a White, Christian country. This change of policy, according to McCloud, not only made America a more diverse place but helped create in "[t]he last decade of the twentieth century . . . a thriving, vibrant, diverse, and expanding American Muslim community." She believes that the success was possible because of the determination of the leaders of the different communities of Muslims to deal with the tensions that exist within their circles.

Focusing on the discourse of the various groups among the Muslims, and taking into account the tensions visible to the inquiring scholar, McCloud identifies two factors as points of conflict. She traces the roots of this tension to the nature of their discourse, to their cross-cultural communication, and to the issues surrounding their definition of Islam in America. After a brief explanation of the theoretical understanding of discourse among human groups, she analyzes how and why the Arab, South Asian, African, African American, and Hispanic Muslims have experienced difficulties in relating to one another. She traces the root cause of their problem to cultural misunderstanding and to the sociological phenomenon Sulayman S. Nyang calls "islandization" of Muslims as their numbers increase and they begin to develop clusters in a given locality.

McCloud argues that, though American Muslims of diverse ethnic background do commingle in the mosques during the celebrations of Eid and at Juma prayers, the social distance between them persists and that the lack of communication beyond this space has led to a sense of alienation from one another. Her observation of this phenomenon leads her to conclude that "[v]arious competitions, internal and external, constitute the factors driving the experience of living as Muslims in U.S. society." She believes that the preoccupation of the various Muslim groups with their own internal and external concern has to some extent shaped their self-definition and self-perceptions as Muslims living in the United States. To help shed some light on this dynamic, the professor puts forth a new way of classifying these large groups of Muslims into "old" American Muslims and "new" American Muslims. Sensing that these two major groups of American Muslims are internally subdivided into first, second, and third generations and that there are many points of convergence between them, she makes the case that the divergent concerns between the two communities are best expressed in the differing attitudes toward American social problems and international issues.

To McCloud, the so-called newer Americans (the immigrants) are "simultaneously diverted by heated discussions on the historical and conceptual frameworks surrounding Muslim thinking on living in the 'West' and the current discourses on the ideas of democracy and the values of Islam." Older Americans (native-born Americans), according to her analysis, are "immersed in working on pervasive, constant American social ills such as rising rates of incarceration, homelessness, gang violence, teen pregnancies, rising numbers of AIDS-HIV cases, lack of health care for the poor, and issues of employment." She maintains that the older American Muslims are also very sensitive to the general tendency between both the immigrant Muslims and the larger society to equate Islam only with Arabs and foreigners.

In her analysis of the newer American Muslims, McCloud notes that this part of the Muslim community in America has many issues that bracket them from the native-born. For example, they are very much involved with the political and cultural problems of their countries of origin; they are still not totally separated from what some scholars called the myth of return; and though they take full advantage of the educational opportunities of the United States, they are still preoccupied with the idea of changing things back home. She sees this long-standing fascination with things back home in the manner in which certain institutions are created to meet those needs. In her view, major drawbacks facing the immigrant Muslims are their lack of adequate attention to the understanding of their cultural and political environment as well as their failure to pay attention to the social problems in their American communities. McCloud traces the sources of some of these issues back to the unfinished business of American Muslim immigrants grappling with the age-old problem of living in dar al-Islam and dar al-harb. Yet she acknowledges the tremendous impact of 9/11 on the American Muslim consciousness. Not only has this tragedy changed the United States forever, but it has created greater opportunities for Americans to hear and know more about Islam and Muslims; Muslims themselves "have sped up their interactions and are beginning in earnest to attempt to know one another." But the author also notes the fact that "[t]hese events have nevertheless hardened further the hearts of those who see Islam and Muslims as a threat to their 'freedoms, rights, and peacefulness' of the United States."

McCloud's chapter touches on a number of issues that complement and reinforce in a different way some of the statements and arguments reflected in chapters 1 and 2. What brings these three chapters together is the fund of theoretical and empirical data they present to our readers who are trying to understand the historical development of Islam in the United States. By plumbing the depths of the historical data about Muslims in majority and minority situations, these three chapters help lay the foundation for the next chapter, by M. A. Muqtedar Khan.

Writing on the question of living on the borderlines between Islam and the West, Khan grapples with a number of conceptual and practical issues that confront the modern Muslims in general and American Muslims in particular. Taking the debate about the clash of civilizations as a point of departure, and working on the assumption that what Samuel Huntington calls a clash is not actually so, Khan argues that this thesis and discourse have "essentially corrupted the American perception of reality and presented it with a deadly option of waging a new global cold and hot war against the entire religion of Islam, nearly fifty-five states, and one-fourth of the world's population." To Khan, the Huntington thesis seems like a "heavy ideological spin" that presents the Palestine struggle in the Middle East, the Kashmiri struggle for freedom, the Algerian struggle for self-determination, the Bosnian struggle for dignity, the Egyptian struggle for authenticity, and the Islamic revolution in Iran against the monarchy "as an attempt by fanatical, essentially evil Muslims to terrorize the world in an attempt to destroy the West and its democratic and liberal ideals."

Khan believes that both the West and the Muslim world are now witnessing the rise to power and influence of the groups he calls the idealists, as opposed to the realists. According to him, the power of the idealists in the United States has become manifest in the field of foreign policy, whereas the power of the idealists in the Muslim world is evident in the present attempt by leaders like President Khatami to build a bridge of reconciliation with the West through intercivilizational dialogue. He also believes that the differences between the idealist and the realist perspectives among Muslims "have had a very profound impact in the way Muslims construct their identity today." Building upon the ideas of other scholars who have historically identified those Muslims who are fascinated with Western ideas as modernists or Islamic liberals, and accepting the notion that those Muslims who opposed Western ideas about modernization are fundamentalists, Khan concedes the validity of both perspectives while criticizing them for their lack of balance. He further argues that "[b]oth elements are to some extent valid and even necessary but only as supplements to a dominant discourse that is both balanced and constructive."

After making these points about the idealists and realists on both sides of the divide between the West and the Muslim World, Khan looks at the question of intercivilizational dialogue. Stressing the fact that such a dialogue is being conducted under circumstances of power differentiation between the two parties, he argues that two hundred years of colonial rule in the Muslim World have indeed transformed the Muslim self-image and self-confidence through the rearranging of the Muslim mental furniture. Added to this pedagogical transformation and cultural deracination are the political disfigurement and balkanization of the Muslim World, especially in the Middle East. It is against this background that Khan tries to understand the discourse between the American Muslims and their adopted country. Arguing from the point of view that Islam and Muslims share much in common with the Western peoples, but realistically recognizing the fact that America and the West exercise control over "the mechanisms of meaning—media, academia, international forums," Khan locates the root cause of the present antagonism on the doorsteps of the elites from the opposing civilizations. The Manichean logic of the two camps has not shown any willingness to accept that the world is not necessarily black and white and that points of convergence and divergence exist. In his view, the power differentials have conspired to make the dialogue not a call for constructive engagement but an opportunity to intimidate the weak and the powerless. In this state of confusion and uncertainly, Khan argues that the emergence of a knowing elite is the silver lining in the present dark cloud. Such men and women have changed the intellectual climate in the Muslim World and beyond to such an extent that "the idea [that] Islam is the solution is gradually bringing political cohesion and moral rigor to growing legions of Islamists." Convinced that there will not be any Marshall Plan for Muslims and no special relationship with the United States as enjoyed by Israel, Khan views the future of Islam in the West and in the Muslim World with guarded optimism. His opportunism is centered on the emergence of the "knowing elites" who have transformed themselves to such an extent that more of them "are comfortable with Prophet Muhammad and Karl Marx, with Ibn Khaldun and Immanuel Kant, Habermas and Ibn Hanbal, and Foucault and Farabi on their shelves than their counterparts from the West."

In analyzing the Muslim presence in the United States after this long discourse on the relationship between the West and the Muslim world, Khan offers a number of conclusions about the nature of the American Muslim experience, describing where he thinks things are heading for Muslims and others in the society. He contends that those Muslims who still have divided loyalties between their adopted country and their country of origin are definitely caught in the cross fire between the antagonists of the clash of civilization thesis. He further argues that whereas intercivilizational dialogue is being initiated by leaders such as Iranian president Khatami, American Muslims are working at the interfaith level. He attributes this state of affairs to the lack of a monolithic conception of the West, a point similar to that of McCloud in her discourse on the dialectics between native-born Muslims and their immigrant counterparts. Like McCloud, Khan also believes that the divergent opinions on and attitudes toward America and the West among the Muslims in the United States have, broadly speaking, divided them between those who see America as a source of moral responsibility and enlightened political process and those who see it as a colonial power and the root cause of Muslim rage and economic and political underdevelopment.

Using the idealists and realists categories developed earlier to differentiate between those national Muslim organizations that are willing to engage America and others unwilling to do so, Khan concludes that these idealists have succeeded in taking full advantage of the U.S. constitutional guarantees to create an Islamic identity for themselves in the United States. In his view, they have not only outmaneuvered the realists (a code name for Islamic fundamentalists and extremists) but have also marginalized them to their small dreamland of Khalifornia. This positive note in the final pages of his essay leads one to conclude that he shares the notion with many Muslims and Muslim-friendly Americans that, though the present predicament of the American Muslims has put them in a fishbowl to be observed meticulously by their fellow Americans and others, the community will eventually weather the current storm and stake their claims successfully in American society. We should also remember his admonition that such an eventuality is going to depend primarily on Muslim understanding of the West and Western understanding of Islam and their compatriots who have chosen to hitch their historical wagon to this metaphysical star of divine guidance.

THE MAINSTREAMING OF AMERICAN MUSLIMS: HISTORICAL AND SOCIOLOGICAL UNDERSTANDING

The first chapter in Part II is written by Ali Mazrui. He addresses the question of Muslim identity in the United States, with special reference to the points of convergence and divergence between the American Muslim experience, on the one hand, and those of the Black American and the Jewish American, on the other. Taking a comparative view of the matter, Mazrui divides his chapter as follows: (1) Comparative Identity and the Jewish Question; (2) Comparative Identity and the Africana Question; (3) Toward Reengaging Muslims and Blacks; (4) In Search of Electoral Carrots and Sticks; (5) Between Political Values and a Moral Code; (6) Between Ideology and Pragmatism; (7) American Islam: Immigrant and Home-Grown. Under each of these headings, he tries to show the paradoxes and ironies in the Muslim experience in America. The first thesis of this chapter is that a comparative approach to understanding the Muslim experience yields a number of insights into the divergent patterns of engagement and assimilation into American society. To Mazrui, an examination of the historical record of the Black American and the Jewish experiences provides an opportunity for American Muslims to see not only how the community is drawn from the diverse races in the society but how also the differential patterns of assimilating and coping in American society could suggest, if not present, models or examples to be studied, understood, and replicated if and whenever necessary.

In elaborating on his argument for a comparative approach, Mazrui reminds us that American Muslims are now almost as many as the Jewish population in the United States. However, he quickly adds that, though the demographic balance is heading toward parity, the political clout enjoyed by the Jewish community is not likely to be matched by the Muslims in the future because of many contradictions in the Muslim community and because of the embryonic nature of the community itself. Many points raised here are familiar to those who have read collections of Mazruiana writings dealing with the Africana experience nationally and internationally. He has stated here and elsewhere that "Muslims in the United States face three cultural crises relevant to their roles as citizens: the crisis of identity, the crisis of participation, and the crisis of values and code of conduct." He believes the crisis of identity of the Muslims in America "involves their determining who they are and how to reconcile their multiple allegiances." The crisis of participation involves decisions about political participation and community life.

Equally important in this set of crises is the crisis of values, which is related to the participation of Muslims in the moral economy of American society.

What is striking about this chapter is how Mazrui has identified many points of convergence and divergence between the Muslim experience and the Jewish or Black experience. He finds that Jews are more politically active in the democratic process, and because of their successes in other areas of life, they have replicated politically what they achieved socially. In other words, Mazrui believes that Muslim self-study should lead them to understand that the politics of numbers is good, but the source of power lies in the ability to mobilize and institutionalize statistical advantage through an effective channeling of votes, cash, and political lobbying resources. He sees a parallel between the present political marginality of a great number of Black voters and the Muslim community. He notes that there are differences between the Black experience and the Muslim experience, although a sizable number of the Muslim communities are from the African American segment of U.S. society. What is a major difference between the Islamically defined community of believers and the racially defined Black community is their divergent attitudes toward American politics and their differing responses to community issues. As has already been stated by both McCloud and Khan in their respective chapters, Mazrui also believes that one point of divergence between the immigrant Muslim community and the Black members of the Muslim community is their foreign policy interest. Except for the case of apartheid South Africa when Muslim organizations such as the American Muslim Council (AMC) and others joined the call for protest against this nefarious system, African American Muslims paid more attention to issues such as "affirmative action, vouchers for schools, the politics of urban renewal, from welfare to workforce, and racial discrimination in such fields as law enforcement and the judicial process." Because of this difference within the Muslim community and between the Muslims and the Jews, Mazrui concludes that Jews and Muslims are divided mainly on foreign policy issues. He further argues that the emerging pattern of Muslim alignments with members of the two dominant political parties suggests Muslims vote with the Democrats on social and welfare issues and with Republicans on family values issues.

In developing his arguments under the seven headings identified earlier, Mazrui arrives at many interesting and insightful conclusions. Not only does he note the role of Islam among the American minorities like the African American, but he also recognizes the manner in which Muslim political power in the country could be enhanced or limited by the politics of engagement between American Muslims and the system, and how Muslims themselves define their identity and engage the other groups within the society. Like some of his colleagues, he, too, feels that there is developing in America "A Tale of Two Islams." He sees this cultural and economic split taking place between the immigrants and the native-born Americans. The division is caused by the forces of history, economics, political psychology, and competing concerns within the larger Muslim community. In developing this thesis, Mazrui provides several examples of how Islam in the United States has been shaped by the peculiar experiences of the African American. He finds evidence for his thesis in Black fascination with the achievements of the emperors and kings of ancient Mali and Ghana. To Mazrui, this is a clear Africana gloriana. According to his argument, the fascination with Islam among certain African Americans was made possible by the fact that blackness and brownness in the United States did not lend itself to significant polarization between the two pigmentation groups as in the Caribbean, where identity with African Islam is stronger among the Muslims of Indo-Pakistani heritage.

Mazrui also focuses on Muslim political involvement during the Clinton and Bush administrations. He thinks the Clintons did a good job of opening the White House to Muslims even though journalists and Muslim opponents such as Steven Emerson tried to paint it negatively. He cites many examples of how he and several Muslim leaders and intellectuals communicated with the U.S. national leadership. As a member of the board of the American Muslim Council, Mazrui had the opportunity to meet former Clinton officials such as fellow Africanist Anthony Lake. He also met politically visible Black leaders such as Minister Louis Farrakhan, especially immediately after the Million Man March. What does the professor learn from his engagement with the United States, and how does his research on this topic affect his vision of American Muslims in the future? As we can tell from his conclusion, Mazrui is telling Muslims to learn from the Jews and the Blacks: "Jews are the America of achievement. Blacks are the America of potential." Caught between these two minorities of race and religion, Muslims should try to develop the potentials in the African American segment of their community and simultaneously cultivate the successes in their immigrant segment to reach the highest achievement goals.

Mohammed Nimer begins chapter 6 on American Muslims in public life by calling out attention to the presence of four to six million Muslims in the country. He goes on to say that this community "has established 1,400 mosques, 200 Islamic schools, and dozens of social service and world relief organizations." According to Nimer, the question of Muslim participation in the political and social institutions of the larger society has continued to occupy the attention of many Muslim leaders and their constituencies. Like his colleagues writing for this volume, he also sees the community split between those willing to engage the larger society and those who are reluctant to do so. Both groups have derived arguments from the Quran and other appropriate sources to press and justify their claims. The Muslims who advocate political participation peg their argument on the need for Muslims to contribute to the moral, political, and social development of American society. Such activities, according to this school of thought, would meet the Quranic injunction calling Muslims to encourage the doing of good and the avoidance of evil. Nimer claims that most of the Muslims embrace this spirit of engagement with the U.S. political system. However, he reminds us that another school of thought also exists within the Muslim community. It tends to see political engagement as a corrupting and defiling exercise in futility. Although advocates of this point of view recognize the fact that not all American values are contrary to Islam, their apprehensions about the corrupting effect on Muslim leaders make them allergic to politics. Nimer concludes this section of his chapter by saying that since the "main object of American Muslim participation in mainstream politics is empowerment," the success of the community in this arena is going "to depend on the degree to which Muslim organizations can institutionalize their work and improve its management."

After examining several surveys done by national Muslim organizations on the issue of political involvement, Nimer tells us a great deal about Muslim efforts at combating discrimination around the country. Not only does he shed some light on the Council on American-Islamic Relations (CAIR) record of Muslim claims of discrimination submitted to local, state, and federal authorities, but he also cites court cases that document the gradual empowerment of Muslims through the affirmation of their First Amendment rights by members of the bench. In elaborating on this theme of Muslim interaction with government agencies, Nimer tells us more about the efforts of national Muslim organizations, such as the American Muslim Council, CAIR, Muslim Public Affairs Council (MPAC), and the American Muslim Alliance, pressing Muslim claims before national leaders. Because of these activities, he argues, Muslims were able to have Eid celebrated at the White House and Iftar (breaking of the fast) at the State Department during the Clinton administration. He also mentions the activities of senators and members of Congress who stood by Muslims during these formative years of political activism.

Nimer devotes a section of his chapter to the question of Muslim interaction with other groups in U.S. society. Singling out MPAC as a leading pioneer in this field of activity, and pointing to its accomplishments in building bridges between Muslims and the members of the other Abrahamic faiths, he concludes by saying that "though the limited resources of the organization could affect its public policy advocate role, its activism has resulted in, among other things, the issuing of statements on counterterrorism, Bosnia, with a focus on the use of rape as a weapon of ethnic cleansing, and the treatment of women under the Taliban, with a focus on separating Islam from the behaviors of the Taliban." Apart from Muslim involvement with the interfaith movement in the United States,

Nimer tells us, there are also attempts by Muslims to make friends and influence people in other areas of life. He believes that most political interaction between Muslims and others has centered on issues of civil rights and freedom of speech. He points to the efforts of national Muslim organizations to collaborate with the coalition led by the American Civil Liberties Union (ACLU) opposing the 1996 Anti-Terrorism and Effective Death Penalty Act, which contained a provision allowing the government to detain individuals based on classified information (popularly known as secret evidence).

The last area of discourse in Nimer's chapter centers on American Muslims and the electoral process. He provides a detailed analysis of this phenomenon, and the data he presents on Muslim contributions to political campaigns, in terms of both financial and moral support, are revealing and illuminating. Here the author indeed gives us a guided tour of this unknown side of the Muslim presence in American political life. Using data from the Federal Electoral Commission, the American Muslim Alliance, and other informants in the community, he pieces together an important tapestry showing the small but growing Muslim effort to carve a niche for Muslims on the American political landscape. Not only does he identify the six most visible national political action groups in the Arab/Muslim communities, but he also tells us about Muslim efforts at participating at the national conventions of the two dominant political parties and in running for office at various jurisdictions.

In chapter 7, Jane Smith deals with the issue of Muslims as partners in interfaith encounters in the United States. Drawing upon a rich collection of interviews with several Muslim leaders and academics, she illuminates a great deal about the phenomenon of interfaith dialogue between Muslims and Christians. Although there are references to Muslim involvement with Jews here and there in the text, the main focus is on Muslim-Christian relations. Working on the assumption that dialogue is basically an invention of the Protestant and Catholic leadership in world affairs, she goes on to explore the origins of this movement in the United States today and how Muslims are grappling with its challenges and opportunities. From the varying opinions gathered through her interviews, Smith concludes that dialogue between the two religious communities has supporters and opponents. Among the Muslims, those who favor dialogue tend to be from a certain background, with certain temperaments, certain attitudes toward the assimilation process, and certain perceptions of the intention of the Christian initiators. Reminding us about the psychohistorical factors and forces that provide the background to this process of dialogue, she argues that the dialogical process benefits from both the change of attitude from the Vatican after the Second Vatican Council from 1962 to 1965 and the acts of reconciliation from the World Council of Churches in the early 1960s.

According to Smith's findings, the vast majority of Muslims would rather not engage in interfaith dialogue, although a small but growing minority has taken a positive stance on this issue and is building structures for greater engagement with other Abrahamic faiths in the United States. Echoing some of the points regarding the theological divide among Muslims on the question of engagement with the political and social institutions of the country, Smith concludes that those from the Salafi and Wahabi orientations are less likely to show any interest in this process.

Specifically, in her view, seven models of interfaith dialogue have emerged since its inception in the United States. The first is the confrontational debate model, which is not widely appreciated by supporters of committed dialogues. The second is dialogue as information sharing, a process that helps bring people together in different contexts and under new circumstances. The third is the theological exchange model that creates the opportunity for both dialogue and *dawah* (Muslims' propagation of their religion) for the Muslim, and dialogue and evangelization for the Christian. The fact that this is a double-edged sword makes it the object of fear for many Muslims who either are not well versed in the ways of the perennial dialoguer or are too fearful of Christian intentions. Smith identifies a fourth model as the ethnical exchange model, which seeks to show the points of convergence between the two faith communities and to encourage their adherents to work together to help solve American moral issues. The fifth model strives to bring the two groups closer together. In her view, proponents of this notion of dialogue "hope that honest conversation among members of the two faiths will not only help find elements that they genuinely have in common but will also lead toward a deemphasis on differences and a reemphasis on sharing and mutuality." Her sixth model focuses on spirituality and healing. She believes this is a small minority who wish to engage others to the point that their spiritual identity is appreciated more than anything else. The seventh model calls for cooperation for addressing pragmatic concerns. This idea of dialogue is popular between Muslim youth, and Smith references many quotes to illustrate her point.

After examining all the issues she raises in her study concerning the nature of dialogue, Smith identifies five benefits of dialogue. She describes dialogue as a path to building trust and friendship, as a balance to the mutually negative images and perceptions entertained on both sides, as a mechanism to change American opinions on and attitudes toward Islam and Muslims, as a means of fostering unity among peoples of faith, as a mechanism for social reform. Next, she describes several problems with dialogue. In her view, dialogue is taking place on an uneven playing field. It is being pursued by Muslims who have yet to develop a conceptual framework for it. Dialogue is also happening when the two parties come together with different concerns and under conditions in which Muslims tend to be suspicious of Christian agendas. She believes that dialogue also suffers from the divergent theological positions of the two groups and from the perceptions of some Muslims that only certain Muslims dominate such encounters between Muslims and Christians. Indeed, it is against this background that she discusses African American Muslims in dialogue and Muslim women and the dialogical process. Her findings help illuminate our understanding of the feelings and thinking of African American Muslims, on the one hand, and Muslim women, on the other.

ISLAM AND THE BLACK EXPERIENCE IN AMERICA

What is interesting about this section of the volume is the manner in which the question of race is tackled by three scholars from three ethnic and cultural backgrounds. Sherman A. Jackson is an African American Muslim scholar of great distinction; Zafar Ishaq Ansari, a Pakistani scholar who heads the Islamic Research Institute in Islamabad, has been studying American Islamic experience for about three decades; and Sylviane A. Diouf is a perceptive scholar of Western African background.

Jackson leads off chapter 8 with his discourse on the African American Muslim identity. He notes that African American Muslims are the largest ethnic group among Muslims and at the same time the largest religious minority within the Black community in the United States. This sociological reality of the Black Muslim poses some interesting questions for study and analysis. Jackson's central argument is that the past, present, and future of Islam among Black Americans can only be understood "in the context of the relationship between Islam and Black religion." For Jackson, "Black religion" is a "sui generis, religious orientation" that developed among Black Americans since their arrival here as slaves. The central and "most enduring" characteristic of Black religion is "its sustained and radical opposition to racial oppression." In other words, Black religion is, at its core, "an instrument of holy protest against racism." Even within Christianity, Black religion retained its original character and identity, including its spirit of struggle for racial equality and justice. As Jackson points out, Black Americans have had a "patently different appreciation of and agenda for Christianity." It is atheological, radical in rejection of racial subjugation, conservative in its social ethics, and rooted in its African heritage "as the locus of its longing and belonging."

Jackson then traces the relationship between Black religion and Islam and examines the positive and negative aspects of this relationship as manifested among African American Muslim today. The dialectic between Black religion and Islam emerges as a major factor in Jackson's argument that Black religion will remain "inextricably woven" into the fabric and future of Black American Islam and will "continue to negotiate its place alongside other sources of Islamic religious authority." But the author also notes some recent changes in the bases of religious authority in American Islam as a result of massive immigration from the Muslim World: Black Americans are losing their "interpretive voice and their effective monopoly over what had functioned as a bona fide, indigenous tradition of 'Muslim' thought and ex-egesis." The pragmatic, folk-oriented religious orientation has been displaced by orthodoxy and by sociocultural realities significantly different from those experienced by African American Muslims.

What Jackson describes here is what Professor Hakim Rashid of Howard University calls the triple quandary situation. This is, African American Muslims are beginning to emerge as a minority within a minority in three distinct situations. They are a significant minority within Black America, a significant minority within the Muslim community, and a significant part of a significant minority along with other non-Whites in the United States.

But the "triple quandary situation," as Zafar Ansari shows in chapter 9, is gradually changing. Ansari identifies several factors that are likely to help African American Muslims play a more important role in the larger Muslim American community and to realize their potential strengths. First, African American Muslims constitute a very large segment of the Muslim population in the United States. Second, African American Muslims have been the first Muslims to have arrived and settled in North America. They have been living in this continent for close to five centuries. Their centuries-long struggle to maintain their faith, identity, and dignity in extremely difficult circumstances is not only a source of pride for all Muslims—and their fellow Americans—but also an inspiration for a better future. Third, their transition from the "Black-centeredness" of the Nation of Islam to Islamic universalism or orthodox Islam has paved the way for their leadership role in the larger Muslim community of the United States. Fourth, the phenomenal growth of the network of Islamic religious and educational institutions and organizations in African American Muslim communities throughout the United States has tended to consolidate their autonomous "religious structure" (i.e., independent of the immigrant Muslims' patronage).

Ansari also notes that in recent decades, African American Muslims have begun to make their mark in the development of Islamic intellectual thought. As is well known, their forefathers in Africa made extraordinarily rich scholarly contributions, especially in the field of Islamic thought and learning. A new generation of African American Muslim scholars—several of them represented in the present volume—is contributing their share to the enrichment of contemporary Islamic thought. Ansari concludes his chapter by pointing out that African American Muslims, compared with their immigrant coreligionists, are placed in an especially advantageous position. They have lived long in the United States "that can justifiably be proud of being" a country that is in the "vanguard of contemporary thought and civilization." They are thus in a position to combine their knowledge of contemporary social sciences and scientific thought with their profound knowledge of Islamic tradition, and to add to that "their vivid awareness of both the sordid and positive aspects of contemporary civilization owing to their presence in America for several centuries." All this eminently qualifies them to take up the challenge of enriching the religious-intellectual tradition of Islam and to assume the leadership role in the growing Muslim communities of the United States.

Chapter 10, Sylviane Diouf's "The West African Paradox," brings to our attention the story of the West African Muslims who, for almost four hundred years, represented 100 percent of the Muslims living in the United States. These were the early Muslims, from Senegal, Gambia, Mali, Guinea, Sierra Leone, Côte d'Ivoire, Ghana, and Nigeria, who remained steadfast under the most brutal conditions of servitude. The West African Muslims are not only the first to introduce and preserve Islam in the United States; they are also among the latest immigrants to join the American Muslim *ummah* (community). In fact, as Diouf documents, "more Africans and perhaps twice as many Muslims arrived in the United States within the past forty years than during the entire era of the slave trade."

Although the West African Muslims constitute the second largest Muslim population after the Asian Muslims in the United States, they are usually overlooked when American policymakers, media, or academia examine the affairs of the Islamic world or even the problems faced by Muslims in the United States. Diouf describes the factors that have contributed to the political, physical, and cultural "invisibility" of this population. Her chapter also explores the history of West African Muslims in the United States, their occupational concentrations, and their religious-cultural institutions in the public square.

Based on an extensive fieldwork conducted in New York City, home to the largest West African Muslim community in the United States, the study explores the issues of faith, ethnicity, gender, and identity in the context of new cultural milieu, economic opportunities, and religious diversity. As Diouf shows, the neighborhood of 116th Street in Harlem, popularly known as "Little Africa," has become a microcosm of Dakar or Lagos. A "self-sufficient enclave" of the West African Muslim community in New York City, the area has become an apt reflection of the community's attachment to its cultural and religious values—shops selling *halal* meat, African cultural and religious creations, African clothes, foods, pictures of religious leaders, prayers rugs and beads, Murid literature—and its participation in modernity—stores providing photocopying service, computer classes, electronic equipment, cosmetics, tax preparation, and calling cards that "link both the *here* and the *there*." A measure of their strength in the trade structure is that both the president and treasurer of the Merchant Association of the 116th Street neighborhood in Harlem are Senegalese. In fact, the New York City officials, police authorities, and community leaders credit the West African Muslim community for turning the neighborhood around from a "boarded-up" and unsafe area to a showcase of prosperous businesses.

Much as they take advantage of the economic and educational opportunities made available by the host society, most West African Muslims tend to distance themselves from U.S. culture, which they perceive as promoting individualism, promiscuity, greed, and violence. What seems to be taking place in the West African Muslim community is not the process of assimilation but a deliberate move toward "accommodation" with the host culture. As Diouf shows in her chapter, Islam and African culture and social values "provide them with a road map to navigate their new world with a sense of control."

ON LOCATING MUSLIMS IN THE AMERICAN LANDSCAPE: DEMOGRAPHIC AND BEHAVIORAL ASPECTS

Scholars of Islam in America have shown considerable interest in recent years in what a magazine article has described as "the number game." The exact number of Muslim population in the United States has been "a matter of curiosity for some, a matter of pride for others and, seemingly, a matter of concern for still others." Studies conducted so far to estimate the Muslim population in the United States have been mostly sketchy and speculative. Also, they are based on designs and methodologies of varying rigor; hence, their estimate of the Muslim population in the United States ranges from three million to ten million. What further complicates the picture is the fact that besides the two major factors of population growth—natural growth and migration—there is this additional factor of conversion, which is often neglected by scholars.

Ilyas Ba-Yunus and Kassim Kone in chapter 11, "Muslim Americans: A Demographic Report," take a critical look at the existing literature on the demography of Muslims in the Untied States and report the findings of their own survey of the American Muslim communities conducted during the spring and summer of 2001 and the summer of 2002. Their study breaks new ground in that it provides fresh data on the educational, income, and professional composition of Muslim communities in the United States.

Ba-Yunus and Kone base their study of the American Muslim population on sixteen different listings of Islamic institutions of worship maintained by hundreds of local, metropolitan, regional, and national Muslim organizations. In addition, 1,315 informants were used to verify these listings. The idea was to bypass survey techniques based on drawing random samples and then to generalize from these samples. Thus, Ba-Yunus and Kone's study is based on 100 percent coverage, a method followed by the U.S. Bureau of Census in its use of the short form. Data collected in their study show that about "5,745,100 Muslim men and women of all ages" live in the United States. In view of the extremely conservative approach that the authors seem to have adopted in the study, and also because of the non-availability of information from more than two hundred Islamic institutions that led necessarily to undercounting, Ba-Yunus and Kone preferred to err in underestimating the Muslim population rather than venturing speculations of higher numbers. A large number of Shia Muslims, including Ismaili Shia, for example, remain undercounted or not counted at all, because of their nonparticipation in Sunni Muslim institutions. A recent study estimates that about 786,000 Shia Muslims reside in the United States. Similarly, the study also does not include several peripheral sects (e.g., Ahmadies, Nation of Islam) that claim to be Muslims but are not generally recognized as such by the mainstream Islamic communities.

Ba-Yunus and Kone's study confirms the general perception about the ethnic diversity of Muslim population in the United States. The largest group of Muslims in America (32 percent) is of Arab origin, followed by the American Muslims—mostly African Americans (29 percent). A close third are Muslims of South Asian origin (28.9 percent), followed by smaller ethnic groups—Turks, Iranians, Bosnians, Kosovars, Malays, and Indonesians. Despite their enormous ethnic diversity, however, American Muslims share some common features in terms of their occupation and residential concentrations. Most of them (86 percent) are concentrated in engineering and electronics, computer science and data processing, and medicine. Like most other new immigrants and many other African Americans, a majority of Muslims prefer to live in metropolitan areas such as Los Angeles, New York, Chicago, Detroit, Philadelphia, Houston, Boston, Dallas, St. Louis, Atlanta, and Washington, D.C., and their adjoining suburbs. One interesting finding of this study is that Muslims are now spilling over into smaller towns of northeast, southeast, and midwest America in growing numbers. This recent shift of the Muslim population from major cities to smaller cities and towns not only indicates the "mainstreaming" of the American Muslim population but also is reflective of the growing demand for Muslim professional talents and skills across the continent.

Chapter 12, written by Ihsan Bagby, deals with "The Mosque and the American Public Square" and focuses on the central Islamic religious institution and its involvement in the larger society. The most important question regarding the mosque's relationship to the public square is whether the mosques in the United States are following a path of isolation from American society and its institutional structures or a path of active participation, accommodations, and involvement. The ideological orientations and cultural directions of mosques in the United States have assumed an added significance in the wake of 9/11 and recently introduced government-sponsored social services under the faith-based initiative.

Bagby's study is based on comprehensive field research of American mosques conducted in 2000–2001 as a part of a wider study of all religious congregations sponsored by the Hartford Seminary. Based on telephone interviews with 416 mosque leaders, randomly sampled from a list of 1,209 mosques, the study demolishes several myths and misperceptions made popular by a section of the media in the post–September 11 debate on the role of Islamic religious institutions in America. The picture that clearly emerges from Bagby's study is that mosque leaders in the United States accept almost unanimously the idea that Muslims must fully participate in American public life and social activities. A majority of mosques, especially African American mosques, are already actively involved in providing community services and participating in outreach activities and interfaith dialogues. In fact, as Bagby's data indicate, the overall rate of mosques' involvement in community affairs is similar to that of other religious congregations, even though mosques are still in their formative phase of development and generally lack the necessary institutional infrastructures associated with social services.

It is obvious from Bagby's interviews with mosque leaders that their primary motivation to advocate community involvement springs from their "deep religious impulse" founded on the Quranic ideals of doing good deeds (Quran 2:82), cooperating with others in righteousness (5:3), commanding good and forbidding evil (3:110), being kind to the needy (4:36), and standing up for the cause of justice (4:135). As Bagby observes, "Mosque leaders do not want to see their mosques as sectarian strongholds where Muslims are holed up against the dominant culture." They want their mosques to become an integral part of the larger American religious landscape and focal points of their contacts with the communities in which they live and raise their families.

While Bagby examines mosques' involvement in community affairs and social services, Iqbal Unus, a longtime institution builder who has been associated with the formation of major national Islamic organizations in leadership roles, critically considers in chapter 13 the internal organizational structures and style of governance in Muslim community organizations (MCOs) in the United States.

From the establishment of the International Muslim Society, later named the Federation of Islamic Associations of the United States and Canada (FIA) by the Syrian and Lebanese Muslim immigrants in 1952, to the watershed event of the establishment of the Muslim Students Association of the United States and Canada (MSA) in 1963, and then the emergence of national advocacy organizations such as the American Muslim Council (AMC) and Council on American-Islamic Relations (CAIR) in the 1980s and 1990s, over 1,600 Muslim community organizations and Islamic centers today dot the American landscape. More than 150 Islamic schools operate on a full-time basis, and dozens of professional, educational, cultural, Islamic-ethnic, and service organizations as well as political action committees and advocacy groups offer Muslims the promise of a bright future. These MCOs, with their own distinctive institutional identity and organizational structures, have now become an integral part of what Alexis de Tocqueville celebrated as the main strength of the American society—the volunteer sector.

Unus groups the MCOs into four major categories: worship and community organizations, welfare and relief organizations, research and professional associations, and advocacy and issue groups. Historically, most of the MCOs were set up largely by immigrant communities to act as a "line of cultural defense." Today, however, they represent diverse facets of the Islamic experience in the United States. Organizationally, some of these experiences were oriented to consultative forms of governance, while others were inspired by charismatic and "situational" leadership. In either case, as Unus shows, "decidedly enthusiastic and sometimes chaotic activism often took the center stage." As is obvious from Unus's study, the search for stability in leadership, institutional design, and modes of governance in MCOs continues to be an ongoing process.

Regardless of how MCOs come into being, whether by individual entrepreneurial initiatives or as branches, chapters, or affiliates of national organizations, formal organizational structures are beginning to take shape, and necessary actions are being taken to establish legal and civic presence for the emerging groups. Good governance is on the top of their organizational agenda today. The new set of rules and regulations issued by the U.S. Department of the Treasury to implement its antiterrorist guidelines after September 11, 2001, have forced many of these MCOs to restructure their organizational designs and decision-making procedures to ensure maximum accountability and transparency. The "back home" models of informal decision-making processes have been replaced by more structured, democratic, and membership-driven result-oriented organizations. Much of this transformation is due to the changing legal landscape for voluntary organizations in the United States, as well as the result of the expanding functions of these MCOs. All in all, the obvious outcome is that the MCOs have today become more "functional elements of the mainstream volunteer sector and worship communities that constitute the mosaic of American civil society."

DIRECTIONS FOR ONGOING RESEARCH

Now that we have described briefly some of the contributions the authors of this volume have made to the understanding of the American Muslim presence in North America, let us examine the implications for future re-

search. Although our contributors have tackled many challenges with respect to the American Muslim presence and are seriously entertaining future research on this subject, we the editors have identified seven issues
that have come to occupy our attention in the last days of this project.

The first is the question of Muslim citizenship and the impact of 9/11 in
the Muslim adjustments to American societal and state demands for assimilation and patriotic commitments. This issue has plagued all immigrants
who have chosen in the past to become U.S. citizens. What is remarkable
about the present state of affairs for Muslims is the convergence of national
and international religious and political forces that are increasingly con-
spiring to question this loyalty, on the one hand, and to appeal to Muslims'
religious sense of solidarity, on the other. Though the Japanese, Italian, and
German immigrants who elected to become U.S. citizens in the last century
faced a similar predicament, their social stigmatization and internment was
more nationalistically inspired than religiously motivated. To put it another
way, one could say that the actions of the U.S. government against these
Americans were taken not to spite the First Amendment but to determine
whether the targeted persons were more committed to their original homeland than to their adopted new country.

The creation of the Homeland Security cabinet post will be historically
identified with the coming to America of Muslims. This is a field of inquiry
that cuts across many frontiers in the academy. Those who are interested
in the history of civil liberties in the Untied States would for a long time be
sharing intellectual space with their colleagues in anthropology, psychology, political science, and international relations. Their common ground
would be how and why the immigration of different racial, religious, national, and ethnic groups into the United States has taken different forms
and shapes due to the changing nature of international society. Here the
impact of globalization on the nature and character of religious pluralism
presents itself as a topic for future research.

The second issue that grows out of our research is the impact of high
technology on human self-perception and self-definition. Unlike the immigrants discussed in this volume and those before them, the present generations of Muslim and non-Muslim immigrants in the United States are creatures of a different social and cultural nature. Rather than immigrating to
the United States and getting dissolved in the ocean of names and faces,
these generations of immigrants are beneficiaries of the CNN factor and the
cell phone phenomenon. This new reality in the patterns and styles of immigration offers scholars and journalists new avenues of research and investigation in the whole process of assimilation, integration, and what some
have dubbed "flexible citizenship."

A third issue that deserves our attention as a research problem is the impact of American immigrants in the economic development of their homes

of origin and in the possible democratization of those parts of the world. What social scientists in the 1960s called the "demonstration effect" might well be at work here. Whether it is myth or reality, only time and serious research can tell.

The fourth issue is the contributions of American Muslims to the age-old American dilemma of race. Our contributors have shed ample light on the issue. However, there are gaps in our knowledge, and the recency of the Muslim community on the American cultural and social landscape makes it dangerous and unwise to say how this population has impacted race relations here.

The fifth research problem that emerges from this study is the question of leadership training and the role and place of the mosque in American society. The chapters in this volume have provided statistical data and analyses about the imam and his congregation. However, much remains to be done in the following areas of inquiry: Who are the imams? Where do they come from? What is the role of the imported imam, and how does he fit in the larger scheme of the assimilation process of the immigrant Muslims? What is the nature of the relationship between the imported imam and the Muslim youth in his community? These and other related issues will occupy the attention of many of us in the coming years.

A sixth area of inquiry is the gender issue and the manner in which American Muslims are grappling with it. The present volume touches on part of the problem, but much remains to be done. There are serious gaps in our knowledge, and secrecy and traditionalism sometimes conspire to block the path of the social scientist bent on unraveling the veils of lies and deception that shroud some of the potential sources of research.

Finally, there is the issue of understanding the problems of Muslim youth and the manner in which their problems can be treated at the national and local levels. Given the diversity of the community and the differences in terms of race, class, and national cultural origins, it is imperative for scholars and journalists to investigate this elephant in the room that has yet to be named and identified properly.

These seven issues point to the opportunities and challenges facing researchers working on issues concerning the American Muslim. Together they show the way to scholars interested in locating Muslims on the American intellectual landscape.

NOTES

1. See Nehemia Levtzion and J. E. P. Hopkins, eds., *Corpus of Early Arabic Sources for West African History* (Princeton, N.J.: Wiener, 2000), 269.

2. See Leo Wiener, *Africa and the Discovery of America* (Philadelphia: Innes, 1922).

3. See George H. Junne Jr., "Neither Christian nor Heathen: Islam among the

African Slaves in the New World," an unpublished essay written by an author based at the Black Studies Department, University of Northern Colorado, Greeley, Colorado, 1995, p. 18.

4. See Allan D. Austin, *African Muslims in Ante-bellum America: A Source Book* (New York: Garland, 1984).

5. See Michael Gomez, *Exchanging Our Country Marks: The Transformation of African Identities in Colonial and Anti-bellum South* (Chapel Hill: University of North Carolina Press, 1998); and Bryan Turner, *Islam in the Black Experience* (Bloomington: Indiana University Press, 1997).

6. See Cedric Robinson, *Black Marxism: The Making of the Black Radical Tradition* (Chapel Hill: University of North Carolina Press, 1983).

7. See Philip D. Curtin, ed., *Africa Remembered: Narratives by West Africans from the Era of the Slave Trade* (Madison: University of Wisconsin Press, 1964).

8. See David Levinson and Melvin Ember, eds., *American Immigrant Cultures: Builders of A Nation* (New York: Macmillan, 1997).

9. See, for example, Philip K. Hitti, *The Syrians in America* (New York: Doran, 1924).

10. Michael A. Koszegi and J. Gordon Melton, eds., *Islam in North America: A Source Book* (New York: Taylor & Francis, 1992).

11. See Abdo El-Kholy, *The Arab Moslems in the United States: A Religion and Assimilation* (New Haven: Connecticut College and University Press, 1983).

12. See Yvonne Haddad and Jane I. Smith, eds., *Muslim Minorities in the West* (Lanham, Md.: AltaMira, 2002); Yvonne Y. Haddad and John L. Esposito, eds., *Muslims on the Americanization Path?* (Atlanta: Scholars Press, 1997); Yvonne Y. Haddad and Jane I. Smith, eds., *Muslim Communities in North America* (Albany: State University of New York Press, 1994); Yvonne Y. Haddad and Jane I. Smith, *Mission to America: Five Islamic Sectarian Movements in North America* (Gainesville: University of Florida Press, 1993); Yvonne Y. Haddad, ed., *The Muslims of America* (Oxford: Oxford University Press, 1991); and Yvonne Y. Haddad and Adair Lummis, *Islamic Values in the United States: A Comparative Study* (New York: Oxford University Press, 1987).

13. See Sulayman S. Nyang, *Islam in the United States of America* (Chicago: ABC International Group, 1999); Jane I. Smith, *Islam in America* (New York: Columbia University Press, 1999); Robert Dannin, *Black Pilgrimage to Islam* (New York: Oxford University Press, 2002); Yvonne Haddad and Jane I. Smith, eds., *Muslim Minorities in the West* (Lanham, Md.: AltaMira, 2002); Baha Abu-Laban and Michael W. Suleiman, *Arab Americans: Continuity and Change* (Belmont, Mass.: Association of Arab-American University Graduates, 1989); and Sameer Y. Abraham and Nabeel Abraham, eds., *Arabs in the New World: Studies on Arab-American Communities* (Detroit: Wayne State University Press, 1983).

I

THEORETICAL PERSPECTIVES ON THE MUSLIM EXPERIENCE IN THE UNITED STATES

1

Toward a Fiqh for Minorities

Some Reflections

Taha Jabir Al-Alwani

Muslim minorities did not attract as much attention in the past as they do today. Muslims would travel as messengers or diplomatic envoys, and as traders or itinerant Sufis. These people would be mainly visitors who would stay for short periods. Those who migrated from Muslim lands for political reasons or as dissidents—and expected to be away for a long time—would usually go to distant places where the influence of the central Muslim authority was much diluted. The more powerful and ambitious migrants of comfortably independent means would travel even to non-Muslim lands, where they would establish their own Muslim emirates, existing as Muslim oases or islands in the middle of non-Muslim oceans. Some communities, like those in the south of France, northern Italy,[2] and other places, were to survive for a long time.

Those Muslims, few as they were, who lived in non-Muslim communities, where political authority was not in their hands and the laws were not based on the Shariah, were mainly indigenous converts. Eventually, they became aware of the significant difference between life in a Muslim community and that in a non-Muslim community. Those who had the means migrated to Muslim lands, while others endeavored to lead as full an Islamic life as possible. They developed a distinct Islamic culture, which might, at times, cause friction with the non-Muslim host community owing to their refusal, if that were possible, to comply with the laws and traditions that conflicted with what they had learned of Islam. Although their new culture might indeed converge in certain aspects with the lifestyle of the host community, the degree of integration was minor and cosmetic. Friction might be provoked by the dominant majority if they attempted to eliminate the minorities' distinctive cultural and religious characteristics so as to absorb them into the non-Muslim society.

3

If the Muslim minorities resisted assimilation, they were likely to be subjected to persecution or enslavement. They would therefore be helpless and lack the means to assert their existence (*al-Nisa:* 98). They would seek *fatwas* (juristic opinions) from their own *ulama* (members of Muslim society's learned class) or from those outside their community, especially during the *hajj* (religious pilgrimage) season. Most of their queries would have been individual and personal. In the past, Muslim minorities were so small and isolated that they were incapable of establishing their own autonomous economic, legal, or cultural organizations and institutions. Their Muslim jurists and ulama were fully aware of a marked difference between the issues and problems of Muslim individuals and groups in a non-Muslim society, and those of a Muslim community living under Islamic law, systems, and traditions. They certainly realized the disparities between the sources of law in Muslim lands (*dar al-Islam* or *dar al-ijabah*, land of compliance) and those of other societies (*dar al-dawah*, land for the propagation of Islam).[2] They understood the impact of the psychological, intellectual, cultural, and juristic differences on life in both environments, thereby obliging the muftis, whether scholars or students, to investigate the evidence. They needed to contextualize that evidence in the light of the prevailing circumstances so as to issue the appropriate fatwas, which could be easily and conveniently applied to this time and space, without infringing the main principles and the general aims of the Shariah.

Therefore, the need for a new *fiqh* (Islamic jurisprudence) for minorities was not as strong in the past as it is today. This was because the "reference community" was never found outside its main country of domicile, and it had not moved to the "land of dawah" except in the limited way described. It was a casual and transient existence that did not attract the attention of jurists to legislate and issue fatwas. It remained restricted and isolated, and its fiqh came to be known simply as the fiqh of "crises" or "emergency."[3]

PUBLIC AWARENESS OF THE SHARIAH

With the popularity of the Quran and its accessibility to the general Muslim public, no matter how rudimentary their knowledge of Islam is, certain standards of Islamic education and culture emerged.

Muslims are aware that the Shariah laws are based on clemency and temperance rather then oppression and severity. They fully realize that the fulfillment of religious obligations is concomitant on human ability (*al-Taghabun:* 16; *al-Baqarah:* 286). Muslims also know that the Shariah permits all that is clean and wholesome and forbids what is harmful, and so it is aimed at making life easier and more convenient. It encourages and promotes good and positive conduct and forbids all that undermines society (*al-Araf:* 157).

The average Muslim understands clearly what is meant by the Quranic statement "He created for you all that is on the earth" (*al-Baqarah:* 29). It confirms the use of all God's bounty with the exception of what has been specifically and categorically forbidden. Permissibility is the norm. The use of everything found in or on this Earth is allowed, as long as it is clean and harmless. What is *halal* and what is *haram* are clearly defined. The gray areas in between are the subject of fiqh, debate, and *ijtihad* (independent reasoning).

The general and universal principles of the Quran created a common, widespread, and accessible culture among all Muslims, which may not be attained by specialists today. In Islam, areas of specialist ijtihad are established and well defined, and the general public is invited to offer its own input. Ordinary people can select the scholar whom they wish to follow and pick from the "common law" the reasons, terms, and restrictions. They follow the scholar in adapting the facts, and there are also matters that they cannot afford to ignore.

For this reason, Muslim society has allowed the rise of the "men of the pen" in contrast to the "men of the sword." However, it has no room for "priests" or "clergy" or a "grand ulama board" to dominate and monopolize the sources of religious knowledge and the interpretation of religious dogma, thereby denying the rest of society access to them and preventing those who were interested from studying, analyzing, and interpreting them. The idea of an elite setting itself up as a reference for religious responsibility and authority is alien to the very nature of Islam. It is something that is rejected by the general public, not to mention the intelligentsia. The Quran is available to all, and no one can monopolize or control access to it. Every reader of the Quran can learn the basics of Islam from it directly.

SHARIAH AND CULTURE

There is a well-established polemical relationship between legislation, whether divine or man-made, and cultural traditions and conventions. These aspects of society influence scholars, researchers, and legislators, just as fiqh and legislation play a role in creating cultures, traditions, and conventions and have a specific long-term impact on them. Muslim minorities live in societies in which these aspects do not stem from Islamic origins, and their Muslim members themselves have no way of completely breaking away from these influences. Even if they succeed in separating themselves with respect to worship and moral conduct, they cannot do so in transactions, economics, politics, and all other general and common areas of society, including education, the media, and other public opinion–forming systems. All this contributes, in varying degrees, to the alienation of minorities from their roots and gradually weakens their bonds with them. To compensate for the loss of the old relationships, new bonds develop within the new geographic environment inhabited by the Muslim minorities.

This is true of the first generation of immigrants. Nevertheless, in later years the old bonds may well be obliterated by the third or fourth generation and become mere bittersweet memories related for entertainment. Thus, the new generations may be completely assimilated into the host communities and disappear altogether, severing their links with their cultural roots, which their fathers and forefathers had made every effort to preserve.

PRESENT-DAY MUSLIM PRESENCE IN THE WEST

It is quite obvious that neither the West nor the Muslims, especially the Arabs, expected to find Islam and Muslims right in the heart of Europe and the United States. These Muslims did not come as conquerors but as immigrants, students, and professionals. They were the citizens and nationals who left their Muslim lands to live in the West, forming a real, settled, and permanent Muslim existence in the United States. The new immigrant communities have a very sincere wish to integrate into the host society, while preserving their religious and cultural identities. Like the rest of the population, they are quite happy and prepared to comply with and respect the law of the land, pay their taxes, assume responsibilities, and benefit from the freedom, advantages and rights provided by the law.

Until September 11, 2001, the United States considered multiculturalism and a multifaith society as positive contributions to its literalism in general. It was the multiculturalism that made the United States a symbol for the whole world. It could rightly assert before all humanity that it was the universal model for integration. This would also justify its assertion that it was the undisputed heir to Hellenism and Roman civilization: a supranational melting pot of cultures and races. It would rightly and deservedly become a world leader, as it has done by what has come to be known as "globalism."

The United States is to be praised for its understanding and welcoming of Islam and Muslims by all levels of society. These include some churches that have offered their premises to Muslims to use for Friday prayers and *Eid* (end-of-fasting celebration) days. The same can be said of certain educational institutions that have welcomed Muslim members and hosted speakers and lecturers to talk about a variety of religious, cultural, historic, and social issues. Prison authorities have welcomed Muslim teachers and preachers to conduct prayers, teach prisoners about Islam, and discuss it with them. They welcome the spread of Islam through the prisons, once they witnessed its positive effects on the prisoners' behavior—for example, by persuading them to abandon drugs and avoid crime. In 1992, the Pentagon approved the appointment of religious instructors inside the three branches of the U.S. Armed Forces. The first minister, Chaplain Abdul-Rasheed Muhammad, was inaugurated in an official ceremony and was followed by others, for a total of fourteen instructors. The number of mosques and Islamic institutions and schools markedly increased, and 1997 was designated the year of the introduction of Islam and the Muslims to the United States.

Many American institutions have opened their doors to Muslims. The first Muslim judge was appointed, and courts began consulting juristic experts when dealing with cases involving Muslim litigants. The former First Lady, Hillary Clinton, employed a female Muslim assistant who wore the *hijab* (traditional dress and headscarf). The first Muslim American ambassador was appointed to Fiji. The Pentagon agreed to modify uniforms for female Muslim officers and privates to include a headscarf worn under the cap. All civilian and military government employees were encouraged to read and learn about Islam before going to Muslim countries so as to avoid offending local sensibilities or cultural traditions and thus provoking a negative reaction toward the United States and its citizens. These efforts have led to a good understanding of Islam and Muslims. Some people have even been inspired to convert to Islam or, at least, to respect it and its followers, to be ready to appreciate their cause, and, in certain cases, to empathize with it.

Cases have been brought before the courts against pressure on Muslim women to remove the hijab or the head cover, all of which were resolved in favor of the Muslim women. Muslim men and women are now clearly visible with their distinctive dress, raising public awareness and interest in their religion, history, and culture. They highlight the positive aspects of Islam that can be passed on to this country, especially in family life, and they practice what I refer to as "the silent dawah."

SEPTEMBER 11: THE AFTERMATH

The shattering events of September 11, 2001, have left everyone in a state of shock. Since then, Muslims and Americans have woken up to a new reality, the like of which has never been known before. The need has arisen, as never before, for a new fiqh dealing with the question of Muslim minorities in the West in particular.

Large numbers of non-Muslim Americans from all strata of society have turned toward learning about Islam from its original sources and from its followers, rather than from others. Numerous churches, universities, and research and study institutions have embarked on inviting imams, professors, and lecturers to speak on Islam and expound its principles, sources, relationship to other religions, and effect on its followers. In addition, speakers are invited to answer questions that are raised by many Americans about Islam, especially those debated in the media relating to the link between

Islamic beliefs and extremism. People wish to know whether Prophet Muhammad (SAAS)[4] taught his followers to be extremists and whether he ordered them to kill their opponents or those who did not believe in Islam. What is the Islamic view of the freedom of the human being? Does Islam exclude freedom of religion? These misconceptions can cause people to judge Islam to be a militant faith, ever advocating fighting, war, and the use of duress to convert others, kill them, or force them to pay protection money. Some have cited the Prophet's battles against his enemies as proof of Islam's militancy.

Nor has all this been enough to satisfy Islam's detractors. Many of them have reverted to established works and references in fiqh and other Islamic sciences to randomly select passages, terms, and statements and interrogate Muslim imams and workers about them. Some of these are as follows:

- Islam divides the world into the "land of Islam" and the "land of war." Does this not mean that Muslims are in a state of continual war with the rest of the world? Does it not give Muslims the right to fight the followers of any other religion whenever they wish and whenever they find themselves strong enough to declare war on others? Were the events of September 11 a result of the Muslims' belief that Americans are infidels and that their country is a "land of war"?
- What about *jizyah* (the "poll tax"), which Muslims insist that Jews and Christians pay with humiliation? It is a degrading tax that infringes people's rights and the freedom to choose the faith in which they believe.
- How about coercing and forcing Muslims who convert to other religions to reconvert to Islam on pain of the death penalty? Is this not the kind of compulsion that you assert is rejected by your faith?
- What about the rights of women, whom Muslims believe to be of inferior minds and lesser religious conviction? A woman's testimony, according to your faith, counts as half of that of a man. What about the right to detain your women in the home, and the right of the man to marry four wives, whereas a woman can have only one husband, whom she has to serve and obey? A woman cannot disobey her husband's wishes or separate from him, because he alone has the right to end the marriage. What about hijab? Do you not see that imposing it on women is a form of humiliation and undermines your trust in them? Does this not confirm the belief that a woman is a second-class citizen who exists solely for the satisfaction of man's sexual desires, bearing and looking after his children, and taking care of his home? Nevertheless, the man is still considered superior to the woman, and he has the last word on whether to keep or divorce her. Moreover, a woman's share of an inheritance is half that of a man. How about depriving women and beating them if they disobey their men?[5]

- What about the amputation of a hand for theft, the stoning to death for adultery, and the killing of homosexuals, using the vilest means such as burning them to death at the stake or throwing them from a great height?
- Why are vile dictatorship, human rights abuses, disease, backwardness, prejudice, and extremism so rife in your countries? Why have all the efforts of development and modernization in your countries failed so miserably? Is not Islam the cause of your backwardness, just as Christianity was the cause of our progress, once we had put it in its rightful place? Why have you failed in adopting democracy? Is this not evidence that the teachings of Islam encourage oppression, dictatorship, class differences, and other similar afflictions?
- Why does Islam teach you that killing yourselves in order to kill civilians in Palestine and New York will lead you to Paradise?

Such misconceptions, questions, and stereotypes need to be intelligently and correctly approached and responded to. They can no longer be dismissed or brushed under the carpet.

LEGAL AND RELIGIOUS FRAMEWORK

Let us begin our discussion by defining the two terms, *fiqh* and *minorities*, that constitute the core of this chapter.

Fiqh

The current usage of the term *fiqh* was not common in the early days of Islam. The term more widely used then was *fahm*, or "comprehension" of the preordained purpose and wisdom of the command of God. In more intricate issues that required closer examination, some would use instead the term *fiqh*, or "understanding." In *al-Muqaddimah*, Ibn Khaldun says:

> Fiqh is the knowledge of God's rules, *ahkam*, regarding the behavior and actions of adult individuals, be they obligatory, forbidden, recommended, abhorrent or permissible. These rules are received from the Qur'an and the Sunnah and the means God has established to ascertain them. The formulation and articulation of these rules, using those means, is what is referred to as fiqh.[6]

The term *fuqaha* (jurists or fiqh practitioners) was not common in those days, either. To distinguish them from their unlearned or illiterate contemporaries, the Prophet's companions who devoted themselves to deduction and the reasoning of religious rules were known as "students" or "readers." According to Ibn Khaldun, "Then the lands of Islam expanded and illiteracy among the Arabs receded due to the spread of literacy. The practice of deduction took hold; fiqh flourished and became a vocation and a science. Thus, 'readers' and 'students' became jurists or *fuqaha.'*"[7]

Minorities

The term *minorities* is a political one that has come into use in contemporary international convention. It refers to a group or groups of state subjects of a racial, linguistic, or religious affiliation different from that of the majority population.

The demands of minorities often include those of the equality of civil and political rights; the recognition of the right to be different and distinctive in beliefs, values, and personal status; as well as such other matters that do not infringe on the overall framework they share with the rest of society. Leaders often emerge among minorities to articulate and express the particular features and aspirations of their group through the following ways:

- The education of the minority group in its history and origins, and the definition of its ethnic characteristics and raison d'être, in order to answer such questions as "Who are we?" and "What do we want?"
- The forging of ties between minority members
- The promotion of educated elite to represent the minority's distinctive culture and traditions
- The establishment and promotion of initiatives to secure the livelihood and social welfare of the group's members following the successful example of Jewish minorities

A "Fiqh for Minorities"

The discussion of a "fiqh for minorities" raises a number of questions:

- Under what discipline should this fiqh be placed?
- What subjects of the social sciences does it relate to, and how far does it interact with other disciplines?
- How did it come to be known as the "fiqh for minorities," and how accurate is this terminology?
- What approach should be adopted when dealing with issues arising from large concentrations of Muslims living outside the geographic and historical Islamic domain?

The fiqh for minorities cannot be included under fiqh as it is understood today—that is, the fiqh of minor issues. Rather, it ought to come under the science of fiqh in its general sense, which covers all theological and practical branches of Islamic law and jurisprudence. This would be in line with the meaning of fiqh used by the Prophet in the hadith: "He to whom God wishes good, He makes him articulate in the religion."[8] Imam Abu Hanifah referred to this knowledge as the "greater fiqh," or macrofiqh, a term that he chose as the title of his great work on the subject.

For this reason, we believe it more appropriate to categorize the fiqh for minorities under fiqh in the macro, or general, sense to avoid the creation of a legislative or fiqh vacuum.

Fiqh for minorities is a specific discipline that takes into account the relationship between the religious ruling and the conditions of the community and the location where it exists. It is a fiqh that applies to a specific group of people living under particular conditions with special needs that may not be appropriate for other communities. Besides religious knowledge, practitioners of this fiqh will need a wider acquaintance with several social sciences disciplines, especially sociology, economics, political science, and international relations.

The term *fiqh for minorities* has, therefore, a precise definition, acceptable from both a religious as well as a conventional point of view. It is not meant to give minorities privileges or concessions not available to Muslim majorities; on the contrary, it aims to project minorities as representative models or examples of Muslim society in the countries in which they live. Based on the rules and fundamentals of this fiqh, a number of parameters have been identified that may define our method in responding to questions from minority members. The main features of these parameters are elaborated further later on in this discussion.

REDEFINING THE QUESTION

When a question relating to minorities is raised, the contemporary fiqh practitioner or mufti will need to understand that he is dealing with a situation beyond the simplistic one of an inquirer unable to obtain an Islamic ruling on a problem he is facing and a scholar who sees his duty as nothing more than giving a fatwa. This is an extremely unscientific approach, inherited from an era when traditional adherence to established doctrine (*taqlid*) was reinforced by illiterate members of society who found it easier to follow and imitate their teachers and their predecessors.

Today, a more logical and scientific approach is required, one that delves deeply into the background of both the query and the inquirer, as well as paying close attention to the underlying social factors that caused the question to be raised. Is the form in which the question has been worded acceptable, or should it be modified and represented as an issue of fiqh to be treated within a comprehensive context that brings into play major

Shariah rules, guiding Quranic principles, higher governing values, and the essential objectives of Islamic law?

Thus, we may be able to appreciate more deeply the Quranic advice not to raise questions whose answers could lead to serious social problems, for these questions are considered the result of negative factors that would only be reinforced should the answers be provided. The Quran has imparted to us a methodical approach by which issues are broken down and questions reconstructed before they are answered. For example: "They ask you about the new moons. Say: 'New moons are means people use for measuring time and for pilgrimage" (*al-Baqarah:* 189). The question, as originally expressed by the Jews of Madinah, was concerned with the physical aspects of the phases of the moon and why they occurred. However, in the Quran it was reconstructed to deal with the functions of the moon, linking its apparent size and orbit with the determination of information such as times and dates constantly sought by mankind.

The whole question then becomes an exercise in education on several levels. First, teach people how to phrase questions accurately so as to elicit appropriate and correct answers. Second, highlight all the elements that shape the question, eliminating those hidden in the inquirer's mind that can be done away with or ignored. Inquirers often have different intentions, and unless the respondent is aware of this fact, he or she can very easily be diverted into giving the wrong response. Inquiries arise for a variety of reasons: There are questions that seek knowledge or information, affirmative questions, rhetorical questions, loaded questions that refute a statement or contradict it, leading questions aimed at exposing the ignorance of the respondent, and so on. Third, prepare the inquirer for receiving the appropriate answer. This approach is evident in the majority of cases where direct inquiries are raised in the Quran (*al-Isaa:* 85, *al-Kahf:* 83, etc.). Inquiry has its own manners that must be observed by both the inquirer and the respondent.

Accordingly, one can appreciate the Prophet's dislike of idle talk and of asking too many questions, or badly phrased ones, that might result in giving the wrong ruling or judgment.

One may then ask, Can Muslim minorities participate in the political life of a host country where the non-Muslims form a majority and where the political system is non-Islamic? An intelligent jurist, appreciating the universality of Islam, the role of the Muslim community in the world, and the necessary interaction between cultures and civilizations in contemporary international life, would decline to respond to a question formulated in this manner. He would change its tone from a negative to a positive one, based on his knowledge of Islam's universal aims and the unique characteristics of both the faith and the Muslim community. Rephrased and restructured, the question would then become, What is Islam's view regarding a group of Muslims who find themselves living among a non-Muslim majority whose system of government allows them to observe and exercise all Islamic obligations that do not threaten public order? Furthermore, the system allows members of the Muslim minority to attain public office, influence policy, assume leadership positions, propagate their beliefs, and set up useful social institutions. Should such a minority relinquish these rights and decline these opportunities for fear of assimilation into the non-Muslim majority or of being influenced by them?

When put this way, the question still satisfies the objectives of the original, but it reflects a sense of responsibility, steering the response toward a more constructive direction. Instead of seeking a license to justify a negative situation, the debate turns to dealing with obligations, positive action, and constructive roles.

THE NEED FOR SPECIALIST IJTIHAD IN THE FORMATION OF A FIQH OF MINORITIES

In recent decades, Muslims have settled in many countries outside Islam's historic and geographic sphere. Within these countries, which have witnessed a growth in the spread of Islam, Muslims are to face new situations that raise many issues far beyond the limited personal ones such as halal food, the sighting of the new moon, or marriage to non-Muslim women. The debate has now turned to greater and much more profound issues relating to Muslim identity, the role of Muslims in their new homeland, their relationship to the world Muslim community, the future of Islam outside its present borders, and how it may go forward to establish its universality in all parts of the globe.

Some may have tried to view these issues as arising out of expediency or the product of exceptional circumstances, forgetting that this approach is extremely narrow and limited. No wonder Muslims find themselves in a sea of confusion, faced as they are with differences in opinion among jurists: some—to varying degrees of strictness—cite differences between life in Muslim and non-Muslim societies (the so-called *dar al-Islam* and *dar al-harb*), and others compare the present with the past and ignore the huge social and historic changes that have occurred. The overall result of these mistaken methods has been to throw the Muslims into confusion and disarray. This, in turn, forced Muslims into isolation and restricted their contribution.

The problems of Muslim minorities can only be tackled with a fresh juristic vision, based on the principles, objectives, and higher values of the Quran in conjunction with the aims of the Shariah—a fresh approach that draws guidance from the authentic Sunnah and example of the Prophet with a view to implementing the principles and values of the Quran. A new methodology for replicating the Prophet's example is needed in order to make his way clearer and more accessible to everyone at all times.

WHAT CAN BE LEARNED FROM THE INHERITED FIQH?

Though varied and rich, the volume of theoretical fiqh bequeathed to us dealing with relations between Muslims and non-Muslims was closely associated with the historic circumstances in which it was developed. It, therefore, is part of its own time and space and none of it can be applied to other substantially different situations. It can only be considered as a precedent to be examined and studied in order to discern the principles on which it was based and that guided our predecessors to produce it. As a precedent, this wealth of jurisprudence is of value to today's jurists to provide them with the skills and methods to respond to the needs of the times. The aim should not be to apply the old fatwas literally but to use them as a guide, learning how to obtain the original principles, the "roots" or *usul*, from which earlier jurists derived and articulated them.

Our pioneering jurists bequeathed to us a golden rule that supports this approach: The changing of rulings should not be censured by the change of time. Many jurists, such as Imam al-Shafei and others, were flexible with certain rulings and opinions, changing them according to the realities of a particular situation or specific reason that arose as they moved from one country to another, or when certain conditions pertaining to the earlier situation had changed, or simply because times had changed. Several innovative jurists indicated that their differences with their own teachers over certain issues were simply due to "the changing of times and situations, rather than to new evidence or reasoning."

The Prophet also set a good precedent when he advised against visiting graveyards but later permitted it, saying, "Visit them because they remind you of the hereafter."[9] The same flexibility was also applied to the storing of meat and many other similar instances.[10]

The Prophet's companions adopted the same approach and never inched from amending or changing their views and rulings whenever they found reason or justification for so doing, due to changes of time or space. Many of the rulings advanced by the four successors of the Prophet included minor as well as major amendments to rulings applied during his lifetime, while some were totally new.[11] Muslims of the second generation followed a similar practice, deviating in their rulings over certain issues from the views of their predecessors.[12]

A study of cases dealt with by the Prophet's contemporaries and their followers clearly shows that they had understood very well the specific purpose, wisdom, reasons, and causes underlying the Shariah. The study, interpretation, comprehension, and application of all religious text should take place within the framework of the purposes and reasons of the Shariah and their underlying wisdom. Insistence on mere linguistic or literal interpretation would not relieve jurists from their responsibility until the ultimate

objectives of the Shariah are served. Rigid or dogmatic attitudes and se-
mantics can only lead to a fiqh similar to that of the Israelites in their argument with Moses (AS)[13] over the sacrificial cow, as related in the Quran.
The need to go beyond the limited fiqh inherited from past generations remains strong for several reasons, some of which relate to methodology and
others to the ultimate objectives (*maqasid*) of the Islamic Shariah.

REASONS FOR A NEW METHODOLOGY

As a first reason for a new fiqh, we must note that some earlier jurists did
not classify the sources of Islamic law in a precise way, one that would fa-
cilitate the deduction of rulings for contemporary issues. Such a system of
classification would consider the Quran as the ultimate and overriding
source of all legislation, the absolute criterion and final reference. It is immutable and incontrovertible. In second place would come the Sunnah of
the Prophet as a complementary and explanatory reference, expanding,
elaborating, and extending the Quranic rulings and principles.

In addition, most jurists overlooked the universality of Islam as a defining factor in their rationalization and analysis of relations between Muslims
and non-Muslims. Their work reflects a certain degree of introversion incompatible with the universality of Islam's eternal message. There has also
been excessive preoccupation with parochial factors of geography and society, strongly associating Islam with the social and geographic environment of its golden era.

Also, the thinking of Muslim jurists with respect to the geopolitical world
map of the time was influenced by contemporaneous historic convention.
They overlooked the Quranic concept of the world and human geography,
and their works thus have tended to be localized and provincial.

Finally, the higher values, principles, and objectives of Islamic legislation
were obscured, reinforcing a partial, fractional, and personalized image of
fiqh. Imam al-Ghazali described fiqh as "a minor science."

REASONS FOR A CLEAR OBJECTIVE

First, in the early days following the time of the Prophet, Muslims were not
used to seeking justice or refuge in non-Muslim lands. The land of Islam
was one, sovereign and secure, with no borders to divide it. Inhabitants
were free to roam from one part of the vast empire to the other without
any feelings of alienation, estrangement, or inferiority.

Second, "citizenship," as the concept is understood today, was unknown
during the heyday of Islamic fiqh. Instead, there were cultural and political

affiliations that were often based on ideological and traditional loyalties. Inter-religious and cultural interactions were undertaken with reserve and caution, mixed with varying degrees of tolerance. Muslims treated non-Muslims as *ahl al-dhimmah*. In other words, non-Muslim citizens, most notably Jews and Christians, could enjoy protection and safety while living in a Muslim state.

Third, there were no established criteria, such as birth, domicile, or mar-riage, for gaining citizenship in another country. Common beliefs and cul-ture were sufficient to confer "citizenship" on new arrivals who would oth-erwise remain as outsiders or foreign to the indigenous society.

Fourth, the ancient world had no concept or experience of international law or diplomatic conventions obliging host countries to protect immigrants or mete out to them equal treatment, except in certain distinguishing matters.

Fifth, the rationale of power was reigning supreme in the relations among ancient empires, including the Muslim empire. Each considered the other as enemy territory which it had the right to overrun and annex, in full or in part. Empires knew no frontiers, and their armies stopped advancing only when the terrain prevented them.

Sixth, our predecessors did not experience the closely connected world we live in today and its interacting cultures and global village atmosphere. Their world was made up of separate "islands," with limited cohabitation or understanding of one another. The "fiqh of conflict" was then prevalent, dictated by the times, but what is needed today is a "fiqh of coexistence" that suits our world in spirit as well as in form.

Finally, some jurists express in their fatwas a kind of resistance or reac-tion to a particular social context that is different from ours of today. A good example of this is Ibn Taymiyyah's views on the need for Muslims to be different from Jewish, Christian, or other non-Muslim groups and his op-position to enlisting their help.[14] One could also cite the early-twentieth-century Algerian ulama's fatwa prohibiting taking up French citizenship. These and other similar opinions stem from a "culture of conflict" that Mus-lim minorities today can better do without.

TOWARD A FOUNDATION FOR A FIQH FOR MINORITIES

In this chapter, I introduce a set of methodological principles that I believe should be taken into account by students of fiqh for minorities. Like all fiqh, this special discipline requires rules and principles of its own.

The science of principles of fiqh, or *usul al-fiqh,* is one of the most no-ble of the theoretical sciences to have been formulated by our pioneering scholars. Imam al-Ghazali describes it well when he writes, "It is a science that combines reason with oral tradition, opinion with religious text, pro-ducing an elegant synthesis of both."[15]

However, when this science first emerged, practitioners applied it as a tool for settling ongoing debates between advocates of hadith and those of reason. From these beginnings, it grew and developed, in the process spilling over into other theoretical as well as practical Islamic sciences in the hope that it might bring these two camps together. Although it was also influenced by other sciences, it continued to retain its original structure, as envisaged by pioneering scholars such as Imam al-Shafie and others. I have compiled a concise history of the development and codification of this science since the publication of al-Shafie's *al-Risalah* up to the present.[16] The main conclusion of my research is that, despite the passing of centuries, the subject has not developed a great deal. Except in works of collation, abridgment, interpretation, and commentary, hardly any significant new contribution has been made.

The main additional contribution worth mentioning here is that of Imam al-Shatibi, who developed some of the ideas of Imam al-Haramayn, al-Ghazali, and others relating to the objectives (*maqasid*) of Shariah. His contribution stands as a significant landmark in the evolution of the theory of fiqh. Modern scholars such as Shaykh al-Tahir ibn Ashur,[17] Allal al-Fasi,[18] Ahmad al-Raysuni,[19] and Yusuf al-Alim[20] developed these objectives of Shariah even further to form a science in its own right, almost independent from *usul al-fiqh*. One hopes, however, that such a separation does not take place in our case, as it did to earlier disciplines such as "General Rules of Fiqh," "Extraction of Secondary Rules from Primary Rules," and "Debate and Disagreement." If this were to happen today, I fear that the science of fiqh theory would revert to stagnation and become yet again a mere collection of philosophical and polemic rules or linguistic and intellectual arguments, or a set of works borrowed from Quranic and hadith sciences. As such, it would no longer be an area for innovation or development but a selection of treatises. The vital science that Mustafa Abd al-Raziq called "Islamic Philosophy"[21] must be reviewed and researched thoroughly in order for it to be forever open and a part of the overall system of Islamic knowledge. It should continue to play its role as laid down by the pioneering scholars who intended it to be the science for new intellectual and juristic innovators and for developing juristic talent that would formulate the Quranic approach.

In defining the fiqh for minorities, I have attempted to highlight the most important aspects of fiqh theory and its methodological limitations that require special attention, without overlooking the rich fiqh legacy, on which I shall aim to build and develop further. The theory of the fiqh for minorities does not ignore the reasoning of the science of fiqh or the rules of extrapolation. It is exercised within the established rules of ijtihad or those of interpretative analysis. What I aim to do is employ the techniques and tools of ijtihad in a way that is compatible with our time and the new explosion in knowledge, the sciences, and means of learning and restore the role of

Shariah in modern life. There is no doubt that the role of ijtihad is to regulate and guide man's actions to accomplish his role as the vicegerent of God on Earth, as God intended. If this is achieved, the end will be positive and conducive to humans receiving the appropriate reward.

The pivotal issue here, then, is the nature, value, quality, and purpose of human actions. This is the fundamental objective of legislation now and in the past, divine or human made. All divine doctrines were aimed at guiding humans' actions to fulfill the purpose of their beings, which is to serve God in the widest possible sense of the word. Such fulfillment shall be reflected in life in the form of prosperity and advancement and in the human heart as pure monotheism, *tawhid,* and as good and constructive behavior.

The whole debate over prophethood and man's need for it, the human mind and its powers and limitations, finite text and infinite events, is related to this central fact. The controversy that has raged on generation after generation can be summarized as follows: Is the human mind independently capable of evaluating human behavior, or should this be a function of divine Revelation alone? Must the two act together in this context in order to identify the relationship between human behavior and God's purpose behind creation? Islam's answer is that the two must work jointly in the evaluation process, because they are complementary and mutually indispensable. The following points should be taken into consideration in the process of formulating a fiqh for minorities:

- Ijtihad (independent reasoning) is an extremely vital function and a distinctive feature of the Muslim *ummah* (community).
- Islam is the first religion to recognize unconditionally the role of the human mind in the evaluation and judgment of human behavior. In fact, it insists on that role, believing that while the origin of the Shariah is divine, its application in the real world of human behavior is human. God says, "For each of you, We have ordained a system of laws and assigned a path" (*al-Ma'idah:* 48).
- Islam considers ijtihad an intellectual state of mind that inspires people to think systematically and according to specific rational methods, and not simply a dogmatic activity constrained within the mere formulation of rules and fatwas.
- Many people these days are advocating ijtihad; the secularists are using it as a pretext to temper and distort the rules of Shariah, and the "traditionalists" to forge a link between the past and the present and revive the Shariah. What is urgently needed today is the ijtihad that prepares Islam and Muslims for a global role in the future.

To establish the foundations of this kind of ijtihad, it will be necessary to recall certain important rules and test their validity on issues relating to minorities. If these are found to be conducive and encouraging, they can be tested in other areas; otherwise, they may be put aside for future research.

Our understanding of religion and religious practice should, in the first instance, be based on the study of divine Revelation, on the one hand, and the real dynamic world, on the other. The Quran guides us to the marvels and secrets of the physical world, while reflection on the real world leads us back to understanding the Quran. We must appreciate how the two interact, contrast, and complement each other.

This is what we refer to as the "combined reading": a reading of Revelation for an understanding of the physical world and its laws and principles, and a reading of the physical world to appreciate and recognize the value of Revelation. The purpose of reading Revelation is to apply the general "key principles" to specific situations and link the absolute to the relative, as far as our capabilities allow. The reader in all cases is the human being, God's vicegerent on Earth, guided by a strong faith in Revelation and an understanding of it, on the one hand, and his or her appreciation of the laws and behavior of the physical world, on the other.[22]

When Imam Ali (RAA)[23] was confronted by the slogan "No rule but God's rule," he responded by saying, "The Quran is a book that speaks only through the mouths of men." This is a fundamental philosophical observation since, in the absence of proper methodology, the meaning and implication of revealed text are determined and influenced by human culture, expertise, knowledge, and experience. This methodology, the "combined reading" in this context, does not come into its own until the metaphysical dimension of life is brought into the fore. Thus, the body of knowledge that is beyond human perception, what the Quran refers to as *ghayb*, is translated into laws and principles to be studied and debated among scientists rigorously and objectively. This is done once we differentiate between what is relatively beyond our perception as human beings, which gradually unfolds with time, and what is absolutely out of the bounds of human knowledge. In this way, we will be able to identify from the Quran itself workable and practical methodologies for such concepts as the "counteraccident" and "counterabsurd" theories, the theory of normism, and the supremacy of the Quran, which makes the Sunnah of the Prophet a practical interpretation of the Quran without any conflict or contradiction in the authority of the two sources.

Once the process of the "combined reading" is under way, we shall find that the noblest values that the two "readings" highlight are the following: monotheism (*tawhid*), purification (*tazkiyah*), and civilization (*umran*). *Tawhid* is the belief in the absolute and pure Oneness of God Almighty as the Creator, Maker, and Everlasting Lord. The second value, *tazkiyah*, relates to man as God's vicegerent on Earth, entrusted by and accountable to him, charged with building and developing the world. He can only achieve this through self-purification. *Umran* is taken to mean the cultivation and development of the world as the arena harnessed for discharging man's mission and the crucible for his trials, accountability, and development.

These values are, in fact, ends in themselves, reflecting God's purpose behind the creation of the world, which was not pointless, and the creation of man, which was not in vain, and God's admonition not to corrupt the Earth. These three values, or objectives, come under the heading of "worship," and it has been necessary to understand and highlight them from the outset as the criteria by which human behavior is judged. Duties and obligations rest on these values and stem from them. They feature very prominently in understanding the Sunnah as well as in the understanding of the work of the companions and the rightly guided caliphs, especially Abu Bakr and Umar. There are countless examples to show how, in their interpretations and fatwas, they had always referred to the main and fundamental principles, fully cognizant of the higher values and objectives of Islam, from which they extracted secondary and specific rulings. This is also frequently found in the fatwas of Imam Ali, and some of Uthman's, and it is clear in all their opinions and interpretations that have reached us. It can also be observed in the fiqh of the following generation who learned from them and their contemporaries.

In defining fiqh terms and the codification of the fiqh literature, however, later generations of jurists were bogged down in dogma and terminology, and they were influenced by the translated works of philosophy and logic. They began to borrow the terms of those works in order to classify duties and obligations as mandatory, obligatory, recommended, preferred, prohibited, forbidden, or otherwise unconditionally permissible. This was done in order to relate these terms to the concepts of reward and punishment, praise and rejection, and so on. Thus, a hiatus was created within the science of fiqh where the fundamental purpose of its rulings was lost until they reemerged in the works of al-Shatibi.

Hence the need to go back to the very beginning and start in the evaluation of human activity with the higher governing values and purposes and then go on to conferring the prescription: "do" or "don't," and so on. We must view rational issues and philosophical terms as secondary, for the risk of overlooking or discarding some of these terms is far less serious than disregarding the higher governing values and purposes.

On another score, we must consider the levels of purpose with reference to responsible adults with regard to "expediency," "priority," and "embellishment," which should be linked to the three higher values: tawhid, tazkiyah, and umran. This will open wide the doors for jurists who are capable of including all new situations under these levels, as was done by Shaykh Ibn Ashur, who listed freedom as one of the main purposes of Shariah. So did Shaykh Muhammad al-Ghazali, who included equality and human rights among its purposes. Other issues also need to be included among the needs and priorities of the Muslim community, and these should be accommodated accordingly.

Jurists have identified certain questions under the heading "Issues Common to the Quran and the Sunnah," and although they standardized their terms, they are, in fact, not the same. The Quranic text is the direct word of God Almighty, the eternal and absolute miracle. It is a sacred text that cannot be allegorically read or interpreted. It was undoubtedly revealed in the language of Prophet Muhammad, but the text bears certain meanings when it is pronounced by God Almighty, a different one when uttered by the Prophet, and yet a third when recited by ordinary human mortals.

For this reason, the words of God and the words of his Prophet must never be unconditionally or unreservedly equated. The important minute differences in nuance between the Quran and the Sunnah do not allow such absolute equality, despite the fact that both of them originate from one and the same source. The tendency to equate between the Quran and the Sunnah has, at times, led to confusion in understanding the true relationship between the two sources. For, although they are not the same, contradiction or conflict between them cannot be possible. The Quran is the source that sets the rules, values, and standards which the Sunnah explains and elaborates further. The Quran, in fact, endorses and legitimizes the other available sources, including the Sunnah, and supersedes them. The Sunnah revolves around the Quran and is closely tied up with it but never surpasses or overrules it.

The confusion in defining the relationship between the Quran and the Sunnah has produced a number of absurd notions, such as the Quran and the Sunnah mutually annul or cancel each other; the Sunnah is the judge of the Quran; the Quran is far more dependent on the Sunnah than the other way around. These claims made the relationship between the Quran and the Sunnah one of precise logic, of either definite or speculative nature, which is contrary to the Quranic description of the relationship. In the Quran, we read, "We have revealed to you the Quran, so that you may make clear to people what has been revealed to them, and that they may reflect" (*al-Nahl:* 44); "We have revealed to you the Book so that you may clarify for them what they had disputed over, and as a guide and a mercy for true believers" (*al-Nahl:* 64); and "We have revealed to you the Book that explains everything and which is a guide and a mercy and good news for those who surrender themselves to God" (*al-Nahl:* 89).

As for sources other than the Quran and the Sunnah, known as secondary or minor sources and estimated to be around forty-seven in number, there is no universal agreement; some of them can be classified under methodology, while others are concerned with interpretation, comprehension, and elaboration. They are used in as far as they support and elucidate the Quran and its objectives and values.

METHODOLOGICAL PRINCIPLES FOR THE STUDY OF THE QURAN

There is a need to propose and develop such principles to assist in revealing more of the purposes of the Quran. This should, in turn, help in building up fiqh rules for minorities as well as majorities. Here are some suggested principles:

1. *Unveiling the structural unity of the Quran by reading it in contrast to the physical universe and its movement.* The Sunnah of the infallible Prophet is viewed as the practical example and an interpretation of the Quran's values in the real world. The Sunnah should also be viewed as an integrated structure in its own right, closely linked to the Quran as an elaboration of its values for relative specific situations.

2. *Acknowledging the supremacy and precedence of the Quran as the judge over all else, including the sayings and actions of the Prophet.* Once the Quran establishes a certain principle, such as tolerance and justice in dealing with non-Muslims, the ruling of the Quran takes precedence. The sayings and actions of the Prophet, in this case, should, if possible, be interpreted to conform to the principle established by the Quran and be subservient to it. One of the examples in this case is the interpretation of a hadith regarding not to return the greetings of a non-Muslim with a better greeting that does not seem to conform to the teachings of the Quran.

3. *Recalling that the Quran has revived the legacy of earlier prophets.* It verifies, evaluates, and expurgates this legacy of all distortions, and then represents it in a purified form in order to standardize human references. This is how the Quran has embraced the whole legacy of previous prophets and taken supremacy over it.

4. *Reflecting on the purpose of the Quran in linking the reality of human life with that which is beyond human perception, or* ghayb, *and discrediting the notion of randomness or coincidence.* This facilitates an understanding of the relationship between the seen and the unseen worlds, the knowable and the unknowable; between the absolute text of the Quran and the real human condition. It reveals part of the delicate distinction between man's humanity and individuality. As an individual, man is a relative being, but his humanity makes him a universal and an absolute one.

5. *Recalling the importance of the factors of time and space.* The Quran emphasizes the sanctity of time by specifying the number of months as twelve and totally forbidding the intercalation of the calendar. It identifies certain lands as sacred and others as sacrosanct. Within this time–space frame, one may come to understand the existence of man since the time of the creation of Adam and Eve until he reaches his ultimate destiny. This existence is the link between the universality of the Quran and that of mankind.

6. *Recognition of an intrinsic Quranic rationale whose rules are infused in its text and that man is capable, with God's help, of uncovering the rules of this rationale that will guide his mind and his activity.* These rules are themselves capable of becoming laws that protect the objective mind against deviation and perversity. The Quranic rationale can provide a common base for human intellectual activity that would help man break away from the hegemony of his own thinking, which is shaped by tradition and blind imitation of previous generations and the attendant tribal consequences.

7. *Adopting the Quranic concept of geography.* The whole Earth belongs to God and Islam is the religion of God. In reality, every country either is a land of Islam (*dar al-Islam*) as a matter of fact or will be so in the future. All humanity is the community of Islam (*ummat al-Islam*), either by adopting the faith or by being a prospective follower of it.

8. *Recognizing the universality of the Quranic mission.* Unlike previous scriptures that addressed specific, localized communities, the Quran began by addressing Muhammad and his close family, then turned to Makkah and the surrounding towns, then to other communities, and finally to the whole of humankind. Thus, it became the only book capable of dealing with contemporary global situations. Any message to today's world must be based on common rules and values, and it must be methodical. It has to be based on rules that govern objective thinking.

9. *Studying very closely the complicated aspects of the lives of people, as the context within which questions and issues arise.* Unless life is understood properly in all its dimensions, it will be difficult to formulate a suitable fiqh theory capable of referring to the Quran and obtaining satisfactory and correct answers. During the time of the Prophet, questions would arise out of various situations, and Revelation would be received providing the answers. Today, the Revelation is complete, and all we need to do is articulate our problems and requirements and then refer to the Quran for answers. We then refer to the Sunnah of the Prophet to understand the context of the Revelation and link the text with the actual situation or incident.

10. *Studying in detail the fundamental principles, especially those relating to the ultimate purposes of the Shariah, in order to incorporate them in the formulation of the principles of a modern fiqh for minorities.* The study must be based on the ultimate purposes and linked to the governing higher values, noting the delicate distinction between the purposes of the Shariah and the intentions of responsible adults.

11. *Recognizing that the inherited fiqh is not an adequate reference for fatwa or the formulation of rules in such matters.* It does, however, contain precedents of fatwa and legislation that can be applied and

referred to for determining approaches and methodologies, as appropriate. Whatever is found to be applicable, useful, and representative of the spirit of Islam may be taken, preserving continuity from the past to the present, without elevating the ruling to the level of Quranic text or taking it as an absolute ruling for the issue in question. It is not a criticism of our predecessors that they did not have answers to issues they had not encountered or events and situations unheard of in their time.

12. *Testing our fatwas, rulings, and opinions in real-life situations.* Every ruling of a fiqh has its own impact on reality, which can be positive, if the fatwa is correctly deduced, or otherwise results in certain setbacks somewhere along the way. The outcome in the latter case would be negative, and the ruling must be reviewed and revised. Thus, the fatwa process becomes one of debate and discussion between the fiqh and the realities of life, which are the ultimate testing ground that will prove how appropriate and practical the fiqh really is.

KEY QUESTIONS

Jurists concerned with a fiqh for minorities need to reflect very carefully on the key questions that arise from this subject, in order to prepare the ground fully and arrive at the true divine rulings, as far as humanly possible. These questions include the following:

- How do members of minorities answer the questions "Who are we?" and "What do we want?" in such a way that accurately reflects their particular situation and the common factors they share with others?
- Under what political system is a particular minority living? Is it democratic, hereditary, or military?
- What kind of majority is the minority living with? Is it authoritarian, consumed by feelings of dominance and possessiveness? Is it a majority willing to achieve a dynamic balance based on carefully considered rules that guarantee minority rights? How significant are these guarantees, and what mechanisms are in place to secure them?
- What is the size, or weight, of the minorities we are dealing with in respect of their human, cultural, economic, and political abilities and resources?
- What is the extent of the interaction between members of the society? Is there interaction between the minority and the majority in resources, industries, professions, and activities (rights and obligations), or is there discrimination based on laws confirming and promoting separation and segregation in all these fields?

- What is the nature of the human geography of the society? Is there interaction? Are there any natural or artificial differences, disparities, or distinctions? Are there certain natural resources peculiar to the minority or the majority, or are these resources common?
- Has the minority any cultural dimension or identity that enables it, perhaps in the long run, to dominate culturally? What would be the effect of this on the majority?
- Has the minority an extended existence outside the shared land, or has it no external roots or extensions? What would be the effect of either case?
- Has the minority any distinctive functions or activities it wishes to preserve, and what are they?
- Is the minority able to perform these activities normally, or does that require institutions and leadership to organize?
- What role do such institutions and leaders play in the lives of the minority? Do they focus more light on the minority's cultural identity?
- Can such institutions turn into a network of interests that enhance the minority's distinctive qualities and persuade it that its cultural characteristics are the factors that identify it as a minority?
- Would such institutions, unconsciously, lead members of the minority to question crucially the value or significance of these distinctive features, ask why they should not be passed on to others, or persuade the majority to adopt them?
- If the minority is a blend of both the historic and the ethnic, how can its identity be defined without risking its people being absorbed into the majority or becoming self-centered?
- How can the minority be educated to deal with the reactions of the majority and absorb the negative fallout without forfeiting the benefits?
- How can the common activities between the minority and the majority be developed and promoted? What areas have to be taken into account in this regard?
- How can the "special" and the "common" cultural identities be preserved and brought together at the same time?
- What must the minority do in order to identify those parts of its culture that could become common? What parts of the majority culture can it adopt? What is the majority's role in this process?

According to these clarifications that relate to the approach and the objectives as well as to the key questions that arise, we can confirm that many of the old opinions that emerged during the times of the empires will not, with all due respect, be of much use to us in establishing a contemporary fiqh for minorities. We nevertheless acknowledge the benefit many of them had specific to their time and place. We must go back to Revelation and the first Islamic model, taking note of the contributions of some fiqh practitioners whose opinion reflected the true spirit of Islam and who succeeded more than others in transcending the restrictions of history. Such opinions, however, cannot be taken as a source for Islamic rulings.

A FUNDAMENTAL RULE IN THE MUSLIM RELATIONS WITH OTHERS

The following two Quranic verses express the golden rule defining the relationship between Muslims and others:

> God does not forbid you to be kind and equitable to those who have neither fought you on account of your religion nor driven you from your homes. God loves the equitable. But God only forbids you to be allies with those who have fought you because of your religion and driven you from your homes and abetted others to do so. Those that make friends with them are wrongdoers. (*al-Mumtahanah:* 8–9)

Ibn al-Jawzi says, "This verse permits association with those who have not declared war against the Muslims and allows kindness towards them, even though they may not be allies."[24] According to Al-Qurtubi, "This verse is a permission from God to establish relations with those who do not show hostility towards the believers or wage war against them. It states that God does not forbid you to be kind to those who do not fight you."[25] Ibn Jarir al-Tabari, pointing out the general reference to non-Muslims of other religions and creeds, says, "The most credible view is that the verse refers to people of all kinds of creeds and religions who should be shown kindness and treated equitably. God referred to all those who do not fight the Muslims or drive them from their homes, without exception or qualification."[26]

The majority of commentators have understood equity to also mean justice. However, Qadi Abu Bakr ibn al-Arabi is of a different view because justice is incumbent on Muslims in the treatment of everyone, friend or foe. He cites the Quranic statement "Let not a people's enmity toward you incite you to act contrary to justice; be just, for it is closest to righteousness" (*al-Maidah:* 8). Ibn al-Arabi understands "equitable" in this context to mean benevolent, by showing financial generosity toward non-Muslims, whereas justice is expected toward those who fight the Muslims as well as those who do not.[27]

These two verses set out the moral and legal foundation-principle with which the Muslims must comply in their dealings with people of other faiths: kindness and justice toward all nonbelligerent communities. All developments and new situations must be judged according to this principle. The relationship between Muslims and non-Muslims cannot deviate from the main framework and the essential purpose for which God has revealed his words and sent his messengers, and this is the establishment of justice in the world. The Quran says, "We have sent Our messengers with manifest signs and sent down with them the Book and the balance, that people may act with justice" (*al-Hadid:* 25). This is an incontrovertible universal principle that applies with respect to the rights of Muslims and non-Muslims alike.

THE ROLE OF THE MUSLIM COMMUNITY

The Quran also describes the Muslim community as the "best nation ever raised for mankind" (*Ali Imran:* 110). This statement indicates that the qualities of the Muslim nation reside in the fact that God has raised it to lead humankind out of darkness and into the light, from servitude to humans to submission to God Almighty, as expressed by Rabi ibn Amir when he addressed the shah of Persia. It is a nation that has been raised in order to lead others and whose nature and role on Earth are intertwined.

Commentators, past and present, have pointed out this link between the nature and the role of the Muslim community. In explaining this statement, Ikrimah says, "The best of mankind [is] for mankind. In the past, people were not secure in other people's lands, but as Muslims, people of any color feel secure among you, as you are the best people for mankind."[28] According to Ibn al-Jawzi, "You are the best people for mankind."[29] Ibn Kathir says, "It means that Muslims are the best of nations and the most obliging towards other people."[30] Al-Nahhas and al-Baghawi also support this view.[31] Abu al-Suud elaborates further by saying, "You are the best community for people which clearly means helpful to other people. This is also implicit in the fact that the Muslim nation was raised for the benefit of mankind."[32] This is the same understanding expressed by al-Khatib: "A feature of the Muslim nation is that it should not keep any beneficial advantage to itself but should share its benefit with other human societies."[33]

With these two qualities, the Muslim ummah's role is not limited by land or confined in space. It has to reach out to others to convey the message of God. Thus, all references to dar al-kufr or dar al-Islam or dar al-harb, as geographic entities, become superfluous and restrictive.

Indeed, the concept of nation, or ummah, in Islamic jurisprudence is not associated with a particular human group or geographic location. It is solely dependent on the principle, even if it revolves around a single person. Thus, the Quran refers to Ibrahim as being "a nation" in his own right. "Ibrahim was a 'nation,' a paragon of piety, an upright man obedient to God. He was no polytheist, [for he was] always grateful for the blessings God gave him. God chose him and guided him to a straight path" (*al-Nahl:* 120–21).

Some classical scholars identified what we mean here and linked those limitations only to the possibility of Islam spreading wide and to the security of Muslims. Islam knows no geographic boundaries; dar al-Islam is anywhere a Muslim can live in peace and security, even if he lives among a non-Muslim majority. Likewise, *dar al-kufr* is wherever Muslims live under threat, even if the majority there adheres to Islam and Islamic culture.

Al-Kasani says, "Our [Hanafi] scholars are agreed that *dar al-kufr* could become *dar al-Islam* once Islamic law is applied there."[34] Qadi Abu Yusuf and Muhammad ibn al-Hasan believe that *dar al-Islam* "becomes *dar al-kufr* if non-Islamic law is implemented."[35] Ibn Hajr cites a view of al-Mawardi in which he goes well beyond this and considers that it is preferable for a Muslim to reside in a country where he can practice his religion openly than living in dar al-Islam because he would be able to attract more people to his faith and introduce it to them, even if by merely living among them. Al-Mawardi says, "If a Muslim is able to practice his religion openly in a non-Muslim land, that land becomes *dar al-Islam* by virtue of his settling there. Settling in such a country is preferable to moving away from it as other people would be likely to convert to Islam."[36]

Imam Fakhr al-Din al-Razi was notably correct in citing al-Shashi's views and taking them as a basis for introducing an excellent alternative to the classification of lands. Instead of dar al-harb, he describes the whole world as dar al-dawah, and dar al-Islam as dar al-ijabah. He also classifies people into *ummat al-dawah,* the non-Muslims, and *ummat al-ijabah,* the Muslims.

STANDING UP FOR ONE'S RIGHTS

God praised the believers for being positive and for standing up for their rights. He praised them for rejecting tyranny and injustice and for refusing to accept disgrace and humiliation. God says, "[A]nd those who avenge themselves when tyranny is incurred upon them help and defend themselves" (*al-Shura:* 39). Commenting on this verse, Ibn al-Jawzi says, "A Muslim must not allow himself to be humiliated."[37] Ibn Taymiyyah notes, "The opposite of avenging oneself is despondency and the opposite of patience is despair; neither patience nor despair are laudable as we can see with many people, including religious ones who incur wrong-doing or witness abhorrent acts. They neither stand up to avenge themselves nor remain patient; they are in fact despondent and despairing."[38]

Hence, acquiescence by Muslims to humiliation, resignation to inferior positions, the adoption of negative attitudes toward others, or withdrawal from proactive interaction with the environment they live in would be in contradiction to the principles advanced by these Quranic statements that call for affirmative and constructive engagement.

FORBEARANCE

Even if the Muslim minority's proactive participation with the majority should entail certain courtesies that may blur or dilute some aspects of the minority's behavior or qualities, other than the fundamentals of its faith, it would be acceptable and pardonable, because without such participation a greater good would be forfeited. This is not a new situation for Islamic fiqh. It was something that Muslim scholars have tolerated ever since the end of the era of the first four caliphs. Muslims were facing two choices: affirmative participation with certain concessions demanded by the reality of the prevailing tyranny, or passive association and withdrawal, leaving the ummah easy prey for tyrants. They opted for the former because of what they knew of Islam's positive and flexible attitude.

In establishing this principle, Ibn Taymiyyah says, "Muslims are required to do their best to cope with the situation. Those who assume office with the intention of pleasing God and serving the objectives of Islam and the interests of the people to the best of their ability, and who try their best to prevent wrong-doing, will not be penalized for what they could not achieve. It is far better that good people are in office than bad ones."[39] He also notes, "Wrong-doing and sinful behavior by some Muslims, rulers as well as subjects, should not prevent others from taking part in good activities."[40] Were he alive today, he would have said "some non-Muslims, rulers or subjects" in accordance with the rationale of legal balance he had adopted and taking into account the changing times.

By the same logic, Ibn Hajar accepted seeking office and canvassing for it, although it is prohibited by the Sunnah, if Muslim interests are threatened or liable to be harmed or squandered. According to him, "Taking office for fear of waste is akin to giving without being asked as this is usually done with no personal greed. Such desire can be overlooked for those who should take office as it becomes an obligation upon them."[41]

LESSONS FROM THE EMIGRATION TO ABYSSINIA

During the early days of Islam, a number of Muslims took refuge in the non-Muslim land of Abyssinia (modern Ethiopia) to preserve their faith. This episode bears particular significance because it occurred at a time when Muslims were weak and while the foundations of Islamic law and fiqh were still being established.

An interesting incident took place during this episode that provides evidence for what Muslim immigrants can do to protect their faith and their interests, gain the confidence and trust of others, and draw their attention to Islam.

In his *Musnad*,[42] Imam Ahmad includes several reports of a lengthy account of how the Quraysh Arabs decided to harass the Muslim immigrants in Abyssinia. They dispatched Amr ibn al-As and Abd Allah ibn Abi Rabiah brimming with gifts and presents to the Negus of Abyssinia and with sweeteners for his patriarchs in an effort to persuade him to hand over the Muslim refugees so that they could forcibly return them to Makkah.

First Amr spoke at the Negus's court and then Abd Allah:

> Your Majesty, a few of our foolish youths have come to your country and deserted the religion of their people but have not embraced your faith. They have come up with a new religion which neither you nor we understand. The nobles of their people, their fathers, uncles and tribesmen have sent us to you asking for them back because they know better what is best for them and what they had done wrong, and had already admonished them.

His patriarchs endorsed what was said and advised the king to hand the Muslims over to them to take back to their country and their people. However, being a fair man, the Negus would not take a decision without hearing the argument of the other side, and so he asked for the Muslims to be brought before him.

When his emissary went to them, the Muslims sought the counsel of one another as to what to say to the Negus when he met them. They decided to tell him all that they knew and what their Prophet had taught them, no matter what the consequences. They went to him, and he called his bishops and prelates, who sat with their holy books open before them. He started by asking the Muslims, "What is this religion that caused you to break away from your people without converting to my religion or to any of the other religions?" Umm Salamah reported that Jafar ibn Abi Talib answered him and said,

> O King, we were a people living in ignorance, worshipping idols, eating carrion meat, committing sins, forsaking our kinsfolk and abusing our neighbors. The strong amongst us exploited the weak. We had been living like that until God sent us a Messenger, one of us, whose pedigree, truthfulness, honesty and purity are well-known to us. He called us to believe in the one God and worship Him and discard the stones and idols we and our fathers had hitherto been worshipping besides Him. He urged us to be truthful in what we say, keep our trust, nurture our kinsfolk, be kind toward our neighbors and desist from offensive behavior and killing. He advised us to avoid repugnant acts, falsehood, taking orphans' property and slandering chaste women. He urged us to worship God alone and nothing else besides Him, and taught us to observe prayer, give alms and fast. We believed him and followed his teachings, but our people set upon us and persecuted us to turn us away from our religion and take us back to idol-worship and the repugnant acts we used to commit. When they overwhelmed and oppressed us and prevailed over us, pre-

venting us from practicing our religion, we came to your country and chose you over all others, desirous to live as your neighbors and hoping, O King, not to be persecuted in your land.

Other reports point out that, on appearing before the king, Jafar departed from convention and did not prostrate himself before the Negus. When asked by the Negus's courtiers why he did not prostrate, he replied, "We prostrate before no one but God Almighty."

The debate ended with the Muslims scoring victory over their opponents, and the Negus was persuaded of the justice of their case. The Quraysh emissaries returned home "humiliated and their argument totally rejected," as Umm Salamah put it. Following this episode, relations between the Muslims and Abyssinia's Christian monarch flourished to the extent that they would pray for his victory against other contenders for his throne. Umm Salamah said, "We prayed to God to help the Negus prevail over his rivals and confirm his rule in his country." The logical consequence of that relationship was that the Negus eventually embraced the religion of Islam.

CONCLUSION

The discussion in this chapter has indicated that the Islamic fiqh relating to Muslim minorities is essentially derived from the general fiqh of Islam as a whole. It is in a similar category to the fiqh of fundamentals, priorities (*al-awlawiyyat*), contrasts (*al-muwazanah*), or realities, or to comparative fiqh, or the fiqh of ethics, and so forth. Accordingly, although this branch of fiqh includes several aspects of the general fiqh, it focuses specifically on issues affecting Muslim minorities living among non-Muslim majorities and endeavoring to preserve their identities under somewhat different customs, legislation, and laws.

It is also common knowledge that every fiqh ruling has its own cultural impact. Indeed, culture stems from fiqh and the laws that govern society. Fiqh and religious rulings also raise questions in an uninterrupted circle of arguments and interpretations, where fiqh, religious legislation, and culture all play interchangeable roles.

A number of methods, means, and tools do exist with which this fiqh can be constructed on sound foundations, and these include the following:

"Fiqh for minorities" is a collective activity and should not be practiced on an individual basis. It is multifaceted, with differing aspects that render any individualistic approach potentially perilous. It involves political, economic, cultural, social, and legal elements.

The fiqh side of it requires appropriate treatment of the facts and issues. No treatment can be correct without consideration of all aspects of the matter in question, a task that cannot be completely fulfilled by a single individual. It requires the collective input of several scientists and specialists from different social and religious disciplines. These people need to scrutinize and study the issue from all angles, especially those of a general nature, that affect the future of Muslim minorities, in order to articulate the problems accurately and seek their solutions in fiqh. Indeed, the fiqh derived for these cases should not be based on partial evidence or facts commonly approved by jurists but should be broadly based on the universal fundamentals of the Quran and Sunnah, as well as the established values and objectives (*maqasid*) of the Shariah. It is, therefore, a varied discipline that can be encompassed or fully understood, as already pointed out, only by someone with a vast knowledge and experience of all other aspects and branches of fiqh.

Specialist seminars can be an effective forum for the development of a minorities' fiqh, provided that they are well planned, enough time is allocated to them, and they are well attended by specialists, researchers, and scholars. The aim is to articulate the various aspects of this field and provide satisfactory answers that can help define the identity of minorities.

Some issues may be developed into research projects for further and deeper study and investigation, with the necessary time and effort devoted to the task. Some issues may be recommended for academic degree studies at the university level, supervised by experts or professors with a specialist's knowledge in the field. For example, a question regarding economics could be dealt with jointly by an economist, a legal expert, and a religious jurist, all dealing with the subject from their own angles.

When seeking or giving fatwas, especially with respect to Muslim minorities, it is generally advisable to accustom people to submitting their questions in writing. A written question is more likely to receive greater attention and be given deeper thought. Specialists responding to these questions are also advised to give written answers to avoid any misunderstanding or misapprehension. People usually interpret things according to their wishes rather than with due objectivity. When inquirers pose their questions in their own particular way, the respondent jurists ought, nevertheless, to ask them to repeat them in writing, even if both parties are on the same wavelength.

Writing usually entails focusing and reflection, and it allows the inquirers to mull over the issues and have greater confidence in explaining their ideas. If the respondents then wish to discuss or clarify those ideas with the inquirers, either over the telephone or face-to-face, to help the inquirers understand fully the implications of their questions, that is all the better. The respondents, in addition, are also required to write down their responses to avoid any misuse or misinterpretation of either the letter or the spirit of their answers. This approach should provide the necessary safeguards for the accuracy and integrity of the questions as well as the answers.

It is also imperative that people are made aware of the importance of fatwas and their impact on the future of Muslim minorities and their relationships with other communities in society, as well as the image of Islam in their own minds and the prospect of its application to them. A fatwa may solve a specific or short-term difficulty for some individuals but raise several others that go beyond individual cases to affect the current and future state of the community as a whole. This awareness of possible conclusions and consequences further emphasizes the need to take account of the principles of the fiqh of priorities and consequences, as well as its other branches, in a manner that is conducive to the correct application of the tenets of Islam.

Jurists must also be fully aware of their environment and their cultural and social surroundings. Some questions on the nature of the minority and the majority living in this environment have already been identified. Fiqh practitioners need to understand these very well to be able to offer appropriate answers that take account of all the surrounding conditions. They must also submit their findings to those directly concerned as well as to other members of the community in the mosques and elsewhere, so that their meaning and implications are fully and clearly understood.

There is also the question of who is most qualified to contribute to the development of fiqh for minorities. I believe that it would be more effective to develop existing institutions and associations of Muslim social scientists, within which departments of fiqh and Shariah for students and practitioners could be established. This would enable traditional jurists and modern social scientists to cooperate and work closely together toward the achievement of the objectives that we have been advocating. This would initiate a debate between the two groups, in which knowledge of the Shariah sources can be passed on to social scientists and the various dimensions of modern social studies that have eluded Muslim jurists may be identified and clarified.

I do not believe that fiqh councils, as they exist today, are adequate, especially since they reproduce old fatwas in contemporary language or use current vernacular. We require original interpretations that respond to the problems of minorities in a way that is free of the negative effects that are usually associated with the fiqh of expediency or crises. For Muslim minorities to be offered solutions to their problems only on the basis of expediency or exceptionality can have harmful consequences that they should be spared. The answer is for groups of experts with differing specializations to come together under the auspices of the associations of social sciences and Islamic studies. They should collaborate on an equal basis without any group being given the impression that it is being exploited or marginalized by the others. In any case, as questions of a political, economic, educational, philosophical, or ethical nature arise, specialists from all sides can be called upon to examine jointly the religious and social aspects of the issues. This arrangement, in my view, would be more effective than fiqh councils limited only to Shariah experts.

Factors of time and space also play an important role in the determination of the nature of the issues being discussed. This is reflected in keeping the field of Muslim minorities' fiqh open for development so as to take account of new circumstances in an ever-changing human condition. This applies to all areas of fiqh, whether macro or micro. The Islamic system is fundamentally open, and changing circumstances do affect the nature of the issues and questions being encountered and put forward. It is often true that these vary even within the same country and the same era. The Muslim minorities fiqh should not, therefore, remain rigid or restricted, but it ought to be open to ijtihad and debate whenever factors emerge that had not previously existed, or were overlooked, when the question was initially raised.

The methods and procedures necessary to develop a fiqh for Muslim minorities should be developed in a number of areas. Some of these relate to the individual or body or council issuing or applying the fatwa, some to the group or community for which the fatwa is issued. For this project to take proper shape and to make the public more aware of the establishment of a fiqh system, we need to respond better to people's problems. We also need to build up a repertoire of knowledge that will enable us to deduce objective principles defining the sources of knowledge and thought models, as well as the essential features of Islamic fiqh for Muslim minorities. To this end, further and wider studies, research, and elaboration are required. This holds true for specific cases as well as the cultural, social, and legal existence of Muslim minorities in their communities.

This type of investigation and research would make this fiqh useful not only for the Muslim minorities but also for the Muslim majorities, who could apply it to their own advantage.

Finally, what I have said so far regarding the fiqh of Muslim minorities is a mere introduction, intended to provoke interest in issues peculiar to Muslim minorities. Since this fiqh is open to debate and discussion, so should be its development, the documentation of its literature, and the elaboration of its means, methods, and tools. These must be open to researchers, scientists, religious scholars, and intellectuals.

NOTES

1. See Shakib Arsalan, *Tarikh Ghazawat al-Arab* (Beirut: Dar Maktabat al-ayat, 1966).

2. See Fakhr al-Din al-Razi, *al-Tafsiral-Kabir,* in which he uses a different concept for "Earth" that I have developed in order to disregard the concepts of dar al-harb and dar al-Islam. This distinction is detailed later. Radwan al-Sayyid, the

Lebanese scholar, has used similar concepts like *dar al-dawah* and *dar al-ijabah* or *ummat al-dawah* and *ummat al-ijabah* in many of his writings.

3. Among the books dealing with this topic is *al-Miyar al-Muarrab wa al-Jami al-Mugharrab an Fatawa Ifriqyah wa al-Andalus wa al-Maghrib*, by Ahmad ibn Yahya al-Wansharishi (died 914 AH) (Beirut: Dar al-Gharb al-Islami, 1983).

4. SAAS—*Salla Allahu Alayhi wa Sallam*: "May the peace and blessings of Allah be upon him"; said whenever the name of Prophet Muhammad is mentioned or whenever he is referred to as the Prophet of Allah.

5. For a new, enlightened approach to this issue, see Abdul Hamid Abu Sulayman, *Marital Discord: Recapturing the Full Islamic Spirit of Human Dignity* (London: International Institute of Islamic Thought, 2003).

6. Ibn Khaldun, *al-Muqaddimah*, 445; see also al-Zubaydi, *Taj al-Arus*; al-Qarafi, *Nafa'is al-Usul, Sharh al-Mahsul, Tabaqat Ibn Sad fi Tarjamat Ibn Umar*; Mustafa Abd al-Raziq, *Al-Imam al-Shafie*, and *Silsilat Alam al-Islam*.

7. Ibn Khaldun, *al-Muqaddimah*, 446.

8. Sahih al-Bukhari: Kitab al-Ilm, hadith no. 69; Sahih Muslim: Kitab al-Zakah, hadith no. 1719.

9. Sahih Muslim.

10. al-Nassa'i, Ibn Majah, and al-Tirmidhi.

11. Examples include the following:

- Grandfather's inheritance. One group considered the grandfather as a "father" and placed him above the brothers. They also differed whether he is entitled to one-third or one-sixth of the estate.
- Suspension of the share of new converts. The Prophet and Abu Bakr included them in Zakah, but Umar did not, possibly in the public good.
- Adjusting the distribution of booty. The Prophet divided the land gained in war among the fighters, while Umar decided to charge a levy for its cultivation to benefit the whole community and the coming generations.
- Suspension of Shariah penalties (*hudud*) in war times. Some Muslim leaders did it to avert defection to the enemy camps.
- Forgoing hand amputation for destitute thieves. Umar pardoned thieves who stole to eat.
- Opting for compensation (*diyah*) for murder following pardon by some relatives, even if others insisted on the death penalty (*qisas*). The Sahabah (companions of the Prophet) encouraged pardon and compensation rather than the death penalty.
- During the Prophet's life, diyah was valued in cash rather than cattle. Umar, however, valued diyah in camels because their market value had risen.
- During Umar's time, stray camels were allowed to roam. When Uthman succeeded him, he ordered that they be valued and traded. If the owner turned up, he was paid the market price for his camels. This was due to new circumstances resulting from the expansion of the Islamic state.
- While acknowledging it was not forbidden (*haram*), Umar disallowed marrying Jewish and Christian women.
- A single pronouncement of divorce was considered final up to the first two years of Umar's reign. But then he concluded that people were abusing the rule and instituted three pronouncements for an irrevocable divorce.

- Imposing fines on manufacturers if they damage or destroy the raw material supplied to them was an issue for debate. Some Sahabah were of the opinion that a penalty equivalent to the value of the damages or lost material should be imposed; others took the opposite view provided the damage or loss is not intentional.
- Benefiting from a security. This was a matter for different views among the Sahabah, dictated by different environments and social developments.

12. Issues over which the second generation had different opinions include the following:

- They opted for penalizing the security holder in case of loss or damage, equivalent to the value of the security.
- The Prophet recommended women to frequent mosques for prayer, but the second-generation ulama preferred them not to do so at night.
- Pricing of goods was rejected by the Prophet, but the second-generation ulama allowed it to protect the ordinary public.
- A divorcé who defaults on his divorce commitments is considered unfit to give witness in legal matters.
- Second-generation ulama rejected witness statements of some relatives for fear of injustice or lack of impartiality.

13. AS—*Alayhi al Salam* or *Alayhim al Salam* (Peace and blessings of Allah be upon him); said whenever a prophet other than Muhammad is mentioned by name.

14. See his book: *Iqtida' al-Sirat al-Mustaqim Mukhalafat Ahl al-Jahim*. See also Mustafa ibn Muhammad al-Wardani, *Al-Nahi an al-Istianah wa'l-Istinsar fi Umur al-Muslimin bi Ahl al-Dhimmah wa'l-Kuffar*. Also see the book by an anonymous author believed to have come from North Africa entitled: *Al-Sawab fi Qibh Istiktab Ahl al-Kitab*.

15. *Al-Mustasfa* 1/3.

16. Taha Jabir Al-Alwani, *Usul al-Fiqh al-Islami* (Herndon, Va.: International Institute of Islamic Thought, 1990).

17. See his book *Maqasid al-Shariah al-Islamiyyah* (Tunis: Al-Dar al-Tunisiyyah, 1972).

18. See his book *Maqasid al-Shariah* (Casablanca: Maktabat al-Wahdah, 1963).

19. See his book *Nazariyat al-Maqasid ind al-Imam al-Shatibi* (Herndon, Va.: International Institute of Islamic Thought, 1991).

20. See his book *Maqasid al-Shariah* (Herndon, Va.: International Institute of Islamic Thought, 1991).

21. See his book *Tamhid li Tarikh al-Falsafah al-Islamiyyah* (Cairo: Lijnat al-Ta'lif wa'l-Tarjumah wa'l-Nashir, 1966).

22. For further elaboration, see al-Alwani, *The Islamization of Knowledge: Yesterday and Today* (Herndon, Va.: International Institute of Islamic Thought, 1995); and *Missing Dimensions in Contemporary Islamic Movements* (Herndon, Va.: International Institute of Islamic Thought, 1996), 14–19.

23. RAA—*Radiya Allahu Anha/Anhu* (May Allah be pleased with her/him); said whenever a companion of the Prophet is mentioned by name.

24. Ibn al-Jawzi, *Zad al-Masir*, 8/39.

25. Al-Qurtubi, *Al-Jami li Ahkam al-Qur'an*, 18/43.

26. Al-Qurtubi, *Al-Jami li Ahkam al-Qur'an*, 28/43.

27. Al-Qurtubi, *Al-Jami li Ahkam al-Qur'an*, 18/43.
28. *Tafsir Ibn Abi Hatim*, 1/472.
29. Ibn al-Jawzi, *Zad al-Masir*, 1/355.
30. Al-Sabuni, *Mukhtasar Tafsir Ibn Kathir*, 1/308.
31. Al-Qurtubi, *Al-Jami li Ahkam al-Qur'an*, 4/171.
32. Abu al-Su'ud, *Irshad al-Aql al-Salim ila Mazaya al-Qur'an al-Azim*, 2/70.
33. Abd al-Karim al-Khatib, *Al-Tafsir al-Qur'ani*, 4/548.
34. Al-Kasani, *Bada'i al-Sana'i*, 7/131.
35. Al-Kasani, *Bada'i al-Sana'i*, 7/131.
36. Ibn Hajar, *Fath al-Bari*, 7/230.
37. Ibn al-Jawzi, *Zad al-Masir*, 7/122.
38. Ibn Taymiyyah, *Al-Tafsir al-Kabir*, 6/59.
39. Ibn Taymiyyah, *Al-Siyasah al-Shar'iyyah*, 167.
40. Ibn Taymiyyah, *Minhaj al-Sunnah*, 4/113.
41. Ibn Hajar, *Fath al-Bari*, 13/126.
42. Details of this account are reported in *Al-Musnad*, hadiths 1649, 14039, 17109, and 21460.

2

Living as a Muslim in a Pluralistic Society and State

Theory and Experience

Omar Khalidi

> It is almost impossible to be a Muslim without either living in an Islamic state or being engaged in a struggle to establish an Islamic state.
>
> —Kalim Siddiqi, *Issues in Islamic Movement, 1984–1985*

> The Constitution of India gives Muslims the right and opportunity to try to change anything in the national constitution or national life which appears to them to be in conflict with Islamic values and to advocate the recognition and adoption of more Islamic values. But their efforts in this direction can only be effective if they speak to the Indian nation not in religious but secular language and argue their case for the reforms which they think are necessary, not on the basis of religious authority but on that of observation, experience and reason.
>
> —Sayyid Abid Husain, *The Destiny of Indian Muslims*

How should Muslims conduct themselves in a pluralistic society? Should their conduct be different in a pluralistic society from the one in which Muslims predominate? Similar questions can be asked about Muslim conduct in a state dominated by others. What does the Quran have to say about these matters? Are there any signposts in the life and career of Prophet Muhammad that can guide the *ummah* (community) in search of answers to these questions? Can one derive clear-cut answers to such questions from Quran and Sunnah? Have the *fuqaha* (Islamic jurists) of the previous centuries something to say about these matters? If so, what are their sources of guidance? Leaving aside pure theory, what is the Muslim practice and experience of these matters?

Finding an answer to these questions is necessary to arrive at a theory of

Muslim interaction within a pluralistic society, where Muslims either are a numerical minority or lack access to formal or informal levers of power or both. Finding an answer to these questions is also an immediate practical necessity, as more than roughly one-third of a billion Muslims in the early twenty-first century are in the numerical minority in many different countries.[1] Further justification for the formulation of Muslim theory of interaction with non-Muslim societies and states is necessary, as some non-Muslim states can and may preempt and co-opt individual Muslims to develop a theory acceptable to a hostile political establishment. Such Muslims are in the Quranic terms *al-munafiqun,* "the hypocrites" (Quran 63:1–2; 63:8).

Source/Basis of Shariah and the Fiqh Al-Aqaliyah

At the risk of repetition, it must be stated at the outset that Islamic law originates from two major sources: divine Revelation (*alwahi*) and human reason (*al-aql*). This dual identity of Islamic law is reflected in the two Arabic designations: Shariah and *fiqh.* Shariah bears a stronger affinity with revelation, whereas fiqh is mainly the product of human reason. *Shariah* literally means "the right path" or "guide," whereas *fiqh* refers to human understanding and knowledge. The divine Shariah thus indicates the path to righteousness; reason discovers the Shariah and relates its general directives to the quest for finding solutions to particular or unprecedented issues. Because the Shariah is mainly contained in divine Revelation (i.e., the Quran and the teachings of Prophet Muhammad or the Sunnah), it is an integral part of the dogma of Islam. Fiqh is a rational endeavor and largely a product of speculative reasoning, which does not command the same authority as the Shariah. The Shariah provides clear rulings on the fundamentals of Islam: the basic moral values and practical duties, such as prayers, fasting, legal alms (*zakah*), the *hajj* (pilgrimage to Mecca), and other devotional matters. Its injunctions on what is lawful and unlawful (*halal* and *haram*) are on the whole definitive, and so are its rulings on some aspects of civil transactions (*muamalat*). But the Shariah is generally flexible with regard to most civil and criminal transactions, such as criminal law (with the exception of the prescribed punishments or *hudud*), government policy and constitution, fiscal policy, taxation, and economic and international affairs. In many of these areas the Shariah provides only general guidelines.

Fiqh is defined as the knowledge of the practical rules of the Shariah, which are derived from the Quran and the Sunnah. The rules of fiqh are thus concerned with the manifest aspects of individual conduct. The practicalities of conduct are evaluated on a scale of five values: obligatory, recommended, permissible, reprehensible, and forbidden. The definition of fiqh also implies that the deduction of the rules of fiqh from the Quran and the Sunnah is through direct contact with the source evidence and necessarily involves a certain measure of independent reasoning and intellectual exertion (*ijtihad*). The ability to use the Quran therefore necessitates the knowledge of Arabic and a certain degree of insight and erudition that an "imitator," or one who memorizes the rules without understanding the implications, could not achieve. A jurist (*faqih*) who fulfills these requirements and has the ability to deduce the rules of the Shariah from their sources is a *mujtahid,* one qualified to exercise independent reasoning.

The rules of fiqh may be divided into two types. First, there are rules that are conveyed in a clear text, such as the essentials of worship, the validity of marriage outside the prohibited degrees of relationship, the rules of inheritance, and the like. These are self-evident and therefore independent of interpretation, yet various schools of thought disagree. This part of the fiqh is simultaneously a part of the Shariah.

Second, some rules are formulated through the exercise of independent reasoning in that part of the Quran and Sunnah that is not self-evident. Because of the possibility of error, the rules that are so derived are not immutable. They are not necessarily an integral part of the permanent Shariah, and the mujtahid who has reason to depart from them in favor of an alternative ruling may do so, without committing a transgression. Only when juristic opinion and independent reasoning are supported by general consensus (*ijma*) does that reasoning acquire the binding force of a ruling (*hukm*) of Shariah.

The schools of law vary in their treatment of the contents of fiqh. Broadly speaking, the body of law is divided into two main categories: devotional matters (*ibadat*) and civil transactions (*muamalat*). The devotional matters are usually studied under the six main headings of cleanliness, ritual prayer, fasting, the hajj, legal alms, and *jihad* (holy struggle); the schools of law do not vary much in their treatment of these subjects. Juristic differences among the schools occur mainly in the area of the civil transactions, which are generally studied under five headings of transactions involving economic exchange of values, equity and trust, matrimonial law, civil litigation, and administration of estates. Crimes and penalties are often studied under a separate heading (*uqubat*) next to these two main categories. As previously noted, the sources of Shariah are two: the revealed and the nonrevealed—first, the Quran; second, the teaching and exemplary conduct (Sunnah) of the Prophet Muhammad, including his sayings, acts, and tacit approval (or lack of condemnation) of the conduct of his Companions and some of the customs of the Arabian society of the seventh century.

The authority of the Sunnah as a source of Shariah as next to the Quran is indicated in Quran itself. Some disagreement, however, prevailed over the precise meaning and authority of the Sunnah until the theologian and jurist al-Shafii addressed the issue in the early ninth century. The legal theory that al-Shafii articulated underscored the normative status of the Sunnah as a source of Revelation that explained and supplemented the Quran.

The nonrevealed sources of Shariah are generally founded in juristic reasoning (*ijtihad*). This reasoning may take a variety of forms, including analogical reasoning (*qiyas*), juristic preference (*istihsan*), considerations of public interest (*istislah*), and even general consensus (*ijma*) of the learned, which basically originates in ijtihad and provides a procedure by which a ruling of juristic reasoning can acquire the binding force of law.

The vast majority of ulama have generally recognized analogy and consensus, but they disagree over the validity and scope of many of the rational proofs that originate in ijtihad. Whether ijma or qiyas, these are merely methods to reach decision based on the texts or the spirit of the Quran and Sunnah. Nothing is acceptable if it contradicts the text or the spirit of these two sources. Any opinions arrived at by individual scholars or schools of Islamic law, including the recognized schools (four Sunni and one Shii), are no more than opinions, and the fatwas are no more than "advice." The founders of these schools never laid exclusive claim to the truth or invited people to follow them rather than any other scholars.

With respect to the question of where a Muslim should live, the Quran does not set forth any guidelines—clear-cut or vague. It does require Muslims to enjoin good and forbid evil, as indicated in 22:41. Presumably this can also mean going outside one's home to teach and preach outside. If we disregard the brief Muslim migration to Christian Abyssinia (615–620) in the time of the Meccan period of the Prophet Muhammad's mission, Muslim minorities came into being as a result of the conquest of non-Muslim lands. Within two hundred years of the Prophet's death, large areas of the Near and Middle East, the Iberian peninsula in southern Europe, and Sicily came under Muslim rule as Al-Andalus[2] where they arrived as conquerors in 711. Similarly, Sicily was conquered in the early ninth century c.e. to be lost in the mid–eleventh century.[3]

MUSLIM MINORITIES: THE CASE OF SPAIN

As is often the case, ethnic and tribal loyalties among Muslims destroyed their political and military power after seven hundred years of rule in 1492, when the last stronghold, Granada, was conquered by Ferdinand and Isabella, the king and queen of Aragon and Castile, respectively, whose marriage united the Iberian peninsula into Spain of the modern world. This did not, however, mean that Muslims no longer inhabited the land that had once been one of the jewels of the Islamic world. Ever since Christian kingdoms had first begun making substantial conquests of Muslim territories in the late eleventh century, ever-larger numbers of Arabic-speaking Muslims had become subjects of Christian kings, who normally encouraged these Muslims to submit to their rule and contribute to the economic stability of their realms. In some areas of Christian Spain such as Valencia, such Muslims, usually known as *mudejares* (apparently from the Arabic *mudajjan*, "one allowed to remain behind"), formed by far the majority of the population long after Christian conquest of these areas. Typically the wealthy and the learned chose to immigrate to Muslim-ruled areas such as North Africa (compare Indian Muslim elite migration to Pakistan after the subcontinent's independence and partition in 1947), so the large mudejar communities were often deprived of their natural leaders. Nevertheless, even as late as the fifteenth century, Muslim scholars of a modest degree of religious learning could be found providing guidance and continuity to the lives of Muslim subjects of the king of Aragon. These Muslims lived within the Spanish Christian kingdoms under a set of regulations that in many ways resembled the *dhimmah* system that governed how Christians and Jews lived within Islamic countries: The mudejares were allowed to continue practicing their Islamic religion; they were allowed to govern the internal affairs of their communities on the basis of Islamic law; they were forbidden to proselytize among the Christians; but they were often encouraged to convert themselves to Christianity. Muslim men were forbidden to marry Christian women, though Christian men could marry Muslim women. Mudejares were subject to special and often especially burdensome taxes; they were theoretically (though rarely in actual practice) required to wear distinctive clothing to indicate their infidelity.

In the early sixteenth century, however, after having expelled the very large Jewish population of the peninsula, the kings of Spain forcibly converted their still large mudejar population to Christianity, though the great majority converted only outwardly, continuing to practice their Islamic faith in private—through *taqiyyah* (dissimulation).

According to the Quran (16:106), fear of persecution is a legitimate excuse for hiding one's faith; one may even verbally renounce one's faith, provided one remains unshaken in one's heart.[4] However, the term *taqiyyah* is usually—and erroneously—associated with and considered a part of the Shiite, particularly the Ismaili creed by the Sunnis. This enormous group of nominal Christians came to be known as Moriscos, and they formed a still highly Islamic sector of Spanish society for about another one hundred years. Though they were generally very productive agricultural laborers or skilled craftsmen, they, too, became troublesome to the rulers of Spain because of their unwillingness to completely assimilate, and in 1609 and 1620, they, like the Jews before them, were expelled from Spain. Some 275,000 Moriscos left their home of nearly nine centuries and settled en masse in North Africa. Though many Spaniards of Muslim ancestry remained on Christian soil, the expulsion of the Moriscos in the early seventeenth century represents the end of any sort of truly Islamic presence in the peninsula until the modern diasporas of the twentieth century.[5]

THE JURISTIC DEBATE: CONSTRUCTION OF THE HOUSE
OF PEACE AND THE HOUSE OF WAR IN THE MEDIEVAL ERA

The fall and eventual expulsion of Muslims from Spain sparked a debate among the ulama about Muslim conduct in areas in which Muslims lacked the power to enforce Shariah either through the sheer force of numbers or through the apparatuses of the state. In fact, the debate had already began since the fall of Islamic Sicily. It can be argued that a life in full conformity with the requirements of Shariah is possible only under an Islamic polity devoted to the application of the divine law in its totality. However, not all Muslims were able to live under the Muslim sovereignty, thus posing the existential dilemma of how to live under non-Muslim rule. Specifically, the status of Muslims as powerless groups under non-Muslim rule can raise the following four questions, among others: Where should Muslims live? How applicable or inapplicable is the full range of Shariah? What is the relationship between the segments of ummah under Muslim rule and those under non-Muslim rule? Finally, what are the rights and obligations of Muslims under non-Muslim rule?

The world according to the classical jurists is divided into the territory of dar al-Islam and dar al-harb, the realms of peace and war, respectively. The Shafii school has added a third category of *dar al-sulh* or *dar al-ahd*, the "territory of truce or treaty," in anticipation of the possibility of peace or agreement between a Muslim state and a non-Muslim one. What determined a territory to be designated as one or the other? The main criterion seems to be that if a territory had fallen under Muslim sovereignty where Shariah is applied, then that territory is part of the dar al-Islam, but it can revert to dar al-harb should Muslim control be lost.

According to the Hanafis, however, there are further conditions. Dar al-Islam becomes dar al-harb after the conquest by the unbelievers, if the laws of the unbelievers are enforced on Muslims, if conquered territory is adjacent to the dar al-harb, and if the lives and properties of Muslims and dhimmis are not safe. This implies that according to the Hanafi jurisprudence, an Islamic region that has been conquered by unbelievers can remain dar al-Islam as long as the conquerors appoint a *qadi* (judge) to administer Islamic law and as long as Muslims and dhimmis are secure as they were under Muslim rule. In other words, Muslim sovereignty is not a precondition for dar al-Islam.

Where Should Muslims Live?

According to Imam Abdallah Muhammad al-Shaybani (749–804), an early Hanafi jurist, the duty to migrate to dar al-Islam was abrogated at the time of the Prophet. Those who converted to Islam but did not migrate to Medina at the time of the Prophet were not allowed to share in the spoils of war. Imam Abu Hanifa (699–767) is reported to have disapproved of Muslims living in non-Muslim territory, presumably due to the difficulties posed in the way of the implementation of the Shariah. The Maliki jurist Abd al-Salam Sahnun (d. 854) of Qayrawan reports that Imam Malik (710–796) strongly disapproved of Muslims even traveling to the lands of nonbelievers for purposes of trade because they might be subject to the laws of the infidels. Submitting to the laws of non-Muslims in Malikite view was an unacceptable proposition. Additionally, it is reported that Imam Malik discouraged Muslims from residing in territory in which the Companions of the Prophet were vilified. Maliki jurists of a later period interpret this to mean that residence in the lands of widespread sin is disallowed.

The views of the Imam al-Shafii (767–820) appear to be different from his Hanafi and Maliki colleagues. According to him, even after the Prophet's migration to Madina, Abdullah bin Abbas, a Companion of the Prophet Muhammad, and others were permitted to remain in Mecca, which was then in dar al-harb. Moreover, the Prophet permitted nomadic tribes to remain outside Madina despite conversion to his faith. It can therefore be deduced that the Prophet would not have given the nomads the choice to remain outside dar al-Islam if it amounted to sin. Therefore, Imam Shafii argued that anyone who converts to Islam in dar al-harb may remain there as long as there is no fear of enticement away from the newly accepted faith. Although Shii works on Hadith generally discouraged Muslim residence outside dar al-Islam, the sixth Imam Jaafar al-Sadiq, when asked if he would die an unbeliever if he entered the lands of unbelief, is reported to have said that he might in fact be able to better serve Islam in a non-Muslim territory! The Andalusian Zahiri jurist Ibn Hazm (d. 1064) disapproved of Muslims entering into non-Muslim territories, unlike the Hanafi jurist Abu Bakr al-Sarakhsi (d. 1090) of Transoxiana. According to al-Sarakhsi, trade with non-Muslims is a necessity for the sake of public welfare, but he cautioned that a Muslim should not sell weapons to non-Muslims. The duty to migrate (*hijra*), while necessary at the time of the Prophet, is no longer necessary. He, however, discouraged permanent Muslim residence in non-Muslim lands due to fears about lack of Islamic ambience. According to Maliki jurist al-Mawardi (d. 1058), "If a Muslim is able to manifest his religion in one of the unbelievers' countries, that country becomes a part of dar al-Islam." Hence, residing in it is better than migrating because it is hoped that others will convert to Islam through him. On the other hand, Ibn Rushd (d. 1122) issued a fatwa prohibiting Muslims to enter or reside in dar al-harb.[6]

In summary, it is fair to say that in general the Maliki jurists opposed Muslim residence in non-Muslim countries, according to the famous fatwa of al-Wansharisi (d. 1508): The territory of Islam, even if unjust, is superior to non-Muslim territory, even if just. He implied that formal association with

Islam is in itself a moral value. The Hanbalis and the Shii Jaafaris argue that if Muslims can practice their religion in non-Muslim territory, migration is not obligatory, in effect making it permissible for Muslims to live there. The Shafii jurists opined that migration may be recommended or not recommended depending on the degree of freedom or autonomy a Muslim enjoys in land not controlled by his coreligionists. The greater the freedom, the higher the permissibility to live outside the realm of Islam.

Applicability or Inapplicability of the Full Range of Shariah

It goes without saying that the extent to which Shariah can be applied to Muslims living in non-Muslim territories is directly linked to the desirability or otherwise of the believers' residence outside the realm of Islam. According to Imam al-Shafii:

> There is no difference between dar al-harb and dar al-Islam as to the laws that God has decreed to his people. He [the Prophet] has not exempted any of his people from any of his decrees, and he did not permit them anything that was forbidden in dar al-harb. What is allowed in bilad al-Islam is allowed in bilad al-Kufr, and what is forbidden in bilad al-Islam is also forbidden in dar al-Kufr. So whoever commits an infraction is subject to the punishment that God has decreed and his (a Muslim's) presence in bilad al-Kufr does not exempt him from anything.[7]

Hanbali and Maliki jurists make similar statements; that is, Islamic law applies to Muslims with equal force wherever they reside. However, the Hanafis differ on a few points. While adultery, theft, murder, defamation, and the consumption of alcohol are prohibited in both dar al-Islam and dar al-harb, the person committing these offenses is liable only before God in the Hereafter, as Islamic courts may have no jurisdiction over crimes committed outside the realm. Even more significant, Hanafi jurists argue that a Muslim residing in a non-Muslim territory may even deal in usury with non-Muslims; may sell or buy prohibited substances such as alcohol, pork, or animals slaughtered in an non-Islamic manner; and may engage in gambling and the like if such acts are legal in the country of residence.

The Relationship between the Segments of Ummah under Muslim Rule and Those under Non-Muslim Rule

It is a cornerstone of Muslim belief that all Muslims are part of one ummah, indivisible on any grounds except in *taqwa* or piety. Therefore, it is not surprising that the vast majority of the jurists agree that regardless of residence, Muslim ummah is simply indivisible into territorial categories—despite the reality of political divisions since the end of the classical caliphate. A related question of historical interest pertained to whether the laws of the Islamic polity applied to a Muslim outside its territories; in other words, to what extent is that person's life and property inviolable? Or, to pose the question in another way, what is the source of a Muslim's inviolability? Does inviolability stem from the simple fact of being a Muslim or from the protection that a Muslim territory provides? To the Hanafis, it stems from the protection that the Muslim territory is able to afford its residents. A Muslim residing in non-Muslim lands enjoys moral inviolability but not necessarily legal inviolability. For instance, if a Muslim kills another Muslim in non-Muslim territory, he or she is not held criminally liable in Islamic courts. The killer is, however, a sinner and is held accountable by God in the Hereafter. The Hanafis concur with this view, reasoning that Islamic courts lack extraterritorial jurisdiction. The Shafii position is that a Muslim is protected regardless of where that person or his or her family is located. The Jaafari and Zaydi schools adopt a similar position in that a Muslim's inviolability stems from his or her membership in the transterritorial world of Islam. Only the Malikis take the position that residence outside the realm of Islam renders a Muslim violable.

The Obligations of Muslims under Non-Muslim Rule

According to Shibli Numani (1857–1914), an eminent scholar from India, Muslims ought to be loyal to the non-Muslim ruler if there is freedom of belief, practice, and propagation of Islam. Quoting Al-Tabari, a muhaditth, he cites the example of the early Meccan muhajirun who took refuge in Ethiopia under the Negus during the early days of the Prophet's call. Evidently during an invasion of Ethiopia, Muslims on their own petitioned the Negus to join his forces to repel the foreign aggression, and prayed for the success of his forces.[8] What should Muslim conduct be in case of a dispute between a Muslim ruler and a non-Muslim ruler? Al-Shaybani and al-Sarakhsi specify that in situations of military confrontation, Muslims residing in non-Muslim territory must publicly renounce their aman and fight to liberate Muslim soldiers who have been captured and enslaved. However, as far as I have been able to ascertain, aside from these two jurists, there is no discussion of this matter in the juristic literature.

MUSLIM MINORITIES: THE CASE OF INDIA

Apart from Spain, the next major region where Muslims acquired political power, gained conversions on a large scale, and founded empires lasting several centuries was India. The case of Indian Muslims is very instructive for understanding Muslim conduct in non-Muslim societies due to the large number (India has many more Muslims than all of the Arab world put together, and roughly as many Muslims live in India as they do in neighboring Pakistan and Bangladesh), as well as because Indian Muslims have contributed to this debate through two centuries of existence under non-Muslim control. Historians often begin the advent of Islam with the invasion of Sindh by Muhammad bin Qasim in 711. In fact, various groups of Muslims arrived in India (theoretically a dar al-harb) from Basra and adjoining areas under the Ummayads, theoretically a dar al-Islam. According to Jalal al-Din al-Suyuti, Muslims appeared on the Konkan and Malabar coasts of western India as early as 699, thus preceding Muhammad bin Qasim by more than a decade, and they remained for centuries under non-Muslim rule.

In other words, whatever the jurists may have said about the binary division of the world into dar al-harb and dar al-Islam, oppression within the domains of the Ummayad caliph ruling from Damascus must have been so severe that it compelled some Muslims to seek refuge outside the world of Islam.[9] In this instance, Muslims were not only free to believe, practice, and propagate their faith but also able to become a self-governing unit within the realm of the Hindu rajas.[10] Through the repeated invasions of northwestern India by Turkish and Afghan chiefs from Central Asia, India came under Muslim rule with the establishment of the Delhi sultanate in the early thirteenth century c.e. Although the Delhi sultanate split in due course into provincial dynasties of Bengal, Delhi, Gujarat, Malwa, and Deccan, Muslims remained in full control.

The story was repeated with the advent of the Mughals in the mid–sixteenth century. It was the arrival of the European nations on the subcontinent first as trading companies and later as military and political powers that ended Muslim rule in the early nineteenth century. What was the Muslim elite's reaction to this development? Before the 1857 Mutiny/Revolt, the situation was unclear, as there was still a Mughal emperor on the throne of Delhi. However, his rule was only nominal, and actual power was in the hands of the British. In 1803, Shah Abd al-Aziz (1746–1824), an *alim* of Delhi, declared the territories between Delhi and Calcutta, which were firmly in the hands of the British to be dar al-harb in an oft-quoted fatwa. Abd al-Aziz was disturbed by the progressive interference by the British with the inherited tradition and practice of Muslim law. His fatwa was issued on the ground that the country was being ruled not by the orders of the Muslim but by those of the Christian rulers. His attitude becomes clearer when his ruling is contrasted with his approach toward the Hindu Marathas under whom India was still dar al-Islam, as they had not replaced the Islamic legal system by one of their own.

Even previous to Abd al-Aziz, the Tariqa e Muhammadi and the Faraidi Movement in Bengal (active during the first part of the nineteenth century) held similar views. Abd al-Aziz's disciple Abd al-Hayyi (1828) was even more specific: British India "was the country of the enemy," for "no recourse is made to our holy law."[11] Despite declaring India as dar al-harb, Abd al-Aziz did not approve of usurious transactions that Hanafis permitted in dar al-harb, nor did he call for *hijrah*, or migration to a dar al-Islam. When asked why he did not call for hijrah, he replied that hijrah required, as a necessary first condition, possession of the means to migrate; it was allowed only if the means were available. Yet Sayyid Ahmad Shahid of Bareli (1786–1831), another disciple of Abd al-Aziz, did organize a hijrah and jihad well before the 1857 Mutiny/Revolt, when he sought to move away from the land of war— the British and Sikh—ruled northern India, to seek an abode in the northwest.

In May 1857, the Indian Revolt/Mutiny by the sepoys failed to overthrow the British power. Although both Muslim and Hindu elite participated or kept aloof from the uprising, the British initially regarded the mutiny as the exclusive handiwork of the Muslims, who allegedly wanted to restore the Mughal emperor. In the early postmutiny years, the British favored various Hindu castes in the army and government employment. The Muslim upper and middle classes wanted to safeguard their opportunities for employment by showing that they, too, could be loyal subjects of the British empire.

The publication of William Wilson Hunter's provocatively titled book *The Indian Musalmans: Are They Bound in Conscience to Rebel against the Queen?*[12] sparked off a lively debate on the question of Muslim loyalty to the non-Muslim state. In upper India, Sayyid Ahmad Khan of Aligarh, Nawab Abdul Latif Khan of Bengal, Nawab Salar Jang in Hyderabad, and Badruddin Tayyibji of Bombay affirmed Muslim loyalty to the raj upon the grant of freedom to practice and propagate their religion, which Queen Victoria had already given in the famous proclamation of 1858. Through the efforts of loyalist Muslim leadership, a rapprochement between Muslims and the British rule was achieved specially with the rise of the Indian— mainly Hindu—nationalism under the leadership of the Congress Party beginning in 1885. Yet many Muslims continued to regard the Ottoman caliph/emperor in Constantinople as their religious-temporal head, which was hotly contested by men like Sayyid Ahmad Khan.

The outbreak of World War I, in which Great Britain and Turkey were on opposite sides, greatly strained Muslim loyalty to the raj. The Ottoman Turkish empire's defeat at the hands of Britain and its allies deeply affected Indian Muslims. A campaign for the support of Turkey was launched in India known as the Khilafat movement (1918–1924). Some ulama actually declared India as dar al-harb. In their memorial to Lord Chelmsford, the viceroy of India in 1919, Mawlana Muhammad Ali and Mawlana Shawkat said:

> When a land is not safe for Islam, a Muslim has only two alternatives, jihad or hijrat. That is to say, he must either make use of every force God has given

him for the liberation of the land and ensure perfect freedom for the practice and preaching of Islam, or he must migrate to some other and freer land with a view to returning to it when it is more safe for Islam. . . . In view of our weak condition, migration is the only alternative for us. . . . This step, which we shall now have to consider with all the seriousness that its very nature demands, will be perhaps most decisive in the history of our community since the hijrat of our Holy Prophet.[13]

Mawlana Abul Kalam Azad, a senior congress leader and scholar, supported the Ali brothers' views. In the summer of 1920, thousands of Indian Muslims under severe emotional stress began to emigrate to neighboring Afghanistan. According to an eyewitness:

It was an unexpected sight of some ferocity that astounded all those who witnessed the events of Saturday morning on 14 August 1920. An excited and highly "truculent" wave of roughly 7,000 people moved from the small frontier town of Landi Kotal to the Khaybar pass bent on crossing the border from India into Afghanistan against all resistance to fulfill their religious duty of emigration from the Land of the Infidels . . . to the Land of Islam. They were chanting religious slogans and hymns to the tune of martial music, some of it Islamic and some profoundly British. "One large company was played out of British India to the tune of the British Grenadiers, played to an old fife!"[14]

Many more followed the stream of *muhajirin*. However, before too long, the Afghan authorities panicked and decided to stop further immigration. As a result of the Afghan measures, the muhajirin began to turn back from Kabul, bitter and impoverished by a long and arduous journey to the land of Islam. Close to three decades later, at the time of British India's partition and independence, seven million Muslims crossed over to Pakistan, the newly created dar al-Islam. For many, real or anticipated discrimination in a largely Hindu India was the motivating cause, for some it was the logical conclusion of their support for a Muslim state, for still others the prime motivation was the employment potential generated by the new country whose native population was largely illiterate. Although no fatwa was ever issued advising Muslims to migrate, some families as far distant from Pakistan as Malabar in the south did leave India.[15]

Even though one of the greatest migrations in the history of humankind, the exodus to Pakistan still left a "minority" of several million Muslims in residual India, making it one of the largest concentration of the Islamic communities. It bears repetition that more Muslims live in India than do in all the Arab states put together. Before we turn to the case of the Muslim minority in postindependence India, we must consider the cases of Russia and the Balkans, from where Muslims migrated in large numbers to Ottoman Turkey.

THE CASES OF RUSSIA AND THE BALKANS

Migrations into the Ottoman Empire began at the time of Russia's annexation of Crimea in 1783 and some forced conversions—exemplified by Muslim-sounding names ending with the Russian suffix *-ov.* Muslims began to leave their ancestral homes largely because they desired to live under the authority of a Muslim ruler rather than the Russian Orthodox czar, but there were compelling economic reasons as well. As the Russian presence in Crimea increased, Muslim peasants became the tenants of new Russian landlords, who tried to maximize their revenue collection from the cultivators. The peasants, and eventually the Muslim aristocrats, who had served in the czar's administration until their places were taken over by the Russians, found salvation in migration.

Emigration intensified after the wars of 1806–1812 and 1829 (with Iran) and especially after the Crimean War of 1853–1856, since Muslims had supported the Ottoman and allied armies in the hope of regaining their old autonomy and independence. After 1812, the Russian authorities, caught in the political and religious fervor of orthodoxy, increasingly sought to rid themselves of the Muslim population by encouraging or forcing emigration or conversion. The last such forced migration came as late as 1944, when the entire Muslim population of Crimea, including Communists and partisans who had fought the Germans in 1941–1943, were forcibly uprooted and moved to Soviet Central Asia, thus continuing the czarist policy.

The anti-Russian resistance of Shaykh Imam Shamil (1850s) led to a new wave of emigration from the Caucasus in 1862. Often referred to as Circassian migration, it actually involved a larger variety of groups than merely the Circassians. The final great wave of migrants from the Balkans into Turkey came after the Turco-Russian war of 1877–1878 and the Balkan wars of 1912–1913. The total number of people immigrating into the Ottoman Empire between 1860 and 1914 was approximately five to seven million. This is, of course, in addition to the exchange of population between Greece and Turkey in the 1920s.[16]

Moving away from Europe to Africa, we find that in Algeria, there was clear agreement about the status of the country: According to Maliki law, there was no doubt that after the French occupation (1847), the country had become dar al-harb, although no large-scale migration occurred, except the exodus of Tilmisan of 1911. In West Africa, Muslims moved to the Sudan and Hijaz in the nineteenth century under similar circumstances, as did some Muslims when eastern Turkistan or Sinkiang was occupied by China in 1950.

In conclusion, what can the experience of various Muslim communities under non-Muslim rule in the medieval and early modern periods tell us? First, whatever be the theory, even when Muslim-ruled territories fell under non-Muslim rule and were declared dar al-harb, most Muslims continued to live under the new circumstances, until religious persecution (as in Spain) forced some to migrate or then were expelled by sheer force of arms. Second, some Muslims migrated to a neighboring region of shared beliefs—Indian Muslims to Afghanistan; Balkan and Russian Muslims to Turkey; West Africans to Sudan, and the like. Yet it is clear that most were content to reside in their homelands if they were granted the freedom to practice Islam. In other words, belief and practice of faith comprised the irreducible minimum—whatever the maximum may have been—over which there could be no compromise. Third, the migration and permanent residence of significant number of Muslims from a putative dar al-Islam such as the Ummayad Empire to India (an obviously non-Muslim land) in the early medieval period demonstrates that Muslims could be and have been oppressed in their own lands. Fourth, many Muslims migrated to the non-Muslim territories for dawah, despite frequent juristic opinion that a Muslim ought not to live in a non-Muslim land. Fifth, except for the Hanafis, who allowed certain Islamic prohibitions (e.g., transactions involving usury; distillation, sale, and the consumption of alcohol; and so on), no other school of law agreed to the lapse of Shariah when Muslims were found to be living in non-Muslim-controlled territories.

Finally, loyalty to the ruler and the defense of the homeland was incumbent upon Muslims, if their beliefs and practices were permitted and their lives and property were safe.

POSTCOLONIAL ERA OF NATION-STATES

For more than two hundred years from the nineteenth to the mid–twentieth century, most of Asia, Africa, and the Middle East were under European colonial rule. At the dawn of freedom in the 1940s–1960s, most Muslims found themselves either in nation-states such as Egypt, Pakistan, and Turkey or as minorities, as in India, China, the former Soviet Union, and Yugoslavia. The simple, neat bifurcation of the world into worlds of Islam and non-Islam may be good in theory, but historical experience shows otherwise. Muslim groups and states have fought with each other over lands and resources or on ideological grounds as much as any other set of religious groups or countries. Some have even aided and abetted non-Muslims against fellow Muslims both as ethnic groups as well as states. The international wars involving Iran and Iraq (1980–1988), the internal wars involving the state and/or ethnic groups or tribal factions within states (Pakistan in 1971, 1980s–1990s; Algeria, Somalia, Turkey, Yemen, Afghanistan [1988–2002]; and the like, have shed more Muslim blood than those involving Muslims and non-Muslims. On the other hand, Muslim states have signed agreements—even treaties of perpetual friendship—with non-Muslim states dating back several centuries.[17] Clearly, dar al-Islam and dar al-harb have been one of the great legal fictions. Many Muslim groups have taken refuge in non-Muslim states when fleeing oppression in dar al-Islam or lack of economic opportunity since the 1950s, exemplified by the cases of the North Africans in France, South Asians in Britain, and Turks and Iranians in Germany. Whatever their origins and exact numbers, roughly one-third out of a billion-plus Muslims in the early twenty-first century are in numerical minority in many different countries.

Apart from the geographic diversity of Muslims, it is obvious that they live or have lived under a long continuum of political systems from liberal democracies—the United States and India—to communist dictatorships—the former Soviet Union and China. How should Muslims conduct themselves in such plural states, particularly in democracies, where they are neither rulers nor ruled but in fact can and do share in the governance. Let us consider two cases: contemporary India and the United States, both of which are governed under conditions of a political/administrative unit—*federal state;* the ideological context within which policy/policies are formulated—*liberalism;* and the policies of secularism in India; separation of church and state in the United States; and the process—*democratic,* through which the policy/policies are implemented.

THE CASE OF CONTEMPORARY INDIA

Indian Muslims have been a large (expected to exceed 150 million by the decennial census of 2001) and an active constituent of national politics and society for a very long time. Throughout the twentieth century, some of their political endeavors have been directed toward achieving internal autonomy in a plural society. The aspiration for autonomy has been sufficiently strong to unite an otherwise extremely heterogeneous population divided by castelike clusters, language, class, sect, and interpretations of Islam. Muslim politics have seldom been monolithic, but a predominant tendency has been devoted to the cause of autonomy entailing a substantial struggle to determine the character and the scope of the state's jurisdiction. This is evident by the fact that even voting for or operating through secular political parties such as the Congress Janata Party, they have done so under the banner of "minority wing" of the respective parties—except the Communist Party of India—Marxist (CPI-M).

Muslims are doctrinally expected to give their primary allegiance to the Muslim ummah—conceived as the community of believers having the responsibility of carrying the divine message to the rest of humankind. Ideally the state, when motivated by Islamic purpose and governed by the

Shariah, becomes coterminous with the community. The duality between the state and the community disappears. Muslims believe that the community enjoyed such wholeness under the guidance of Prophet Muhammad and four Khulafa Rashidun—the rightly guided caliphs. For the rest of the Islamic history, the story has been very different. The state has appeared, at best, as an embodiment of organized political-military power of particular Muslim groups deployed on behalf of Islamic causes, but above all for the defense of Muslims and the particular territory that they inhabit; at worst it has been—and more often than not—a source of oppression and exploitation illustrated by the cases of dictatorships and monarchies in our own times.

Of all the world religions, Islam is perhaps unique in having an acute concern for power, and Islamic political theory generally assumes Muslim political-military ascendancy whether Muslims be few or many. If they should not enjoy ascendancy, the Islamic political theory insists that they must, failing which as a community it must be wholly autonomous: a state within a state, to put it bluntly—the equivalent of the Ottoman millet system in reverse! The relationship between Muslims and the non-Muslim state is contractual, except for the moral obligation of defending it materially and militarily when unjustly attacked by non-Muslims. The concepts of "majority" and "minority" are entirely alien to Muslim political thought, as was the case in Europe until the French Revolution. They derive from a different tradition—secular humanism—in which the guiding principle of political community is the territorial nation-state, in which the state is viewed as the embodiment of the moral unity of the citizens. As the carriers of the divine message of God, Muslims are expected only to expand by dawah, not to shrink by disbelief. Thus, the idea that Muslims could be a fixed, permanent minority is a stranger to Islam, since all territories not under Muslim rule were treated as borderland of a worldwide dar al-Islam destined by God eventually to encompass all humanity.

The Muslim position is therefore analogous to that of the Communists during the heyday of the Soviets between 1917 and 1991. In contrast, India's national constitution adopted in 1950 by an elected assembly rests on a different principle. Like other secular/Western/European constitutions, it incorporates the citizens into state structure individually to stress individual rather than collective rights and duties, and applies impersonal and universalistic principles in regulating relationships within their authoritative arenas. The Indian constitution rests on the principle of a territorial nation constituted by citizens, irrespective of religious or any other identities. The Indian state embodies the moral unity of its citizens and lays claim to their primary allegiance by virtue of it. Instead of a confederacy of religious, ethnic, or cultural groups, it has substituted the idea of fundamental rights—and the rights of religious/linguistic minorities despite the efforts of the Hindu militants to the contrary. In the political sphere, it has instituted fluid majorities and minorities not irrevocably hostile to each other. Thus, India has remained true to its constitution in theory, at least, and true to its democratic governance for the most part—except the "Emergency" nightmare of two years in 1975–1977.

How have Muslims responded to the Indian polity: a secular state with citizenship as the cornerstone of political community? There is little doubt that the postindependence political order has presented a major challenge to the hitherto-established Muslim political thought. As the nationalist movement grew under a largely upper-caste Hindu Indian National Congress, Muslims under the leadership of the Muslim League (and similar organizations in princely India) sought religious and cultural autonomy pertaining to the practice and propagation of Islam, preservation and perpetuation of the Urdu language, political representation, and reservation in government jobs. The failure of the Indian National Congress to concede some of these demands led to the hardening of Muslims' stand, leading to the partition of the country and the creation of Pakistan. The creation of Pakistan not only did not solve the problems of Muslim minority in India but worsened them—reducing its numbers, consequently weakening them politically, causing massive dislocation of populations and several thousand deaths in widespread violence. Yet, the writers of the Indian constitution, by conferring equal citizenship, and the resulting membership of the moral-political community have required Muslims to define their relationship with that community in terms other than Islamic.

In medieval India, Muslims or at least their elite were or thought of themselves as the dominant group; certainly this remains a self-image if nothing else.[18] During the colonial period, they shared the burden of being the subject of alien rulers with others. In contemporary India, they are neither the dominant group nor the unequal subjects of a hostile ruler but cocitizens of an avowedly secular polity. Here Muslim response has been governed not by the liberal theory of the state but by the urge to preserve, perpetuate, and increase the group autonomy. India's democratic system provides the opportunity to the community to manipulate the political process to its advantage—by bloc voting, for instance. Needless to say, the text of the Indian constitution is far from reflective of political realities exemplified by the pogroms of Muslims in many parts of India, particularly the ones that took place in Mumbai in 1992–1993 and in Gujarat in spring 2002.

The dominant Islamic model for a pluralistic society was and remains the *millat* system, which recognizes religious communities, with their separate laws, as legitimate and protected constituents of the society, dominated militarily and politically by Muslims. Indian Muslims have not theorized directly about the jurisdiction of the Indian state in their own society, but through their practice helped determine its character in four areas: (1) political representation to the state; (2) state jurisdiction in matters of personal/family laws of marriage, divorce, and inheritance; (3) secularism; and (4) national integration, all of which are represented in the experience of the world's largest Muslim minority and thus highly significant for Muslims as minorities everywhere.

Political Representation to the State

As noted earlier, according to the jurists, society is divided into the realm of Muslims and non-Muslims. From this division it follows that those who are of the group are best qualified to speak for the group in a legislature. Within the context of Islamic values, it is more important to Muslims to be represented by Muslims than by elected, politically accountable non-Muslims.[19] In contrast, the liberal theory tends to regard representative institutions as the repositories of national consensus, which is periodically renewed by elected majorities. The liberal view distinguishes sharply between a representative's political commitments, on the one hand, and his or her religious, racial, or cultural affiliation, on the other. Indian Muslims have historically adhered to the view that those representing the community must come from within its own ranks and even from within its own platform.

At the dawn of the twentieth century, the Indian nationalists, led by the Congress Party, demanded the British colonial authorities to introduce some democratic institutions in the country based on the universal franchise, arguing that the will of the numerical majority ought to be the will of the people. The British answer was that Western political institutions had grown up in a particular society—homogenous England—and could not be transferred to another one so different in composition as India, which was not a nation but a subcontinent composed of many nations. For the vocal Muslim leadership, representative government on the Western model, as demanded by the Congress, meant the permanent subjugation of the Muslim minority to Hindu majority. They demanded separate electorates so as to ensure the Muslims a share of power in the new framework of government. The 1909 act granting the separate electorates was a curious compromise in that it conceded to the Muslims their own desired method of representation despite the intense opposition of the Congress, but at the same time it established the principle of majority rule.

The question was insistently asked, How are the rights of minorities to be safeguarded, particularly on community-sensitive questions? This is an issue that received little consideration in the nineteenth-century British liberal political thought, which the Indians had drawn from. Liberal political thinkers had been concerned with the rights of *minority opinions,* but the issue in India was very different. It was not the question of dissenting opinion and individual freedom but the enforcement by government of not merely the ordinary business of law and order but a whole range of religious and social practices of permanent groups, not temporary clusters of opinions. As soon as the British withdrew and partition drastically reduced Muslim numbers in India in 1947, the Congress Party set about to abolish the separate electorates through its majority in the Indian Constituent Assembly. Despite the spirited opposition of Muslim League leaders such as Muhammad Ismail and his colleague from Madras, the Hindu-dominated Constituent Assembly rejected the demand for the retention of separate electorates in May 1949.[20] Half a century later, Begum Qudsiya Aizaz Rasul, the woman who was co-opted by the Constituent Assembly to move the resolution abolishing separate electorates, regretted her historic decision.[21]

Secularism and State Jurisdiction in Matters of Personal Law

Not only did the Constituent Assembly abolish the separate electorates, but it also wrote an Article 44 in the chapter on "Directive Principles of the State Policy" in the national constitution to which most Muslims objected. This article directs the state to secure a uniform civil code for all regardless of religious difference. But since it is a "directive principle," it is specifically outside the realm of justice. The possibility of replacing the Shariah-based Muslim personal law (applied by the British Indian courts) with a uniform civil code as demanded by a vocal segment of an odd combination composed of right-wing Hindu parties and left-wing secularists is looked upon by the majority of Muslims as a threat to their religious identity.

For many Muslims, the issue here is more fundamental. The issues are not the desirability or otherwise of the reforms in the personal law but whether a state controlled by non-Muslims can be permitted to interpret and make changes in the Islamic laws. Many Muslims assert that the laws of religious groups are parallel to those of the state and enforceable by it. This position is clearly modeled after the Prophetic precedent of the *muahadah* (pact) with the Madinan Jews, which was between two different communities to live their own lives, rather than the two to participate in constructing a life in common. Significantly, the Jamiat al-Ulama-I Hind, the Congress Party's ally during and after the struggle for independence, conceived of the future constitution of a free India as a contract between the Muslim community of India and the non-Muslim others. The idea of a nation-state was simply absent in the thinking of the Jamiat.

Contrary to the Jamiat's hope and desire, the Indian elite conceived of a democratic state, not a federation of ethnic-religious corporate entities. The constitution of India was going to be a contract between the individual and the state, not concerned with group entitlements—except the Scheduled Castes and Tribes, mostly Hindu. This is because there is a great deal of confusion in India and other liberal democracies between the concept of religious freedom, one of the most cherished rights that has emerged in the long struggle of the individual against the church in the West, and group rights. Religious freedom in the language of the Indian constitution means the right to practice and propagate one's faith, without hindrance from the state, whereas most Muslims interpret it to mean that the government should in effect support through law the family laws and customs that a community claims are basic to its internal life. It is a widely held, vehemently asserted belief among Muslims that their personal law is an intrinsic part of their religion, that it represents a perfect code for all. No one has the right to change it, certainly not a legislature controlled by non-Muslims.

As noted earlier, a bizarre combination of anti-Muslim Hindu right-wing parties and secularists had been clamoring for the change in Muslim personal law since independence. Matters came to a head when in 1985 the Supreme Court of India handed down a decision, which at the first glance looked unremarkable. Muhammad Ahmad Khan, a lawyer, had appealed a judgment that required him to pay indefinite maintenance to his former wife Shah Bano Begum. Two judges of the Supreme Court referred the case to a larger bench to decide whether the Criminal Procedure Code of 1973 (which punishes former husbands not paying maintenance to former wives) had been interpreted correctly and whether that code was in conflict with the 1937 Shariat Act. The court in fact determined that Khan did owe maintenance (alimony) to his divorced wife, as it argued that the Criminal Procedure Code of 1973 makes no exception for an individual's personal law and that it was therefore intended to be applied to all parties regardless of religious affiliation. According to the Muslim Personal Law, Khan was required to pay maintenance to his former wife for three months only—the period of *iddat,* or the menstrual cycles, but no more, whereas the Criminal Procedure Code of 1973 provided for maintenance of a divorced wife who had not remarried and/or needed support. Most Muslims saw this decision as an undue interference in the family law of Islam.

The Supreme Court's judgment unleashed a nationwide controversy. Muslim public opinion was mobilized and led by the Muslim Personal Law Board representing all shades of opinion within the community except the secularist. To be sure, there was/is a minority opinion within Muslims who argued for either a reinterpretation of the Muslim family laws or a change in it altogether. That opinion is represented by some Bollywood actors, singers, academics, journalists, and public figures of various kinds. So intense was the polarization of opinion on this question that Shah Bano Begum herself publicly withdrew her claim to maintenance and demanded that the Indian government overturn the Supreme Court's judgment in her favor! In doing so, she conveyed her and the community's preference for Islamic family laws over those of the Indian legislature. "How could I be right," she argued, "when my qawm's [nation's] leaders say that I am wrong!"[22]

Bowing to the Muslim public opinion—because of its voting power—the Indian government overturned the Supreme Court's decision. It passed the

Muslim Women (Protection of Rights on Divorce) Act in May 1986, which asserts the supremacy of Muslim Personal Law over the Criminal Code with regard to divorce.

Like the stand on the question of divorce law, the Muslim position on the issue of adoption followed a similar path. In June 1972, the Indian law minister, H. R. Gokhale, introduced a bill in the Rajya Sabha, the upper house of the parliament, to regulate the adoption of Indian children. This proposed legislation was in compliance with Article 39 of the constitution, which requires the state to protect children and youth against exploitation and against moral and material abandonment. In the "Statement of Objects and Reasons" accompanying the bill, the minister stated that the "bill seeks to provide for a uniform law of adoption applicable to all communities."[23] It raised all the issues, religious and political, that had agitated Muslims for half a century or more: the threat to Muslim personal law and consequently to Muslim identity. It also raised the problem of what Islam permitted and how far Muslims should be allowed through a permissive legislation to opt out of the Shariah and whether the state should assist them in doing so.

The bill was referred to a joint Select Committee of Houses of Parliament, consisting of forty-five members, only three of whom were Muslims. The committee was commissioned to receive representations from interested individuals and organizations and collect evidence from witnesses having interest in the subject and submit its report to the parliament. The committee labored for four years, during the course of which it examined memoranda from fifty-nine organizations and eighty-five individuals drawn from all parts of India.[24] Interestingly, a majority of the organizations making representations to the committee belonged to Muslims.[25]

The adoption issue greatly roused Muslim public opinion, which was galvanized by the Muslim Personal Law Board constituted in December 1972 by a variety of organizations drawn from all parts of India. The board expressed its opposition to the application of the bill to Muslims on the ground that it was specifically prohibited in Islam.[26] The three Muslim members of the Joint Select Committee—all belonging to the Congress Party—submitted minutes of dissent, giving Islamic reasons for their opposition to the application of the bill to Muslims. They claimed that a vast majority of Muslim opinion was opposed to adoption being made legally permissible for Muslims because it was expressly prohibited by the Quran (33:4), and one of them argued that the fact of changes being made in the Muslim personal law in other Islamic countries (e.g., Turkey, Tunisia) will be of no use here, that many of those countries were ruled by dictators who paid no heed to the people's opinion, while India, being a democracy, must respect the nearly unanimous Muslim demand.[27]

Disagreeing with the predominant Muslim opinion, a minority Muslim opinion supported the proposed bill's comprehensive application; since the proposed legislation was only permissive, not mandatory, they contended, it did not infringe the Muslim personal law. It was argued by the same minority group that the bill expanded the legal rights of Muslims who wished to avail of the adoption possibility. In response, the majority opinion argued that such a possibility ought not to be made available to Muslims. In the words of Muhammad Jamilurrahman, one of the three members of the Joint Select Committee, "Muslims as a community should not have the option to get out of or run away from the applicability of any of the provisions of the Muslim Personal Law."[28] Other arguments produced in favor of exemption of Muslims from the scope of the bill were that it would violate the freedom of religion guaranteed to them by the constitution (Article 25) and that it would affect the Muslim law of inheritance and the Muslim law of marriage.

The Joint Select Committee rejected the plea of its Muslim members that Muslims be exempted from the scope of the bill, but the Muslim political opposition to it was so strong that the Congress government did not proceed with it in its original form, and with the change of the government at the center to the Janata Party in 1977, the bill was withdrawn. The new Adoption Bill presented to the parliament in 1980 expressly excluded Muslims from the scope of the bill. Against the majority of his coreligionists, M. H. Beg, a former chief justice of India, expressed himself strongly against exempting Muslims from the scope of the new bill. He argued that exclusion of Muslims from the bill rendered it unconstitutional, as it will deny to Muslims the equal protection of law. He took the position that an individual's right to deviate from the view of the majority of his religious community ought to be recognized as part of religious freedom.[29] Unlike Justice M. H. Beg, Abu Shoaib Rizvi contended:

> The personal status assigned to an individual by the court is not by virtue of his religion but by virtue of his belonging to a particular group or community. When a person declares his religion before the court, by implication he claims membership of a community whose internal structure is based on a particular set of personal laws. The courts administer these laws in deference to the wishes of the community, which is sovereign in this field. The community may claim that its laws are a part of, or derived from the religion. But that is an internal matter for the community. . . . The community is one of the federative [*sic*] units of the state, contributing its own law, enjoying a limited sectional jurisdiction and making demands over the judicial and executive organs of the state to implement these laws.[30]

This is the clearest summation of the millat system in the Indian context. What it tells us is that in the Indian Islamic thought—if not in Islamic thought itself—a theory of state is not fully developed. The state is often equated with administration or the executive branch of a government. A Muslim, according to this theory, is not a citizen but a member of the ummah. The Islamic ummah is not a political community. A handful of Muslims who have written on the theme of the Islamic state have argued that an Islamic polity must be grounded in justice and strive to ensure the well-being of its population subject in its jurisdiction, that sovereignty rests with God, and the rulers are merely trustees administering it for the good of the population.[31] The Muslim position on the family laws determines the Muslim view of the proper scope of the authority of the state and discloses the preferred form for it. The entire question of personal law is closely related to the issue of secularism, to which we now turn.

SECULARISM: ANTIRELIGION OR RELIGIOUS NEUTRALITY

Secularism, entailing in its Western definition the separation of religion and politics and thus freeing the state from sectarian conflict, was seen by the founders of the Indian republic as the political solution to the historical problem of religious cleavage in India. The state retained the right to regulate aspects of the religious institutions but guaranteed freedom of religion and protected the cultural interests of the minorities. They also expected that secularism would promote national integration (i.e., bring about a greater and increasing harmony among the different constituents of the Indian population) and over time establish a modern political community. Moreover, the state became directly involved in the reform of Hinduism, the majority religion in India. The Indian Constituent Assembly abolished untouchability, *sati* (widow burning), dowry, all social customs—if not religious practices— associated with Hindus. Through further legislation, the Indian elite also permitted entry into temples closed to various lower castes and untouchables. Through the Hindu Marriage Act, the minimum marriage age of the Hindu women was also fixed, thus abolishing child marriages. In other words, the state took a proactive role in the reforms of a particular religion.

Since most of the articulate Muslims were resigned to a state dominated by non-Muslims, no objection was raised to the legislative reforms of Hindu practices, but they are unwilling to extend the same right to legislatures to interfere in Islamic affairs. Most Muslims would like to interpret secularism as merely a mechanism for complete state neutrality in the religious matters of all religions. The state ought to be religion-free in totality. It should neither penalize nor reward one religion at the expense of the other. Secularism is understood as a "utilitarian expediency" which under conditions of a pluralistic population is acceptable, even desirable, but not its denial of religion.[32] The state should not encourage or discourage any or all religious belief or practice, nor should it be in the business of reforms or interpretation of religion, except public safety. In other words, it should not occupy the same space as religion. In practice, however, we have seen that in India, the state has been actively involved in what can be seen as religious reform. Sometimes, it has even encouraged the singing of Hindu hymns—such as Vande Mataram—in schools and over state-controlled television and radio, much to the resentment of Muslims. At least in one case, the Indian government rebuilt a Hindu temple—Somnath in Gujarat—which was allegedly destroyed by Mahmud Ghaznawi, a Turco-Afghan invader in the medieval period. Many Muslims would agree with sociologist T. N. Madan's argument "that neither India's indigenous religious traditions nor Islam recognize a sacred-secular dichotomy in the manner in which Christianity does"[33]; instead, "[a] decentralized polity, a positive attitude towards cultural pluralism, and genuine concern and respect for human rights would be, perhaps, the best guarantors of Indian secularism, understood as inter-religious understanding and the state policy of non-discrimination and of equal distance (not equal proximity) from the religious concerns of the people."[34]

If, as shown earlier, Muslims do not want the state to interfere in their religious matters and family laws derived from religion and thus claim a large zone of legal autonomy, how do they propose to participate in the public affairs of the country, particularly since many of their spokespersons claim that Islam is a comprehensive religion, a complete way of life, presumably not excluding matters of governance? It is a recurring theme in contemporary Muslim discourse that Islam does not make a distinction between religion and politics. What do the proponents of this assertion mean?

One obvious implication is that Islam is not just an otherworldly religion but lays down for Muslims what is obligatory, recommended, permissible, disapproved, and prohibited. The believers are of course expected to conduct their lives accordingly. The other implication could be that no great significance attaches to the political arena as political activity is subsumed under religious activity; that is, when a Muslim acts politically, he is in fact acting religiously in political sphere. Islam is thus not a religion in the restricted post-Enlightenment sense of belief, worship, rituals, and the like. It is taken by Muslims to be a comprehensive, complete religion encompassing the entire range of human needs, situations, and activities. Islam in a Hegelian sense is a positive religion—a religion of commandments. Thus, Muslim participation in the public affairs of any country ought to emanate from this understanding that when a Muslim acts politically, he or she should religiously as well, whether so combining the two seemingly unrelated motivations is comprehensible to others or not. In the Indian situation, Sayyid Abid Husain has articulated this position very well, particularly

if they [Muslims] live as an integral part of the nation and discharge their civic or national duties as sincerely and zealously as they do their religious and communal duties with the realization of moral values (which are really Islamic values), the dualism in their thinking would disappear and they would regard every act which is meant for the material or moral welfare of God's creatures, whether they are Muslims or non-Muslims, as a religious act.[35]

Given the long history of intergroup antagonism in India, the bloody events of the subcontinent's partition, and the perennial Hindu-Muslim violence, it is not surprising that Sayyid Abid Husain cautions his fellow Muslims to couch their words and deeds in terms other than their own. "But their efforts in this direction can only be effective," he says, "if they speak to the Indian nation not in religious but secular language and argue their case for the reforms which they think are necessary, not on the basis of religious authority but on that of observation, experience and reason."[36] In conclusion, then, a Muslim's participation in the Indian public affairs—including matters of governance—can be based on the Islamic principles of enjoining good and forbidding evil.

By the same token what is a sound practical advice in the Indian context is equally applicable in the American situation as well. The Quranic concepts of *adl, qist* (Quran 16:90, 5:8), and *mizan* (justice; Quran 6:152, 7:85, 11:84, 11:85, 55:9) can be translated and applied to contemporary situations. By these Quranic justifications, it would be imperative for Muslims to work zealously for causes such as economic development, poverty alleviation, promotion of education, advancement of gender equity, interreligious group harmony, and the like, both through participation in the political process as well as through nongovernmental voluntary organizations, charities, and professional networks. In fact, given the Islamic understanding of religion and politics as being an undifferentiated whole, Muslims—in common with orthodox Christians and Jews—have a potential advantage over other groups, as Muslim participation in the political process would have direct Quranic sanction. Muslims should participate in the political process in India not merely out of expediency but with the higher purposes of working for the greater good of the country, as there is no inherent clash of interests between Muslims and others, certainly not in general economic and human development. By so doing, Muslims would be fulfilling an Islamic obligation as well as protecting and promoting their own interests in purely religious and cultural affairs from the encroachment of Hindu chauvinist forces.

Moving from India toward the West, we now consider the case of the emergence (or reemergence) of Muslim communities, and the issues they raise in a country with many similarities in the political system (liberal democracy; separation of religion from politics), if not in the composition of the society and its values.

THE UNITED STATES: NEW MEDINA OR A FATAL SHORE?

Given the absence of religious affiliation as a category for census enumeration, no one seems to know how many Muslims there are in the United States, just as we do not know how many Baptists or Jews there are. Whatever be the current estimates—six to eight million—they certainly exceed the population of some of the smaller Muslim majority states. Like Muslims in the rest of the world, culture, language, sect, and the duration of presence in the United States quite naturally differentiate American Muslims. Muslim ethnic/national composition in America at the dawn of the twenty-first century rivals the one found during the hajj in Mecca only seasonally every year. By estimate, the majority is composed of newly converted or reverted African Americans, followed by mostly recent, post-1965 immigrants and their descendants.

With its usually thriving and expanding economy, occasional labor shortages in certain sectors, and a superb educational system, the United States has long been a magnet for oppressed people everywhere, including Muslims. Some Muslims can even look to this country as an escape from religious persecution (India) and genocide in cases like Bosnia, other parts of the Balkans, and Chechnya. For most immigrant groups—other than Catholics, Jews, and Blacks—the "problem" in the United States is one of cultural preservation and perpetuation versus the continuum of integration—assimilation in a society largely assumed to be based on Judeo-Christian values.

For other groups like Muslims, American society poses another challenge: surviving the challenge of assimilation in a society known for a high capacity for absorbing immigrants in a sponge-like manner. This challenge takes several forms or phases over generations: preserving one's religious beliefs and practices to a high degree among the first-generation immigrants, perpetuating them in the subsequent generations, and even expanding Islam among fellow Americans through dawah.

Before we explore possible approaches or strategies for surviving the challenge of assimilation, let us consider the various and competing paradigms of U.S. society. Historically, "Anglo-conformity" was perceived as the norm throughout the nineteenth century and first half of the twentieth. In this paradigm, mostly European national and ethnic groups emulated the English norms in all walks of life except church affiliation. Later on, intellectuals defined the goal of U.S. society as a melting pot in which identities of the old world were dissolved to create a new transnational American identity. Pretty soon it was discovered that there were too many "unmeltables"! In 1955, American Jewish scholar Will Herberg promoted the idea of an America with equal religious conglomerates: Protestant, Catholic, and Jewish.[37] Given that Herberg was writing at a time when the Muslim presence was either small or unrecognized, it is possible that he would have even included Muslims if he were to write in the late twentieth century.

In contemporary America, one can see at least two paradigms seeking acceptance. The first comes from the proponents of the religious right wing of the Christian fundamentalists shared to a degree, or aspects of it, by some Jewish groups and some politicians. This paradigm perceives America as based primarily on the religious and cultural values of Christianity and Judaism. Even granting that the American wall of separation of church and state would be affected by the societal composition (Protestants, Catholics, and Jews up to the 1960s), this model has come under criticism due to the ever-expanding diversity of the United States. Contemporary liberal America boasts not merely of Christians and Jews but increasingly of Muslims, Hindus, Sikhs, and Buddhists, not to speak of agnostics or atheists. A society modeled only after Judeo-Christian values (assuming there is only one interpretation) will consign the contemporary and future population segments with distinct values and faiths to the periphery.

The other paradigm advocates a pluralistic society that celebrates diversity. Its critics fear the sharpening of ethnic identities already present—for instance, in the various ethnic enclaves all over the United States—and favor new limits on immigration. This paradigm would naturally appeal to those Muslims wanting to preserve their faith, perpetuate it in the next generations, and expand it by spreading it among the unbelievers. As far as the first generation is concerned, most Muslims who arrive committed to Islam are likely to remain so to various degrees. The degree to which they practice Islam in America may also be conditioned by their past commitment in the land of birth and socialization. Additionally, for many Muslims their religion and culture/nationality are also two sides of a coin, both equally valid: being a Yemeni often also means a Muslim, just as it is the case with Turks and Pakistanis, although we know that there are non-Muslims in all those countries. The first generation would be more likely to remain Muslim also because of an attachment to the culture of their native lands, as Muslims would in common with other immigrant groups. Because of the need for a group to socialize with, sometimes to enter business relationships with through ethnic networks, for cultural satisfaction, all will work for group identity, as one's self-esteem and belonging are tied to similar people—members of one's ethnic/national group. In other words, the attachment of immigrants to their culture is an asset and would help them preserve their faith, but it can also be a liability for Muslims, as it may impede growth of a transnational Muslim consciousness in the Untied States.

Barring the exceptional cases of Blacks (due to a distinctly visible race) and Hispanics, a concentrated group in a specific location (e.g., the Southwest) with easy access to Spanish-speaking Mexico, no other significant group has been able to perpetuate its identity to a high degree. Despite a huge array of institutions and resources, many Jews feel threatened by the loss of membership in their group through large-scale intermarriages. The fate of isolated Arab groups in Quincy and Springfield, Massachusetts, and Detroit, Michigan, and Albanians in Connecticut, Michigan, Illinois, and elsewhere is hardly encouraging, as most of these groups have assimilated. Even granting that these groups had substantial numbers of Christians among them and that they arrived well before a time when Muslim communities were not as widespread as they were in the 1990s, it is still instructive that their assimilation happened despite living in a geographically compact space.

Scholars and journalists repeatedly assert and the community's own spokesmen claim that Islam is the fastest-*growing* religion in the United States. Is it possible or probable that Islam may be the fastest-*shrinking* religion among the second generation? Next to nothing is available in the literature about the extent of perpetuation of Islam in second-generation Muslims. No one has any idea about the number of "lapsed" Muslims. Similarly, we have no idea about the extent to which Muslim men and women have chosen to marry or live together with non-Muslims. Nor does anyone know about the number of cases where second-generation Muslims have in fact converted to Christianity.

Sociologists often claim that the third generation of immigrants, secure in American soil, rediscovers the roots. Will this be true of religious affiliation as well? It remains to be seen. Certainly there is a dearth of information about individuals and families reverting back to Christianity after having converted to Islam, especially among African Americans. There certainly are fears about such occurrences and plentiful anecdotes. Since it is a taboo topic of extreme sensitivity, most Muslims, including many in the leadership, have tended to bury their heads in the sand. Since the events of 9/11, there is an upsurge of anti-Muslim stereotypical propaganda on TV, in the newspapers, over the Internet, and everywhere else. In a generally hostile environment, immigrant Muslims may withdraw into the safety of the ethnic cocoons, leaving their children to face the music. Will the United States be the new Medina, as Ismail R. Faruqi hoped it would be, or will it prove to be a fatal shore where first-generation Muslims see their progeny swallowed by the postmodern culture of contemporary America? How can Muslims prevent their first generation from disappearing in the cultural swamp that America is?

In the following section, I offer what seem at the present to be some of the options. First, at the level of belief and practice, Islam needs to be taught and practiced as a seamless whole, transcending time and space. The word *religion* is too restricted to show the entire range of human behavior that the Arabic word *aldin* encompasses, including what is called a value system. Great stress ought to be laid on aspects of Islam, which involve group worship such as the prayers, particularly the Friday prayers. The emphasis on family and the collective ummah over the individual needs to be stressed. The inordinate individualism in contemporary America has been and will be especially harmful for anyone valuing family and group solidarity. Excessive individualism is not at all a moral ideal but pure egoism, leading to family breakups. Inculcating the idea that Islam is beyond time, space, and ethnic and national identities would promote loyalty to the doctrinal unity at an early age. Thus, when these children come of age, unlike their immigrant parents, the second-generation offspring would be receptive to the possibility of large-scale intermarriages between men and women of different cultural heritage united by faith and by the common upbringing in the United States, facilitated by socialization at mosques and Islamic community centers. Large-scale intermarriages between second-generation American Muslims are desirable from the point of view of generating supranational Muslim communities. As a first step toward the ideal, it can start as widespread intermarriages between, for example, the Egyptians and the Lebanese or between the Indian and the Pakistani/Bangladeshi Muslims. In this project, the first-generation/immigrant parents would have to make a number of adjustments for the sake of the survival of Islam in the next generation. These include but are not confined to matters of material culture such as dress, language, food, music, and the like. As far as dress is concerned, a practicing Muslim would insist only on the idea of *satr* (cover) rather than a particular national style or fashion.

Language retention through loyalty is neither Islamic nor practical. While there would be no disagreement among Muslims about the virtue of learning Arabic as the language of the Revelation, only the classical Quranic Arabic merits that status. As far as conversational Arabic is concerned, there are more than one version. No particular version of Arabic can command Muslim loyalty on Islamic principles, anymore than can Urdu or Kurdish. Language can create communication barriers among different groups of believers and is therefore undesirable in the American context. Moreover, as a century-old experience has shown, most Arab Americans (regardless of religion) have not been able to retain their parents' language.[38]

As people become more cosmopolitan, they are likely to experiment with foods of different cultures while retaining a core cuisine from which they draw their daily nourishment. For Muslims, any halal food and drink is acceptable. In any case, like language, food habits and choices of the old lands are modified or altered for an American palate even if not discarded altogether in the second generation.

If as a result of Islamic education and training of the second generation it remains Muslim, and if this generation chooses to find spouses from within Muslim communities, there is a chance of the fusion of different groups into a Muslim community, which would have all or most characteristics of a religious-national group possessing distinct values and lifestyle, particular behavioral patterns, distinctive customs and traditions, recognizable styles of dress, and the like. Care must be taken to see that this new "*homo Islamicus*" is as far removed from any one national/ethnic culture as possible and as close as possible to the Islamic values, so that this group at once erects a boundary between itself and others but always has a gate through which those desiring entrance into the new Medina can gain access through conversion to Islam as a result of dawah.

Needless to say, this is theory; putting it into practice to achieve the desired results would not be easy. But if this model or some version of it were not translated into action, what are the alternatives? Or what is happening now that is likely to intensify? It is no secret that American Muslims are divided into a large number of ethnic/national communities and sects. Further compounding the division are various interpretations of Islam in practice: Tablighis, Salafis, Sufis. If the immigrant Muslim groups remain preoccupied with the affairs of their native lands, each ethnic/national group will divide its energies and resources to the neglect of pressing matters at home, resulting in a bunch of highly fragmented communities. Indeed, such is already the case. The danger of such fragmentation carrying over into the next generation is also real. If, on the other hand, the second generation retains Islam at least to the degree that their parents did, then Muslims would emerge as a large and cohesive group like Jews, Catholics, Hispanics, and Blacks. Otherwise, American Muslims may simply repeat the experience of the numerous previous diasporas through the life cycles of genesis, development, and extinction, with an insignificant minority holding on to the faith and culture of their parents and grandparents.

PARTICIPATION OF MUSLIMS ON THE PUBLIC SQUARE

As the number of Muslims in the United States increases, the likelihood of Muslim participation in the U.S. political system and its consequences becomes an issue worthy of attention. Up to now, Muslims in the United States for the most part have had very little influence on American politics. Although by the dawn of the twenty-first century there is a consensus within the community about participation in public affairs, it is worth considering arguments presented against Muslim involvement.

Three strands can be seen in the argument of those opposed to public participation. The first is a group that sees the United States as a virtual Kufristan, a land of the unbelievers. The followers of Tabighi Jamaat, Hizb al-Tahrir, and the Khalifornians represent this group. The Tablighi Jamaat, a loosely knit organization founded in India in the 1930s, is now a transnational organization. The Tablighis confine themselves to teaching, preaching, and practicing the ritualistic elements of Islam. The Tablighi focus is only on males who they think are lapsed Muslims, hoping to bring them back to the mosques. The Tablighis are averse to any debate or discussion on matters other than the rituals, and they have stuck to that theme with remarkable consistency. Implicit in the preoccupation with the rituals is that nothing is to be gained by participation in politics, since the first priority is the observance of the basic rituals. In any case, how can anyone look up to the nonbelieving legislators when Allah is the sole lawgiver? The framing of the law is the prerogative of God, and humans cannot take up that task; therefore, participation is haram, as the Quran, supplemented by the Sunnah, is complete Shariah—so where is the need for further laws? The Tablighi position may seem like déjà vu to many Americans familiar with the beliefs and practices of the Amish. Participation in lawmaking, whether at the local, state, or federal level, amounts in the Tablighi perspective to playing God. It is noteworthy that the Tablighi behavior is uniform whether in India and America or Pakistan and Bangladesh—predominantly Muslim and non-Muslim countries, respectively.[39]

The America-as-Kufristan argument is in some ways similar to the second type of opposition, the isolationist argument articulated by an African American Muslim, Jamil Abdullah Alamin (the former H. Rap Brown). According to him, "the priorities of the Muslim community should be the pillars of faith, especially prayer, and the formation of an ideal Islamic community inside, but separate from, the larger American society."[40] Alamin's argument is supported by Tariq Qureishi, a former director of the North American Islamic Trust of the Islamic Society of North America. Qureishi is reported to have remarked:

> Those people who insist on entering U.S. politics say it on the presumption as if they were some kind of Jews who have to work for some state of Israel . . . and then watch the process. But philosophically speaking it is not possible. The process will assimilate you, and then adopt you, and then change you to its own objective. . . . Even if you are ideologically very well indoctrinated, you will have to make compromises here and there.[41]

Echoing the Tablighi argument, Amer Haleem, the former Egyptian editor of *Islamic Horizons,* describes the United States "as a system organized by design to elevate the will of man above the will of God."[42] The only "political activity" Haleem is willing to sanction would be to simply "address political bodies, politicians, and more importantly the public directly on the issues."[43]

Finally, there are those who proclaim the necessity of a caliph to whom a Muslim must give *bayah* (allegiance). Proponents of participation are many. The foremost theoretician may be Taha Jabir Alalwani, the Iraqi American mufti and an academic scholar. He categorically states that "it is incumbent upon Muslims to participate in politics effectively in America; they need to do it for the following reasons: to protect their rights . . . to support fellow Muslims around the world . . . to spread Islam's message, and finally to express the universality of Islam."[44] Unlike the Tablighis and the isolationists, he describes the United States as "a country that respects the freedom of all religions," whose "cultural patterns are still open to influence from Islam," which "provides an opportunity to contribute to its growth."[45]

An even more forceful advocate of Muslim participation is a political scientist from India, M. Abdul Muqtadir Khan. Citing the American Constitution (which says, "We the people of the United States, in order to form a more perfect Union, establish justice, secure domestic tranquility, provide for the common defense, promote the general welfare, and secure the blessings of liberty to ourselves and our posterity, do ordain and establish this constitution for the United States of America"), Khan asks, "What is in this constitution that an Islamic state would not like to provide to its people?"[46] Judging by the favorable coverage of the efforts to urge Muslims to participate in the political process as seen in the American Muslim press, and good turnout at Muslim-sponsored fund-raisers for public office candidates in mid-2000, it appears that those advocating active isolation from the political process are in a minority.

The weakness of the opposition to participation, however, does not make the task any easier, as the next biggest hurdle that those favoring participation would find is far more formidable. That hurdle pertains to developing an agenda for political action and participation. Just as it is difficult for Muslims in countries such as Pakistan, Iran, Saudi Arabia, and elsewhere to define what is meant by an Islamic state and a democratic, nonviolent way to establish such a state, so would establishing a Muslim agenda for political action also face considerable difficulty. Their in-group unity is hampered because of diversity of their national origins and because of their relatively new experience—except that of Indian Muslims—with the notion of evolving compromises in a democracy. Muslims with longer exposure to democracy are likely to be more comfortable with the peculiarities of the American political system—including coalition building.[47] Immigrant groups from different Muslim and non-Muslim countries are likely to assign varying priorities to matters of their primary interest. Issues primarily of a religious nature—zoning controversies relating to mosques, for example—can be dealt with locally. Problems involving discrimination on the basis of religion, nationality, color, gender, and so forth, have a long history of legislative, court, and executive action in this country, and Muslims are increasingly taking advantage of the preventive measures already in place. Second-generation Muslims are even less likely to be worried about problems of discrimination and alienation than their parents were.

Then the question arises if immigrant Muslims remain engrossed about matters of their old countries, African Americans Muslims about issues of urban America, will there be, can there be, an agenda of Muslim origin but affecting the United States nationwide? What could be some of the issues on that agenda? Not coming up with a specific agenda of national significance and then struggling for its acceptance and enforcement would reduce Muslims to one more interest group among the many. That would be surely quite a comedown for a community claiming to be the carrier of the divine message urging good and forbidding evil.

CONCLUSION

Whether seen through the prism of Islamic jurisprudence or the experience of Muslims in actual time and space, Muslims can and should be able to live in total harmony with the predominantly non-Muslim environment of India as well as the United States. Despite the recurring riots and pogroms in India and the troubling environment of post-9/11 events in the United States, Muslims have no choice but to live in the societies they have chosen to. After all, there is no dar al-Islam anywhere where they can migrate, given the lack of peace and economic opportunities just about everywhere in the Muslim world.

NOTES

I am very grateful to Theodore P. Wright Jr., professor emeritus, Department of Political Science, State University of New York–Albany, as well as the anonymous reviewer for comments on a draft of this chapter.

1. Syed Z. Abedin and Saleha M. Abedin, "Muslim Minorities in Non-Muslim Societies," in *The Oxford Encyclopedia of the Islamic World,* ed. John L. Esposito, vol. 3 (New York: Oxford University Press, 1995), 112.

2. W. Montgomery Watt, *A History of Islamic Spain* (Edinburgh: Edinburgh University Press, 1965).

3. Aziz Ahmad, *A History of Islamic Sicily* (Edinburgh: Edinburgh University Press, 1975).

4. Mustansir Mir, *Dictionary of Quranic Terms and Concepts* (New York: Garland, 1987), 54.

5. This section draws on John Boswell, *Royal Treasure: Muslim Communities under the Crown of Aragon in the Fourteenth Century* (New Haven, Conn.: Yale University Press, 1977).

6. This section draws on Khaled Abou El Fadl, "Striking a Balance: Islamic Legal Discourse on Muslim Minorities," in *Muslims on the Americanization Path,* ed. Yvonne Y. Haddad and John L. Esposito (New York: Oxford University Press, 2000), 47–64.

7. Imam al-Shafii.

8. Shibli Numani, "Musalmanaon ko Ghayr Madhab Hukumat ka Mahkum ho kar Kiyon kar Rahna Chahiye" (How Should Muslims Live under Non-Muslim Rule), in his *Maqalat e Shibli* (Azamgarh: Dar al-Musaniffin, 1932), 167.

9. Omar Khalidi, "Konkani Muslims: An Introduction," *Islamic Culture* 74, no. 1 (January 2000): 127–53.

10. Muhammad Hamidullah, "Ex-Territorial Capitulation in Favour of Muslims in Classical Times," *Islamic Review* 38 (1950): 33–35.

11. M. Naeem Qureshi, "The Ulama of British India and the Hijrat of 1920," *Modern Asian Studies* 13, no. 1 (1979): 41–59.

12. Published in London by Allen Lane, 1871.

13. Muhammad Ali Jauhar, cited in *Muslim Self-Statement in India and Pakistan, 1857–1968,* ed. Aziz Ahmad and G. E. von Grunebaum (Wiesbaden: Harrassowitz, 1970).

14. Dietrich Reetz, *Hijrat: The Flight of the Faithful* (Berlin: Arabische Buch, 1995).

15. Omar Khalidi, "From Torrent to Trickle: Indian Muslim Migration to Pakistan, 1947–1997," *Bulletin of the Henry Martyn Institute of Islamic Studies* 16, nos. 1–2 (January–June 1997): 32–45.

16. Kemal H. Karpat, "The Hijra from Russia and the Balkans: The Process of Self-Definition in the Late Ottoman Empire," in *Muslim Travelers, Pilgrimage, Migration, and the Religious Imagination*, ed. Dale F. Eickelman and James Piscatori (Berkeley: University of California Press, 1990), 131–54.

17. James P. Piscatori, *Islam in a World of Nation States* (Cambridge: Cambridge University Press, 1986).

18. Theodore P. Wright Jr., "Identity Problems of Former Elite Minorities," *Secular Democracy* 5, no. 8 (August 1972): 43–51, reprinted in *Journal of Asian Affairs* 1, no. 2 (Fall 1976): 58–63.

19. Farzana Shaikh, "Muslim Political Representation in Colonial India: The Making of Pakistan," *Modern Asian Studies* 20 (1986): 539–57.

20. See Omar Khalidi, *Indian Muslims since Independence* (New Delhi: Vikas, 1996).

21. My interview with the Begum Sahiba, Lucknow, December 12, 1999. See also my "Begum Qudsiya Aizaz Rasool: An Extraordinary Life," *Radiance*, December 9–15, 2001, pp. 15–17.

22. Shah Bano Begum's statement in *Ayina e Ayyam*, Sholapur, January 4, 1986.

23. H. R. Gokhale, who served as minister of law and justice in the Indira Ghandi administration, introduced a bill in 1972 in the Rajya Sabha (Indian Parliament) dealing with the adoption of Indian children.

24. *The Adoption of the Children Bill, 1972, Report of the Joint Select Committee* (New Delhi: Rajya Sabha Secretariat, 1976).

25. *The Adoption of Children Bill, 1972, Report of the Joint Committee*, 33.

26. Minnatullah Rahmani, *The Adoption of Children Bill, 1972: A Review* (Monghyr, Bihar: Personal Law Board, 1974).

27. *The Adoption of Children Bill, 1972, Report of the Joint Committee*, x.

28. *The Adoption of Children Bill, 1972, Report of the Joint Committee*, xiv.

29. *Fourth Annual Report of the Minorities Commission* (New Delhi: Minorities Commission, 1983), 208–29.

30. *Radiance*, March 18–24, 1984, p. 11.

31. Abul Ala Mawdudi, *Islami Hukumat ki Tarah Qayim Hoti Hay* (Lahore: Markazi Maktabah Islami, 1953); Rahimuddin Kemal, *The Concept of Constitutional Law in Islam* (Hyderabad: Fase, 1955).

32. Ziya ul Hasan Faruqi, "Indian Muslims and the Ideology of Secularism," in *South Asian Politics and Religion*, ed. Donald E. Smith (Princeton, N.J.: Princeton University Press, 1966), 139.

33. T. N. Madan, "Secularism in Its Place," *Journal of Asian Studies* 46, no. 4 (1987): 747–49.

34. T. N. Madan, "Whither Indian Secularism," *Modern Asian Studies* 27, no. 3 (1993): 697.

35. *The Destiny of Indian Muslims* (New Delhi: Asia, 1965), 161.

36. *The Destiny of Indian Muslims*, 161.

37. Will Herberg, *Protestant, Catholic, Jew: An Essay in American Religious Sociology* (Garden City, N.Y.: Doubleday, 1955).

38. Mohammed Sawaie, *Arabic Speaking Immigrants in the United States and Canada* (Lexington, Ky.: Mazda, 1985).

39. Based on conversations with Tablighi friends in India, Pakistan, and the United States during an ijtima in Delhi, Lahore, and Boston in the summer of 1995.

40. Steve A. Johnson, "Political Activity of Muslims in America," in *The Muslims of America,* ed. Yvonne Y. Haddad (New York: Oxford University Press, 1991), 113.

41. Amer Haleem, "Path to Peace: Calling to Allah in America," *Islamic Horizons* 16 (December 1987): 29.

42. Haleem, "Path to Peace," 30.

43. Haleem, "Path to Peace," 30.

44. Taha Alalwani's fatwa sent by e-mail by the Boston Muslim Network on June 1, 2000.

45. Taha Alalwani's fatwa.

46. Muqtadir Khan, "Why Muslims Must Participate in American Politics," *Preview Themestream,* July 8, 2000; available at www.ijthad.org.

47. Karen Leonard, "South Asian Muslim Leadership of American Islam," in *Sojourners to Citizens: Muslims in Western Diasporas,* ed. Yvonne Y. Haddad (New York: Oxford University Press, 2002).

3

Conceptual Discourse

Living as a Muslim in a Pluralistic Society

Aminah Beverly McCloud

Whereas the "Middle East" has for centuries been a pluralistic culture along with "a convergence point of major religions," the West has in its modern history been largely homogeneous until the last forty years. As a home of immigrants, U.S. immigration law has served to keep its society White and predominantly Christian. Non-Whites and non-Christians have never been preferred as immigrants, though people of other faiths have been well tolerated. On the other hand, even though Muslims from the Middle East are used to the presence of other faiths and people from different ethnic groups, they have in most cases been members of the majority faith and ethnicity. American Muslims come from all over the world and represent every philosophical, theological, and political strain in Islam. They are Sunnis, Shias, and Sufis. They are also traditional and very modern. For many of those who moved into the worldview of Islam from another faith or none, living in a pluralistic society is proving contentious, as they are used to racial differences but find themselves in a problematic religious space. Additionally, American Muslims are faced with the challenge of moving from their ethnic centers to a multiethnic whole.

The last decade of the twentieth century witnessed a thriving, vibrant, diverse, and expanding American Muslim community. This success was possible because of the determination of many in mosques and organizations across ethnicities and despite serious tensions within and across ethnic communities. Discussion of these tensions and some potential resolutions are the subjects of this chapter. As we map the various discourses and their effects, what we see is a community in process in a pluralistic society. As we examine the tensions, two factors emerge as points of conflict. Both of these points of friction are centered on discourse, cross-cultural communication, and issues surrounding the definition of Islam in North America.

Discourse includes both the verbal and the nonverbal. It is not only the collection of those things said; it is those gestures or silences we act out whether we are verbal or silent. Furthermore, it is that whole set of etiquettes and history that inform and determine our modes of communication. Discourse is also that learned set of information that gives us our way of valuing and discerning truth from falsehood that shadows in the background as we communicate.

Each culture has its own discourse, and cross-cultural communication is a difficult enterprise. For example, Arab, South Asian, African, African American, and Hispanic Muslims have experienced the difficulties in getting to know each other and in collaborating in social and political endeavors. Lack of experience of each other's culture has resulted in reciprocal misunderstandings. Ethnic communities have come together on Juma, at Eid celebrations, and at fund-raising events. Once inside, they segregate into ethnic/language groups for comfort but generally feel discomfort with continuing not to know each other.

Plural societies are not multicultural (as that implies an equal standing among the cultures present); they are competing societies. Groups compete for services, opportunities, and recognition. Competition for these things in turn compels groups to hide individual differences as they seek recognition as a group and not to seek to know one another. Ethnocentrism is often the result of the absence of cross-cultural engagement.

For Muslims, the coming together of ethnic communities from all over the world has been one expectation of *hajj* (pilgrimage), even though the focus of hajj is God. Even in the Middle East, where Muslims of different ethnic groups are in contact with each other and their encounters are frequent, there is little need for purposeful, sustained engagement, as there is no public competition or need for recognition. Various competitions, internal and external, are some of the factors driving the experience of living as Muslims in U.S. society.

Each ethnic group of Muslims has particular internal issues further complicating cross-cultural communication and engagement of others in the larger public square. Researchers have usually divided the Muslim community into indigenous and immigrant, even though each group contains at least three generations, and neither has a monolithic voice. For purposes of this chapter, let us reclassify these large categories as "other" and "newer" American Muslims regarding their American experiences, while ethnicities remain the same. Major ethnicities among the newer American Muslims are Arabs, South Asians, and Africans, and the older American Muslims include African Americans, European, and Hispanic Americans. Inside the larger categories we can isolate a few issues that directly affect cross-cultural engagement.

Newer American Muslims are still engaged with the processes of immigration itself. Though many families include generations born in the United States, there are still large numbers of family members living in the homeland, necessitating involvement in its affairs. They are simultaneously diverted by heated discussions on the historical and conceptual frameworks surrounding Muslim thinking on living in the West and the current discourse on the ideas of democracy and the values of Islam.

Older American Muslims are immersed in working on pervasive, constant American social ills such as rising rates of incarceration, homelessness, gang violence, teen pregnancies, rising numbers of AIDS-HIV cases, lack of health care for the poor, and issues of employment. They also see their efforts in Islam and its establishment in the United States being erased by the focalization in both the Muslim and larger plural public space on Islam = Arab and Muslim = immigrant. Concerns with erasure have coalesced into discourse on authority and the authoritative in Islam. Additionally, just as newer American Muslims have to contend with the problems of family left behind, the older American Muslims have to contend with the presence of non-Muslim family members. Both groups bring their issues to the common Muslim public space and subsequently to their experiences living in a pluralistic society.

NEWER AMERICAN MUSLIM CONVERSATIONS

Newer American Muslims are from all over the world. Some are from countries where Islam is a minority religion and others where Islam is the state religion. Status as either minorities or majorities always contributes to a group's psychological makeup regarding perceptions of ability for success and influence. Immigration to a Western society mediates some of this because there is no history. While the individual brings a life with a particular status, it does not translate into the same currency in the new society. For example, most societies have families whose wealth is immeasurable, whose reputation of influence and prestige is well known, and to whom deference is expected and given. Arrival in the United States largely erases the past as family name is unknown; thus, the wealth is considered new, and deference, though sometimes expected, is rarely given.

United States' immigration policies have encouraged skilled immigrant labor with a preference for professionals, thus inviting people from a certain class. The absence of preferential treatment usually given to the upper and middle class leads to competition for recognition in available spaces. One such space in the United States is the mosque. Sulayman Nyang, in his text *Islam in the United States of America,* describes the issues of mosque leadership. He defines four basic categories: imam-led, president-led, group leadership, and hybrid styles.[1] These leadership styles often reflect status and Islamic philosophical understanding. Those groups who want to mimic home have an "imam-led" community. Many times this leader has been hired from "home" and has little knowledge of U.S. society or English, but his community feels comfortable as it tries to replicate home. Algorithms for community issues are time-honored methods from home, and these communities of Muslims often have the most difficulty negotiating life in another place. Other leadership styles are frequently indicators of serious mediations between the known and the new public spaces. Members of these communities in many cases are reconciled to their U.S. status but see their American experience as more than fear of acculturation/assimilation. They usually envision a dynamic reciprocity between cultures. They see themselves in a process that includes the family demands from back home and the needs of their current home.

Inside each ethnic group, people have come to know each other. A community of Arabic speakers may be composed of as many as twenty different cultures. One tool of colonialism was to divide and conquer. As colonial powers created new borders for their territories in the Arab world, they also used a variety of tools to create mistrust and disdain between cultures. In the United States, these cultures have the challenge of recognizing this fact and using Islam to foster trust and appreciation. They are in the process of getting to know each other. For example, a variety of factors contribute to the Indian-Pakistani divide, including colonialism, and minority versus majority status. Added to all of this are issues of class. Class structures, though present in the United States, are fairly well masked by the effects of market capitalism. Class in the United States, as in the rest of the world, is about knowledge and the ability to influence the running institutions, government, and media. As mentioned earlier, class is also about expectations and privilege. While newer American Muslims struggle to redefine their personal expectations and notions of privilege, they also experience relatively intimate living and worshiping with a diverse body of Muslims.

Juma prayer and hajj are the traditional sites of an intentional, though temporary, equalizing of class among Muslims. In the plural public space of the United States, almost the entire space is equalized, as TV stars, basketball players, Nobel Prize winners, politicians, muggers, and so on, all occupy the space and may live in the same neighborhood. Increasing diversity in the public space has caused some contentious encounters, because the various cultural cues are often misunderstood. The large diverse community of Muslims has the same experiences. Simultaneously, newer American Muslim families are intimately involved in the affairs of the old home.

Many newer American Muslims responded to opportunities for education, employment, and stable lives but remained committed to reform in countries of origin. Consequently, a number of charities emerged to assist in relief for families, earthquakes, and refugee camps and to sponsor building projects. The enormity of the stresses associated with relief and sponsorship keeps newer American Muslims engaged along with nascent attempts to influence the U.S. government to assist in these endeavors. These efforts coupled with an ignorance of the demands of social responsibility in the West have caused newer American Muslims to ignore the social problems in their American communities. As a result, they have not been considered effective citizens, thus creating another stress for community members.

Possibly two underlying ingredients contributing to the complexity of the concerns here are the inherent instability of living in a country that has a negative conception of Islam and Muslims coupled with Muslim's own conceptions of living as minorities. Muslims in South Asia and the Arab world have decades of old discourses on both modernity and living as minorities in the West. Both of these discourses have come under critical review and spawned new discourses. We are most interested in the discourse on living as minorities.

The conceptual framework that surrounds living as a minority is phrased *dar al-harb* versus *dar al-Islam* (the land of war versus the land of submission to the Will of God). The implied hostility here generally refers to the absence or presence of Islamic law as guidance in public affairs. These rubrics, if accepted as true renderings of reality, present both theological and practical challenges in conception and articulation. The phrase *Darul-Islam* has been used for centuries to describe an ideal. One Muslim scholar living in the West, Tariq Ramadan, asserts:

> Early in Islamic history, some 'ulama drew a specific geography of the world, distinguishing dar al-Islam (abode of Islam) from those which were not under Islamic rule called dar al-harb (the abode of war) stating that it was not possible for Muslims to live in dar al-harb except under some mitigating circumstances.[2]

Though the phrases reflect a particular geographic division of the world, this division has not reflected the divisions of power and the subsequent realities of Muslims for a few centuries. By this I mean that the abode of Islam is described as a place of Muslim rule that is just and in which Muslims are safe from tyranny. There is no such place in the Muslim world today or yesterday. The realities of the Muslim world are filled with inequities of power and resources. Muslims are struggling against many rulers and governments created by fleeing colonial powers and the vagaries of global capitalism and Western neocolonialism. Again quoting Tariq Ramadan:

> The concept of Dar al-Islam is a hindrance today within the Muslim world. Even when we speak of Dar al-'ahd [the House of Treaty, which stipulates that Muslims living as a minority among unbelievers should live peacefully but without truly joining these societies], it means peaceful coexistence but it also

promotes this kind of binary vision, "us and them." It does not allow us to feel that we are part of the Western societies, that we are sharing with others our values and belonging.[3]

In the West, especially the United States, the questions around the conceptions of dar al-Islam or dar al-harb are mute except in the minds of a few. Yet, there has been little involvement of newer American Muslims in society. One possible answer to this reality may just lie in understandings of community. In the Muslim world, community is family—nuclear and extended. Thus, the community is not a geographic space; rather, it is a network of kinship. In the United States, the community is defined by geographic boundaries and by named neighborhoods. This difference in conceptualization of a community may be one unconscious reason for lack of involvement. Perhaps a shift needs to happen in the conceptual worlds of newer American Muslims. Some of the other conceptual worlds inside Islam are beginning to collapse due to living in a pluralistic society. Ethnic communities' cultural Islam is often held up for scrutiny both from inside and outside the Muslim community. Issues of authority and the authoritative have emerged as one primary set of concerns.

Which cultural adaptation of Islam will define Islam for the United States? Will the Quran prevail as the guidance for Muslims? The struggle is earnest as the stakes are high. One of the demands of living in a religiously and ethnically pluralistic society is that believers explain their beliefs and practices and that they be accountable for observable deviations. Claims about religious belief and practice are especially under scrutiny against observations of racism, questionable treatment of women, and even assertions regarding the playing of music and denials of indulgences in alcohol or gambling. Responses to the ambiguities have generally been conflicting. Counterclaims of color-blind communities, excellent treatment of women, abstinence from alcohol, and so on, are viewed by the general American public as hypocritical. The problems encountered by newer American Muslims are of diversity of thought/practice and an unrelenting scrutiny by the West. While certainly some of the behaviors of some Muslims are consciously blatantly racist and misogynist, for most, their behaviors are the result of ignorance and a preformed opinion of ethnic groups in the American public space. Whatever the source of any of these problems, Muslims have acknowledged their existence and are working feverishly to eradicate them. Many of the newer American Muslims have consciously visited the communities of older American Muslims for Juma prayers and social events. Ethnic organizations have opened themselves up to a multiethnic presence. These ventures are starting points for the process of coming to know one another. The issues of authority, however, remain paramount.

Arab American Muslims have laid claim to the most rights to define Islam, since they are the guardians of the language of the Quran. South Asians lay their claims in ownership of national Islamic organizations. Other newer American Muslims, because of small numbers, are marginalized. The claims of the single authority of the Quran are under attack by Western scholars who are asserting that the Quran is not complete or has been corrupted in magazines such as *Atlantic Monthly*.[4] Media have declared Islam and Muslims violent, irrational, anti-American, and antimodern. Newer American Muslims have been inundated with questions about violence and terror in Islam, while they themselves are experiencing ongoing terror and violence from the government. Since September 11, 2001, their communities have experienced arbitrary arrests and detentions, violence to property and persons, and terror.[5] They have witnessed the suspension of their constitutional rights and serious curtailment of their civil liberties. The Japanese community in many cities has even come to mosques to sympathize and share their history of being attacked by the U.S. government. Needless to say, the freedoms of living in the United States are under siege for this community.

Responses to these incursions and the presence of a McCarthyesque atmosphere surrounding the newer American Muslim community have been fully American. Muslim organizations and individuals are suing individuals, organizations, and government agencies for discrimination, profiling, unlawful arrest, unlawful seizure of property, invasion of privacy, and harassments. The public space has become unlawful and capricious regarding newer American Muslims. Older American Muslims have generally been erased from the picture of Islam and Muslims in the United States. This reality has set off a number of responses.

The community of older American Muslims is not a homogenous community, either, as it is composed of African, European, Hispanic, and Native Americans. While their nationality is the same, their Islamic adherences differ. They are also Sufis, Shias, and Sunnis and represent every philosophical, theological, and political strain in the Muslim world. Some are ardent advocates for the disenfranchised, while others are concerned solely with the affairs of the *ummah* (world community of believers). They also are second and third generations distinguished by their ongoing fight against being rendered invisible regarding Islam. Living in a pluralistic society for these communities also translates into living with other Muslims. These Muslims are already accustomed to living in the United States' pluralistic society.

The conceptual discourse of older American Muslims can be placed in at least four categories: (1) the psychological experience of moving into the worldview of Islam, (2) learning Arabic and the Islamic sciences, (3) engagement with other Americans in tackling American social ills, and (4) defining Islam for America. As one of the younger communities to join the ummah, older American Muslims are struggling with many of the same challenges that other communities faced when first accepting Islam. Their struggles are heightened, perhaps, by the nature of a pluralistic society.

Little has been written analytically about the psychology of moving into the Islamic worldview. A few autobiographies describe the encounter with Islam and Muslims but little of the trauma of separating from family in many cases or the discomfort with the "foreign" language and behaviors. The move into Islam is often a solitary event without family celebration and frightening on many levels. Many older American Muslims did not move into Islam as an act subsequent to prolonged study or stay in the Muslim world. For those in this category, love for Islam came from reading a translation of the Quran and the frequent or occasional company of Muslims in a mosque. Explaining Islam to family members who know nothing of the religion and even less about its beliefs and practices or who may have believed the negativity that surrounds Islam and Muslims in film and other media. Many of the newer American Muslim leaders teach that membership in the ummah requires the severing of ties with Christians and nonbelievers, thus leading new Muslims to believe that they can no longer interact with family at all. Severing ties with family is traumatic, as is changing one's name and the possibility of losing inheritances. But putting these matters aside, there is trauma in learning a whole new way of life. Despite these struggles, most older American Muslims have succeeded in remaining Muslim and many have attempted to reestablish family ties after some time.

Learning Arabic well enough to read the Quran in the absence of qualified teachers who can teach it as a second language is a serious challenge. Most Arabic teachers are students who come and go, leaving students with the rudiments such as the alphabet. Attempting to lead a life as a Muslim without some intimacy with the Quran is a serious difficulty for the spiritual life. Older American Muslims complain but have not in any large numbers engaged themselves fully in learning the Arabic of the Quran. This shortcoming also has weighed heavily on their ability to legitimate themselves in the Muslim or American public square. Mosque leadership, organizational leadership, and Muslim representation in certain spaces require Quranic recitation, and the inability to recite or read Quranic Arabic puts one at a disadvantage. One obvious reason behind this apparent shortcoming lies in the American phobia of languages other than English; another reason is the paucity of course offerings in many cities in the United States. The fact remains that older American Muslims must make the learning of Arabic one of their priorities if they want to become visible in Muslim spaces and as representatives of Islam in this pluralistic society. The aversion to learning Arabic so that there is knowledge of the Islamic sciences further makes these communities dependent on cultural interpretations of Islam, which may be and usually are problematic.

One fundamental problem in the emergence of an American definition coming from older American Muslims is that there is not enough knowledge of Islam, its history, and its cultural accretions. There is however, a nascent but growing group of older American Muslim scholars of Islam. As this community grows with assistance from some among the newer American Muslims and those in the Muslim world, communities will get stronger and perhaps more visible. Older American Muslims have begun in recent decades to establish communities in the Muslim world and are, though still in small numbers, increasingly traveling to the Muslim world to study. What older American Muslims have excelled in is their participation with social agencies that work with the disenfranchised.

Employed as social workers, teachers, police officers, drug counselors, abuse counselors, physicians, and community advocates, older American Muslims bring Islam to urban America. Most new Muslims learn about Islam through their interactions with older American Muslims. In these spaces they represent Islam without the requirement of Quranic recitation or Arabic speaking. Contributions at this level are seen as a priority, as one primary Islamic understanding is to push for social justice. In these spaces, Muslims are seen as disciplined, just, and God-fearing people who will stand up for the rights of others. Many neighborhoods across the United States have welcomed the Muslims because they know that there will be a decrease in crime and criminal behavior. What older Muslims must do is transfer this knowledge and success to newer American Muslims, and newer American Muslims must see these activities as worthy of their efforts. The challenge lies in place of residence. Older American Muslims tend to live in urban areas, whereas many newer American Muslims live in the suburbs. This difference is a challenge that can easily be overcome and foster some of the learning of cross-cultural communication.

As with newer American Muslims, their older counterparts have not sought to learn the cultural gestures of their partners in faith, either. Many declare that Muslims in the Muslim world who have immigrated to the United States are "just racist" and leave it at that. There is little self-reflection on how American gestures are often rude and incomprehensible to others. To enter the contest of defining Islam for America, however, multicultural knowledge is high on the list of skills that older Muslims must acquire.

What is Islam, and who is authorized to articulate it? These questions comprise a pervasive discourse in the community. Muslims know that Islam has no formal hierarchy but often find themselves in competition with one another to act as "the leader." Even though pluralism is evident in U.S. society, the rules for inclusion and active participation take their forms from Christianity and the public spaces demand "someone in charge" to contact or represent. One large contingent among older American Muslim communities, African Americans, has had a peculiar history.

The religion and philosophy of the Nation of Islam, founded in the early

1930s by Elijah Muhammad, has marked every African American Muslim. The marginal Islamic practice and Black Nationalist tendencies of the Nation of Islam for many decades along with intense scrutiny by the media of their rhetoric have served to castigate all African American Muslims. Whether it is racism or ignorance that places all African Americans who move into the Islamic worldview into one group, this labeling has hindered African American voices on issues surrounding Islam in the United States. Even the Nation of Islam suffers a stigma as it moves toward Sunni Islam. The conceptual world of America and of newer American Muslims relegates all participation in Islam by African Americans to categories of protest against racism and poverty. Other communities of African American Muslims have permitted these conceptualizations to grow and ironically have nurtured them by working with the Black community in protesting discriminations. In many ways, African and Hispanic Americans participate in pluralistic America, but only as marginalized actors who are tainted by the racial lines White America draws and who are often only permitted to speak or are listened to only about racial matters.

The responses to media attention to the Nation of Islam as irrational and Islam as the religion of newer American Muslims have always been mixed. Some of the social activities of the Nation of Islam, such as its reputation regarding drug rehabilitation, are marks of success that all want a share in, while most of their rhetoric surrounding Elijah Muhammad and Fard Muhammad is condemned. The recent discourse on Warith Deen Muhammad as a "prophet" has caused the same kinds of condemnation. Still others have feared Minister Louis Farrakhan of the Nation of Islam taking the Nation along the path of mainstream Islam because of his charisma and outspokenness. Striking a balance among a Muslim's family, ethnic, and religious concerns is very much a concern of all Muslims, especially those living in a pluralistic society. Nevertheless, authority in Islam remains problematic in the United States, as the events of September 11, 2001, proved beyond a doubt.

THE AFTERMATH OF 9/11

The events of 9/11 marked a watershed for the United States and its domestic and foreign policies. It also changed the American Muslim community forever. Newer American Muslims are still in shock and sadness over the tragedies and living in terror of the aftermath. Older American Muslims are in shock and sadness over the tragedies and struggling to quickly learn about the reform and antimodern movements in the Muslim world. Both communities, however, see these events as opening a door for them to the larger American society and each other.

Since those tragic events, knowledge of Islam and Muslim cultures has risen dramatically, as have sales of the Quran and books on Islam. Other religious communities have given their support to Muslims in their neighborhoods who have been terrorized by the government and requested lectures and books from the local mosque. Newer and older Muslims have sped up their interactions and are beginning in earnest to attempt to know one another. These events have nevertheless hardened further the hearts of those who see Islam and Muslims as a threat to the "freedoms, rights, and peacefulness" of the United States.

Media discourse on Islam and Muslims has been irrational and incendiary, as frequent use has made *terrorism* synonymous with *Islam*. Supported by the government, the media has changed the conceptual framework of understanding Islam. With rhetoric that claimed that "a war on terrorism was not a war against Islam," the U.S. government expressed in the media that all of the terrorism in the world had its base in the Muslim world, and some of that world had moved to the United States. Talk-show hosts and facilitators openly ridiculed even the definition of the word *Islam*. Other Americans have been led to believe that Muslims hate them and are among them to do them harm. Now that the United States is under a constant state of alert for terrorism, Muslims are leading precarious lives.

Muslim Americans have found themselves under fire in a conceptual war in which they have no weapons. Muslims, in their decades in the United States, have produced community newspapers and books on Islam but did not pool their resources to buy media outlets. In the face of an onslaught against Islam, they cannot defend themselves or assert themselves in any sustained way. As events in the Muslim world dominate news, Muslim Americans are not commentators or analysts. Muslims are coming together, and some members of other faiths are supportive of their plight. Muslims, older and newer, have no doubt that Islam will flourish in the United States but worry about the kind of community that will represent it.

NOTES

1. Sulayman S. Nyang, *Islam in the United States of America* (Chicago: ABC International Group, 1999).

2. Tariq Ramadan, *To Be a European Muslim* (Leicester, England: Islamic Foundation, 1999), 99.

3. Tariq Ramadan in an interview with *Salon* magazine, on February 15, 2002.

4. See *Atlantic Monthly* 283, no. 1 (January 1999): 43–56.

5. See www.cair-net.org for information regarding these events.

4

Living on Borderlines

Islam beyond the Clash and Dialogue of Civilizations

M. A. Muqtedar Khan

The concept of civilization has resurfaced and is now engendering a global discourse. The civilizational discourse is wide in its scope. It is philosophical and sufficiently profound to suggest a rethinking of the global human self and advance rudimentary theories of a global ethic. It is also mundane enough to become a central concept around which American foreign policy in the post–Cold War era can be anchored. As the vulnerabilities of the nation-state become obvious and its durability becomes suspect, international political theorists have increasingly sought to find alternate polities around which world politics can be organized. The phenomenon of globalization and the acceptance of global economic interdependence has also reduced the utility of the doctrine of state sovereignty, making porous borders and fluid polities commonplace. It is in an attempt to help theorize as well as give direction to the postnationalism world politics that the conception of civilizations is being invoked.[1]

While the global condition is highly volatile and in a constant flux, thereby escaping theoretical formations, there is an emerging consensus that we are living in a world experiencing "glocalization"—simultaneous forces of globalization and localization or integration and disintegration. Economies are going global, while identities are increasingly anchored in the local.[2] Either nation-states are sacrificing sovereignty to merge into large political-economic unions like the European Union (or sometimes just economic unions, such as the North American Free Trade Agreement [NAFTA]), or sovereignties are imploding to create substates as in the former Soviet Union and the former Yugoslavia. Theory seems to follow process, and international political theorists are also responding by heading in opposite directions. Those excited by the promise of globalization and integration are talking about a civilizational dialogue, and those seeking to defend the local fear a clash of civilizations.[3]

For analytical purposes, I shall employ two concepts from international relations (IR) theory to explain the nature of the civilizational discourse. At its most fundamental level, IR theorists divide perspectives on world politics into two categories: the realist and the idealist.[4] Realists are theorists whose ontological beliefs are highly pessimistic. They assume, following Thomas Hobbes and Hans Morgenthau, that the state of nature is a war of all against all. In the realm of international relations, which is beyond the borders of the nation-states, they do not recognize any higher authority and assume that world politics is conducted in a state of anarchy. This grim diagnosis of the nature of the international arena leads to even grimmer conclusions. Since there is no higher authority that one can appeal to for justice and order, actors can rely only on self-help. The best means to ensure this is through power maximization (or balancing of power), and therefore world politics is reduced to power politics, and interest is best understood in terms of capabilities. As a result of these assumptions, realists believe in the singular importance of power and expect conflict rather than cooperation with other actors in any system. For the realists, power is the key to security and peace, and order comes through hegemony and domination.[5]

The idealists, on the other hand, have a rather benign view of human nature and human interaction. They believe that conflict is often the cause of misunderstanding or miscommunication. While there may be no higher authority in the arena of world politics, idealists are confident that the growing economic interdependence and the emergence of global governance through multilateralism and international institutions will preclude conflict and enhance cooperation. Therefore, for idealists, communication or interaction and not power is the key to a more peaceful and prosperous future. While realists are usually suspicious of the intentions of other actors, idealists are more willing to accept actors at face value and trust them to play their part in joint ventures. Thus, based on their assumptions about world politics, realists have advanced a discourse that fears a clash of civilizations, while idealists have proposed a dialogue of civilizations.[6]

In the subsequent sections, I identify the authors and the central principles and arguments of the two discourses. But first I underscore some of the limitations of the two approaches. To begin with, we must understand that both realists and idealists, in their attempts to clarify each other's relative theoretical positions, often articulated in opposition to the other approach, have boxed themselves in hard-core ontological assumptions that are far from reality. The realities of world politics are somewhere between the expectations of the two approaches. The ontological dogmatism of the two approaches precludes their practitioners from recognizing that while limited civilizational contests are taking place in the geopolitical arena, civilizational dialogues also are taking place in the sociological arena of identity construction.[7]

Realists undermine the virtues of any dialogue and constantly argue that in the face of a security threat, power and its judicious exercise alone can guarantee security,[8] whereas liberals insist that not only is a dialogue of civilizations possible, but it is also necessary and the only way to preclude conflict and enhance peace and security. Both realists and idealists desire security and peace, the former through a preemptive clash or strategies of containment and the latter through a United Nations–sponsored dialogue between nations that will enhance mutual understanding and respect for each other's values and cultures. In advancing their claims, the realists ignore the power of ideas and meaningful exchanges, and the idealists underestimate the logic of power. Realists do not really give peace a chance through a religious adherence to realpolitik (power politics), and the idealists fail to recognize that in the presence of significant disparities of power, a genuine dialogue is impossible.

CLASH OF CIVILIZATIONS?

In a 1993 article that gained great currency worldwide, Sam Huntington advanced the thesis that with the end of the ideological conflict between capitalism and communism the world would now face the prospects of a civilization struggle between the dominant West and others who sought to undermine the West or replace it.[9] In his article, Huntington basically employs realist understanding of world politics to an imaginary political arena wherein a handful of civilizations compete with each other for global domination.[10] Huntington's primary concern in this article was to provide the United States in particular and the West in general a new grand theory that would help guide their foreign policies in the post-Soviet era. After the end of the Cold War, the United States and its allies were at a loss to even understand their international interests and foreign policy concerns. Huntington's suggestion that the next threat was a civilizational challenge to Western domination from an emerging alliance between Islamic and Confucian nations identified a new threat that would not only keep the West politically united and give its military alliance, NATO, another raison d'être but also would prevent the possible decline of the West and sustain the globalization of Western values.

Huntington's article was received by realists everywhere as one demonstrating Copernican insights. Indeed for several years, American and Western foreign policy experts saw nothing but the specter of an Islamic threat armed by nuclear weapons and missiles provided by China. But Huntington was also widely criticized for his analysis that on closer scrutiny failed the tests of reason and history. His use of history was selective and even erroneous. His definitions of cardinal concepts such as civilization seemed to lack clarity as well as purpose. Even if his reading of history and use of reason lack rigor, there is an intuitive value to his argument that cannot be rejected entirely. Yes, the idea of defense of a civilization has played a major role in global conflicts in the past. For example, Western Christendom did launch a global war called the Crusades at the behest of arguments advanced by Pope Urban II that were not very different from the one's advanced by Huntington. This is a historical fact that mysteriously eluded Huntington, who in my opinion used the idea of civilizations as a cover to simply argue that resurgent Islam and an intransigent China alone continue to resist Western domination, and they should be crushed before they join forces to present stronger resistance.

Huntington's argument is not new. Bernard Lewis, in an article titled "The Roots of Muslim Rage," made a similar point as to how Muslims entertain serious reservations against Western values and harbor resentment against the West for colonial excesses and intend to seek revenge.[11] He even used the subtitle "Clash of Civilizations" to underscore his claim about how Western and Islamic values were poles apart and would always prevent peaceful coexistence between Islam and the West. Lewis and his cohort of policy entrepreneurs have been trying to cast the Middle East conflict as a clash between Islam and the West, ostensibly to recruit Western power in an attempt to crush the contemporary resurgence of Islam. Many friends of Israel, like Pipes, Emerson, Lewis, and Miller, saw the Middle East conflict as a zero-sum game between Islam and Israel. And in their desire to provide Israel with Western protection they joined the Huntington bandwagon and nurtured the clash of civilizations thesis and propagated the myth of a global Islamic threat to the West and Western values.[12]

As a result of their endeavors, the United States in the mid-1990s saw itself engaged in global skirmishes with Islamic movements, in Central Asia, the Middle East, South Asia, and Afghanistan. The United States increasingly found itself in alliance with undemocratic forces in Turkey; in Algeria, it found itself standing by as Russia committed gross injustices in Chechnya in the name of crushing Islamic fundamentalism, and also creating new and unnecessary enemies such as Osama bin Laden. However, thanks to the wise council of many reasonable American scholars such as John Esposito, John Entelis, and John Voll, and sensible and pragmatic diplomats such as Robert Pelletreau, the myth of the Islamic threat was not only exposed but Islam was seen with new eyes and found to be an intellectual and moral (civilizational) challenge and not a threat. Islamic resurgence according to these scholars was not a threat to the West but an authentic expression of Muslim desire for self-determination.[13]

The clash of civilizations discourse essentially corrupted the American perception of reality and presented it with the deadly option of waging a new global cold and hot war against the entire religion of Islam, nearly fifty-five states and one fourth of the world's population. The heavy ideological spin presented the Palestinian struggle for a national homeland, the Algerian struggle for self-determination, the Kashmiri struggle for freedom, the Bosnian struggle for dignity, the Egyptian struggle for authenticity, and the Islamic revolution of Iran against monarchy as an attempt by fanatical, essentially evil Muslims to terrorize the world in an attempt to destroy the West and its democratic and liberal ideals. In many ways the United States itself was undermining democracy and liberalism in its own institutions and through its policies as it sought to fight Islamic resurgence everywhere.[14]

Three developments, however, significantly changed the American approach as idealists gradually gained more influence over American foreign policy and realists became marginalized. The first development was the realization that globalization is making geopolitics second to geoeconomics and identity politics. American focus has shifted from the realist domains of security and power politics to the idealist arena of economic cooperation and cultural exchange. America needs the world both as a market for its goods and as a supplier of cheap labor and expert talent to sustain its economy and power. It could not afford to wage a war against one-fourth of the world's population. By demonizing Islam it was creating support and allies for a small band of militias who were creating security problems for the United States and its allies everywhere as manifest in the bombings of U.S. embassies in Africa. The altered strategy recommended by idealists—recognize the greatness of Islam and its contributions to human civilization while surgically isolating sources of political violence (described often as terrorism when directed against U.S. interests)—has paid better dividends. Violence and attacks against the United States have nearly diminished, and the Lewis–Huntington clash of civilizations has been reduced to the clash between the United States and Osama bin Laden.

Among Muslim thinkers, too, one finds the same dichotomy between idealists and realists. Idealists among Muslims often focus on the positive aspects of the West such as democracy and human rights, and the realists tend to concentrate on Western colonialism and foreign policy excesses.[15] Thus, one finds a Muhammad Abduh who remarked that in many ways the West was "Islam without Muslims,"; one also finds an Ayatollah Khomeini who argued that the West, the incarnation of Satan himself, was responsible for the decline of the Muslim World and is its number one enemy. Interestingly, Iran in the twenty-two years since its Islamic revolution has moved from a realist like Khomeini to an idealist like Khatami. Muslim idealists are keen to have a dialogue with the West while realists are preparing for a clash.

The differences between the idealists and the realists and their different perspectives of the West have had a very profound impact in the way Muslims construct their identity today. Muslim intellectuals and thinkers have all had to contend with the power of the West and the power of Western ideas while interpreting and understanding the condition of the Muslim *ummah* (community). Many of them openly admired the West for its achievements in the arena of civil society as well as science and technology and have even remarked that the West was "Islam without Muslims." For them the West was indeed worthy of emulation in many areas such as democracy, human rights, and respect for the rule of law and for their dedication to science. This conception of the West has resulted in a genre of literature widely known as Islamic modernism when the theory of modernization was popular. Now in the age of liberalism, this Islamic tendency is referred to as Islamic liberalism.[16]

Other Muslim thinkers have found the West responsible for the moral and material decline of the Muslim world. They blame Western imperialism and the era of colonial domination for the present backwardness and lack of self-government in the ummah. They imagine it as the embodiment of Satan and have postulated Islamization as complete rejection of all that they see as Western, including democracy and freedom of speech. These thinkers are widely represented as Islamic fundamentalists in the West and are often contrasted with Islamic liberals.[17] Both discourses have an element of truth in them, but both suffer from a lack of balance. While the former suffers from a lack of self-esteem and exaggerates the virtues of the West, the latter confuses polemics and diatribe against the West for Islam. Both elements are to some extent valid and even necessary but only as supplements to a dominant discourse that is both balanced and constructive.

DIALOGUE OF CIVILIZATIONS?

Dialogue between Islam and the West is an interesting idea indeed. However, is it possible given the difference in power between the two entities? It is this issue that I wish to raise while exploring the possibilities of a dialogue between civilizations. But before that, I examine this treatment of West and Islam as two exclusive entities. When most people use the term *civilization,* they are generally referring to a culturally and historically homogenous society. While *civilization* is extremely ambiguous, most people do manage to conjure some shared meaning when the term is used. That will suffice to initiate a dialogue. However, I do not believe that Islam and the West are two easily distinguishable civilizations.

The present set of values and normative preferences that constitute "the West" are traced back to the classical wisdom of ancient Greeks and the Judeo-Christian ethic. This reading of the evolution of the West often denies the contribution of Islamic civilization to the emergence of modernity in Europe. However, more and more scholars are now challenging this intellectual bigotry. Still many, like Sam Huntington of Harvard and Bernard Lewis of Princeton, would like to posit Islam as a passive inheritor and transmitter of Greek values and wisdom to the West.[18] A rejection of the intellectual passivity of Islamic civilization makes Islam one of the three fundamental sources of "the West—ancient Greek philosophy, the Judeo-Christian ethic, and Islam. The proximity of Islamic values to Judeo-Christian values further cements my contention that Islam is a major philosophical stakeholder in the modern West.

Two hundred years of colonization of Muslim lands by the West has had a significant impact in the transformation and evolution of contemporary Muslim political and philosophical sensibilities. The dislocation of traditional forms of education and their replacement with Western structures of pedagogy alone have changed the way many Muslims look at the world and at their faith. The redrawing of borders by the Imperial West alone introduced a new political sentiment—nationalism—into the Muslim world, a sentiment that has singularly undermined the political cohesiveness and communal unity of what used to be the Islamic civilization. While Western values and their sociopolitical processes were often imposed, they have been effective in instituting significant changes in the Muslim psyche. Thus, the West, too, has had a major share in shaping (or disfiguring) the character of the contemporary Muslim world.[19]

The West was, however, only partially successful in this endeavor, and therefore the Muslim world today manifests, simultaneously, fragmented forms of tradition and modernity. It has become a mosaic of the past and the present. It is at once modern and traditional. The Muslim world is both a Western and an Islamic civilization.[20] The various conflicts and crisis in the Muslim world today is an attempt by an ancient, once-cohesive civilization to reconcile its internal incongruity and inconsistency. The mass migration of Muslims to the West and their remarkable success in not assimilating into the local culture have further added an Islamic hue to the various shades of culture that make the present West. With over twenty million followers (more than the Dutch, Belgians, Swedes, or even Jews), Islam in the West is rapidly becoming as important an issue as Islam and the West.

Thus, to a great extent, Islam and the West are "shared civilizations." They have shaped and continue to reshape each other. They remain interconnected and codependent due to their common historical experiences and, more important, due to the cross-pollination of ideas that have shaped their political and normative ethos. But these transfers of values, ideas, philosophies, and cultural ethos have not taken place through what is normally understood as a "dialogue." The West learned from Islam through its admiration of the powerful Muslim empires and their economically and culturally vibrant societies that they encountered in their Crusades against Islam. Muslims have been influenced by the West after being humiliated in the battlefields and after their lands were colonized. Even today, Muslims learn from the West to emulate their "methods" to regain Islam's past glory.

While these transcivilizational transfers of knowledges sound romantic, I must remind readers that it happened under *relations of power*. This intellectual exchange involved ugly Crusades, parasitic colonization, and brutal wars of independence. Knowledges were shared in the midst of conflict, not through cooperation. Civilizations, it seems, learn under domination. *The very idea of a dialogue presupposes an environment free from domination and intimidation.* The question, then, that confronts the civilizational dialogue is, Do the present conditions in world politics represent a domination- and intimidation-free climate? Can those who are involved in such a dialogue ignore the realities of power and organize events where everyone gets to know everyone? World politics is not a company picnic where one chats pleasantly with the boss's wife.

In most places, Muslims and the West are engaged in relations of power.[21] The United States and its allies have imposed sanctions against many Muslim countries. Western forces are poised in a rather intimidating fashion in the Persian Gulf. The West is on the wrong side of many conflicts where Muslims are involved, in Chechnya, Palestine, and Sudan. Many prominent members of the Western elite have threatened to crush Islamic resurgence. Many Muslims, too, threaten dire consequences. Moreover, the economic and military capability of the West exceeds that of the Muslim world by such a margin that any talk of Muslim capability to resist Western intimidation rings hollow. The control that the West has on global sources of information and the *mechanisms of meaning*—media, academia, international forums—allows it to maintain a tight rein on how the world is perceived and what forms of communications take place.

There is much talk about freedom of speech and expression and about the virtues of pluralism in the West, but these values are for domestic consumption. Internationally, expression is tightly monitored. Propaganda dominates truth. International pluralism is not tolerated as slogans about the globalization of Western values, democracy, individualism, secularism, and economic liberalism become defining principles of activist foreign policies. Any difference is construed as a global threat, and there are attempts to eliminate them. A look across the map will clearly indicate that any state that is different is under siege. The world under Western hegemony has no room for difference. Ape the West, or face the West. The first option requires no imagination, but the second demands capability. Look at Iran and Cuba or Sudan. They all face stringent international sanctions. This is not in any way a defense of these states and their human rights records. The way the West relates with Israel, China, and Russia suggests that human rights may be important, but they are not significant enough to be deterministic of foreign policy. Interstate relations are never entirely contingent on how states treat their own populations. Then, discounting human rights records, what the West seems to oppose is resistance to Western ideology.

If the West and Islam share a lot in common, as I argued earlier, then what separates them? It is the difference in their capability and the ideological necessity of their respective leaders to emphasize difference rather than identity. It is only by emphasizing difference that Western elite can justify policies of domination against a different, foreign, and inferior other. For instance, the constant vilification of Iran is based on it being a totalitarian and nondemocratic regime. If for some reason Iran were to become an ally (say, to counter a new belligerent Russian posture toward the Middle East), the same Iran would be appreciated for having a French-like revolution, for eliminating monarchy and taking significant strides toward democracy with its Majlis. What is emphasized is clearly a function of realpolitik. It is also by emphasizing difference that the Islamic elite can mobilize support for regime change. For the Islamist proximity to the West has become a barometer of legitimacy. They can delegitimize any regime by calling it a Western puppet. Any intellectual leader can be demonized merely by insinuating Western or Zionist connections. Thus, difference between Islam and the West, a major barrier to productive dialogue, is a source of power for elite in both cultures. This is a standard operating procedure for Islamists as well as traditional Mullahs.

The possibilities of dialogue cannot be conceived in a power vacuum. It is, I believe, contingent on realities of power. Can weaker civilizations dialogue with the West that so strongly intimidates "the other"? Can anyone negotiate with a player that cannot tolerate any difference? The West has also displayed a tendency to prefer intimidation to dialogue when the power differential is heavily favorable. For instance, the United States would dialogue with the Soviet Union, and it prefers *engagement* to sanctions with China. But it refuses to dialogue with Iran; it imposes sanctions across the board with no sensitive for behavioral change. It refuses to let up until the other completely transforms itself. Iran is a pathetically weak state when it comes to meeting the U.S. challenge. Though I must concede that Europe, like Japan, has maintained a "critical dialogue" with Iran. Many would agree that Europe and Japan are more dependent on Iranian oil and imports, and this gives Iran the power to demand more respect from them. But against the United States it enjoys no such leverage. The present China and the former Soviet Union are militarily more powerful states, who could be ideological rival as well as maintain a dialogue with the West, unlike the Lilliputs—Iran, Sudan, and Cuba.

Power implicates dialogue in domination because it uses dialogue to legitimize domination. Gramsci and Machiavelli both talked about the two faces of power.[22] Power to them was like a centaur, half human and half beast. The beast is the ability of the dominant player to use coercion to establish its will over the other, whereas the human face of power is the capacity to persuade the other, through economic concessions or normative criticism, to alter its values and adopt the values of the dominant player. This form of power is insidious, pervasive, and invisible. It legitimizes domination and makes power relations more stable over time. Dialogue with the subaltern (the group being dominated) is employed to understand their interests and shape them to proximate the interests of the dominant group. Dialogue also establishes the superiority of the master's values and emphasizes the need for the subaltern to emulate the master's values. This in Gramscian terms is *hegemony*—the moral and intellectual leadership of the dominant group. The dialogue with the master often convinces the subaltern that resistance is futile. For a while the master seeks legitimacy; it will always reserve its capability to use coercion if hegemony fails.

The dialogue between a powerful West and a weak Islam may only serve the purpose of convincing Muslim elite that they recognize the superiority of Western values and embrace them, and in return they may join the cadres of the global elite and get the opportunity to share some of the West's success and glory. However, that does not seem to be the case as one clearly sees a new kind of Muslim elite successfully resisting being co-opted by the West. Some Western scholars, Sam Huntington and Paul Kennedy of Yale, believe that the West is declining.[23] They fear that the gap between the West and the rest is lessening to the extent that its hegemony is being challenged. In a material sense, this may be the case given the economic growth of the Pacific Rim and China. But it does not hold true with respect to the Muslim world. The oil powers are weak and now completely dependent on the West for their security. Traditional powers such as Iran and Iraq are today pale shadows of what they were a decade ago. Pakistan is in turmoil, as is Algeria. What, then, is the source of power that is enabling some Muslims to resist hegemony and to dialogue with the West?

I contend that it is the growing moral and intellectual cohesiveness in certain sections of the Muslim world. The emergence of the new intellectual elite—the Islamists—and their ability to generate new ideas that simultaneously empower them and liberate them from the intellectual prisons have plagued the secular intellectuals and the traditional Ulema. The growing conviction among some Muslims that the solution to their problems must come from within has enabled them to shrug the inferiority complex that has plagued Muslims since colonization. The idea that Islam is the solution is gradually bringing political cohesion and moral vigor to growing legions of Islamists. The periodic success in counterhegemonic efforts, such as the Iranian revolution, the successful hijacking of Sudan, the successful politicking in Turkey, and the confidence in Malaysia, further cements the convictions that Muslims must take their destiny in their own hands. There is going to be no Marshall Plan for Muslims or special relations as enjoyed by Israel (which has received over $75 billion in aid from the United States, equivalent to 4.5 Marshall Plans). The very intent to rely on "self-help" is a liberating and empowering experience. It is also an indication of maturity.

Thus, Muslims, without manifesting any palpable shift in capabilities, have become a more powerful community than before. It is the presence of a "knowing elite" and its commitment to self-transformation that is the new source of power that Islamists have found. Muslims today have performed an interesting feat. They have both physically as well as epistemologically traversed across civilizational boundaries. More Muslims are comfortable with Muhammad and Marx, with Khaldun and Kant, Habermas and Hanbal, and Foucault and Farabi on their shelves than their counterparts from the West. There are, I must concede, some Western scholars of Islam who have demonstrated the rare quality to transcend their cultural context and understand Islam. I have had the honor and pleasure to work with two of them, John Esposito and John Voll, but in spite of their huge impact, they are exceptions and not the norm. It is this ability to be comfortable with one's Islamic heritage and also enjoy the cognitive capacity to engage with Western philosophical discourses, constructively and critically, that is the greatest source of power for the contemporary Muslim intellectual.

I had once asked the Egyptian philosopher Hasan Hanafi, When would we know that the process of decolonization was complete? And he had replied, "Muqtedar, when we become knowing beings." Professor Hanafi, I think we are getting there. The presence of a knowing elite who is cognitive and comfortable with the plurality of epistemologies and philosophical traditions, yet strongly aware of who they are, is a sure sign that the knowing beings are here. It is this development, the emergence of the New Ulema (John Esposito's idea), that is generating a discursive balance of power despite the tremendous imbalance in material capabilities. If the West can recognize this new dimension of the Islamic civilization, then the possibilities of dialogue are very real indeed. But this is still contingent on the West recognizing Islamism—the genuine desire of millions of Muslims to find ways to live life according to Islam—as a legitimate force and not equate it to the extremism of a minority.

The most significant development in this encounter of civilizations is the growth of Islam in the West. There are at least thirty-five million Muslims in the West, including seven million in the United States. Muslims in the West, particularly those who entertain the twin goals of retaining their Islamic identity and gaining acceptability in the Western mainstream, have indeed transcended the dichotomy of clash or dialogue of civilizations. They are living on the borderlines of both the civilizations, their feet in the West, their hearts with Islam, and are creating through their very existence a discourse that is beyond either clash or dialogue of civilizations. Describing their existence as a syncretism of both civilizations would merely trivialize their identity. Western Muslims are not just an amalgam, a potpourri of East and West; they are indeed a reinvention of what it constitutes to be Western as well as Muslim. They are not just Muslims who live in the West or Westerners who believe in Islam. They are Muslims who are redefining what it means to be a Muslim, and they are also Westerners who are reinventing what it means to be Western. In constructing this new identity, Western Muslims are going beyond the conservatism of the realists and the liberalism of the idealists.[24]

LIFE ON THE BORDERS OF CIVILIZATIONS: ISLAM IN THE UNITED STATES

Muslims who live in the United States and strongly identify with their Islamic identity are faced with a perplexing existential dilemma. Who do they belong to? They are not part of the Western cultural mainstream and are also not a part of the Muslim political and social mainstream; they live on the margins of Western as well as Islamic civilizations. If they see themselves as Western, then they suffer from cultural alienation; and if they imagine themselves as a part of the Muslim world, then they feel exiled. In a sense, as long as Muslims in the United States adhere to their Islamic identity, they will experience this double exile from the West (culturally) and from the ummah geographically as well as politically. Perhaps the emerging global village will eventually eliminate both physical and metaphysical distances, but the competing forces of localization suggest against betting on it.

The discourses on dialogue or clash of civilizations are essentially motivated by geopolitical dimensions and competing material interests that shape the foreign policies of the United States and the West, on one hand, and the strategically located and oil-rich Muslim Middle East, on the other. The issue of Israel and the plight of Palestinians further exaggerate the relationship between the two civilizations, since both perceive Israel as a frontier post of the West. American Muslims whose futures are linked with the West and whose hearts still remain anchored in the Muslim World are in many ways caught between the cross fire. While they are certainly not subscribers of the clash of civilizations thesis, they are also not exactly engaged in the civilizational dialogue.

American Muslims are engaged in interfaith but not intercivilizational dialogue. Perhaps the most important reason behind this is because, unlike the Muslims in the traditional Muslim world, American Muslims do not have a monolithic conception of the West. They are more acutely aware of the internal contradictions within U.S. society but are also able to see the significant differences between European and American approaches to Islam,

Israel, and Muslim minorities. They are also concerned with the immediate
task of living in an environment that at once offers freedom and dignity as
well as hostility. They are focused on finding their rightful place within the
American mosaic while retaining their Islamic identity. In essence, American
Muslims, by existing in and engaging with the Western ways in such a sustained and systematic fashion, have gone beyond the civilizational discourses.

The task of finding a respectful and meaningful communal existence in
the United States has compelled American Muslims to reimagine America
and rethink their conceptions of the self. In the process, not only has a balanced view of the United States emerged but also a new identity—the
American Muslim identity. The American Muslim identity has not yet stabi-
lized. It remains deeply contested, and, not surprisingly, the divisions about
what constitutes the meaning of an American Muslim are between Muslims
who are realists and those who are idealists.

There are clearly two images of America—"America the democracy" and
"America the colonial power"—that exist in Muslim minds. Muslims who focus on the "inside" are fascinated and excited by the political freedom available to its citizens. They understand and appreciate the vitality of its economy, its culture, its ethics of competition and free enterprise. Most of all, they
are deeply enamored by what they call Islamic values in action such as consultative governance (democratic processes), religious freedom, and cultural
and political pluralism. For these Muslims, the relative opportunity to practice Islam and build Islamic movements and institutions in the United States,
when compared to the presently autocratic Muslim world, remains the most
thrilling aspect of American life. And it is to this aspect that they respond. *For
them, America is liberal, democratic, tolerant, and multicultural.*

There is a competing image of America. Muslims who focus primarily on
U.S. foreign policy see America as an evil force; a colonial power domi-
nating the Muslim world, stealing its resources, depriving it of its freedoms
and right to self-determination. Many Muslims also believe that the United
States is anti-Islam and seeking to globalize its immoral culture. They find
America's uncritical support of Israel, even as Israel oppresses and massacres Palestinian children, as proof of its evil motives. The complete devastation of Iraq and the incredible hardships caused by the United
States–sponsored sanctions are seen as further evidence of American intentions to destroy and eliminate Islam and Muslims. These Muslims have
trouble reconciling America's benign attitude toward Muslims at home with
the consequences of its malevolent foreign policy.[25]

The leadership of Islamic movements such as the Islamic Society of North
America (ISNA) and Islamic Circle of North America; of Islamic political institutions such as the Council of American-Islamic Relations (CAIR), American Muslim Council (AMC), and American Muslim Alliance (AMA); and of
Islamic intellectual initiatives such as Association of Muslim Social Scientists

(AMSS) and the North American Fiqh Council, all share the first image of America. It is not that they are indifferent or blind to U.S. foreign policy excesses. They recognize it, are critical, and frequently voice their displeasure and condemnation of the United States' uncritical support to Israel and the inhuman sanctions against Iraq. But they also understand the need to build a strong, vibrant, and thriving Islamic community here. And in the interest of establishing Islam in the United States, they focus more on the "inside" rather than the "outside" of America. In defining the goals and interests of Muslims in America, the aforementioned institutions have emphasized the "America the democracy" identity over "America the colonial power."

The difference between these two images is essentially based on where Muslims imagine their homes. Those who still see the countries of their origin as "home" are more focused on U.S. foreign policy and are resentful toward and distrustful of the United States. Those Muslims who imagine the United States as their home and the homeland of their progeny are more concerned with establishing Islam in the country and are excited by the opportunities they see. Muslims who wish to make America their homeland dominate American Muslim leadership. Largely due to this group, Islamic activism, in the area of politics and in the realm of religious life, is well on its way toward what one may call Americanization.[26]

ASPIRATIONS OF THE AMERICAN MUSLIM COMMUNITY

Muslims who entertained a negative image of America were genuinely surprised by the relative freedom they enjoyed in the United States. Muslim immigrants who started coming to the United States from the early 1960s had already tasted the elixir of Islamic revivalist fervor and also tasted the brutality and autocracy of their own governments, which were interested in either crushing or co-opting emerging Islamic movements. Several members of the various Islamic movements such as the Muslim brotherhood and the Jamaat-e-Islami came to the United States, and many of them soon discovered the epochal opportunity that the United States provided.

In a society where there was political and religious freedom, Muslims could quickly organize and freely establish Islamic movements that were constantly repressed in the heartlands of the Muslim world. While there was deep hostility and prejudice toward Islam and Muslims, these attitudes were nothing compared to the stifling character of despotic regimes in Egypt, Iraq, Iran, Saudi Arabia, Libya, Sudan, and Palestine (under Israeli colonialism). The easiest and often the only way for these Muslims to come to the United States was through the route of higher education.

They came, they got their Ph.D.s, in natural and social sciences, and they stayed to create a crucial mass of intellectual Muslim elite in the United

States. The nature of the immigration became a filtering process allowing only the better-educated and intellectually sophisticated individuals to enter from the Arab world. Add to this the flow of Muslim professionals and scholars escaping poverty and poor economies from India, Pakistan, and Bangladesh, and you have a Muslim leadership capable of articulating enlightened self-interest and formulating a far-reaching vision for the revival of Islam and Islamic values.[27]

The Islamists who found themselves in leadership positions in the emerging American Muslim community essentially had one overriding goal: to revive the Islamic civilization.[28] They strongly believed that the key to reviving Islamic civilization was the intellectual revival of the ummah. Thinkers like Ismail Farooqi and his Islamization of Knowledge project, and Seyyed Hossein Nasr and his Islamic philosophy and Islamic sciences project, are indicative of this thinking. The establishment of the Association of Muslim Social Scientists (AMSS)[29] was the first step toward establishing this revivalist thinking within some kind of institutional setting. The lack of freedom for rethinking the Islamic civilizational project and to indulge in serious rejuvenation of the stagnant Islamic sciences was not available in the Muslim world.

The freedom available in the West led to further institutional development of this revivalist agenda and led to the establishment of the International Institute of Islamic Thought (IIIT) in Virginia and the Islamic Foundation in Leicester, United Kingdom. They are both think tanks dedicated to intellectual revival of Muslims. The idea was simple: The freedom of religion and thought in the West and in America in particular would be utilized to produce Islamic ideas and ideology and then exported back to the Muslim world, where it would be tested or introduced, hoping to stimulate and galvanize social and religious reform. Both centers produce prolific literature in the forms of books and journals on various aspects of Islamic sciences and social sciences. The most spectacular of such endeavors was the establishment of the International Islamic University (IIU) of Malaysia.

IIU Malaysia is a product of American Muslim expertise and Malaysian resources. The president of IIIT, who was also a founder member and president of AMSS, AbdulHameed AbuSulayman, left the United States to take over as the rector of IIU Malaysia. He took with him not only the ideas of Ismail Farooqi, the Islamization project, but also many Muslim social scientists and intellectuals who had bloomed in the free and challenging environment of American academia. There he sought to unite the so-called secular and sacred sciences in an attempt to create a generation of Muslim students well versed in modern as well as traditional knowledges, the essential ingredient for the reconstruction of a thriving Islamic civilization.[30]

Muslim leaders of this generation also created Islamic political organizations like CAIR, the American Muslim Council (AMC), Muslim Political Action Committee (MPAC), Kashmiri American Council (KAC), American Muslim Alliance (AMA), and American Muslims for Jerusalem (AMJ)[31] to use the resources of the American Muslim community to fight for freedom, democracy, and self-determination in the Muslim world. These organizations are trying to increase their political and economic influence in the United States in the hope that it can be leveraged to improve the condition of the Muslim world.[32]

In the United States, the emerging leadership realized that the single most important goal was not to assimilate and disappear into the great melting pot, like those who had come before them. The need to defend and consolidate Islamic identity became the number one goal in the United States. *Muslims were not here to assimilate. They were here to be accepted.* Thus, the development of the American Muslim community in the last three decades, at least among the immigrants, can be divided into two phases. The first phase entailed *consolidation of the Islamic identity;* the second phase entailed *making an impact* on the American society.

To realize these goals, nearly 2,000 Islamic centers and over 1,200 Islamic schools mushroomed within the last three decades. Several Islamic movements, such as the Islamic Society of North America (ISNA), Islamic Circle of North America (ICNA), and Islamic Assembly of North America (IANA), emerged to galvanize momentum and fervor in adherence of Islamic practices so that the Islamic identity of the immigrant community did not dissipate. Traditionalist movements like the Tablighi Jamaat, a movement that focuses on ritual purity and revival, have taken roots along with the Naqshbandi Sufi movement.[33]

The leadership of the intellectual elite, the resonant echo of the Islamic revivalist fervor of the Muslim world, the gradual transformation of the United States from melting pot to a multicultural society and the rapid rate of conversion of Americans, both White and Black, all provided energy and momentum for the sustenance of Islamic practices in the nation. Unlike other ethnic immigrant and religious communities, the Islamic community has enjoyed the great advantage that comes from conversions. When the Italians and the Greeks and others came to the United States, they also struggled with the issue of assimilation and identity. But unlike the Muslim community that wins new converts, there was no such case of Greek Americans or African Americans converting to Italian ethnicity or Anglo-Saxon Americans becoming Greek American. Even as assimilation took away many, reversion and conversion to Islam brought many new believers within the fold and kept the critical mass of the community sufficiently large to preclude complete assimilation.[34]

We can summarize the aspirations of American Muslim leadership as follows:

- Defending the Islamic identity of Muslims in the United States against assimilation
- Developing intellectual and political resources capable of making significant social and political changes in the Muslim world

In the pursuit of these goals, the American Muslim identity has gradually emerged as the community coped and adjusted to challenges within and without the community.[35]

INTERNAL AND EXTERNAL CHALLENGES

The American Muslim leadership realized that the challenges to becoming fully accepted and respected participants in American democracy were two-dimensional. They were *barriers to acceptance* posed by ignorance of Islam and prejudice toward Arabs and Muslims widespread in American society and nurtured meticulously by its political leadership and media.[36] They also realized that there was *resistance to adjustment* within the community itself that would pose as a major barrier to engagement with the American mainstream. Both the challenges, internal and external, had equal impact on both goals that the American Muslim community had set for itself.

RESISTING ASSIMILATION

Prejudice against Islam in the American mainstream presented several barriers to the practice of Islam. Every time there was a major political development in the Middle East, American newspapers and TV shows would unleash attacks on Islam and its values. Islam was and is still presented as an irrational, undemocratic faith opposed to equality, freedom, and peace. The Western imagery of Islam as antithetical to Western values had made it difficult for Muslims in the past to declare their commitment to Islam in public.

The demonization of Islam in the media and the prejudice, hatred, and intolerance it bred, made practicing Islam in the public arena a dangerous prospect.[37] Muslim women could not wear the headscarf in schools, at shopping malls, or in workplaces. Muslim women wearing headscarves were usually screened at the interview stage. If they started wearing scarves after they got the job, they were often fired without any reason. Teachers would object and send Muslim girls home for wearing the headscarf. Girls were punished when they refused to wear revealing clothes in gym classes or in the swimming pool. Social interactions in the workplace, which often takes familiarity between people of different gender as given, was alien to many Muslim women. Ignorance of Islamic gender practices also led to deliberate or unintended discrimination of Muslims. Work environments that lack sensitivity to Muslim needs tend to become hostile.[38]

Men faced discrimination for wearing beards and caps and for wanting a longer break on Fridays to offer the congregational Friday prayers. Both men and women had trouble getting days off for Islamic festivals. Many

Muslim scholars and intellectuals faced discrimination while seeking jobs in higher education and while writing on politics, particularly on Middle Eastern issues, from an Islamic perspective. The pressure to "become normal," to consume alcohol at parties, to eat nonhalal food, or to participate freely in mixed environments remains very high. Muslim men in responsible positions found that their careers could be jeopardized because Islamic etiquette and dietary laws socially marginalized them.

The ignorance about Islam and the hostility toward it presented and continues to present several challenges. The pressure to assimilate to normalize was and still remains very high. Many Muslims started using Americanized versions of their names to hide their Islamic identity and even their "foreignness." Muhammad became Mo, Jeffery became Jeff, Ali became Al. But others resisted and sometimes made a breakthrough, and at other times paid the cost. As children were born, Muslim families realized that American public schools offered reasonable education at no cost, but they did not inculcate Islamic values. The food was not halal; the stories and the lessons were based on either Christian folklore or secular ethos. Children found it difficult to resist wanting to be like their peers. And most parents struggling to establish themselves in their careers found that they had little time to provide their children with the religious and cultural education that they needed.

Many Muslims were neither disturbed nor concerned with this. They were happy with their material success and tried to gain acceptance in the mainstream culture by distancing themselves from Islam and Islamic practices. For those who were not keen on defending their Islamic identity, life in the United States was wonderful. Many had realized the American dream, and all that was left was to enjoy the prosperity and freedom available in America. A large segment of this group returned to Islam in big ways once their children grew up and began to manifest some of the social ills of American society, such as sexual promiscuity, drug use, moral indifference, and other negative behaviors. Some still remain assimilated, finding themselves on the fringe of both the Islamic society in the United States and American society.

But there are many Muslims who came to the United States for political and economic reasons and are determined to resist assimilation. They answered the call from the Islamists and Muslim intellectuals and *dawah* (propagators of Islam) workers to join the various Islamic movements that mushroomed in the 1970s and 1980s. The first thing that Islamists did was to take over the National Arab Students Association and dissolve it. They replaced it with the national Muslim Students Association (MSA). The National MSA and its branches in various campuses started working with local communities to establish small Islamic *halaqas* (study circles) and *musallahs* (prayers centers) in classrooms or rented apartments.

Gradually, with the help of the Muslim leadership that was graduating from schools and outgrowing the MSAs, these small communities started establishing Islamic centers. Fortunately, in the late 1970s the Gulf states had become cash-rich with the rise in oil prices. Many of them gave generously to Muslim communities all over the world, seeking to establish mosques and Islamic schools. Some of the most important Islamic centers, like the Islamic centers in Washington, D.C., and New York, were built with generous donations from them.[39]

With some foothold in communities and universities, Islamic movements began to fight against the pressure to assimilate. In the 1970s and 1980s, the response was purely defensive, as the primary focus was to build large numbers of Islamic centers and Islamic schools. Islamic centers and their activities kept the adults in touch with their beliefs and their heritage, and Islamic schools taught Islamic values and inculcated Islamic practices among the young. Today there are over 2,000 Islamic centers and over 1,200 Islamic schools in North America.[40]

These centers also became the hubs for activities by Muslims who in their countries of origin belonged to various Islamic movements. For example, the Tablighi Jamaat, an Islamic movement focused on Islamic rituals, quickly took root in many mosques, especially in Florida, Chicago, upstate New York, and New York City. This apolitical and mildly spiritual movement is one of the biggest Islamic movements in North America, with over one hundred thousand participants. It is a loose network of activists who encourage each other to pray regularly.

Similarly, ISNA and then ICNA also expanded, centering their activities on Islamic centers. Gradually, all the Islamic movements began holding annual national and regional conventions that bring scholars from North America and the Muslim world to large convention centers where thousands of Muslims converge every year to listen to lectures on Islam and participate in various community- and faith-related workshops. Currently, the annual convention of ISNA attracts over thirty-five thousand participants and over a thousand scholars. The regional Tablighi *ijtimas* (gatherings) attract anywhere between ten thousand and fifteen thousand attendees. ICNA averaged between ten thousand and twelve thousand participants at its annual conventions. At all these conventions, Muslim scholars and intellectuals from North America and the rest of the Muslim world mingle with American Muslims and each other, providing a sneak preview to the Islamic civilization that Muslims dream about.

THE STRUGGLE FOR "AMERICAN ISLAM"

The transition of American Muslims from a fragile group focused on defending its identity to an intrepid community determined to make an impact has not been without contention. There is still no consensus in the community over several issues. To understand the political dynamics and the various contentions, it is important to return to the two images of the West that Muslims currently entertain: America as a democracy and America as a colonial power. For the purpose of this discussion, I use the term *Muslim idealists* to describe Muslims who pay more attention to American democracy. Those who give American imperialist tendencies overseas greater significance in conceptualizing American identity will be identified as "Muslim realists."

The relationship between the two groups, Muslim idealists and Muslim realists, can best be described as a love–hate relationship. On practical issues concerning the defense of Islamic identity, such as establishing and maintaining Islamic centers and schools, these two groups cooperate fully, and the community appears to be seamless. But on political issues, these two groups break apart and do not see eye to eye on any issue. It is safe to say that, while on preserving belief and rituals these two groups have common ground, they clearly entertain different conceptions of the role of Muslims in the United States.

Muslim Realists and America

Muslim realists see the United States as an evil empire dedicated to global domination. In this decade alone, they have seen the United States benefit from the Iran–Iraq War and then destroy the most advanced Arab nation in the Gulf War and making billions of dollars in profit by billing Muslims for that war. They have seen how the United States–led sanctions have gradually squeezed the life out of Iraq, killing hundreds of thousands of Muslim children. Recently they watched in horror as the Israeli military killed over 350 protesting Palestinians using a war machine that has benefited from U.S. aid, which is about $4 to $6 billion every year and has exceeded $80 billion in total.

They could not believe their senses as they read report after report in the media blaming the Palestinians for dying and listened in amazement as the United States, the so-called defender of human rights, refused to blame or admonish its ally Israel. Muslim realists are incensed with the United States for having an utter disregard for Muslim lives and Muslim society. The media demonizes Islam, everyone gets away with defamation of Muslims, and when the president needs to divert attention from his private life, he chooses to fire cruise missiles at Muslim nations.

Most important, Muslim realists are not impressed with America's democracy or its values of freedom and pluralism. They point to the secret evidence act, used only against Muslims, which violates both these values by not allowing defendants full access to due process of law. They see American society as immoral, sexually decadent, greedy, and exploitative of the weak at home and abroad. Philosophically, they do not appreciate the value of freedom and tolerance; theologically, they disagree with democracy as a means of political governance. For them, democracy is an institution that legitimizes the basic instincts of humanity and is an affront to divine laws. They describe the American system as *kufr* (a system against the laws of Allah or the Islamic Shariah) and reject it totally.

The frustration and animosity that they feel as a consequence of American foreign policy excesses are translated into a rejection of all that is American and Western, including democracy and religious tolerance. The hostility toward the United States is also extended toward people of other faiths and makes them suspicious and paranoid even when they see the United States doing something right, such as intervening against a Christian state to protect Muslims in Bosnia and Kosovo. Some of the realists are disingenuous in their explanation about religious freedom in the United States and argue that all the positive things that are happening to Muslims in America are from Allah, and American values of tolerance, freedom, and democracy have nothing to do with it since they are just empty slogans. They, of course, do not apply the same determinist approach in explaining the misfortunes of Iraqis or the Palestinians. The bad things that are happening to them are not from Allah but a consequence of American and Israeli colonialism.[41]

There is an element of hypocrisy, too, in the manner in which the realists conceptualize their own role in the United States. They maintain that, since the American system is not divinely ordained and is not geared toward realizing the Islamic Shariah (they ignore the fact that in theory both the U.S. Constitution and the Islamic state seek justice, protection, and the moral and material well-being of their citizens), participation in that system constitutes (in their minds) violation of Allah's decree in the Quran (5:45) that Muslims shall not rule by anything other than what Allah has decreed. Participation, they argue, means endorsement of the system; therefore, they are opposed to Muslim participation in American politics.

Even though they reject the entire system, they have no qualms about participating in the American economy. They take jobs, pay taxes (to support the system), and some of them even start businesses in the system where, like the polity, the economy is also un-Islamic. When quizzed on this inconsistency and pressed further by suggestions that since they disapprove of the system they should migrate (which is an Islamic thing to do), the realists resort to accusing Muslim idealists as agents of the State Department and of being in league with the enemies of Islam.

They argue that American Muslims must participate in an effort to revive the institution of Khilafa, which will magically take care of all Muslim problems. Some of the realists have organized themselves under the banner of Hizb-ul-Tahreer, a fringe political movement that advocates a narrow and harsh interpretation of Islam. Tahreer has been shut down in most Muslim countries, recently in Pakistan. The only places where they are free to pursue their activism in the open and without any fear of state reprisal is in the West, specifically, the U.K., the United States, and Canada. Ironically, Tahreer condemns the West for its belief in democracy and freedom, yet it is this very belief in freedom that has helped them escape political extinction.

In the last few years, the realists have focused their attention on preventing the Muslim idealists from bringing Muslims into the American mainstream. However, their attempts to create intellectual and political ghettoes have failed, as more and more Muslims are participating in the American political process.[42]

Muslim Idealists and the American Muslim Identity

Muslim idealists have not only transformed American Muslims from a marginal, inward-looking immigrant community to a reasonably well-organized and well-coordinated interest group able not only to fight for its rights but also to begin asserting its interests at the national as well as international levels. The key to Muslim idealists' success has been their understanding of the West and their liberal vision of Islam.

Muslim idealists were quick to grasp the significance of the constitutional guarantee of religious freedom in the United States. They used this in the beginning to organize institutions and movements solely focused on preserving the Islamic identity of Muslims. They were aware that Muslims who had come before them had been culturally assimilated and had lost all connection to Islam. But as more and more Muslims came to the United States and answered their rallying call, they began to see a dream—a dream of a "model Muslim community" practicing Islam as well as playing a role of moral leadership, guiding not only other Muslim communities but also Western societies toward a life of goodness and God consciousness.

What they see in America is not just the imperialist impulse but also the respect for law and fellow human beings. They are aware of the double standards that Western nations employ while treating their own citizens and others differently. But this practice was not new to them. They have witnessed their own societies employing separate standards while dealing with people. They are frustrated with the United States when it does not fulfill its commitments to democracy and human rights in the Muslim world but are quick to acknowledge that Muslims are better treated here than in their own countries. They have seen democracy, pluralism, and cultural and religious tolerance in action and are fascinated by its ability to resolve political differences peacefully. They admire the American state for its commitment to consultation and desire to rule wisely through deliberation. They wish that Muslim societies, too, would be able to escape the political underdevelopment from which they currently suffer and rise to manifest Islamic virtues and, like the United States, present the world with a model worthy of emulation.

Muslim idealists have had several successes. First, they were able to quickly assume leadership positions in nearly every avenue of American Muslim activism. Whether it is in the political arena or in religious affairs, Muslim idealists hold sway. Second, they have been able to advance a vision for the American Muslim community, which makes American Muslims proud of themselves and galvanizes them to contribute their money and time in the pursuit of this vision. Their greatest achievement has been their liberal interpretation of Islam.

Through thousands of seminars, persuasive articles in monthly magazines and Islamic center newsletters, lectures at regional and annual conventions of ICNA, ISNA, AMC, CAIR, MSA, MYNA (Muslim Youth of North America), workshops and leadership retreats in the last thirty years, and the Friday Juma prayers across the nation, Muslim idealists have campaigned to alter the way Muslims think about the United States and about Islam itself. They have fought for the legitimacy of their ideas against traditional scholars and battled against the siege mentality that had prevented Muslims from opening up and taking a fresh look at the world as well as themselves from the new place that they were in now.

In these three decades, Muslim idealists have shifted the Muslim communities' focus from battling the West to building bridges with it. They have rejuvenated the tradition of *ijtihad* (independent thinking among Muslims) and now openly talk about *fiqh al-akhliat* (Islamic law, or interpretation of the Shariah for places where Muslims who are in the minority).[43] They have emphasized Islamic principles of justice, religious tolerance, and cultural pluralism. They have Islamized Western values of freedom, human rights, and respect for tolerance by finding Islamic sources and precedence that justify them. A very good example of this tendency is the establishment of the Center for the Study of Islam and Democracy (CSID) that explores common ground between Islamic governance based on Shariah and Shura and idealistic governance that emphasizes rights and consent.

In the battle for American Islam, Muslim idealists have enjoyed a resounding success. They have gradually marginalized the realists and rendered their arguments and positions illegitimate. There are still pockets of resistance that are confined largely to Internet-based discussion groups or websites. In the run up to election 2000, the struggle between the two types of Muslim elite in America had intensified. But the realists have been completely isolated. Muslim idealists succeeded in mobilizing Muslims to register to vote, and they voted in large numbers, making a difference in the crucial state of Florida. Today American Muslims are not only eager to participate and make an impact; they have made an impact already.

The realists do not have any program or vision that would attract Muslims. Their call to establish Khilafah is without substance and lacks credibility. They themselves spend their resources in attacking Muslim idealists for "inventing an American Islam" in conjunction with American scholars like John Esposito and Yvonne Haddad who emphasize the "softer side of Islam." Their activism is now limited to harassing Muslim activists and trying to place hurdles in their paths.

As a new generation of Muslims joins the community, the influence of Muslim idealists is consolidated. While the new generation is familiar with the problems of the Muslim world and its bill of complaints against the West, life as they know it is in the West, with all its pluralities and inconsistencies. They are strongly in the corner of the idealists and truly manifest that "third identity"—American Muslims. They are proud to be Muslims and Americans.

They are not Americans who are Muslims or Muslims who are born in the United States. They are American Muslims. They believe in Islam; they are idealistic; they respect human rights and animal rights and share the concern for the environment. They are economic and political liberals and social conservatives. They believe in the freedom of religion and the right of all peoples, ethnic as well as religious, to be treated equally. They are aware of their economic and political privileges and grateful to Allah for it. They dream of making changes in Muslim attitudes as well as Muslim conditions so that their fellow Muslims can also learn the bliss of practicing Islam by choice and without any fear of the state or a dominant group.[44]

Beyond the Idealists and the Realists

The West is essentially like a centaur—half-human and half-beast. The human face of the beast allows the West to appreciate the virtues of democracy, equality, and freedoms of speech and religion. It provides it with the moral basis for protecting and treating its own citizens with utmost respect and dignity while also striving hard to advance their interests—understood in terms of political and material development. The bestial dimension of the West has led it to commit huge crimes against humanity. The world wars, the Holocaust, colonialism, imperialism, slavery, and racism are just a few of the crimes that the West has committed or, to a much lesser extent, continues to commit outside its borders. These elements of the West are puzzling. How can a society that has so much respect for the human life at home be so determined to allow the steady elimination of innocent Iraqis? How can a society that stands for equality and democracy allow so little freedom to other societies to disagree with it?

Today in an era of globalization, all civilizations are forced to live in intimacy. Also, millions of Muslims now live in the West, and many others live in a close embrace of the Western ways of life. Understanding the puzzle that is the modern West is essential because its enormous power, both material as well as cultural, has attained hegemonic proportions. There is very little resistance, except from some Islamists and some Asianists, to the growing influence of the West on the cultural and moral fabric of this planet. We not only have to understand the modern West in a more balanced way but also develop a discourse for the reconstruction of Islamic identity that is neither weakened nor distracted by the enormous shadow of the West. Until we as Muslims can go beyond blind imitation of the West or outright rejection of its values, we will not be able to construct an Islamic self, independent of Western influence. It is essential that we develop a positive and constructive understanding of the "other." Only through such a positive and creative act will we be able to reconstruct a vibrant and meaningful self.

It is therefore doubly important that Muslims in the West develop a "firsthand" understanding of what the West really is. It is rather ridiculous that Muslims who have been living in the United States for decades put aside their own experiences and, to understand the West, turn to the polemics of Muslim intellectuals of the 1960s who have not experienced the contemporary West. Only those who have had a sustained experience of the West and have witnessed both its human and its bestial dimension can develop a meaningful understanding of it. Others will continue to rely on caricatures, one way or the other.

What does it mean to have a balanced view of the West? It means that we do not throw out the baby with the bathwater. Because Muslims are upset that the United States has chosen to be friends with Israel and not with the Arabs, just because the United States has committed crimes against Iraqi children, we must not reject democracy, human rights, respect for freedom, and the rule of law.

A balanced view of the West should recognize the material impulses that shape many of the Western foreign policy choices and resist as well as condemn them. But in an endeavor to resist the Western domination, we must not foolishly reject the laudable results of their moral impulses manifest so elegantly in their self-governing, rights-respecting societies. A balanced view of the West will rise far above simple associations. Because democracy is found in the West, it should not be labeled "Western." Now we can find Islam in the West, too—does that mean Islam, too, is Western? A balanced view of the West will seek to understand the sources of Western values and also their implications of social welfare before passing judgment on them. A balanced view of the West is essentially a considered and enlightened opinion of Western institutions and practices that does not allow negative emotions to cloud one's rational faculties.

Only when such an attempt to understand the West is made by Muslim intellectuals as well as the general public will the basis of a healthy Islamic identity emerge. Until then, reactions to the West will continue to subvert the construction of Islamic identity. In this chapter, I have argued that American Muslims (idealists) through their sustained engagement with the American and Western way have not only developed a balanced view of the West but have succeeded in reinventing themselves as a middle nation.

NOTES

1. Richard Betts, ed., *Conflict after the Cold War* (New York: Macmillan, 1994); Walter C. Opello Jr. and Stephen J. Rosow, *The Nation-State and Global Order* (Boulder, Colo.: Rienner, 1999).

2. M. A. Muqtedar Khan, "Constructing Identity in 'Glocal' Politics," *American Journal of Islamic Social Sciences* 15, no. 3 (Fall 1999): 81–106.

3. See Samuel Huntington, "The Clash of Civilizations?" *Foreign Affairs* 72 (Summer 1993): 22–49; H. H. Saunders, "The Virtues of Sustained Dialogue between Civilizations, "*International Journal on World Peace* 18, no. 1 (2001): 35–44; Marc Lynch, "The Dialogue of Civilizations and International Public Sphere," *Millennium: Journal of International Relations* 29, no. 2 (Spring 2000): 307; Ejaz Akram, "International Conference on Dialogue of Nations," *American Journal of Islamic Social Sciences* 17, no. 3 (2000): 135–37.

4. These concepts operate at the most basic level. In its most sophisticated incarnation, IR theory distinguishes among classical, structural, and neorealists and among liberals, liberal internationalists, and neoliberal institutionalists. But for the purpose of this argument the fundamental distinction between the ontological assumptions that realists and idealists make about the nature of things is sufficient.

5. To understand the theoretical and philosophical underpinnings of political realism as applied to international relations (realpolitik), see Hans Morganthau, *Politics among Nations* (New York: Knopf, 1948); Edward H. Carr, *The Twenty Years Crisis: 1919–1939: An Introduction to the Study of International Relations* (New York: Harper & Row, 1964); Kenneth Waltz, *Theory of International Politics* (New York: McGraw-Hill, 1979). I believe that the famous Islamic theory of international politics postulating conflict between *dar al-harb* (house of war) and *dar al-Islam* (house of peace) advanced by the classical jurist Al-Shaybani is also a realist theory of international relations. For a discussion, see M. A. Muqtedar Khan, "Islam as an Ethical Tradition of International Relations," *Islam and Christian-Muslim Relations* 8, no. 2 (July 1997): 177–92.

6. For some examples of idealist literature, see Terry Nardin and David Mapel, eds., *Traditions of International Ethics* (Cambridge: Cambridge University Press, 1993); Mark R. Amstutz, *International Ethics: Concepts, Theories, and Cases in Global Politics* (Oxford: Rowman & Littlefield, 1999); Mervyn Frost, *Ethics in International Relations: A Constitutive Theory* (Cambridge: Cambridge University Press, 1996).

7. For a discussion of ontological dogmatism and the sociological turn in the study of international politics, see M. A. Muqtedar Khan, *Identity and Choice in International Relations: A Constructivist Theory of Agency and Action* (Washington, D.C.: Georgetown University, 2000). Also see Yosef Lapid and Freidrich Kratochwil, eds., *The Return of Culture and Identity in IR Theory* (Boulder, Colo.: Rienner, 1996).

8. Realists such as Daniel Pipes and Judith Miller have consistently argued for a military solution to the Islamist challenge to the current political status quo in the Muslim world. See Daniel Pipes, "There Are No Moderates: Dealing with Fundamentalist Islam," *The National Interest* 41 (Fall 1995): 48–57; Judith Miller, "The Challenge of Radical Islam," *Foreign Affairs* (Spring 1993): 43–56. Idealists such as Muhammad Khatami, the present president of Iran, and Anwar Ibrahim, the former

finance minister of Malaysia, have called for a dialogue of civilizations to remove any misunderstanding between Islam and the West and to enhance mutual understanding and respect. See the chapter on "Religious Belief in Today's World," in Muhammad Khatami, *Islam, Liberty and Development* (Binghamton, N.Y.: Binghamton University Press, 1999). Also see Khatami's address to UNESCO in New York at www.unesco.org/dialogue2001/en/khatami.htm, September 5, 2000; and Anwar Ibrahim, *The Asian Renaissance* (Kuala Lumpur: Times, 1997).

9. Bernard Lewis, "The Roots of Muslim Rage," *Atlantic Monthly* (September 1990): 47–54.

10. His only departure from the realist paradigm was at the level of analysis. Realist theorists of international relations are state-centric and seek to balance power between states. Huntington chose a supranational entity—a civilization—as his level of analysis, and his realpolitik was the dynamics of power between clusters of states constituting competing civilizations.

11. Lewis, "The Roots of Muslim Rage" *Atlantic Monthly* (September 1990): 47–54.

12. For a systematic analysis of the various positions on Islam and the West and who claims what, see M. A. Muqtedar Khan, "Policy Entrepreneurs: The Third Dimension in American Foreign Policy Culture," *Middle East Policy* 5, no. 3 (September 1997): 140–54. Also see M. A. Muqtedar Khan, "US Foreign Policy and Political Islam: Ideas, Interests and Ideology," *Security Dialogue* 29, no. 4 (December 1998): 449–62.

13. See John Esposito, *Islamic Threat: Myth or Reality* (New York: Oxford University Press, 1999). Also see Khan, "Policy Entrepreneurs."

14. Arthur L. Lowrie, "The Campaign against Islam and American Foreign Policy," *Middle East Policy* (September 1995): 210.

15. See M. A. Muqtedar Khan, "Islamic Identity and the Two Faces of the West," *Washington Report on Middle East Affairs* (August–September 2000): 71; available at www.washington-report.org/backissues/08092000/0010071.html.

16. Charles Kurzman, *Liberal Islam: A Source Book* (New York: Oxford University Press, 1998); Leonard Binder, *Liberal Islam: A Critique of Development* (Chicago: University of Chicago Press, 1988); Katerina Dalacoura, *Islam, Liberalism and Human Rights* (London: Taurus, 1998).

17. See Ibrahim Abu-Rabi, *Intellectual Origins of Islamic Resurgence in the Modern Arab World* (Albany: State University of New York Press, 1996); Mir Zohair Husain, *Global Islamic Politics* (New York: HarperCollins, 1995); Ali Rahnema, ed., *Pioneers of Islamic Revival* (London: Zed, 1994); Mehrzad Boroujerdi, *Iranian Intellectuals and the West* (Syracuse, N.Y.: Syracuse University Press, 1996).

18. Indeed, one of the most prominent of Western thinkers who claimed that Islam played a passive role in the emergence of the modern West is none other than Bertrand Russell himself. See Bertrand Russell, *A History of Western Philosophy* (New York: Touchstone, 1972), 427. For a completely antithetical thesis, see W. M. Watt, *The Influence of Islam on Medieval Europe* (Edinburgh: Edinburgh University Press, 1972).

19. See John L. Esposito and Mohommed A. Muqtedar Khan, "Religion and Politics in the Middle East," in *Understanding the Contemporary Middle East,* ed. Deborah J. Gerner (Boulder, Colo.: Rienner, 2000), 324–25. Also see Esposito, *Islamic Threat,* 48–50.

20. See the chapter "When Worlds Collide: Muslim Nations and Western Moder-

nity," in Akbar Ahmad, *Islam Today: A Short Introduction to the Muslim World* (London: Taurus, 1999), 96–162.

21. Graham Fuller and Ian Lesser, *A Sense of Siege: The Geopolitics of Islam and the West* (Boulder, Colo.: Westview, 1995).

22. See Barry Hindess, *Discourses of Power: From Hobbes to Foucault* (Cambridge, Mass.: Blackwell, 1996).

23. See chapter 4, "The Fading of the West: Power, Culture and Indegenization," in Samuel P. Huntington, *The Clash of Civilizations and the Remaking of World Order* (New York: Simon & Schuster, 1996); Paul Kennedy, *The Rise and Fall of the Great Powers* (New York: Fontana, 1989).

24. A sampling of the following works can provide a fair understanding of emerging Western Muslims: Jane I. Smith, *Islam in America* (New York: Columbia University Press, 1999); Phillip Lewis, *Islamic Britain: Religion, Politics and Identity among British Muslims* (London: Taurus, 1994); Alija Ali Izetbegovic, *Islam between East and West* (Indianapolis: American Trust Publications, 1984); Gilles Kepel, *Allah in the West: Islamic Movements in America and Europe* (Stanford, Calif.: Stanford University Press, 1997); Yvonne Haddad and Adair Lummis, *Islamic Values in the United States* (New York: Oxford University Press, 1987); Gerd Nonneman, Tim Niblock, and Bogdan Szajkowski, eds., *Muslim Communities in the New Europe* (Ithaca, N.Y.: Cornell University Press, 1996); Yvonne Y. Haddad, ed., *The Muslims of America* (New York: Oxford University Press, 1991); Tomas Gerholm and Yngve Georg Lithman, *The New Islamic Presence in Western Europe* (London: Mansell, 1988); Amber Haque, ed., *Muslims and Islamization in North America: Problems and Prospects* (Beltsville, Md.: Amana, 1999); John L. Esposito and Yvonne Y. Haddad, eds., *Muslims on the Americanization Path?* (New York: Oxford University Press, 2000).

25. See Khan, "Islamic Identity and the Two Faces of the West," 71.

26. Haddad and Esposito, eds., *Muslims on the Americanization Path?*

27. For historical accounts of how the American Muslim community emerged over the years, see Sulayman S. Nyang, "Islam in America: A Historical Perspective," *American Muslim Quarterly* 2, no. 1 (Spring 1998): 7–38. Also see Omar Altalib, "Muslims in America: Challenges and Prospects," *American Muslim Quarterly* 2, no. 1 (Spring 1998): 39–49.

28. Review the main themes in the works of some of the most prominent Islamic thinkers in North America, such as Fazlur Rahman, Ismail Farooqi, Seyyed Hossein Nasr, Taha Jabir Al-Alwani, and the desire to revive the Islamic civilization will be the dominant theme. *Islamic Horizons,* the main journal of ISNA, dedicated an entire issue in March/April 1999 to the memory and ideas of Hassan Al-Bannah, the founder of Muslim Brotherhood of Egypt and a prominent figure in twentieth-century Islamic revivalist movements.

29. "A Forum Rebuilds: AMSS Serves as a Platform for Discussion of Issues Facing Muslims," *Islamic Horizons* (January/February 1999): 17.

30. For a review of IIIT's endeavors, see Jamal Barazinji, "History of Islamization of Knowledge and Contributions of the International institute of Islamic Thought," in *Muslim and Islamization in North America,* ed. Haque, 13–33.

31. To learn more, visit these organizations on the Internet: CAIR, www.cair-net.org; AMC, www.amconline.org; AMA, www.amaweb.org; MPAC, www.mpac.org; KAC, www.kashmiri.com; AMJ, www.amjerusalem.org.

32. See M. A. Muqtedar Khan, "Collective Identity and Collective Action: Case of Muslim Politics in America," in *Muslims and Islamization in North America*, ed. Haque, 147–59.

33. To learn more about the Islamic movements of North America, visit their websites: ISNA, www.isna.net; ICNA, www.icna.org; IANA, www.iananet.org; Tablighi Jamaat, www.almadinah.org; Naqshbandi Sufi Movement, www.naqshbandi.org.

34. See Smith, *Islam in America*, 65–71.

35. Defense of Islamic identity and the well-being of the Muslim world are the dominant themes in the American Muslim discourse. Examples of works expressing these sentiments are Yvonne Haddad, "The Dynamics of Islamic Identity in North America," in *Muslims on the Americanization Path?* ed. Haddad and Esposito, 19–46; Fahhim AbdulHadi, "Protecting the Future of Islam in America," *Islamic Horizons* (March/April 1999): 30. Also see Sarvath El Hassan, "Educating Women in the Muslim World," *Islamic Horizons* (March/April 1999): 54–56; "Muslim in the West Serving Muslim Worldwide," *Islamic Horizons* (January/February 1998): 47; Altaf Hussain, "Youth and the Emerging Islamic Identity," *The Message* (June/July 1999): 21–22.

36. See Edward Said, *Covering Islam: How the Media and the Experts Determine How We See the Rest of the World* (New York: Pantheon, 1981). See also the following chapters in *Muslims and Islamization in North America*, ed. Haque: Ahmadullah Siddiqui, "Islam, Muslims and the American Media," 203–30; Jack Shaheen, "Hollywood's Reel Arabs and Muslims," 179–202; and Ibrahim Hooper, "Media Relations Tips for Muslim Activists," 231–56. For some recent examples of media bias against Islam, see M. A. Muqtedar Khan, "Public Face of Bigotry," *Washington Report on Middle East Affairs* (November/December 2000): 72.

37. Read the chapter on "The Public Practice of Islam" in Smith, *Islam in America*, 173–76.

38. See Ambereen Mirza, "Muslim Women and American Choices," *Islamic Horizons* (May/June 1999): 50; Kathleen Moore, "The Hijab and Religious Liberty: Anti-Discrimination Law and Muslim Women in the United States," in *Muslims on the Americanization Path?* ed. Haddad and Esposito, 105–28. For more on the positive role played by Muslim women in the Untied States, see Ghazala Munir, "Muslim Women in Dialogue: Breaking Walls, Building Bridges," *Muslims and Islamization in North America*, ed. Haque, 337–41.

39. I am grateful to Ahmad Totonji, the secretary-general of the International Institute of Islamic Thought, for filling me in on the early history of the MSA. Totonji was the general secretary and the president of the National MSA in its formative years in the late 1960s. He has also played a major role in its development over the years and is still one of its major patrons.

40. See Abu Sameer, "Some Milestones in Islamic Education in North America," *The Message* (May 2000): 33–35; Mohamed Ismail, "Islamic Education in the Weekend and Full-Time Islamic Schools," *The Message* (May 2000): 41–42; Nassir Ali-Akbar, "Challenges Faced by Islamic Schools," *The Message* (May 2000): 29–30.

41. Because the realists are not as well organized as the idealists and lack scholars participating in mainstream scholarship, it is not easy to refer to any of their published works as indicative of their values. A book by Ahmad Ghorab, *Subverting Islam: The Role of Orientalist Centers* (London: Minerva, 1996), is often sued a major

source book by the realists. However, one can easily learn about their views by the discussions they carry out over the Internet. Some of the archives of their views can be found at http://political.islam@listbot.com and at http://islam.guardian@ listbot.com.

42. Also see Abdul Basits's critique of the realists in "How to Integrate without Losing Muslim Identity," *Islamic Horizons* (March/April 1998): 32–34.

43. See Yusuf Talal Delorenzo, "The Fiqh Councilor in North America," in *Muslims on the Americanization Path?* ed. Haddad and Esposito, 65–86. See, for example, Yusuf Talal Delorenzo, Fiqh and Fiqh Council of North America, at http://islam.org/ Politics/Shariah.htm#S2.

44. See M. A. Muqtedar Khan, "The Manifest Destiny of American Muslims," *Washington Report on Middle East Affairs* (October/November 2000): 72. This article was published in several periodicals and on many websites. But for a fascinating discussion of American responses to this article, see the version in FreeRepublic.com, at www.freerepublic.com/forum/a39f129590fe4.htm (accessed 2002).

II

THE MAINSTREAMING
OF AMERICAN MUSLIMS:
HISTORICAL AND SOCIOLOGICAL
UNDERSTANDING

5

Muslims between the Jewish Example and the Black Experience

American Policy Implications

Ali A. Mazrui

Muslims in the United States face three cultural crises relevant to their roles as citizens: the crisis of identity, the crisis of participation, and the crisis of values and code of conduct. The crisis of identity involves their determining who they are and how to reconcile their multiple allegiances. The crisis of participation involves decisions about how far to be active in community life and public affairs. The crisis of values concerns a general code of ethical conduct and of policy preferences—ranging from Muslim attitudes to abortion to Muslim concerns about homosexuality. In this chapter, I consider each of these three crises in turn, but bearing in mind that in real life they are interrelated and intertwined.

In relation to these three concerns of identity, participation, and code of conduct, American Muslims are best studied *comparatively*. As identities, Jews and Muslims are mutually exclusive categories. One cannot be both a Muslim and a Jew. On the other hand, Blacks and Muslims are overlapping identities. Indeed, at least a third or more of the population of Muslims in the United States are either African American or African.[1]

As U.S. Muslims struggle to define themselves in America, they may have lessons to learn from both the Black experience and Jewish self-definitions. On the issue of political participation, Jews and Blacks in the United States are contrasting paradigms. American Jews may well be the most active participants of all major groups in the American political process. Jews participate not merely in the final voting but also in the choice of candidates for the primaries, in the debates of the issues, and in making political financial contributions to the candidates or parties of their choice. Between elections, Jews are also exceptionally participatory in trying to influence policy options in Congress, the White House, and state legislatures.

On the other hand, African Americans are among the least participatory of all American voters. The majority of them do not have faith in the electoral process or in the political system as a whole. A large proportion of African Americans are also too poor to read newspapers, follow political trends, or have the time to be politically active citizens.[2] American Muslims are caught between these two paradigms of massive Jewish engagement and substantial Black disengagement from the political process.

The most emotional issues for Jews and Muslims have in the past been related to foreign policy. Jews vote in American elections partly on the basis of which candidate is more committed to the state of Israel. American Muslims are emotionally involved in such foreign policy issues as Palestine, Kashmir, Iran, Afghanistan, and Iraq.[3]

African Americans, on the other hand, are much more concerned with such domestic issues as affirmative action, vouchers for schools, the politics of urban renewal, from welfare to workfare, and racial discrimination in such fields as law enforcement and the judicial process.[4]

Jews and Muslims in the United States are therefore divided mainly on foreign policy issues. They are certainly on opposing sides in the Israeli-Palestinian conflict. African Americans and Muslims are united mainly on race and civil liberties. Since September 11, 2001, the prejudices of "driving while Black" have been compounded by the bigotry of "flying while Muslim."

Because of their well-earned success, U.S. Jews are a powerful minority in the American political process. Because of their history as a disadvantaged racial group, African Americans are a relatively marginalized minority in the American political order. U.S. Muslims would like to be like the Jews in level of success (vertical admiration) but are not keen to be integrated with them (horizontal empathy).

In the American system, African Americans are not a collective role model (because of vertical marginalization). But U.S. Muslims and African Americans have been exploring ways of solidarity (horizontal interlinkage). Let us explore more fully the relationships between Islam and the Black experience, on the one hand, and Islam and the Jewish experience, on the other hand.

COMPARATIVE IDENTITY AND THE JEWISH QUESTION

Muslims in the United States have begun to outnumber Jews in the twenty-first century.[5] The two groups were already numerically neck-and-neck (about six million each) in 2000. However, contemporary Muslim influence on U.S. foreign and domestic programs continues to be only a fraction of the influence exercised by Jewish Americans. This is partly because Jewish identity is consolidated enough to be focused and probably because Jewish Americans are more strategically placed in the economy, in the media, in institutions of higher learning, and in the political process.[6]

From the point of view of response to public affairs, Muslims in the United States respond to four principal identities in themselves. First, Muslims respond to the emotional pulls and sentiments of their own *national origins* (e.g., as Pakistanis, Indonesians, Iranians, Somali, or Egyptians).[7]

Second, Muslims also act in response to their *racial identities,* given the race-conscious nature of American society. Among U.S. Muslims the racial factor has historically been particularly immediate among African Americans, who currently constitute more than 30 percent of the Muslim population of the United States.

Third, U.S. Muslims try to influence policy as *Muslims per se*—such as the activities of the American Muslim Council, which is based in Washington, D.C. The council has served as a lobby on both the Congress and the federal government on issues that have ranged from Bosnia to the Anti-Terrorism Act or the Patriot Act and their implications for civil liberties. Since September 11, 2001, U.S. Muslims have also felt exposed to new kinds of Islamophobia.[8]

Fourth, American Muslims may also act, quite simply, as Americans. As concerned or patriotic U.S. citizens, they may take positions on the size of the federal budget, or on how to deal with the trade imbalance with China, or the future role of the North Atlantic Treaty Organization, or how to deal with large-scale corporate corruption.

In all these four identities (national origins, race, religion, and U.S. citizenship), American Muslims have become more organized and less inhibited since the last quarter of the twentieth century than they ever were before—with the possible exception of the followers of the Nation of Islam, who have never been politically inhibited since they first came into being in the 1930s. Even the impact of September 11, 2001, has not forced U.S. Muslims back into a low-profile national role.

In some respects, U.S. Muslims view U.S. Jews as a role model—a successful minority. Are Muslims in the United States comparable to Jewish Americans? What do they have in common, and where do they differ? Both Muslims and Jews are anxious to avert being completely overwhelmed by the dominant Christian culture. Both Muslims and Jews are nervous about intermarriage across the religious divide. Both Muslims and Jews wish to retain a degree of cultural autonomy and distinctiveness within the wider *educational* system.

These generalizations about Muslims apply to Muslim immigrants from Pakistan, Egypt, Nigeria, Saudi Arabia, Bangladesh, Indonesia, Malaysia, Brunei, and elsewhere. On such issues they are concerned as *Muslims.* These groups have formed such Pan-Islamic organizations as the American Muslim Council, the Council on American-Islamic Relations (CAIR), the American Muslim Alliance, the Association of Muslim Social Scientists, the

Association of Muslim Scientists and Engineers, the International Institute of Islamic Thought in Washington, D.C., and the Islamic Society of North America (ISNA). I am a member of the Governing Board of the American Muslim Council, Washington, D.C., and have been chair of the Center for the Study of Islam and Democracy, Washington, D.C.

The annual conference of ISNA attracts more than twenty thousand participants. This is clearly a Pan-Islamic event and not confined to national origins.

The *American Journal of Islamic Social Sciences* (published from Washington, D.C.) does sometimes carry articles of relevance to policy and politics. Volume 12, number 3, of fall 1995, for example, included short pieces on "Islam and the West" and "Business Ethics: The Perspective of Islam." The journal is a joint publication of the Association of Muslim Social Scientists and the International Institute of Islamic Thought.

But in what sense are Muslims in the United States different from Jews? Although both American Jews and American Muslims have diverse national origins, Jews in the United States have become Jews first and national origins second, whereas Muslims are still national origins first and Muslim identity second.

It is partly a function of *time*. After all, Iranian Jews, for example, may be as Iranian as they are Jews. They will one day become more Jewish than Iranian in the United States. Will Pakistani Muslims in America one day become more Muslim than Pakistani? Is it a case of socioreligious evolution?

Muslim identity in the United States is more recent than Jewish identity. It remains to be seen whether Islam will overshadow national origins. Today, Polish Jews, British Jews, and Jewish Moroccans are identified as Jews in the United States. But while Muslims and Jews share a cultural predicament in the United States, they do not share the same status in the political economy. The Jews are well represented in Congress. They are also well represented in the print media and television, and they have a substantial presence in the commanding heights of university education. This is quite apart from the Jewish economic muscle in banking, trade, and production.

With regard to the numbers game, the *New York Times* put it in the following terms as far back as August 1995: "Muslims now outnumber Episcopalians [Anglicans] 2-to-1. With six million adherents, Islam is expected to overtake Judaism as the largest non-Christian religion in the United States by the end of the decade."[9]

The Muslim community in the United States is also facing a crisis of participation. Blacks are an example of underparticipation. Jews are a model of effective participation.[10] But is it religiously legitimate for the believer to be politically active in a system of government which is not only non-Islamic but is potentially anti-Islamic from time to time? Should a Muslim agree to vote under the U.S. Constitution and against the background of the role of the United States' controlling if not intimidating many Muslim countries? In the 1990s alone, American bombs and missiles fell on Iraq, Afghanistan, Sudan, and even Pakistan.

We could use some of the categories of medieval Islamic jurists who divided the world between *dar al-Islam* (the abode of Islam) and *dar al-harb* (the abode of war). Are Muslims in America an enclave of dar al-Islam lodged in the body politic of dar al-harb? Where does the political participation of dar al-Islam fit into the political process of dar al-harb? Or should we abandon altogether these medieval Islamic divisions of the world as being outdated? What is clear is that deliberate Muslim self-marginalization in the United States would give additional power to the pro-Israeli lobby, reduce the protection of Palestinians in the American political process, and dilute the foundations of religious tolerance in the United States.

Once again Muslims are caught between the lessons of the Black experience and the attraction of the Jewish example. African Americans outnumber not just Jewish Americans but Jews of the whole world added together. Indeed, the population of African Americans is on its way toward being double the population of world Jewry.[11]

Yet partly because African Americans grossly underutilize the American political process and have allowed themselves to be taken for granted by both the Democrats and the Republicans, the influence of African Americans is only a fraction of its own potential—and certainly far less than the influence of their Jewish compatriots.[12]

COMPARATIVE IDENTITY AND THE AFRICANA QUESTION

Meanwhile, Islam continues to expand in numbers in the United States, both within the world of the Nation of Islam and among mainstream denominations. What is the lure of Islam to the Black experience?

Among diaspora Africans of the Western Hemisphere, there have been two routes toward re-Africanization. One route is through Pan-Islam—the transition chosen by Elijah Muhammad and Malcolm X. The other is the route directly through Pan-Africanism—the transition chosen by Marcus Garvey and the Rastafari movement. Ras (Prince) Tafari was the title and name of Haile Selassie before his coronation as emperor of Ethiopia. The land of Bilal (the first African convert to Islam) is in competition with the legacy of Muhammad.

One question that arises is why Islam and the legacy of Bilal have made much more progress among North American Blacks than among Blacks in the West Indies. The second question is why African traditional religion, or beliefs rooted in sacred Africanity, sometimes appear to be more visible in the Caribbean than among Africans of North America.

One major variable was the tendency of African Americans to equate brown with Black. No sharp distinction was made in the Black American paradigm between brown Arabs and Black Africans. Indeed, until the second half of the twentieth century, almost all "colored people" in North America—whether they came from Africa or Asia or elsewhere—were treated with comparable contempt. When someone like W. E. B. DuBois argued that it was not Blacks who were a "minority" but Whites, he had added up the teeming millions of Asia with the millions of Africa to give the colored races a massive majority in the *global* population.

If the transition from brown Asian to Black African was so smooth within the Black American paradigm, the transition from Africanity to Arabness continues to be even easier. Indeed, of all the religions associated with Asia, the one that is the most *Afro-Asian* is indeed Islam. The oldest surviving Islamic academies are actually located on the African continent—including Al-Azhar University in Cairo, over a thousand years old. The Muslim Academy of Timbuktu in what is today Mali is remembered by Pan-Africanists with pride.

Nigeria has more Muslims than any Arab country, including the largest Arab country in population, Egypt. On the other hand, there are more Arabs in Africa as a whole than in Asia. Indeed, two-thirds of the Arab world lies in the African continent.[13]

Given, then, the tendency of the Black American paradigm to draw no sharp distinction between being Black and being colored, Islam's Africanness was not too diluted by its Arab origins. Elijah Muhammad, Malcolm X, and Louis Farrakhan have sometimes equated Islamization with Africanization. North American Black Muslims have seen Mecca as a port of call on the way back to the African heritage, as well as a stage on the way back toward God.

Islam in the Caribbean, on the other hand, is partly in competition with Ethiopia as a Black Mecca. Moreover, race consciousness in the Caribbean does not as readily equate Black with brown as it has historically done in the United States. The Caribbean historical experience was based on a racial hierarchy (different shades of stratification) rather than racial dichotomy (a polarized divide between white and colored).[14] Arabs in the Caribbean racial paradigm therefore belonged to a different pecking order from Africans. Indeed, Lebanese and Syrians were more likely to be counted as White rather than Black. Because of that, the Arab origins of Islam were bound to be seen as being in conflict with Islam's African credentials.

Moreover, the Caribbean has a highly visible East Indian population, a large proportion of whom are Muslims.[15] When I gave a lecture in Georgetown, Guyana, some years ago, on the subject of Islam in Africa, the overwhelming majority of my audience were not Afro-Guyanese (eager to learn more about Africa) but Indo-Guyanese (eager to learn more about Islam). The Black population in Guyana and Trinidad has a tendency to see Islam neither as African nor as Arab but as *Indian*. The result is a much slower pace of Islamic conversions among Caribbean Africans than among African Americans. Caribbean Blacks are less likely to see the Muslim holy city of Mecca as a spiritual port of call on the way back to the cultural womb of Africa. On the contrary, Mecca is more likely to be perceived as a stage of cultural refueling on the way to the Indian subcontinent. Ironically, Ethiopia, the land of Bilal, is the de facto "Mecca" of the Rastafari followers.

Indigenous African religiosity has often prospered better in the Caribbean than in Black America. Why? One reason is that cultural nationalism in Black America is rooted in *romantic gloriana* rather than *romantic primitivism*. Gloriana takes pride in the complex civilizations of ancient Africa; primitivism takes pride in the simplicity of rural African village life. In the words of Aime Cesaire, the Caribbean romantic primitivist of Martinique who coined the word *negritude:*

Hooray for those who have invented neither powder nor the compass,
Those who have tamed neither gas nor electricity,
Those who have explored neither the seas nor the skies . . .
My negritude [my blackness] is neither a tower nor a cathedral;
It plunges into the red flesh of the soil.

While this idealization of simplicity can capture the Caribbean mind, it seldom inspires the imagination of the African American. The dominant North American culture is based on the premise of "bigger, better and more beautified." Black rebellion against Anglo-racism, therefore, seeks to prove that Africa has produced civilizations in the past that were as "big and beautified" as anything constructed by the White man. Muslim civilization is seen as an African legacy.

In this cultural atmosphere of gloriana, African indigenous religion appears capable of being mistaken for "primitivism." Indigenous African rituals appear rural and village derived. While Yoruba religion does have an impressive following in parts of the United States, and its rituals are often rigorously observed, the general predisposition of the Afro-American paradigm of nationalism is afraid of appearing to be "primitive."

The Islamic option is regarded by many African Americans as a worthier rival to the Christianity of the White man. Parts of the Quran seem to be an improvement on the White man's Old Testament. The Islamic civilization once exercised dominion and power over European populations. Historically, Islamic culture refined what we now call "Arabic numerals," invented algebra, developed the zero, pushed forward the frontiers of science, and built legendary constructions from Al-Hambra in Spain to the Taj Mahal in India. Black America's paradigm of romantic gloriana is more comfortable with such a record of achievement than with the more subtle dignity of Yoruba, Igbo, or Kikuyu traditional religion.

There is a related difference to bear in mind. Cultural nationalism in

Black America often looks to ancient Egypt for inspiration—perceiving pharaonic Egypt as a *Black* civilization. Caribbean Black nationalism has shown a tendency to look to Ethiopia. The Egyptian route to Black cultural validation again emphasizes complexity and gloriana. On the other hand, the Ethiopian route to black cultural validation can be biblical and austere.

The most influential Ethiopic movement in the African diaspora has indeed become the Rastafari movement, with its Jamaican roots. This reveres Bilal's land of Ethiopia without Bilal's legacy. Named after Haile Selassie's older titled designation, the Jamaican Rastafari movement evolved a distinctive way of life, often austere, but sometimes drugged. Curiously enough, the movement's original deification of the emperor of Ethiopia was more Egyptian than Abyssinian. The fusion of emperor with God-head was almost pharaonic. The ancient kings of Egypt built the pyramids as alternative abodes. The divine monarchs did not really die when they ceased to breathe; they had merely moved to a new address. To die was, in fact, to change one's address and modify one's lifestyle. In this sense, the original theology of the Rastafari movement was a fusion of Egyptianism and prebiblical Ethiopianism. The resulting lifestyle of the Rastas, on the other hand, has been closer to romantic simplicity than to romantic gloriana. In North America, the Rasta style is still more likely to appeal to people of Caribbean origin than to long-standing African Americans with their grander paradigm of cultural pride. Bilal's land sometimes casts a stronger spell than Bilal's Islamic legacy.

Pan-Africanism and Pan-Islamism are still two alternative routes toward the African heritage. The Ethiopianism of the Rastas converges with Bilalism as Black Islam. After all, Islam first arrived in the Americas in chains—for it was brought to the Western Hemisphere by West African slaves. If Alex Haley is correct about his African ancestor, Kunta Kinte was a Muslim. So Haley assures us in *Roots*. In reality, the Haley family under slavery was better able to preserve its African pride than to protect its Islamic identity. Slavery damaged both the legacy of African culture and the legacy of Islam among the imported Black captives. But for quite a while Islam in the diaspora was destroyed more completely than was Africanity.

Yet I still remember my halal breakfast with the boxer Muhammad Ali in the Bilal Restaurant in Philadelphia in December 1992. The legacy of Bilal is Black Islam. The legacy of Bilal's country is Ethiopianism. Islamization and Africanization in North America are still perceived as alternative routes to the cultural bosom of the ancestral continent.

Within the political process of the United States, on the other hand, African American Muslims are, or can be, a bridge between other Muslims and the African American community at large. The comparison with the Jewish experience remains part of the national background. While Jews are the America of achievement, African Americans are the America of potential.

In population size, American Muslims generally are more like Jewish Americans—seven million or less. In power and national influence, American Muslims are more like African Americans—very limited representation in the citadels of power. Neither Muslims nor Blacks have a single senator on Capitol Hill.

In the economy and the liberal professions, non-Black American Muslims are becoming more and more like Jewish Americans—driven by the pursuit of the American dream and the achievement motive.[16] In access to the news media and influence on mainstream opinion, American Muslims are more like African Americans—relatively marginalized.

In universities and research institutions nationwide, the Jewish presence is remarkable in size and impact. The Black presence in higher learning is well below its potential and its impact is still modest. The Muslim presence is just beginning.

The Jewish presence in the higher echelons of the civil service of the United States, and among career diplomats, is impressive and constitutes a major input into policy formation. The Black presence in diplomacy and the civil service has increased considerably in response to affirmative action policies, but it is still a fraction of the Jewish leverage. The Muslim presence in the American foreign and diplomatic service has at best just begun.

American Muslims generally and African Americans historically have continued to be adversely affected by a crisis of underparticipation. Many Blacks have lost faith in the American political process for *racial* reasons. Many Muslims have disengaged from the political process for *religious* reasons. As cultural minorities in a liberal democracy, should Blacks and Muslims reexamine their policies on participation?

TOWARD REENGAGING MUSLIMS AND BLACKS

The largest Muslim minority in the world is in South Asia. This is the minority of some one hundred and twenty million Muslims in the Republic of India.[17] In spite of the periodic massacres of Muslims by Hindus in India, political participation by Muslims in the wider political process is one of the shields protecting Muslim interests.[18]

One of the factors that has influenced most political parties in India to be tolerant toward Muslims has been the voting leverage and participation of this 12 percent of the population. Had Indian Muslims opted out of politics completely, Indian Muslims would have been more marginalized and perhaps even more victimized than ever.

The following distinctions need to be made concerning Muslims and U.S. laws:

- (1) Can Muslims live in the United States without *obeying* U.S. laws? Can they refuse to pay U.S. taxes, even if the taxes are not remotely Islamic? (2) Can Muslims become *U.S. citizens* without allegiance to the U.S. Constitution, which is not Islamic? (3) Can Muslims insist that their money should not be used in wars against Muslim countries abroad?
- Since Muslims in the United States cannot long endure without *obeying* U.S. laws, should they not try to influence the process of *making* those laws? Voting for members of Congress and for the president constitutes part of the process of influencing the *making* of those laws—and not merely obeying the laws. Even those militant opponents of Muslim voting in U.S. elections do have to obey U.S. laws.
- The third domain is not merely Muslims voting but also Muslims running for office. This would be a process of Muslim empowerment. If elected, Muslims would not only be more directly affecting the making of the laws. The Muslims would also be influencing the *implementation* of the laws and their *enforcement.* Over time, the judicial and legal system of the United States would become more sensitized to the Muslim experience and related issues.

The central underlying question is that once American Muslims have recognized that they have to obey the laws of the United States, almost all of which have nothing to do with the Shariah, the next question is whether Muslims should strategize to help influence the *making* of those laws and their *implementation* in the hope of making those laws more sensitive to the multicultural and multireligious nature of the population of the United States.

There is another nagging question: If Muslims cannot be voters in the United States, can they even be *lawyers* or legal consultants? Do opponents of Muslims voting in U.S. elections have sons or daughters training to become U.S. lawyers?

If it is *haram* (forbidden under the Shariah) to be a voter in a U.S. election, is it ten times haram to be trained as an expert in U.S. law and practicing it? Is a Muslim American lawyer who is devoting his or her time defending Muslim clients committing at least a *double* haram?

On the other hand, if we concede that Muslims may become attorneys and lawyers in the United States, why should not Muslims become voters also? Voting is connected with law at many different stages and in many different respects.

What we have here is the complex interrelationship among lawmaking (the legislature), law interpretation (the judiciary), and law implementation (the executive). Voting is part of the process of choosing who makes these laws, who interprets them, and who implements them. The logic of the legal process is intertwined with the logic of the electoral process.

The logic of saying that it is haram to seek to influence lawmaking in the

United States would make it haram to have Muslim lawyers practicing under U.S. law. It would also make it close to haram to obey the laws of the land. Such advice would be dangerous indeed for a Muslim minority living almost anywhere in a primarily non-Muslim country.

The conclusion to be drawn is that it is to the unmistakable advantage (*maslaha*) of a Muslim minority to seek ways of influencing governance in the direction of greater enlightenment.

Like Jews, Muslims located in the United States have worldwide obligations since they are geographically located in the most powerful country in the world, with an immense capacity to either harm or benefit the rest of the coreligionists worldwide.

The United States could either do such positive things as helping Afghanistan get rid of Soviet occupation or do such negative things as bombing Khartoum and Tripoli when there is suspicion of so-called Sudanese and Libyan "terrorism."

The United States can either look the other way and let Iran arm Bosnian Muslims against Serbian genocide, or the United States can pass illegal legislation penalizing third world countries for trading with Iran and Libya. American Jews have succeeded in making the United States and its courts be a defender of Jewish interests worldwide.

American Muslims need to be active enough to monitor and influence American policy in a similar way not only in domestic affairs but also in foreign affairs. The self-denial of voting power by some U.S. Muslims is an exercise in political castration.

Had the United States in the twentieth century had very few Jewish citizens, the history of Israel and the Middle East would have been vastly different. Without a large and powerful Jewish lobby *within* the United States, U.S. generosity toward Israel would probably have substantially evaporated. At the very minimum, the United States would have spent less money on arming Israel, used fewer vetoes to defend Israel at the United Nations, been more attentive to Palestinian and Arab concerns, and been more publicly critical of Israeli atrocities. Jewish activism in U.S. politics produced pro-Jewish results.

American Muslims may never equal the power of the Jews in the U.S. system, but the Muslims may one day help provide some counterbalance in policy formation. Muslim participation and empowerment within the U.S. political system is therefore vital not only for the sake of Muslims themselves but also for the sake of the wider *ummah* (community) worldwide, and for the sake of enriching the pluralism and global representativeness of American civilization.

But how should Muslims vote? For one thing, Muslims should avoid the mistake that African Americans have made for much of the twentieth century—that of being predictably for one political party and having nowhere

else to go. In recent decades African American votes have been too predictably identified with the Democratic Party—with the result that neither
party has tried very hard to court their vote. They have simply tried not to
alienate them completely.

Muslim voters should behave differently. They should use the vote as a
leverage to reward those who take Muslim concerns seriously and to punish those who ignore those concerns. In some years, more Democrats may
deserve Muslim support than Republicans; in other years, the Republicans
may turn out to be the more Muslim-friendly.

In the *congressional* elections of the years until 2020, Muslims should vote
candidate by candidate—and not by political party. The American Muslim
Alliance has the ambition of having one Muslim senator elected by 2008.

Muslims in each congressional constituency, in each senatorial constituency, should examine the candidates according to (1) their record,
(2) their policies and pledges, and (3) their degree of sensitivity to Muslim
concerns at home and abroad.

At the congressional and Senate levels in the years until 2020, Muslims
should vote by candidates and not by party affiliation.

IN SEARCH OF ELECTORAL CARROTS AND STICKS

What about the presidential election when it ever comes? Since this is a crisis of political participation, we must confront the issue head-on. There will
always be two specific candidates close to the elections. Will one of them
be more Muslim-friendly than the other?

In the elections of 2000, should Muslims have rewarded Bill Clinton by
voting for Al Gore—rather than invest in the unknown quantity of George
W. Bush? Clinton had gone further than any other president in U.S. history
to give Islam some standing as an integral part of American society. But this
was Clinton not as a Democrat but as a pro-Muslim initiator. He had started
the process of going beyond the political convention of treating the United
States as a Judeo-Christian community only. In personal behavior, Clinton
fell below Islamic standards of family values, but in official behavior, he
was a particularly ecumenical president of the United States.

During his administration, President Clinton recognized a major Islamic
institution within the United State: the fast of Ramadan. He sent an open letter to believers wishing them a blessed fast. Under the Clinton watch, the
White House for the first time ever celebrated Eid al-Fitr to mark the end of
Ramadan at which Hillary Clinton recognized the increasing expansion of
the Muslim community within the United States and wished Muslims well.

Under Clinton's watch, the United States decided to look the other way
when the Islamic Republic of Iran was arming the government of Bosnia in

the face of an illegally imposed arms embargo by the United Nations in spite of Serbian aggression.

Also during this administration, the first Muslim chaplains of the U.S. military were appointed—with the major participation of the American Muslim Council. Arab and Muslim Americans met with the president of the United States and discussed issues of Arab and Muslim concern. Moreover, Muslim representatives were received by Anthony Lake of the National Security Council and explored with him the implications of U.S. policy toward Bosnia.

Indeed, under Clinton's watch enemies of Islam began to accuse the White House of extending hospitality to Hamas and socializing with mujahideen. Clinton stuck his political neck out for Muslims of America. While in foreign policy Clinton was no less friendly to Israel than any other U.S. president, in domestic policy he was more Muslim-friendly than any other president in the history of the United States. Did Muslims repudiate Clinton by voting for the Republican George W. Bush?[19]

To Be or Not to Be Politically Active in a Non-Muslim Society

The burden of our analysis has been that U.S. Muslims cannot afford to be politically neutral. But they should reward the party that has helped them and punish a party that betrays their interests. In 2000, Muslims did not reward the Democrats for a Muslim-friendly Clinton administration. The Muslims gambled on Bush instead.

In terms of national origins, Arab Americans have been politically active since before Israel was born. Americans of Arab origin have included Christians (e.g., the consumer advocate Ralph Nader) as well as the more politicized Muslim Arabs. In the struggle to prevent the partition of Palestine before 1947–1948, both Christian and Muslim Arabs lobbied hard in favor of "undivided Palestine." To the present day, the Arab American population in the United States is more Christian than Muslim, on balance.[20]

But after Israel was created, the "Palestinian cause" in the United States became increasingly identified with Muslims on their own. This coincided with a period of unprecedented Jewish rise in influence in the American political process—to the second half of the twentieth century.

Although the number of Arabs within the U.S. population rose from 1948 (the year of Israel's creation) to 1967 (the year of the Six-Day War), Arab impact on U.S. foreign policy probably declined during that period. This was almost certainly in direct proportion to the impressive expansion of the influence of the pro-Israeli lobby on Capitol Hill and on sections of the federal government during those years. Many Arab Americans also chose to keep a low profile out of fear of Zionist extremists and of other zealots of Middle Eastern politics.

What changed in the last quarter of the twentieth century was that Arab Americans became less inhibited, felt less politically intimidated, and were more sophisticated in skills of utilizing the American political process. However, today they are still subject to some of the tensions and divisions of the wider Arab world. They have also become more vulnerable to prejudice and ethnic profiling since September 11, 2001.

The foreign policy issue on which South Asian Muslims in the United States feel most strongly about is perhaps Kashmir. There is constant lobbying on Capitol Hill either for resolutions to censure India for human rights violations in Kashmir or for legislative action in search of a solution. There is also a constant flow of brochures, pamphlets, and news updates on Kashmir not only targeted at Congress but also distributed widely to campuses, news media, and other contributors to policy formation. Now that India and Pakistan have become nuclear powers, there is anxiety that Kashmir might become a nuclear trigger in the years ahead.

While the majority of South Asian Muslims in the United States favor self-determination for Kashmir or union with Pakistan, a minority of Muslim citizens of India would rather see Kashmir remain part of India. It is worth remembering that India today has more than a hundred and twenty million Muslims (the fourth largest concentration of Muslims after Indonesia, Pakistan, and Bangladesh). Many Muslims of India are ambivalent about Kashmir. Do they want Kashmiris to have self-determination and risk depriving India of its only state with a Muslim majority? Or would they rather have Kashmir remain part of India and strengthen the plight of other Muslims in India? Muslims from India who have become U.S. citizens betray the same ambivalence about Kashmir.

However, those American Muslims who favor the status quo for Kashmir have decided to keep a low profile—especially since most of them are appalled by the human rights violations often perpetrated by the Indian troops in Kashmir and by Hindu militants in Gujerat. The most vocal American Muslims on Kashmir are those who favor self-determination for the embattled people of that province.

From the point of view of racial identity, the great majority of Muslims in the United States are, of course, people of color. Their position on apartheid in South Africa before the 1990s was almost unanimous. There was Muslim consensus that the United States should impose and maintain sanctions against the racist regime in Pretoria (as it then was). The American Muslim Council went into a kind of strategic alliance with TransAfrica, led by the African American activist Randall Robinson. TransAfrica was by far the more active U.S. organization against apartheid. But many Muslims supported Robinson. And the American Muslim Council held a major conference in the 1980s on the theme "Islam against Apartheid" with major international speakers, including Muslim activists from South Africa itself.

The United States was persuaded (especially by TransAfrica and its allies) to impose wide-ranging sanctions on the racist regime in South Africa. The sanctions lasted until after Nelson Mandella was released and the African National Congress was legalized in the 1990s. Imam Warith Dean Mohammed, the African American Sunni crusader, played an important role in consolidating the Muslim crusade against apartheid and racism.

The most race-conscious of all those who call themselves Muslims in the United States are, however, the followers of the Nation of Islam, currently led by Minister Louis Farrakhan. Foreign policy was part and parcel of the birth of the movement, for the founder was an immigrant reportedly born in Mecca, who arrived in the United States in 1931. Was Farrad Muhammad an Arab? In pigmentation he was very fair, but he identified himself with the Black people of the city of Detroit.

Farrad Muhammad disappeared without a trace in 1934. His successor as leader of the Nation of Islam was Elijah Muhammad.[21] The foreign policy tests came with the outbreak of World War II. Elijah Muhammad enjoined his followers that as Muslims they had no obligation to fight for the flag of the United States. He was imprisoned from 1942 to 1946 because of that position.

The dilemma between Islam and the flag in the United States continued afterward. The boxing champion Muhammed Ali, a follower of the Nation of Islam, refused in 1967 to fight for the United States in Vietnam. He was convicted and stripped of his championship in retaliation. He in turn reportedly threw away his Olympic gold medal in protest. It was not until 1971 that the Supreme Court of the United States revoked his conviction and helped restore his championship title, by protecting his religious freedom and freedom of expression under the American Constitution. At the 1996 Olympic games in Atlanta, Ali was also ceremonially honored with a replacement of his ostensibly "lost" Olympic medal.

I and other AMC colleagues spent five hours with Minister Louis Farrakhan at his home in Chicago in January 1996, which was, of course, after the Million Man March of October 1995. Did the Million Man March have foreign policy implications? Farrakhan told us that soon after the march he had received congratulations from Muamar Qaddafy, the head of state of Libya. Qaddafy was most impressed by the success of the march.

Farrakhan also told us about his plans to tour both the Muslim world and Africa. He started the tour the following month—stirring much debate in the United States when he was reported to have visited Iran, Iraq, Syria, and Libya, which were regarded with particular hostility by the U.S. government.

When Libyan sources reported that Qaddafy had offered Farrakhan $1 billion for his movement, and Farrakhan confirmed this offer on his return to the United States, there were demands in Congress that Farrakhan be compelled to register as a "foreign agent." Farrakhan retorted that he would be prepared to discuss such a possibility if several members of Congress would similarly register as agents of the state of Israel. In any case, Qaddafy's proposed $1 billion to the Nation of Islam was for schools, clinics, and social services, and not for political lobbying or political activism, Farrakhan insisted.[22] The wrangling continued inconclusively.

When U.S. Muslims behave as Muslims (heirs of the Hijrah, the Prophet's migration to Medina), and when they behave as concerned Americans (heirs of the *Mayflower*), they have operated under a number of paradoxes. Let us examine those paradoxes affecting codes of conduct.

BETWEEN POLITICAL VALUES AND A MORAL CODE

The first paradox is that while American secularism is good news for Muslims (separating church from state), American libertarianism is bad news for Islam (e.g., the latest American debate as to whether same-sex marriages should be legally recognized nationwide as they already are in Hawaii).

The Democratic Party in the United States is more insistent on separating church from state, including its opposition to prayer in schools. This draws some Muslim parents toward the Democrats, since the Muslim parents do not want their kids to be under peer pressure to recite Christian prayers.

On the other hand, the Republicans generally are stronger on traditional family values and are more opposed to sexual libertarianism. This draws many Muslims (especially immigrant Asians) to the Republican Party. Most Muslims share Republican concerns about abortion and gay rights.[23]

The second paradox concerns the legacy of the Clinton administration. We have mentioned that while Clinton's administration had been no more pro-Israel than any other U.S. administration since Lyndon Johnson, this same Clinton administration had domestically made more friendly gestures toward U.S. Muslims than any previous administration. We referred to the president's greetings to Muslims during the fast of Ramadan in 1996. We referred to the first lady hosting a celebration of Eid al-Fitr (the festival of the end of Ramadan) in the White House in April 1996 and 1998. Vice President Al Gore visited a mosque in the fall of 1995. And the first Muslim chaplain to serve the ten thousand Muslims in the U.S. Armed Forces was sworn into the Air Force under Clinton's watch. Clinton also appointed Osman Siddiqui as the first Muslim ambassador of the United States to Fiji, Nauru, Onga, and Tuvalu.

The Clinton gestures toward Muslims were sufficiently high-profile that a hostile article in the *Wall Street Journal* in March 1996 raised the specter of "Friends of Hamas in the White House"—alleging that some of the president's Muslim guests were friends of Hamas and supporters of the Palestinian movement. The critic in the *Wall Street Journal* (Steve Emerson) had a long record of hostility toward U.S. Muslims. His television program on PBS entitled *Jihad in America* (1994) alleged that almost all terrorist activities by Muslims worldwide were partially funded by U.S. Muslims. President Clinton's friendly gestures to Muslims probably infuriated this self-appointed crusader of Islamophobia.[24] But did Clinton start a process of recognizing Islam as part of America that may survive even the impact of September 11, 2001?

The third paradox facing U.S. Muslims is that in *foreign* policy, the Republicans in recent U.S. history before September 11, 2001, had been greater friends of Muslims than have Democrats—whereas in *domestic* policies the Democrats are probably more friendly to Muslims than the Republicans. We shall return to that thesis soon.

The fourth paradox concerns the two Islams in the United States—indigenous and immigrant. But let us first return to the first paradox. In the United States, Western secularism has protected minority religious groups by insisting on the separation of church and state. That is a major reason why the Jews in the United States have been among the greatest defenders of the separation of church and state. Any breach of that principle could lead to the imposition of some practices of the religious majority—like forcing Jewish children to participate in Christian prayers at school.

In discussing the role of American Muslims qua Muslims (heirs of the Hijrah), we have to look more closely at their moral concerns in relation to American culture. Curiously enough, American secularism is indeed good news for Muslims in the United States. The bad news is the expanding arena of American *libertarianism*. Secularism in the political process does indeed help protect minority religions from the potential intrusive power of the Christian Right. On the other hand, expanding American libertarianism in such fields as sexual mores alarms both the Christian Right and Muslim traditionalists in the United States.

These moral concerns in turn have consequences on how American Muslims relate to the wider political divide between Republicans and Democrats in both foreign and domestic policies.

Since the 1990s, more and more American Muslims are registering to vote and seeking to influence candidates in elections. On such social issues as family values and sexual mores, Muslims often find themselves more in tune with Republican rhetoric and concerns. On the need for a more strict separation of church and state, which helps protect religious minorities, it is the more liberal Democrats who offer a better protection to Muslims. Let us look at these contradictions more closely.

The First Amendment permits religious minorities to practice their religions in relative peace. Of course, like all doctrines, secularism has its fanatics who sometimes want to degrade the sacred rather than permitting it. But at its best a secular state is a refuge of safety for minority religions. It is in that sense that American secularism is a friend of Muslims living in the United States.

But while secularism is a divorce from formal religion, Muslims see libertarianism as a dilution of spirituality. One can be without a formal religion and still be deeply spiritual in a humanistic sense. John Stuart Mill and Bertrand Russell were without formal religion, yet each had deeply spiritual values. Albert Schweitzer, the Nobel laureate for peace, was at times an agnostic—but he was deeply committed to the principle of reverence for life, even protecting the lives of insects in Africa.

Religion has been declining in influence in the West since the days of the Renaissance and the Enlightenment. But it is mainly from the twentieth century that *spirituality* in the West has taken a nosedive. From an Islamic perspective, America has become not only less religious but dangerously less spiritual. America has become not only more secular but dangerously more libertarian.

It is the libertarianism that is regarded as a danger to Muslims living in the Western Hemisphere. There is the libertarian materialism of excessive acquisitiveness (greed), libertarian consumption (consumerism), the materialism of the flesh (excessive sexuality), the materialism of excessive self-indulgence (from alcoholism to drugs). These four forms of libertarianism could result in a hedonistic way of life, a pleasure-seeking career.

What is more, Muslim parents fear that American libertarianism is likely to influence the socialization and upbringing of the next generation of Muslim children—excessive levels of acquisitiveness, consumerism, and diverse forms of sexuality. It is because of all these considerations that Islam within the United States feels threatened less by American secularism than by American libertarianism.

BETWEEN IDEOLOGY AND PRAGMATISM

But there are also the political and ideological shifts in power in the Western world as a whole—between liberals and conservatives, between Tories and Socialists, between Democrats and Republicans. American Muslims have been sensitive to those shifts internationally. What does the end of the Cold War mean for the Muslim countries? In much of the Western world in recent times, it is not simply a case of more conservative parties winning elections; the whole political systems in France and Britain have been moving to the right. Muslims worldwide have wondered about the implications of all these developments and changes for Islam today.

American Muslim leaders follow global trends with mixed feelings. What used to be major socialist or internationalist parties have not only shrunk in support—they have also diluted their left-wing orientation. Communism is crippled. A party of the right may lose an election—as the Tory Party has done in Britain in the last general election—but it lost to a Labour

Party that is a much more conservative force today than it was thirty or fifty years ago.

Indeed, the leader of the British Labour Party had already persuaded the party to get rid of clause 4 in its constitution—a clause that had for so long committed the party to the socialist ambition of nationalizing the means of production, distribution, and exchange. In France, when the late socialist president François Mitterand was ailing, so was his old style of socialism. The system had not only moved to the right—it had become a little more racist. There is also more Islamophobia in France today than there has been at any other time in the twentieth century. The move to the right has coincided with greater anti-Muslim and anti-immigrant sentiments.[25]

What about the United States? Is it simply a case of the Republicans winning greater control of the Congress? Or are all three branches of government moving to the right with only minor variations between the two parties? Was the Clinton style of "New Democrat" a reflection of the force of conservative influence? Is the U.S. system as a whole going conservative—and how is it going to affect Muslims? Is the shift short-term or long-term?

In France, the move to the right has triggered off some degree of xenophobia, or hostility toward foreigners. French cultural xenophobia has included Islamophobia. In Germany, xenophobia has included Turkophobia, or hostility toward the Turks—which in turn has included elements of Islamophobia. Turkish houses have been fire-bombed, and Turks have died at the hands of German neo-Nazis. U.S. Muslims are bracing themselves for similar chauvinism against immigrants. After the Oklahoma City bombing, at least 227 hate crimes were committed against Muslims, according to the Council for American-Islamic Relations. Muslims braced themselves for more hate crimes after the atrocities against the U.S. embassies in Kenya and Tanzania in 1998 and since September 11, 2001.

In the United States, changes in regime between Republicans and Democrats has had historical paradoxes. In Middle Eastern politics, Republican administrations in the twentieth century sometimes showed greater ability to stand up to Israel than have Democratic administrations. American Muslims have noted that.

In 1956, it was Republican President Dwight Eisenhower who insisted on a halt to the occupation of parts of Egypt by Britain, France, and Israel—and compelled the Israelis to withdraw from the Sinai, which they had occupied in the Suez War of 1956.

It was the first President George Bush who put his foot down against the indirect use of American money on illegal Jewish settlements on Arab occupied lands. George H. W. Bush did lead Desert Storm against Iraq in the Gulf War of 1991, but perhaps no U.S. president (Republican or Democrat) would have permitted Iraq to annex Kuwait. What is more, a Democratic president might have authorized a march onto Baghdad.

On the other hand, it was a Democratic president, Harry S. Truman, who gave the U.S. green light in 1947 for the creation of the State of Israel—setting the stage for fifty years of Arab-Israeli wars, Palestinian suffering, and mutual hatreds.

It was Democratic president Lyndon Johnson's administration that helped Israel (with logistical intelligence) win the June war of 1967 in six days, which resulted in the occupation of Arab lands in Gaza, Sinai, Golan Heights, and the West Bank. It was Democratic president Bill Clinton who came closer than any U.S. president toward giving silent legitimization to Jewish settlements in occupied Arab territories. Clinton did once even consider recognizing Jerusalem as the capital of Israel (a brief temptation). The Clinton administration was for a while more militant in trying to isolate Iran internationally than previous U.S. administrations had been since the Islamic revolution in 1979. The election of Muhammad Khatami as president of Iran in 1997 began to tip the scale. Khatami was more liberal.

It was, on the other hand, Republican Richard Nixon who took a position sympathetic to Pakistan and against India in the Indo-Pakistani conflict in 1971 when Nixon was in power. Nixon was hated in India for it. What all this means is that in foreign policy, the Republicans before George W. Bush were often greater friends of the Muslim world than the Democrats. Did September 11, 2001, change this particular equation?

But domestically the Democrats are the party of minorities and the secular state. And so although Muslims have not emerged very explicitly as a political minority, the party most likely to be sensitive to domestic diversity is the Democratic Party. If Muslims are discriminated against or harassed at home within the United States, the Democrats are more likely to come to the rescue than the Republicans.

In foreign policy, on the other hand, the Republicans in the twentieth century were greater friends of the Muslim world than were the Democrats. The antiterrorist legislation proposed and signed by the Clinton administration was probably both a matter of domestic policy and foreign policy. The divide between Republicans and Democrats was therefore even. Since September 11, 2001, Muslim and Arab profiling has been done by a Republican administration.

AMERICAN ISLAM: IMMIGRANT AND HOME-GROWN

In places like Britain, France, and Germany, *both* Islam as a civilization and local Muslims as residents are widely regarded as foreign even when the Euro-Muslims are citizens of the European countries. In the United States, half the Muslim population will soon consist of descendants of families who have been Americans for hundreds of years. A third of Muslims in the

United States are already African Americans. This creates a different situation from that of Europe.

In Europe, both Islam and Muslims may be regarded as foreign; but in the United States, such an equation is increasingly difficult. Islam may be new, but its followers will include millions who have been part of American history for two or three hundred years. The African American Muslim population is expanding significantly.

But even the immigrant half of the Muslim population of the United States is operating in a country of immigrants anyhow—unlike the immigrant Muslims of France, Britain, and Germany.

In the United States, it has been possible for an immigrant with a heavy foreign accent to become the most outstanding nonpresidential American statesman of the second half of the twentieth century—Henry Kissinger, the brilliant Jewish secretary of state under President Nixon.

So even the immigrant Muslims in the United States are, in that special American sense, less foreign than the Muslim immigrants in Europe. But there is no doubt of the reality that the United States faces a "Tale of Two Islams."

I use *indigenous* in the United States in this chapter to describe people who have been American for at least two centuries. We might therefore conclude that indigenous American Muslims are mainly African Americans, with a small percentage of white Americans.

Immigrant Americans, for the purposes of this chapter, are those who have been part of American society for less than a century. Immigrant American Muslims are mainly from Asia, the Middle East, and Africa in recent times. Some are from Muslim Europe.

While indigenous American Muslims are highly sensitive to issues of domestic policy in the United States, immigrant American Muslims are more sensitive to the *foreign* policy of the United States.

The problem of low-income families among *indigenous* Muslims may be above the national average; that is, there are too many poor families. On the other hand, the proportion of families in the professional class among *immigrant* Muslims (teachers, lawyers, doctors, engineers, etc.) may be above the national average.

Indigenous Muslims (especially African Americans) tend to rebel against the mythology of the American dream as a pursuit of personal advancement in conditions of economic freedom. Immigrant Muslims, on the other hand, seem to be like Jewish Americans—disproportionately persuaded that there is more opportunity than oppression in capitalism.

Indigenous American Muslims are new to Islam but old to America (though Islam did once arrive in the Americas with enslaved Africans in chains). Today, African American Muslims are fully Americanized but not always fully Islamized. Warath Dean Mohammed is among those who are both fully American and fully Muslim.

With immigrant Muslims, the situation is the reverse. They are old to Islam but new to America. They are often substantially Islamized but not yet fully Americanized.

Indigenous American Muslims are overwhelmingly *unilingual*—speaking only English (standard or dialect or both), though they often learn some modest Arabic for purposes of Islamic ritual. Immigrant Muslims are often bilingual and even trilingual. At home they may even speak more than one *European* language. Lebanese Americans may speak French, Arabic, as well as English.

Indigenous American Muslims are weak economically, but as African Americans they have considerable potential political leverage. After all, the population of African Americans generally is much larger than the population of the Jews of the whole world added together. Yet at the moment the influence of African Americans on U.S. foreign policy is only a fraction of the influence of Jewish Americans. Will the difference in leverage narrow in the twenty-first century? Will African American influence reflect the political importance of Islam among American Blacks?

If indigenous Americans are currently economically weak but potentially strong politically, the immigrant Muslims may be in the reverse predicament. They may be politically weak but with considerable potential for economic and professional leverage.

The population of indigenous Muslims may expand as a result of the new Republican attacks on welfare, Medicaid, and the safety nets that had once been provided for the Black poor. More poor Blacks may turn to Islam. On the other hand, the population of immigrant Muslims may decline as a result of more strict laws against immigration from all parts of the world. Muslim immigration may also suffer from how the new antiterrorist legislation is actually implemented on the ground. Individual immigration officers might be encouraged to be particularly harsh to visa candidates from the Muslim world in the aftermath of September 11, 2001.[26]

But when all is said and done, the two sets of Muslims in the United States (indigenous and immigrant) are in the process of being forged into the largest Muslim nation in the special hemisphere of Christopher Columbus, the Americas. In 1492, the Islamic presence in Spain was ended, and Christopher Columbus opened up the Americas for the West. Five hundred years later, an Islamic presence was trying to establish itself in the lands that Columbus had helped open up for Spain and the West. Was history indulging its ironic sense of humor all over again? The heirs of the Hijrah became simultaneously heirs to the *Mayflower.*

In foreign policy, the four identities of U.S. Muslims play their part. The issue of national origins, the membership of a racial group, the power of religious affiliation, and the moral concerns of U.S. Muslims as ordinary Americans—such a confluence of identities is part of the politics of pluralism, part of policy formation in a liberal democratic order.

But in the final analysis the cultural dimension of the American Muslim experience is not simply this crisis of *identity*. It is also the simultaneous and interrelated crises of *participation* and *code of conduct*. It still remains a drama in three acts. Act I: Am I an American Muslim or a Muslim American? Which comes first—and under what circumstances? Act II: Do I accept to be a participant in the American constitutional process? Act III: Is my code of conduct as a Muslim compatible with my code of conduct as an American?

I have sought to demonstrate in this chapter that one approach toward understanding Muslims in the American public space is to view Muslims *comparatively*. The Muslim predicament in the United States is caught between the lessons of the Black experience and the power of the Jewish example.

Jews are the America of achievement. Blacks are the America of potential. Muslims are caught between the pursuit of their potential and the lure of ultimate achievement. The struggle for readjustment continues.

NOTES

This study is indebted to the author's previous work on American Muslims and policy formation in the United States.

1. Jonah Blank of the *U.S. News & World Report* points out, "The two largest Muslim groups in the United States are native-born African-Americans (42 percent)." See Jonah Blank, "The Muslim Mainstream," U.S. Department of State, International Information Programs, July 20, 1998; available at http://usinfo.state.gov/usa/islam/a072098.htm.

2. According to the United States Census Bureau, African American voter participation in congressional elections in 1998 was 40 percent, a 3 percent increase from 1994. U.S. Census Bureau, "African Americans Defy Trend of Plunging Voter Turnout, Census Bureau Reports," July 19, 2000. In the 2000 presidential elections, "The voting rate for African American citizens increased by 4 percentage points, to 57 percent. . . . The voting rate for all citizens was 60 percent." U.S. Census Bureau, "Registered Voter Turnout Improved in 2000 Presidential Election, Census Bureau Reports," February 27, 2002.

According to Human Rights Watch:

Among Florida's African American residents, the impact of the state's disenfranchisement laws is particularly dramatic: 31.2 percent of Black men in Florida—more than 200,000 potential Black voters—were excluded from the polls. Assuming the voting pattern of Black ex-felons would have been similar to the vote by Black residents in Florida generally, the inability of these ex-offenders to vote had a significant impact on the number voting for Vice President Gore. ("US Election 2000. Losing the Vote: The Impact of Felony Disenfranchisement Laws," November 8, 2000.)

The poverty rate of African Americans in 2000 was 22.1 percent, significantly higher than the national average of 11.3 percent during that same year. See U.S. Census Bureau, "Nation's Household Income Stable in 2000, Poverty Rate Virtually Equals Record Low, Census Bureau Reports," September 21, 2001.

In higher education, the total 1,640,700 Blacks enrolled in degree-granting institutions in the United States in 1999 comprised 11.5 percent of all students enrolled.

See U.S. Department of Education, National Center for Education Statistics, Higher Education General Information (HEGIS), "Fall Enrollment in Colleges and Universities" surveys; and Integrated Postsecondary Education Data System (IPEDS), April 2001.

3. Reporting on Jewish Americans' lobby for Israel, Lisa Richardson of the *Los Angeles Times* writes:

> The success of Jewish groups in helping to defeat two longtime African American members of Congress has further frayed the damaged relationship between leaders of black and Jewish organizations. In the wake of Tuesday's ousting of Rep. Cynthia A. McKinney in a Georgia Democratic primary, some African American political activists and leaders are expressing outrage at Jewish organizations that targeted McKinney because she had expressed pro-Palestinian sentiments about the Middle East crisis. McKinney lost to Denise Majette, a former state judge who is also black but benefited from out-of-state contributions from Jewish groups and crossover voting by Republicans. Also this year, another black member of Congress, Rep. Earl F. Hilliard of Alabama, who had pro-Arab support, was defeated by Artur Davis, who was funded by backers of Israel. ("Political Ties between Blacks and Jews Strained," *Los Angeles Times*, August 23, 2002)

Jeff Phillips reports that 88.7 percent of Muslim Americans want an independent Palestinian state. See his "Muslims 'Key' to US Elections," U.S. Department of State, International Programs, August 29, 2000; Available at www.usinfo.state.gov/usa/islam/phillips.htm.

4. For more analysis of African Americans' political participation in the United States, see Jeremy D. Mayer, *Running on Race: Racial Politics in Presidential Campaigns, 1960–2000* (New York: Random House, 2002).

5. In August 1995, the *New York Times* estimated the U.S. Muslim population to be six million. See the front-page article on Islam in the United States, *New York Times*, August 28, 1995. The television program *Frontline* also points out, "The estimated 5–7 million Muslims in the United States include both immigrants and those born in America (three-quarters of whom are African Americans)." See "Portraits of Ordinary Muslims: United States," *Frontline*, PBS Television, May 9, 2002.

6. In an article in the Saudi Arabian English-language online newspaper *arabnews.com*, Mark Weber, the director of the Institute for Historical Review, examines the achievements and political influence of Jewish Americans in the United States. He quoted Jewish author and political science professor Benjamin Ginsberg as saying, "Since the 1960s, Jews have come to wield considerable influence in American economic, cultural, intellectual and political life. Jews played a central role in American finance during the 1980s, and they were among the chief beneficiaries of that decade's corporate mergers and reorganizations."

> Today, though barely 2 percent of the nation's population is Jewish, close to half its billionaires are Jews. The chief executive officers of the three major television networks and the four largest film studios are Jews, as are the owners of the nation's largest newspaper chain and the most influential single newspaper, the *New York Times*. . . . The role and influence of Jews in American politics is equally marked. . . .

Jews are only 3 percent of the nation's population and comprise 11 percent of what this study defines as the nation's elite. However, Jews constitute more than 25 percent of the elite journalists and publishers, more than 17 percent of the leaders of important voluntary and public interest organizations, and more than 15 percent of the top ranking civil servants.

Two well-known Jewish writers, Seymour Lipset and Earl Raab, pointed out in their 1995 book, *Jews and the New American Scene*:

> During the last three decades Jews [in the United States] have made up 50 percent of the top two hundred intellectuals . . . 20 percent of professors at the leading universities . . . 40 percent of partners in the leading law firms in New York and Washington . . . 59 percent of the directors, writers, and producers of the 50 top-grossing motion pictures from 1965 to 1982, and 58 percent of directors, writers, and producers in two or more primetime television series.

The influence of American Jewry in Washington, notes the Israeli daily *Jerusalem Post*, is "far disproportionate to the size of the community, Jewish leaders and U.S. officials acknowledge. But so is the amount of money they contribute to [election] campaigns." One member of the influential Conference of Presidents of Major American Jewish Organizations "estimated Jews alone had contributed 50 percent of the funds for [President Bill] Clinton's 1996 re-election campaign."

See Mark Weber, "A Look at The Powerful Jewish Lobby," *arabnews.com*, July 14, 2002.

Richard Cohen, a columnist for the *Washington Post*, also notes in an article that "At the elite Ivy League schools, Jews make up 23 percent of the student body. They are a measly 2 percent of the U.S. population." See "A Study in Differences," *Washington Post*, May 28, 2002.

7. For an overview of Muslims in the United States, see Yvonne Y. Haddad, *The Muslims of America* (New York: Oxford University Press, 1991).

8. Other groups and organizations established by Muslims in the United States to correct stereotypes and influence policy include the Committee for American-Islamic Relations, based in Washington, D.C., and the Muslim Public Affairs Council; see "Muslims Learn to Pull Political Ropes in U.S.," *Christian Science Monitor*, February 5, 1996, p. 10.

9. James Brooke, "Amid Islam's Growth in the U.S., Muslims Face a Surge of Attacks," *New York Times*, August 28, 1995, p. A1.

10. According to an article by the Religion Writers Association, "In the 2000 election, Dr. Saeed [Dr. Agha Saeed is President of the American Muslim Alliance] counted nearly 700 Muslim candidates across the United States, of which 152 were elected. This year he estimates that about 70 American Muslims are running for office." See "9/11 Fallout: Muslims Fall Back from Seeking Office," www.*religionwriters.com*, August 26, 2002. For more analysis on American Muslims' political participation in recent years, see Alexander Rose, "How Did Muslims Vote in 2000?" *Middle East Quarterly* 8 (Summer 2001).

According to the Joint Center for Political and Economic Studies, the total number of Black elected (federal, state, substate regional, county, municipal, judicial, and law enforcement and education) officials in the United States in 2000 was 9,040.

See "Black Elected Officials" at www.jointcenter.org/DB/detail/BEO.htm (accessed in 2000).

Of the Jewish Americans' political participation, Stephen Steinlight of the American Jewish Committee, writing on immigration issues and a concern of diminished Jewish political power in the United States, points out, "Not that it is the case that our disproportionate political power (pound for pound the greatest of any ethnic/cultural group in America). . . . Jewish voter participation also remains legendary; it is among the highest in the nation. Incredible as it sounds, in the recent presidential election more Jews voted in Los Angeles than Latinos." See Stephen Steinlight, "The Jewish Stake in America's Changing Demography," Center for Immigration Studies, October 2001.

11. According to the U.S. Census Bureau, the number of residents in the United States who reported as African American alone or in combination with one of more other races in the 2000 Census was 36.4 million. U.S. Census Bureau, "African American History Month: February 2002," January 17, 2002. According to the prime minister of Malaysia, Mahathir bin Mohamad, there are currently thirteen million Jews in the whole world. Mahathir bin Mohamad, "The Muslim World Is Hopelessly Weak," *International Herald Tribune*, July 30, 2002.

12. In the 2000 presidential election, 90 percent of African Americans voted for the Democratic candidate, Al Gore. See "National Coalition's Efforts Lead to Upsurge in Black Voter Turnout," National Coalition on Black Civic Participation, November 10, 2000.

13. According to the *World Factbook,* as of July 2001, the total estimated population of Algeria, Egypt, Libya, Morocco, Sudan, and Tunisia was 182.9 million (source: compiled from the *CIA World Factbook,* 2001). These six African countries alone, which are part of the Arab League, make up the majority of that organization's widely reported total population of 281 million.

14. For more analysis on racial stratification in the West Indies, see J. A. Rogers, *Nature Knows No Color-Line,* 3d ed. (New York: Helga Rogers, 1952), 3–26. This book was reprinted by Macmillan in 1972, with an introduction and commentary written by John Henry Clarke.

15. For example, as of July 2001, Trinidad and Tobago and Guyana have populations of 1.16 million (40.3 percent East Indian) and 697,181 (49 percent East Indian), respectively. Moreover, Trinidad and Tobago and Guyana have Muslim populations of 5.8 percent and 9 percent, respectively (source: compiled from the *CIA World Factbook,* 2001).

16. According to a study by the Center for Immigration Studies, in 2000, Muslims constituted 73 percent of Middle Eastern immigrants to the United States. (This study includes as Middle Easterners immigrants from Afghanistan, Bangladesh, Pakistan, North African countries, and Mauritania.) According to the study, Middle Eastern immigrant men in the United State have median earnings of $39,000, slightly more than the $38,000 average for native workers. Moreover, 19 percent of Middle Eastern immigrants own their own businesses, compared to 11 percent of natives. Steven A. Camarota, "Immigrants from the Middle East: A Profile of the Foreign-born Population from Pakistan to Morocco," Center for Immigration Studies, August 2002.

17. India's Muslim population is now estimated at 150 million. Thomas L. Friedman, "Where Freedom Reigns," *New York Times,* August 14, 2002.

18. For more analysis on Hindu-Muslim relations in India, see Peter Van Der Veer

and Kevin Michael Doak, *Religious Nationalism: Hindus and Muslims in India* (Berkeley: University of California Press, 1994).

19. According to an American Muslim Alliance (AMA) postelection survey, "more than 80 percent of the Muslim Americans cast their votes for George W. Bush [in the November 2000 presidential election]. About 10 percent voted for Ralph Nader." In Florida, where the presidential election was won officially by "537 votes out of 5.8 million cast" (J. Lantigua, "How the GOP Gamed the System in Florida," *The Nation,* April 30, 2001), the AMA reports, "Of the 100,000 Muslims in Florida, about 60,000 are eligible voters, . . . an exclusive exit poll of Florida Muslims, 91 percent of those polled indicated that they had voted for George W. Bush." AMA Election Report, "Muslim Vote," Freemont, Calif., November 12, 2000; available at www.amaweb.org/election2000/ama_election_report.htm.

20 The Arab American Foundation reports that, of the nearly three million Arab Americans in the United States, Christians comprise 77 percent (Catholic 42, percent; Orthodox, 23 percent; and Protestant, 12 percent), and Muslims comprise 23 percent. Helena Samhan, "Arab Americans," *www.aaiusa.org/definition.htm*; article originally printed in *Grolier's Multimedia Encyclopedia* (2001).

21. For a biography, see Malu Halassa, *Elijah Muhammad* (New York: Chelsea House, 1900).

22. See the reports in the *Amsterdam News*, February 3, 1996; *New York Times*, February 22, 1996; *Afro-American*, February 10, 1996; *Chicago Tribune*, February 22, 1996; *Chicago Defender*, February 1, 1996, among others.

23. According to a Zogby International survey of 1,781 Muslims entitled "American Muslim Poll, Nov/Dec 2001," Muslim and Republican Party voters in the United States share similar social values. According to Zogby International, "American Muslims are conservative on many issues. They support the death penalty (68 percent); oppose gay marriages (71 percent); support making abortions more difficult to obtain (57 percent); oppose physician assisted suicide (61 percent), and support banning the sale and display of pornography (65 percent). . . . American Muslims support prayer (53 percent) and the display of the Ten Commandments (59 percent) in schools, and they support vouchers to send children to private schools (68 percent)." See Zogby International, news release, "American Muslim Poll, Nov/Dec 2001," December 19, 2001; available at www.projectmaps.com/PMReport.htm.

24. Steve Emerson's article appeared in the *Wall Street Journal*, March 13, 1996, p. 14.

25. Even liberal intellectuals in France opposed the freedom of Muslim girls to wear headscarves. For one analysis of this event, see Norma C. Moruzzi, "A Problem with Headscarves: Contemporary Complexities of Political and Social Identity," *Political Theory* (November 1994): 653–72.

In addition, the European Union is preparing to take harsh immigration measures against third world countries. According to the *Singapore Strait Times* newspaper:

Efforts to forge Europe-wide policies to tackle illegal immigration suffered a setback when EU governments split publicly over linking aid to cooperation on tackling illegal migration. At a meeting on Monday the foreign ministers of France, Sweden and Finland opposed British, Italian, Dutch, Spanish and German-backed plans to make the European

Union's 9.3 billion euro ([Singapore] S$15.7 billion) development aid budget conditional on repatriation agreements. "The EU does not go this far when it comes to violations of human rights and the war on terrorism, so it is sending the wrong signals going so much further on illegal immigration," said Swedish Foreign Minister Anna Lindh. . . . The dissenters however want the EU to focus on giving incentives in extra aid and technical support to Third World countries that help stem the flow of asylum seekers and economic migrants. Shocked by a surge in support for anti-immigration populist parties across Western Europe, EU leaders are rushing to find ways to get tough on the influx of an estimated 500,000 illegal migrants a year into the bloc. (*Singapore Strait Times*, "EU Nations Split over Linking Aid to Migration Curbs," June 19, 2002)

26. The number of temporary visas issued to Middle Easterners (except Israel) and South Asians by the U.S. State Department between September 11, 2001, and March 31, 2002, and temporary visas issued the same time last year declined by 41.2 percent, from 315,120 to 196,190. Joseph A. D'Agostino, "U.S. Has Given 50,000 Visas since 9-11 to New Visitors from the Middle East," *Human Events*, December 8, 2001.

6

Muslims in the American Body Politic

Mohammed Nimer

The American Muslim community has experienced rapid growth over the past three decades. Estimates of the Muslim population in the United States range from five to six million. The community has established some 1,200 mosques, 300 ethnic associations, 200 student groups, 200 Islamic schools, 100 community media outlets, and 50 social service and world relief organizations. Moreover, Muslim public affairs groups have emerged locally and nationally since the early 1990s, working to defend Muslims against discrimination and defamation, to give them voice in the public arena, and to represent their views before governmental and non-governmental bodies.

Leading Muslim organizations are in favor of involvement in American public life. Even groups focusing on the development of religious institutions are engaged in voter registration activities. The Islamic Society of North America (ISNA) and the Muslim American Society (MAS) host voter registration booths in their annual conventions. Muslim public affairs groups, most of which have been established since 1990, have made strides in shaping Muslim attitudes in favor of greater involvement in America's political and legal institutions. These groups include the American Muslim Council (AMC), Council on American-Islamic Relations (CAIR), Muslim Public Affairs Council (MPAC), American Muslim Alliance (AMA), and Muslims for Good Government. This chapter is an examination of how American Muslim groups have related to the American political process, focusing on their public concerns, relations with others, and participation in the elections.

CHALLENGING DISCRIMINATION

The growth of Islam in the United States has not always been welcome. The overly unsympathetic portrayal in the entertainment industry compounds the problem for Muslims. As a result, a number of mosques have been subjected to attacks and threats in crisis periods; others, however, have been attacked in noncrisis times. The Islamic Center in Springfield, Illinois, suffered an arson attack on June 6, 1995, causing an estimated $30,000 in fire and heat damage.[1] The Huntsville Islamic Center was broken into on July 16, 1995. Islamic religious texts were ripped, computers were damaged, and other equipment was stolen. The level of damage rendered the mosque unusable for the immediate future.[2] Masjid Al-Momineen in Clarkston, Georgia, was vandalized on September 11, 1995, resulting in broken windows, damaged light fixtures, and the discharge of fire extinguishers, as well as Satanic symbols burned into the mosque's carpet. Six days later, police caught one suspect, who admitted responsibility for the incident.[3] The Islamic Society of Greenville, South Carolina, was set ablaze on October 21, 1995. The South Carolina Law Enforcement Division ruled the case as a suspected arson and estimated the damage at $50,000.[4] The same day, vandals spray-painted an obscene anti-Islamic message on the exterior of Flint Islamic Center/Genesee Academy in Flint, Michigan. The vandals spray-painted a vulgar sexual reference to God, using the word *Allah*. Although the police said that there were no suspects in the incidents, the Genesee County Sheriff's Department promised Muslim community leaders that it would increase patrols in the area.[5]

In West Springfield, Massachusetts, bottles were thrown into the local mosque. The community claims that vandalism has increased ever since the minaret and the dome of the mosque have been completed.[6] In another vandalism incident, at the Islamic Center in Fort Collins, Colorado, which was well covered by local television stations, good police work has led to the capture of those responsible for the attack on the mosque on January 28, 1998. A reward offer of $1,000 by the local Muslim community may have contributed to the arrest of two men, who have been charged with vandalism and criminal mischief. In most other cases, however, no one has been caught or charged. In Austin, Texas, a ram head was thrown in a mosque on May 30, 1998. The Mosque of El Barrio in New York was broken into and robbed of a stereo on June 28, 1998. Also, vandals broke the windows of the mosque in Amarillo, Texas, on July 30, 1998, but were caught by the police.

The terrorist attacks of September 11, 2001, were followed by the worst wave of anti-Muslim violence in the United States. CAIR reported receiving more than 1,700 complaints of harassment and hate crimes in the two months after the attacks, including a dozen murders. The U.S. Department of Justice confirmed that there was adequate evidence of anti-Muslim hate as a motive in three killings.[7] South Asians, especially Sikhs who wear beards and turbans and usually are mistaken for Muslims, were also attacked.

Mosques in particular have been targeted. In Irving, Texas, nine shots were fired at the Islamic Center of Irving on September 12, 2001, breaking the windows and damaging the furnishings. The community asked the police to investigate it as a hate crime, but the police told them they would record it as a regular crime. In Seattle, Washington, Idriss Mosque was subject to an attempted arson on September 13. The suspect in the attack was caught and charged with attempted arson. In Cleveland, Ohio, twenty-nine-year-old Eric Richley of Middleburg Heights rammed his Ford Mustang through the Grand Islamic Mosque of Cleveland on September 17. The front wall collapsed, causing an estimated $100,000 in damage. On March 25, 2002, Charles Franklin, a forty-one-year-old carpenter, drove a truck into the Islamic Center of Tallahassee at Florida State University. The man left the scene after the crash but was caught by the police later. Luckily, no one was injured in the crash, which occurred thirty minutes before evening prayers.

Other attempted attacks were more alarming, as they involved planning and organization. Two board members of the Jewish Defense League in California were caught by federal agents with explosives ready to be planted at a local mosque and the offices of Arab American congressman Darrel Isa and MPAC. In another incident in Florida, a thirty-seven-year-old doctor plotting to bomb mosques in Florida was arrested on August 23, 2002. Press reports said deputies found explosive devices, including hand grenades and a gasoline bomb with a timer and a wire attached, and a cache of up to forty licensed weapons, including .50-caliber machine guns and sniper rifles, inside the man's home. They also found a list of fifty Islamic centers and organizations in the state, mostly in the Tampa Bay area. Later a second man was arrested for his role in the plot.[8]

Muslims in the workplace have also increasingly complained of discriminatory treatment and denial of constitutional rights. A 1996 survey of members of the ISNA, one of the largest Muslim community groups in the country, asked, "Have you ever discussed with an employer or a teacher any matter that relates to the religious practices of yourself or any of your children?" Sixty-one percent answered yes. Another question asked, "Can you describe any specific matter or request that you discussed with officials at work or school regarding religious practices?" Three-fourths of the responses centered around religious accommodation in schools and the workplace. They mentioned being allowed to perform their prayers, to celebrate their holidays without penalty, to follow their dietary requirements, and to observe other religious requirements without fear of discrimination. They also indicated the need for greater public awareness about Muslims and what their religion has contributed to human civilization.[9]

Some Muslims have taken their employers to court over issues of religious accommodation. In a number of cases, the courts have affirmed the right of Muslims to religious practices. On October 4, 1999, the Supreme Court decided to reject the appeal of lower court ruling in favor of bearded Muslim police officers against the Newark Police Department's no-beard policy, which handed the American Muslim community perhaps the most significant legal victory since the prisoners' rights movement in the sixties.[10] The earlier ruling, issued by the United States Court of Appeals for the Third Circuit Court, *Fraternal Order of Police v. City of Newark,* stated, "Because the Department makes exemptions from its policy for secular reasons and has not offered any substantial justification for refusing to provide similar treatment for officers who are required to wear beards for religious reasons, we conclude that the Department's policy violates the First Amendment."[11] This accommodation of an element in Islamic law within America's secular legal tradition may embolden Muslims calling for greater religious tolerance toward the Islamic faith.

Still, many practicing Muslim employees often face the choice between job and religion. Although the Civil Rights Act of 1964 requires employers to provide reasonable accommodation of employees' religious practices, the law is not self-enforcing. Corporate personnel policy manuals often lack appreciation for religious accommodation requirements of their employees. Companies usually prefer to deal with this area on a case-by-case basis but do not commit themselves to enacting procedures to prevent incidents of discrimination. As a result, Muslim women wearing the *hijab* (loose-fitting clothing with head covering) complain repeatedly that they are denied jobs because of their dress. Some have successfully used the agency of the Equal Employment Opportunity Commission to reassert their right to religious accommodation. Other Muslims have simply opted for nonconfrontational responses, mainly because they are unfamiliar with the law or lack the financial resources to seek legal remedies.

Another area where Muslims have started to raise concerns is the public school system. Although Islamic schools are increasing in numbers, the overwhelming majority of Muslim students attend public schools. Muslim students complain that schools do not provide for time and space to offer their prayer. School districts exercise discretionary powers in implementing religious accommodation policies. These regulations tend to reflect federal interventions such as the Equal Access Act, which allows students in middle and high schools to establish extracurricular clubs. In some districts this act has allowed Muslim high school students to organize Friday prayers. In other districts, however, time restrictions do not permit students to meet at the religiously appropriate time for the prayer. Other Muslim concerns include the lack of alternative food items when pork is offered in school lunches. Also, Muslims point out that social study textbooks often contain misrepresentation of Islam and Muslims.

At the national level, CAIR, which was established in June 1994, has defended Muslims discriminated against in schools and the workplace. CAIR has used moral persuasion and public pressure in resolving almost two hundred cases of discrimination and lack of religious accommodation experienced by members of the Muslim community. Complementing this community service effort, CAIR has published a series of booklets offering practical suggestions on how to accommodate Muslim religious practices in the workplace, schools, and hospitals. It also challenges misrepresentation and defamation of Islam and Muslims in the marketplace. Since 1996, CAIR has issued an annual report logging incidents of anti-Muslim discrimination and violence on account of such ethnic and religious features as beard, complexion, accent, name, birthplace, and national origin.[12] CAIR's 1999 report noted that despite the persistence of discrimination, an increasing number of employees have eased their objection to Muslim women's hijab.[13]

Local Muslim activism has led to increased public awareness and brought some changes in school policies. For example, the Newark-based Majlis Ash-Shura of New Jersey (Council of Mosques and Islamic Organizations) produced a handbook designed to educate New Jersey's 2,600 public schools about Islamic religious practices. The Department of Education in the state agreed to let the Muslim council distribute the booklet to public schools.[14] Later, the Paterson County School Board voted to close schools on the two major Muslim holidays. The Muslim Education Council in Fairfax County, Virginia, has successfully lobbied the county school board to mark pork items in school lunch listings, to offer Arabic classes, and to issue a directive allowing Muslim students to wear more modest clothing during gym classes. Efforts by Imam Ghayth Kashif led to a decision by Prince George's County Public Schools in Maryland to the inclusion of the beginning of Ramadan, Eid al-Fitr, and Eid al-Adha on the school district's calendar of religious holidays.

GOVERNMENT RELATIONS

AMC has led the way in developing relations with the various branches of the government. It recognized the value of making sure that Muslim imams, like rabbis and priests, are invited to offer the opening prayer before congressional deliberations. With the help of Representative Nick Rahhal, Imam Siraj Wahhaj of New York opened the 1991 Congress with a prayer. This coincided with the height of the Gulf War crisis. The AMC leadership decided that it was time to bring public attention to the status of uniformed Muslims, especially those serving in Desert Storm and Desert Shield. AMC intended to assure that Muslims in the military have access to Qurans and Islamic books and can visit the holy places in

Mecca. The Pentagon informed an AMC delegation that Muslims in the military are in need of chaplains to lead their prayer and offer spiritual and religious advice.

After the war, AMC complained that President George H. W. Bush recognized Muslims abroad in his address on the occasion of Eid, but he did not address Muslims in this country. Six months later, with the facilitation of Representative John Sunnunu (R-N.H.), AMC received an Eid greeting message on a videotape from the president. Under President Bill Clinton, the White House continued sending these greetings to Muslims in the United States and around the world. AMC, however, still wanted the White House to conduct a ceremonial celebration of Eid as it does Christian and Jewish holidays.

The first-ever Ramadan *iftar* (breaking of the fast meal) on Capitol Hill was held in 1996 and attended by congressional representatives, their Muslim aides, and AMC members. In the same year, First Lady Hillary Clinton hosted a celebration of Eid, inviting Muslim leaders and their families. The White House under George W. Bush continued marking the two occasions, and after the September 11 attacks, the administration has begun to view them as occasions to reach out to a global Muslim audience. The White House invited ambassadors of Muslim-majority countries to iftar, and in 2002 President Bush made the first-ever Eid visit to a mosque. Eid greetings are offered in seventeen languages on the White House website.

Muslims across the board have welcomed these symbolic gestures but have longed for more substantive interactions. AMC has coordinated regular town meetings between members of local Islamic centers and elected officials. With this visibility, AMC has participated in meetings at the White House and other departments of government. AMC's call for increased government appointments of American Muslims has prompted the Clinton administration to appoint, in 1999, Osman Siddiqui to be the first-ever Muslim ambassador representing the United States in Fiji, Nauru, Tonga, and Tuvalu. That year's appointments also include Laila al-Marayati, who served on the United States Commission on International Religious Freedom, and Ikram Khan, who became a member of the Board of Regents for the Uniformed Services University of the Health Sciences. In 2002, President Bush appointed Elias Zerhouni, an Algerian-born radiologist at Johns Hopkins University, to head the National Institutes of Health.

State and local Muslim involvement resembled the work of national organizations promoting greater public recognition and inclusion of the American Muslim community. In Michigan, the state house of representatives opened its first session after the 1999 summer recess with the invocation of a Muslim, R. M. Mukhtar Curtis, a spokesperson for the Islamic Center of Ann Arbor. Muslims in the Detroit–Ann Arbor metropolitan area constitute perhaps the largest single concentration of the Muslim population in the United States. In the state of Ohio, the Islamic Council of Ohio, with the cooperation of other Islamic centers, organizes an "Islamic Day in Ohio" event. The day is celebrated every year in a different city, allowing Muslims to meet with state and local officials, media representatives, and other members of the interfaith community.[15]

Despite such local and national initiatives, Muslims have pointed out that senior government officials have failed to confront anti-Muslim speech in their own departments. For example, in one incident aboard the aircraft carrier U.S.S. *Enterprise,* the secretary of defense ignored a Muslim request of a proper disciplinary action against a crew member who inscribed on a missile designated for an attack on Iraq, "Here's a Ramadan present."[16] In another incident, an American Muslim requested that the Senate Republican Policy Committee rebuke anti-Muslim policy analyst James Jatras, who suggested that the very presence of Muslims in the United States is a "population infiltration" and that NATO policy in the Balkans was foolish because it offered aid to Muslims. The Idaho senator Larry Craig, chair of the Senate Republican Policy Committee, stood by his aide, claiming that his views are merely protected speech and that disagreement is only part of the democratic process. The National Republican Committee refused to even comment on the controversy. To Muslims who saw Jatras's remarks as a form of bigotry, the Republican responses reflected a lack of sensitivity toward non-Christians among senior party leaders.

Muslims have also been critical of some government initiatives that they believe unfairly targeted members of their community, especially when Muslim and Middle Eastern travelers reported that they have been singled out for extra scrutiny at airports. Most airport complaints were reported following the government's intrusive implementation of the Computerized Automated Passenger Screening (CAPS—known as passenger profiling), initiated by the White House Commission on Aviation Safety and Security following the crash of TWA Flight 800. Although the use of passenger profiling has diminished when authorities concluded that the TWA crash was due to mechanical failure rather than sabotage, the program has been reactivated with every terrorism threat, most notably after the terrorist attacks of September 11, 2001.

Another discriminatory policy has become known as secret evidence. Since the enactment of the 1996 antiterrorism law, several individuals of Arab and Muslim heritage have been detained based on classified information that they have not been allowed to challenge in court. Hundreds of Middle Eastern and South Asian immigrants were detained and deported on charges of visa violations after the 9/11 attacks. Many others, including some American citizens, were questioned in connection with the investigation— also under a shroud of secrecy that has been challenged in the courts.

Realizing that effectiveness in meeting local and national challenges requires collaboration, Muslim public affairs groups established in 1998 the American Muslim Political Coordination Council (AMPCC). One of the council's first undertakings was to start dialogue with the Council of Presidents of Arab-American Organizations, an ethnicity-based umbrella group. The two community bodies prioritized their shared public concerns, identifying secret evidence, voter registration, and Jerusalem as the top issues. September was declared Arab and Muslim voter registration month. On October 23, 2000, the AMPCC-PAC, a recently established political action committee, decided to endorse the presidential candidacy of George Bush after he criticized the Clinton administration for introducing secret evidence in the deportation of U.S. permanent residents.

Despite the heightened public pressure on Muslims after September 11, 2001, community groups have openly criticized the Bush administration for ignoring the community until the 9/11 disaster. They also criticize him for having introduced the Patriot Act of 2001, which they believe erodes civil liberties and clearly contradicts promises candidate Bush made before the elections. In particular, critics have charged that the act gives the executive branch the power to detain immigrant suspects for lengthy periods of time, sometimes indefinitely. Critics have also pointed out that the act allows the executive branch to circumvent the Fourth Amendment's requirement of probable cause when conducting wiretaps and searches. Under the current law, critics say, persons and organizations searched could be U.S. citizens who are not suspected of any wrongdoing. The law permits personal or business records to be seized for an investigation without prior evidence of connection to terrorism or criminal activity.

Still, Muslims have applauded government efforts on behalf of hate crime victims following the terrorist attacks. Indeed, President Bush has set the tone of tolerance toward Muslims; Congress strongly supports that sentiment. The House of Representatives passed a resolution condemning bigotry and violence against Arab Americans, American Muslims, and South Asians in the wake of September 11. Local and federal authorities acted with resolve against the anti-Muslim backlash. They have taken measures to monitor, investigate, prosecute, and even prevent incidents. Police departments across the country stepped up patrols around Muslim facilities. Local and federal agencies responded quickly to stem the rise of anti-Muslim hate crimes.

INTERACTIONS WITH OTHER GROUPS

Institutions that affect Muslim life in the United States have their social roots in ethnic, religious, and business communities. Muslims realize that they cannot ignore the groups to which coworkers, classmates, government officials, teachers, and law enforcement agents belong. Thus, Muslims have recognized the need to reach out to other groups to foster greater understanding. In a number of Islamic centers, such moves have grown out of necessity, as churches have offered mosques the use of their parking lots to help compensate for the lack of parking space, especially at Friday prayer services. Many Islamic centers around the country are members of local and regional interfaith groups. These groups exchange speakers who introduce their faith to other groups and send delegations to attend religious celebrations of other faith communities.

One of the leading Muslim groups in interfaith relations is MPAC. Headed by Maher Hathout, a physician with considerable religious knowledge, the center has offered a forum for interfaith dialogue. Groups invited to speak at the forum include local and national Jewish organizations, the National Conference of Catholic Bishops, and the National Council of Churches of Christ. Still, the feeling of being engulfed with barrages of misinformation about Islam and Muslims in the media and in the discourse of leaders permeates the activities of MPAC. As executive director Salam Al-Marayati puts it, "We have to deal with issues that are given high profile by the public."[17] Thus, the council has issued statements on counterterrorism, Bosnia (with a focus on the use of rape as a weapon of ethnic cleansing), and the treatment of women under the Taliban (with a focus on separating Islam from the behavior of the Taliban).

Most political interactions between Muslims and others center around issues of civil rights and freedom of speech. Muslim groups such as CAIR, AMC, and MPAC joined the coalition led by the American Civil Liberties Union (ACLU) opposing the 1996 Anti-Terrorism and Effective Death Penalty Act, which contained a provision allowing the government to detain individuals based on classified information (popularly known as secret evidence). Although the effort did not succeed, Muslim participation offered an opportunity for Muslim groups to experience firsthand the inner workings of lobbying and coalition building.

Immediately following the passage of the secret evidence law, the federal government detained a number of Muslim activists. The ACLU has accused the Immigration and Naturalization Service (INS) of illegally detaining Nasser Ahmad and seeking to deport him based on classified information. Ahmad had worked as a paralegal in the defense of Omar Abdel Rahman during his trial in the World Trade Center bombing case. Ahmad, who had been seeking political asylum in the United States, has never been charged or accused of any terrorist activity. The ACLU filed a lawsuit seeking his release and asked that the INS be prohibited from using classified information to deport immigrants.[18] Most recently, a judge threw the government case against Ahmad, ruling that he cannot be deported based on secret evidence.[19] Other cases of secret evidence include Mazen al-Najjar, a Palestinian journal editor suspected of association with anti-Israel groups, and Anwar Haddam, an Algerian suspected of incitement to violence against the military government in his home country.

Such cases proliferated after September 11; due to government secrecy, no agency was able to keep track of them all. Mazen al-Najjar, who was released less than a year before the terrorist attacks, was rearrested on the same old immigration charges and later was secretly deported to Lebanon. The civil liberties coalition, however, grew exponentially, and, in addition to Arabs and Muslims, almost every other minority group in the country has joined.

Relations with the Jewish community have been fractious, as issues of disagreement have overshadowed areas of collaboration. The American Muslim Council has endorsed a statement drafted by the American Jewish Congress on religion in public schools.[20] In another instance, the American Jewish Committee in Los Angeles joined the Women Coalition against Ethnic Cleansing. Leading the effort to formulate this alliance was the Muslim Women League. The group compiled information and testified in Congress on the rape of Muslim women during the Serbian attacks on Bosnian towns.[21]

Still, Israeli occupation of Arab lands remains the major source of conflict. While pro-Israel groups have cultivated a tradition of an uncritical support of Israel, Muslims are becoming increasingly vocal in their criticism of U.S. support for Israel. When American Muslims for Jerusalem (AMJ) threatened fast-food restaurant Burger King with boycott over a franchise in the Jewish settlement Maali Adomim, the Anti-Defamation League (ADL) called the boycott entirely inappropriate and contrary to the peace process. AMJ believes the ADL position is promoting the continuance of occupation and thus runs against the advancement of peace.

The American-Israel Public Affairs Committee (AIPAC) has listed a host of American Muslim and Arab American groups as "Israel detractors." Many Muslims believe Jewish groups place the issue of Israel ahead of any common concerns in dealing with fellow American Muslim citizens.

Pro-Israel groups have used their influence to block American Muslim access to government. The Washington office of the ADL and the Zionist Organization of America (ZOA) opposed the invitation of CAIR and MPAC to participate in meetings of the State Department's newly established Office on International Religious Freedom. Opposition of pro-Israel groups to Muslim involvement in public debate extended to areas unconnected to the Palestinian-Israeli conflict. Daniel Pipes, head of the Middle East Forum, opposed the publication of an article describing anti-Muslim attacks following false accusations that Muslims bombed the Murrah Federal Building in Oklahoma City in 1995. The intended venue for that article was the *Muslim Politics Report,* published by the Council on Foreign Relations.

Most recently, major Jewish groups opposed the appointment of Laila al-Marayati, of the California-based Muslim Women League, to the Commission on International Religious Freedom. They cited al-Marayati's weak stand on terrorism as the reason. Also, all major Jewish groups, including the Council of Presidents of Major Jewish Organizations, opposed the nomination of Salam al-Marayati, of MPAC, to the National Commission on Terrorism. Al-Marayati had expressed the view that Israeli repression of the Palestinian people has led to a violent reaction among the Palestinians. His condemnation of attacks against noncombatants was not seen by pro-Israel groups as sufficient evidence of his opposition to terrorism.

This action by the Washington-based Jewish groups, however, triggered dissent among Jewish leaders, especially after editorials in major national and California newspapers, including the *Washington Post* and the *Los Angeles Times*, criticized pro-Israel groups and U.S. representative Richard Gephart, who withdrew the nomination. Rabbi Alfred Wolf of the Skirball Institute, which is administratively linked to the American Jewish Committee, whose national office opposed the nomination of Salam al-Marayati, along with three other local rabbis, disagreed with the view of the East Coast Jewish leaders, arguing that it is not in the best interest of the Jewish community to block the nomination. A dialogue initiative between Muslims and Jews in California that started before this incident received a further push. The dissenting West Coast rabbis have engaged local Muslim imams and other leaders in a discussion over what they call "a code of ethics," which decries rumor mongering and prejudice and calls for a fact-based discourse.[22]

The aftermath of September 11 marked a bottom low in Jewish Muslim relations, as a number of pro-Israel groups became worried about the favorable spotlight that was cast on Muslim community organizations. Rabbi James Ruden of the AJC wrote a piece entitled "Can American Muslims and Jews Get Along?" at AJC's website, suggesting that Jews should not have contacts with Muslims unless they believe in the right of Israel to exist. In Connecticut, the AJC even refused participation in an interfaith event because it viewed the invited Muslim speaker as unfriendly to Israel.

A *Los Angeles Times* article that became a national story said that since September 11, pro-Israel groups have supplied media outlets with reams of information designed to discount the credibility and significance of Muslim American organizations. Evidence shows that some American Jewish leaders view the very growth of Islam in America as a threat to their influence on U.S. policy on the Middle East. Even prior to September 11, AJC executive director David A. Harris wrote, "We dare not underestimate the Arab and Muslim lobbies [in America] or delude ourselves as to their ultimate objectives. The stakes are too high. The call for action by American Jewry . . . is clear."[23]

Nevertheless, local Jewish and Muslim congregations in various parts of the country held joint meetings. On the West Coast, on the 2001 Eid al-Adha, one of Islam's most important holidays, a day dedicated to the remembrance of Abraham, Los Angeles Muslims and Jews met to remind themselves of their common patriarch. On the East Coast, members of the Baltimore Jewish Council visited the Islamic Society of Baltimore on January 23, 2002, during an interfaith exchange evening.

Catholic-Muslim relations have been much more conciliatory, perhaps reflecting a historical worldwide trend since the mid-1960s. The Vatican had issued *Declaration on the Relations of the Church to Non-Christian Religions*. The document, which represents an attempt by the Vatican to recognize the legitimacy of other religions, states:

> The Church has also a high regard for the Muslims. They worship God, who is one, living and subsistent, merciful and almighty, the Creator of heaven and earth. . . . For this reason they highly esteem an upright life and worship God, especially by way of prayer, alms-deeds and fasting . . . for the benefit of all men, let them together preserve and promote peace, liberty, social justice and moral values.[24]

Despite uneasiness with some Catholic figures, such as Richard Neuhaus and William Bennett, who support the clash of civilizations notion, Muslim groups have recognized other Catholic voices and have cooperated with them on common ground issues. The Islamic Center of Long Island, one of the largest Muslim communities in New York, joined the Catholic League for Religious and Civil Rights in October 1998 to protest *Corpus Christi,* a play that depicted a Jesus-like figure engaging in sexual acts with his disciples. The protest did not call for a ban on the play, attempting only to assert that the denigration of religious values must be challenged. This shared concern emanates from a realization that secularism is no longer limited to the separation of church and state but has gone to the point now where religious communities encounter hostility from those who oppose any public expression of religion of any kind.[25]

A number of Muslim groups have maintained dialogue with groups from various Protestant denominations. For example, CAIR and the General Board on Church and Society of the United Methodist Church (General Board) started meetings on February 2, 1998, with the two groups exchanging public speeches, published columns, and office visits. CAIR initiated the dialogue as part of a conscious effort to survey the playing fields of politics. Nine million strong, Methodists are the second largest Protestant denomination in the United States, whose general conference has adopted resolutions in the past in favor of increased tolerance and religious accommodation of Muslims. In the public policy arena, the Methodist Church view of the natural world is concerned with the protection of the environment. The Muslim way of life is essentially conservationist. The Quran and the tradition of the Prophet Muhammad are replete with warnings against waste and overspending—moderation in consumption is a supreme value.

On the drug crisis, the General Board on Church and Society advocates prevention and treatment. Across the country, Muslims are actively involved in programs that include conducting youth programs in inner cities, patrolling neighborhoods, and distributing educational literature to prevent drug abuse.

On the matter of prayer in public schools, both Muslims and Methodists believe in the right of students to initiate prayer activity, but they oppose the imposition of a generalized prayer in classrooms and other school meetings. Such dialogue initiatives have brought some fruits. On occasions, the various groups issued joint statements. In 1999, the General Board on Church and Society, along with the Catholic League for Religious and Civil Rights and the Interfaith Alliance, cosponsored a letter to Senate majority leader Trent Lott, asking him to take a stand on bigotry among conservative Republicans.[26]

Contacts between Muslims and the Christian Right have been uncertain and highly confrontational at times. For example, Pat Robertson, the founder of the Christian Coalition and host of the *700 Club* cable show, said on October 27, 1997, "to see Americans become followers of, quote, Islam is nothing short of insanity." This remark set off a campaign of protest by a wide spectrum of groups. Muslim groups joined the Interfaith Conference of Metropolitan Washington and People for the American Way, a group that monitors Robertson and other politically active Christian groups, in denouncing Robertson's remarks.[27] Robertson had slandered the Islamic faith as early as 1990 and puffed up his rhetoric after September 11 when he called the Prophet of Islam a killer and a robber.

Contrary to the conduct of Pat Robertson, who has exhibited clear anti-Muslim bias, officials of the Christian Coalition, which he founded, have tried to court Muslims in the 1998 elections. On October 12, 1998, David Spady, the executive director of the Christian Coalition of California, met with representatives of the United Muslims of America and officials of the Islamic Society of Orange County, asking them to distribute the coalition's election literature to Muslim voters. Moreover, groups associated with the Christian Coalition have in the past joined Muslims in action. For example, Concerned Women for America has joined the International Association for Muslim Women and Children in coordinating a conservative response during the Beijing Women Conference held in China in 1996.

Father Richard Neuhaus, editor of *First Things,* a journal dedicated to discussing the role of Christianity in public life, published a scathing anti-Muslim article in the October 1997 issue of the journal. The piece promoted the idea that Islam is the chief enemy of the West. Muslims responded rapidly by a flux of letters protesting this bellicose attitude. In the February 1998 issue of the publication, Neuhaus clarified that he thought dialogue with Muslims has become increasingly imperative and that he only meant to make the point that Christianity is closer to Judaism than to Islam, because "Islam is not, as Judaism is, an integral part of the Christian understanding of the story of salvation."[28] But Neuhaus did not explain how this theological position translates into a warning against a Muslim bogeyman threatening Christianity and the West. Nevertheless, Muslims viewed his partial retreat as a signal that a cool-headed dialogue might still be open.

Other expressions of anti-Muslim sentiment by non-Muslim leaders came mainly from conservative groups. For example, an analyst with the Hoover Institution, a right-wing policy research group, called immigrant Muslims a "security threat" to the United States.[29] While public debate is crucial to the formulation of policy options and the making of political alliances, it is elected officials who eventually make policy decisions.

AMERICAN MUSLIMS AND THE ELECTIONS

Financial contributions to political candidates serve as another measurement of Muslim involvement in the political process, although there is an inherent difficulty in identifying donors by their faith. A subset group of CAIR members offers a convenient alternative method of examining American Muslim contributions to political candidates. The CAIR 2000 membership list of individuals includes 1,200 unique last names. Matching these surnames against Federal Election Commission data yielded a total of 7,784 contributions from individuals with the surnames in the CAIR list from January 1995 to May 2000. Once the data were refined, the net came down to 5,653 contributions totaling $3,898,075. The breakdown of the contributions by year is shown in table 6.1. These data, however, are not a comprehensive account of the general Muslim contributions to political campaigns, because many other surnames of Muslims do not appear on CAIR's list.

While many individuals supported the political campaigns of candidates directly, others channeled their contributions through political action committees (PACs). PACs organized by Muslim and Arab Americans, shown in table 6.2, range from the less significant groups such as the American League of Muslims, which contributed $147 in 1999–2000, to the Pakistani Physicians PAC, which received $75,950 in 1997–1998 and $8,985 in 1999–2000 (as of September 1). The other PACs organized by Muslim and Arab Americans include the Albanian American PAC, whose collections to-

Table 6.1   Number of CAIR Surname List Contributions by Amount and Year

Year	Number of Contributions	Sum ($) Contributions
2000 (up to May)	474	295,249
1999	1,179	848,075
1998	1,158	716,174
1997	572	433,850
1996	1,467	1,032,740
1995	803	571,987
Total	5,653	3,898,075

Sources: CAIR 2000 Surname List; www.fec.gov; information taken in October 2000.

taled $54,900 in 1997–1998 and $17,600 in 1999–2000; the Arab American PAC, which received $32,940 in 1999–2000; the Arab American Leadership PAC, which collected $91,900 in 1997–1998 and $44,600 in 1999–2000; and the National Association of Arab Americans, which received $3,250 in 1997–1998 and $200 in 1999–2000, apparently before it merged with the American Arab Anti-Discrimination Committee. Searching the terms *Kashmiri, Iranian, Palestinian, Lebanese, Syrian, Turkish,* and *Bosnian* did not return any results—meaning there are no PACs collecting and dispersing funds using the name of any of these ethnic groups. There are state-level PACs, but these do not appear in the list of federally registered groups.

Arab and Muslim PAC collections are small not only in real terms but also in comparison to contributions by individuals. The CAIR list contributors outspent community PACs by a ratio of 10:1. However, since there is no monitoring agency tracking all local activities, it is hard to ascertain the extent to which contributions are the outcome of organized activity. Many local activists hold fund-raising functions in which donors write checks directly to candidates selected by the host. One such political fund-raiser is Abdulrahman Alamoudi, who sent an invitation to potential donors to support Senator Spencer Abraham of Michigan in the 2000 elections. Rationalizing his choice of candidate, Alamoudi writes:

> Spencer Abraham is the only Arab-American Senator . . . who has fought secret evidence, . . . introduced a resolution condemning prejudice against Islam and recognizing the contribution of Muslims to American society (S.Con Res. 133). He also called for the issuance of a Ramadhan stamp, . . . called President [Clinton] to visit Pakistan in his last visit to [South Asia], and stood for reforming immigration law.[30]

Financial activity by PACs increased during the 1997–1998 election cycle, according to figures compiled by the Federal Election Commission (FEC).

Table 6.2   Muslim PACs in Two Election Cycles

PAC	1997–1998 Received ($)	Spent ($)	1999–2000 Received ($)	Spent ($)
Arab American Leadership PAC	91,900	77,050	44,600	32,500
Arab American PAC			32,940	9,000
National Association of Arab Americans	3,250	6,150	200	2,470
American League of Muslims			0	147
Pakistani Physicians PAC	75,950	2,500	8,985	0
Albanian American PAC	54,900	42,100	17,600	15,100
Total	226,000	127,800	104,325	59,217

Source: www.opensecrets.org/pacs/index.htm; information taken in October 2000.

From January 1, 1997, through December 31, 1998, 4,599 PACs raised $502.6 million.[31] When compared to all PACs, Muslim PACs look very small, as their contributions account for only 0.04 percent of the total reported collections of PACs. Comparing Muslim community PACs to ideological and single-issue PACs, the picture looks a bit brighter, although it shows that Muslims are still trailing far behind. The average contribution per ideological/ single issue PAC in 1999–2000 was $50,749; the community PACs under study averaged $9,870.[32]

As for political parties, the Democrats received $357,506 and the Republicans $249,672 in the 1998 and 2000 elections. The disparity is hard to explain, since Muslims in general do not have an innate affinity to either party. As more information becomes available, it is important to observe whether this becomes a pattern of Muslim political contributions. In total, the parties received $607,178 from the CAIR list members, or 16 percent of the total individual giving. This sum, however, if distributed across the three election cycles, is 22 percent more than the average amount given by individuals to community PACs per election season. This indicates that political party machinery may have done a better job than Muslim PACs in courting individual Muslim contributors.

Still, the group of individual donors under examination contributed to a cross section of about one thousand candidates during the 1996, 1998, and 2000 election cycles. Some politicians, however, received a disproportionate amount of contributions. Tim Johnson, the Democratic senator from South Dakota, received $116,050, of which $74,900 was contributed during the 1996 election season. Johnson ran successfully, partly due to the help of Muslims, against incumbent Larry Pressler, who, in the name of curbing nuclear proliferation, had authored an amendment proposing sanctions on Pakistan tougher than those applying to other countries, especially Pakistan's rival India, pursuing a similar nuclear program.

Beneficiaries of other issue-driven giving included Republican representative Tom Campbell and Democratic representative David Bonior, who received $40,085 and $61,975, respectively. The bulk of the contributions to the two from the group under study followed the congressmen's introduction of HR 2121, known as the Secret Evidence Repeal Act. Some contributions to congressional candidates were driven by local concerns. Members of Dar al-Hijrah Islamic Center in Falls, Virginia, have organized three fund-raising events in support of Jim Moran and Tom Davis, who had sent letters to Fairfax City officials opposing a motion by Falls Church residents to revoke the user permit of the mosque.[33] FEC records show them receiving $16,520 and $4,830, respectively, from CAIR list members, both above the average of $3,900 per candidate given in the three election cycles.

Other factors motivating political contributions are also present. Spencer Abraham, whose ethnic heritage and weight within Republican ranks have overshadowed his substantive commitment to community concerns, received $91,100, almost equal to what Bonior and Campbell got together. Other top receivers include Texas senator Phil Gramm, who collected $46,675 from CAIR list members, and New Jersey senator Robert Torricelli, who collected a total of $86,735. Although the contribution to Gramm does not bear direct connection to community-based issues, the givings to Torricelli were justified in terms of a stance against those who defame Muslims. New Jersey Muslims decided in 1996 to support the reelection of Torricelli after his opponent publicly slighted the Muslim community.[34]

The top receivers, those who received $40,000, collected about $1.3 million, one-third of all contributions. The top recipients were ethnic candidates, community PACs, political party committees, presidential candidates, and a few congressional candidates whose support in the community has been linked to Muslim concerns. The rest of the money was contributed to candidates in virtually all states. In other words, two-thirds of the contributions were given to congressional district candidates—a decent measure of individual Muslim interest in state-level involvement.

Muslims have participated in the electoral process as candidates as well. The website of American Muslim Alliance (AMA), whose main purpose is to promote Muslims seeking public office, lists eleven Muslim candidates running in various local, state, and congressional districts in the 2000 elections. The only Muslim congressional hopeful was Eric Vickers, a St. Louis lawyer and member of the board of directors of AMA. He received 6 percent of the vote in his congressional district in the Democratic Party primary on August 8, 2000, while the winner, William Lacy Clay Jr., received 59 percent of the vote.[35] Eleven members of the group of financial contributors under examination contributed $5,900 to his campaign, a modest sum for a congressional contest.

Other Muslim candidates have won some electoral seats at the state and local levels. In 1996, Larry Shaw became a state senator in North Carolina—the first Muslim ever to occupy such a position in any state. Several other Muslims have won city council seats, including Yusuf Abdus-Salaam in Selma, Alabama; Lateefah Muhammad in Tuskegee, Alabama; Yusuf Abdul-Hakeem in Chattanooga, Tennessee; and Nasif Majid in Charlotte, North Carolina. According to the American Muslim Alliance, two dozen Muslims were elected to party conventions at precinct, county, state, and national levels in 1996. In the 2000 election, twenty-eight Muslim delegates attended the Democratic Convention, and four went to the Republican Convention. More Muslim candidates ran for state legislatures, some of whom showed more promise than others. For example, Abdul Karim Muhammad, an accountant, a Democratic Party functionary, and a member of the Detroit Citizens Review Committee, ran in the 2000 primary for the first district seat of the legislature in Michigan. He received 800 votes, whereas the primary winner got 1,500 votes. (In this traditionally conservative district, the top Republican vote getter received four thousand votes.) Other Muslim candidates have had better luck. Saggy Tahir, a Republican, won a state house seat twice, in 2000 and 2002.

CONCLUSION

The main objective of American Muslim participation in mainstream politics is empowerment. Attaining this goal, however, depends on the degree to which Muslim organizations can institutionalize their work and improve its management. In this respect, national Muslim public affairs groups are facing tremendous challenges in their attempt to gain political clout. Local efforts, the backbone of any future success, are in worse shape. Their activities are usually scant and ad hoc in nature. For example, Citizens for Equal Justice in the Middle East in Dallas, Texas, ceased to exist after it successfully challenged the *Dallas Morning News*. AMPCC has declared September a national voter registration month for the Muslim community, but it has not attempted to measure the response of local communities. There are signs of some improvement, however. AMC was able to mobilize only half a dozen Islamic centers in its 1996 voter registration drive; the number increased to two dozen in the 1999 campaign.[36]

Muslims realize that the game of power in the United States is dependent on votes and money, which, due to the relative small size of the Muslim community and its recent experience in political participation, means that Muslims are not likely to become a significant political force any time soon. These challenges, however, must be seen as part of the normal experience of any starting organizations. Still, Muslim public affairs groups have been able to make stereotyping of Muslims a matter of public debate, have been able to resolve many incidents of discrimination and defamation, and have demonstrated ability to mobilize support for their concerns regarding the treatment of Muslims by government, media, and civic groups.

Moreover, efforts of Muslim public affairs groups, as modest in strength as they may be, have sparked a debate around very signficant issues related to Muslim integration into a predominantly non-Muslim society. While isolationists have dismissed such contacts as futile, others stressed that the Prophet Muhammad had set the example of recognizing non-Muslim groups as social entities that have rights and duties and can be taken as allies on matters of common good. For most Muslims, the perception of relations with others in terms of tension between Mulsims and non-Muslims is giving way to a more engaging vision that identifies actions and views with specific groups rather than broad religious communities.

As a result of interfaith and civic encounters, Muslims have gained greater acquaintance with the public square and engaged some of its players, managing to initiate dialogue with diverse groups on issues of common interest. Whether the issue is Jerusalem, defamation, or discrimination, they mainly touched sensitive matters related to Islamic beliefs and practices. Robert Fowler and Alan Hertzke, writers on religion and politics in America, have predicted that Muslims may join like-minded groups in what is known as the Religious Right opposing secular forces.[37] Evidence shows that Muslims have entered alliances on an issue-by-issue basis. It is too early to predict how and whether a Muslim consensus can be developed in favor of a strategic place for the community in the American body politic, as the main thrust of the American Muslim public discourse is preoccupied with combating prejudice and ignorance.

NOTES

1. *St. Louis Post-Dispatch,* June 17, 1995.

2. *Huntsville Times,* July 16 and 17, 1996.

3. *Atlanta Journal/Constitution,* September 16, 1995.

4. *Greenville News,* October 22, 1995.

5. *Flint Journal,* October 23, 1995.

6. *Union News,* October 25, 1996.

7. Department of Justice Press release, August 28, 2002; available at www.usdoj.gov/opa/pr/2002/August/02_crt_497.htm.

8. *St. Petersburg Times,* September 27, 2002.

9. Findings of the survey paint a picture of the average ISNA member as a young, highly educated professional who lives in a middle-class, family-oriented, and possibly ethnically diverse household. However, only a small percentage of African American Muslims identify with the organization, as ISNA draws its membership primarily from immigrant and practicing Muslim populations.

10. For more details on the prisoners' rights movement, see Katherine Moore, *al-Mughtaribun: American Law and the Transformation of Muslim Life in the United States* (Albany: State University of New York Press, 1995).

11. *Fraternal Order of Police v. City of Newark,* App. No. 97–5542.

12. CAIR, *The Status of Muslim Civil Rights in the United States* (Washington, D.C: Author, 1998), 6–11.

13. CAIR, *The Status of Muslim Civil Rights in the United States* (Washington, D.C: Author, 1999), 2–10.

14. *The Record,* February 15, 1999.

15. Interview with Andy Amid, secretary of Islamic Council of Ohio, September 18, 1999.

16. The Associated Press distributed a photo with the aforementioned inscription on December 21, 1998.

17. Interview with Salam Al-Marayati, September 15, 1999.

18. *New York Times,* September 10, 1997.

19. *New York Times,* November 11, 1999. The newspaper reports that in a declassified testimony of an FBI official, the government argued against Ahmad's release, fearing that he might gain respectability in the Arab and Muslim community.

20. *"Religion in Public Schools: A Joint Statement of Current Law,"* n.d.

21. Interview by the author with Laila al-Marayati, president of the Muslim Women League, on May 16, 1997. The league is affiliated with MPAC.

22. Interviews with Rabbi Alfred Wolf and Salam al-Marayati, September 30, 1999.

23. *Jerusalem Report,* May 28, 2001.

24. Vatican, "Declaration on the Relations of the Church to Non-Christian Religions," October 28, 1965.

25. Address of K. Whitehead at the CAIR Panel, "Muslims and Catholics: Challenging Anti-Religious Bias," October 14, 1998; "Religious Expression in the Public Schools," testimony by William Donohue, president of the Catholic League for Religious and Civil Rights befor the United States Civil Rights Commission, May 20, 1998 (published in *Catalyst* [July/August 1998]: 8–9).

26. The letter was published as an adverstisement in the *Washington Times* on June 29, 1999.

27. *Washington Post,* November 8, 1997.

28. *First Things* (February 1998): 64.

29. James Philips, "Islamic Terrorists Pose a Threat," in *Urban Terrorism,* ed. A. E. Sadler and Paul Winters (San Diego, Calif.: Greenhaven, 1996), 62–65.

30. Abdulrahman Alamoudi to Nihad Awad, September 22, 2000.

31. Federal Election Commission news release, June 8, 1999; available at www.fec.gov/press/pacye98.htm.

32. This is based on a total of $19,030,964 contributed by 375 ideological/single-issue PACs to federal candidates; FEC news release, June 8, 1999.

33. Interview with Bassam El-Estewani, September 28, 1999.

34. *Washington Report on Middle East Affairs* (July/August 1998): 9–10.

35. See www.washingtonpost.com/wp-dyn/politics/elections/2000/states/mo/house/mo01/index.html.

36. Interview with Manal Omar of AMC, October 25, 1999.

37. Robert Fowler and Alan Hertzke, *Religion and Politics in America: Faith Culture and Strategic Choices* (Boulder, Colo.: Westview, 1995).

7

Muslims as Partners in Interfaith Encounter

Jane I. Smith

While Muslims in the American public square are increasingly becoming involved in interfaith or multifaith activities, over the past several decades their most common form of engagement with another faith tradition has been through interactions with Christians in a variety of settings. So-called dialogue has taken a range of forms, has been initiated (primarily by Christians) for a variety of reasons, and has elicited a number of different kinds of responses from members of the American Muslim community. It is with these forms and responses that this chapter is concerned.

The legacy of Muslim-Christian interaction is marked by many centuries of fear and misunderstanding. Christians have struggled to determine whether this new religion arising centuries after the establishment of Christianity is a heresy, a tool of the devil, or a true and valuable contribution to human religious history. Christian polemics about Islam throughout the Middle Ages and extending to modern times have demonstrated a great deal more suspicion and derision than appreciation, from the treatises of the scholastics to the outrageous popular tales perpetuated about the founder of Islam and his followers.[1] For their part, Muslims divided the world into the realms of *dar al-Islam* (the region in which the laws of Islam rule) and *dar al-harb* (literally "the realm of war," or that inhabited by non-Muslims). Christians, along with Jews, have been called "People of the Book" and treated as special (although second-class) citizens in the Islamic state. Muslim polemic, however, has always insisted on the "truth" of the Quran as correcting and superceding the Torah and the Gospel that are currently in use by the Jewish and Christian communities.

A number of specific occurrences in the centuries of Christian-Muslim encounter have added to the storehouse of misunderstanding and mistrust.

The Crusades, historically of much greater importance to Christians than to Muslims, have now taken on new meaning for Muslims as they contemplate waves of Western Christian intrusion into Muslim lands. More recently this intrusion has taken the form of persistent evangelistic missionary activity, which Muslims perceive as another attempt to destroy the religion of Islam, of Western imperialism and colonization of Muslim territories, of the so-called orientalism of much Western scholarship about Islam, and most lately of Western Christian political and moral support of the Zionist presence in the heart of the Muslim Middle East.

Muslim memory of these activities is enhanced and encouraged by the rhetoric of revivalist Islam in many countries today and reinforced by those American Muslims who are encouraging members of the community to take an isolationist stand and eschew involvement in American public life. Added to this, of course, is the clear recognition on the part of all Muslims living in the West of the persistent negative stereotyping of Islam on the part of the American media, of the prejudice and fear that continue to linger and be manifested in the general public, and of the deep concerns they themselves have about elements of Western society and the dangers of becoming too deeply involved in its ethos. All of these factors come to play as Muslims reflect on whether they wish to, or feel that it is appropriate to, become engaged in Christian-Muslim dialogue and, if so, what the nature of that involvement should be.

Dialogue initiatives in the United States have been taken primarily by Roman Catholic and Protestant Christians. For Catholics, the Second Vatican Council from 1962 to 1965 signaled the start of new ways of thinking about and relating to other religions, and its statement that the Catholic Church "has a high regard" for Muslims clearly pointed toward a dramatically new orientation in Catholic response to the religion of Islam. The legacy of a painful past was to be put aside in favor of new ways of achieving mutual understanding.[2] The Secretariat for Non Christians, later called the Pontifical Council for Interreligious Dialogue, has been the vehicle for promoting this new attitude and for formulating new initiatives at dialogue. In the 1960s, guidelines for dialogue between Christians and Muslims were published, and they have since been revised several times.

The establishment of the World Council of Churches (WCC) in Geneva, Switzerland, in 1948, whose members include Protestants and Orthodox but not Roman Catholics, provided the opportunity for other forms of Christian dialogue with Muslims. The first such organized dialogues took place in the late 1960s, and they have continued regularly in various parts of the world, with various agendas and different constituencies. The name of the WCC unit concerned with interfaith dialogue has changed several times; most currently it is called Inter-Religious Relations and Dialogue. Other efforts at interfaith conversation and cooperation have arisen in many different countries and regions.³ To some extent, these conversations have affected the nature of the dialogue in the United States, and American Muslims occasionally have participated in them. For the most part, however, the dialogue that has grown up in this country has been its own creature, encouraged and guided by Christian agencies abroad (especially Rome and Geneva) but responding to the issues that have been raised by Christians and Muslims who live in the United States.⁴

American Muslims have expressed a variety of concerns over involvement in Christian-Muslim dialogue, which is elaborated in this chapter. Many prefer not to become involved with such activities. In a recent study on mosques in America, however, researcher Ihsan Bagby of Shah University found that 65 percent of respondents indicated that they have participated in an interfaith dialogue or program and 37 percent in an interfaith social service project.⁵ Those Muslims who do want to dialogue are clear in saying that their coreligionists who continue to consider Christians and Jews to be *kafirs* (nonbelievers, or rejecters of faith), despite their status as People of the Book, not only do not want to be part of any dialogue but really have no business doing so anyway. It seems clear that the more Muslims acknowledge their sense of "belonging" in the United States, and the more they involve themselves in the public square as attested to by the elements of the current MAPS project, the more they are going to find themselves drawn into interaction with members of other faith traditions. As MAPS codirector Sulayman Nyang observes, "Interfaith is an indirect way of indexing American Muslims, i.e. of seeing the degree to which they have been acculturated."⁶ Walid Saif, a participant in Christian-Muslim dialogue sessions of the WCC, argues that "the more one is secure in his/her own identity, the more is he able to be more inclusive."⁷ Saif's description seems to apply to most of the Muslims who have elected to become involved in Christian-Muslim dialogue in the American context.

MODELS OF MUSLIM-CHRISTIAN DIALOGUE IN THE UNITED STATES

The purposes for which interfaith encounter has been proposed naturally serve to determine the nature of the dialogue. In the United States, a range of such purposes continues to be evidenced, resulting in a number of "types" or "models" of engagement. Within these models different themes and issues emerge, which are examined later. Here we will consider some of the models that have characterized American Muslim-Christian conversation, recognizing that a few have been on the scene for decades while others are just emerging. The naming and descriptions of these categories are my own.

The Confrontation/Debate Model

Debate and confrontation, generally of a theological nature, have characterized Muslim-Christian encounters since the earliest days of Islam. Historically, such encounters were not what could be called friendly discussions designed to promote better understanding of the other, but debates for the purpose of disproving the validity of the other's faith and belief system. Recent immigrants from parts of the world in which tensions between Christians and Muslims are high have experienced this kind of confrontational dialogue and sometimes expect to replicate it here. The WCC has been explicit in denouncing the debate model as an inappropriate vehicle for interfaith dialogue, urging a movement away from each side trying to prove its own religious truth in contrast to the other and toward a dialogue of mutual respect and understanding.[8]

On the whole, debate is not a model that is much appreciated in the American context, and most Muslims are clear in articulating that it is not appropriate for the promotion of genuine interfaith understanding. It is important, they say, to get beyond argumentation that fosters an "I am right and therefore you are wrong" attitude.[9] Or as Ahmad Sakr of the Foundation for Islamic Knowledge tells his readers in *Da'wah through Dialogue,* "Allah has reminded us to use the best approach when we are talking with People of other Faiths. In this regard Allah says in Surah Al-'Ankaboot (The Spider): 'And dispute not with the people of the Book, except with means better (than mere disputation).'"[10]

Dialogue as Information-Sharing Model

Within a range of different possibilities, this model seems to be the most common form of Muslim-Christian encounter. Longtime dialogue participant Sanaullah Kirmani of Towson University calls it "the safest form of 'dialogue.'"[11] As Christians become aware of the reality that Islam is the fasting growing religion in the United States and that Muslims are increasingly visible in all walks of Western life, churches and denominations are recognizing the importance of better understanding their new neighbors. Many Muslims find themselves invited to attend gatherings at which they are asked to talk about the basic beliefs and practices of Islam. They, in turn, may be told about some of the ways in which American Christians observe their own faith.[12] Often a single Muslim is featured as an invited "guest" in a predominantly Christian gathering, thus becoming the focus of Christian attention. One convert to Islam reports that she is often asked to participate in such sessions because she can speak the language of Christians as well as explain Islam. Dialogue is limited in such gatherings to a kind of question-and-answer session, during which participants try to make sure that basic information has been imparted. Many Muslims indicate that they are getting tired of the superficiality of this model. "Such explanatory sessions are frustrating because they are not really dialogue," reported a Shiite woman from Detroit. "It's time to get down to more serious discussions."[13]

Some Muslims are experiencing a new context for information sharing, however, that they see as a possible model of dialogue. This is the opportunity provided in the college or university classroom. Ali Asani of Harvard University, for example, says that he has found himself engaged in serious dialogue with his Muslim and non-Muslim students and that often it has provided a helpful experience for Muslim students who are struggling to find their identity as Muslims.[14] Imam Talal 'Eid of the Islamic Center of New England confided that he has learned from participating in Asani's course some of the ways in which it is possible to "do dialogue" with non-Muslims.[15]

It should be noted that the fact that many Muslim children are now enrolled in Catholic parochial schools, and that some Christian children go to Muslim schools, suggests the possibility of dialogue at a completely different level. Public schools are also providing opportunities for Muslim children (and often their parents) to talk to other students about their holidays and customs at appropriate times in the Islamic ritual cycle.

The Theological Exchange Model

For a number of years, certain Christian groups have encouraged the kind of dialogue in which deeper conversation is held about elements of faith within the traditions of Christianity and Islam. This model has been particularly effective in the annual regional meetings of the National Conference of Catholic Bishops, organized by its interreligious relations director, John Borelli. Participants in these dialogues, who attend on a regular basis and get to know each other well, exchange perspectives on a number of different theological themes.[16] Some Muslims, such as Islamic Society of North America (ISNA) former president (as of this writing) Muzammil Siddiqi of the Islamic Society of Orange County, California,[17] feel that the theological exchange model is still a very important mode of Muslim-Christian encounter. Others are not so sure, persuaded that this model does not work very well for Muslims, because theology is not their primary concern and is not always of great interest to them. Several have said frankly that they think theological dialogue is a waste of time. Unlike some Christians, Muslims generally do not engage in theological dialogue because they expect to learn something helpful to their own spiritual development. "Do Muslims want to 'grow' from the dialogue?" asks Sheikh Ibrahim Negm of the Islamic Center of Valley Stream, New York. "No, they want dialogue for information but not for personal growth."[18]

Lurking behind the concerns of some Muslims over this kind of theological exchange is the fear that Christians are subtly using the dialogue forum to continue their efforts at evangelization of Muslims. Those with experience particularly in international sessions know that despite their rhetoric, for some Christians dialogue has not replaced efforts at conversion but only provides a more covert opportunity for extending it. They worry that Muslims who have had little experience in such theological exchanges will not be prepared to understand what they fear to be the underlying agenda. Most Christians and Muslims who engage in theological dialogue, of course, are quick to affirm that the context should *not* be one in which judgments are made or persuasion attempted.

The Ethical Exchange Model

Some Muslims, most notably the late Ismail al Faruqi, have been adamant that the appropriate arena for discussion between Christians and Muslims is not theology but ethics.[19] This view has not prevailed within either community to date, but it is clearly gaining in popularity. Concerns for the decline in morality in American society, long feared by Muslims and usually seen as an inevitable concomitant of the rise of secularism in the West, have put ethics on the agenda as a matter of crucial importance for many. In general, Muslims express themselves as convinced that if Christians were to observe the ethical injunctions of their own religion more strictly, many of America's social problems might be alleviated. In any case, they understand that an examination of the ways in which Christians and Muslims can look to the resources of their traditions to provide ethical and moral guidance in the new century would be a profitable endeavor. And as advancements in medical science—for example in the field of bioethics—raise disturbing questions in both communities, some Muslims urge a coming together to share resources and perhaps to find common guidance.

The "Dialogue to Come Closer" Model

Proponents of this type of dialogue, both Muslim and Christian, hope that honest conversation among members of the two faiths will identify elements of commonality, leading to a deemphasis on differences and a reemphasis on sharing and mutuality. It must be said, of course, that most Muslims are very nervous about this kind of approach, finding it dangerous and expressive of exactly what they most fear about dialogue. We should not, they say, make any moves that will tend to blur the distinctions between our two communities. In its worst form, they believe, such conversations may lead to a kind of syncretism that Christians and Muslims on the whole have tried hard to avoid.

A few Muslims, however, are willing to go out on a limb and affirm the importance of this kind of exchange. "Most Muslims don't want it," says Plemon Amin of the Atlanta Masjid of Al-Islam, "but I think it is where we have to go."[20] He articulated this position clearly several years ago at a Christian-Muslim dialogue held at the International Denominational Center in Atlanta:[21] "Allahu Akbar means that God is greater than anything I imagine about God. No matter how I rise up in my religious and spiritual understanding, God will still be greater. That opens the door for me to have relationships with people of other faiths because they can have an insight on God that I don't have." Describing experiences in what he calls "academic dialogue" in Washington, D.C., Sanaullah Kirmani describes times when dialogue among members of different faith traditions helped deepen and increase individual faith commitments. "We can learn from each other, consciously or unconsciously coming closer to each other," says Irfan Ahmad Khan of the Council of Islamic Organizations in Markham, Illinois.[22] For most Muslims, however, this model will probably appear dangerous.

The Spirituality and Moral Healing Model

A small number of Muslims are interested in coming together with Christians for the purpose of pursuing issues of spirituality or what is sometimes referred to as moral healing. This model is very close to the prior one. Sometimes it is associated with an examination of modes of traditional psychology. As Laleh Bakhtiar of KAZI Books, whose own work is with young women in the area of psychology and healing, puts it, "It is developing dialogue in terms of virtues and vices that we all share."[23] For others it means pressing forward together into a deeper form of spiritual experience, which necessitates that participants be at more or less the same "level" of spiritual interest and understanding. An imam expressed such a desire during a dialogue of African American Christians and Muslims in Hartford several years ago. "My hope is always that we be prepared to discuss things at a more transcendent rather than a specific [i.e., issue-oriented] level. We need to address issues that touch the soul, heart, and mind. Do we have the spiritual character to have a true openness that is based on what is eternal and transcendent or not?" Again, most Muslims are not at a point where they are willing to commit themselves to such pursuits, and are openly nervous about them.

The Cooperative Model for Addressing Pragmatic Concerns

For many in the American Muslim community, the time for talk is over, and interest lies in "getting something accomplished together." Aminah Carroll of Stephenstown, New York, says, "As actions are a form of connected community, perhaps shared community action projects one of the deepest forms of dialogue."[24] One person called this the "common enemy" approach—addressing issues that are germane to the wholeness of both groups. This is

especially true of many younger people, as discussed below. It also characterizes the attitude of some who have had long experience participating in
Muslim-Christian dialogues and have become discouraged at what they feel
to be a lack of much progress. They feel that it is now time for people of faith
to join together in doing community work such as fighting drugs, delinquency, and other social ills. "That way," says Rula Abi Saab of the University
of Akron, "they can see that the 'other' is very much part of the social landscape and can't be ignored."[25]

Sometimes very innovative programs are being developed between and
among religious communities, such as a Canadian venture described by
Liakat Takim of the University of Miami that brings people in cold weather
off the streets to spend one week sheltered in a mosque, another in a
church, another in a synagogue. "Such a program fosters a belief in humanity," says Takim.[26] Muslims and Christians are working together in several major cities to help resettle Muslim refugees. Some have found that
while working together on projects may be more useful than "one more
conversation," the struggle is to find a project that works and to which
everyone can feel committed, as well as to find ways to reflect together
about what has been done.

One of the very practical issues of common concern that is being addressed by a number of the Christian-Muslim dialogue groups around the
country is that of intermarriage: how to counsel young people who are
contemplating such a marriage, what kinds of support can be offered by
the respective communities for couples of mixed faiths, and what concerns
should be addressed in terms of the children of such marriages.

THE NATURE OF THE DIALOGUE

As I have talked with Muslims about their involvement in Christian-Muslim
dialogue, a number of different themes have emerged. These themes are
suggested in the following categories or topics, again according to my own
designation.

The Range of Muslim Perspectives on Dialogue

As indicated earlier, most Muslim leaders believe that the majority of
Muslims in the United States are really not interested in interfaith dialogue,
either by inclination or by ideology. Those who would identify with what
is perceived as a growing Wahhabi or Salafi influence in this country are
among the Muslims who would probably decline the dialogue. This is of
particular concern to Muslims who fear that such influence, especially on
the youth in many American mosques, will deter a new generation of

young people from engaging in what they consider to be a very important activity.[27] Those who do not want to be involved sometimes argue that part of the doctrine of Islam is being loyal strictly to Muslims, and they fear that somehow that loyalty might be compromised were they to engage in real dialogue. Others are convinced that they have no need for such conversations, that there is really nothing to talk about since Islam provides them with all they need to live in Western society.

More Muslim leaders visible on the national scene, however, seem to be getting involved in dialogue efforts. (Skeptics question whether their interest is piqued more by the opportunity to form political connections than for religious reasons.) Leaders of major Muslim organizations such as the ISNA (encouraged by both former president Muzammil Siddiqi and Secretary General Sayyid Saeed) are generally very supportive of dialogue efforts, as are many members of the Islamic Circle of North America. Some Muslims with whom I spoke expressed concern that the more conservative organizations that are involved in the dialogue ultimately are more interested in *dawah* (Islamic propagation) than in building bridges of understanding. The question of the relationship of dawah and dialogue is a complex one for Muslims, as is that of dialogue and evangelization for Christians, and opinions vary widely. Some Muslims are deeply convinced that any effort at dawah must be strictly abandoned if dialogue is to be successful, and they draw a clear line between Muslims who are seriously interested in interfaith conversation and those who are only interested in conversion. Others are persuaded that if one is not able to speak honestly and with conviction about one's deepest beliefs there can be no effective dialogue, and if it constitutes dawah, then so be it. "If I experience something that I think is good," said an African American Imam in Hartford, "then it is un-Islamic for me not to try to share it. . . . This is what Islam is. It may be perceived as proselytism, but we must tell you what we believe. God will ask us at the judgment, 'Why didn't you say so-and-so when you had the opportunity to do it?' I believe that the same integrity exists for Christians."

Prolific author and speaker Jamal Badawi insists that the Quran makes it incumbent on Muslims to convey the message of Allah in its final form to all humanity, but he also insists that "We are not talking here about conversion. I do not like that word." While Badawi does not use the term *dawah*, it is clear that is what he is talking about.[28] Or as Fawaz Damra, the imam of the Islamic Center of Cleveland, puts it, "Dawah can't stay outside the door. It takes integrity, courage, and patience to speak honestly."[29] As yet there has been little sustained conversation within the Muslim community itself about the relationship of dawah and dialogue, although a few individuals such as Isma'il al Faruqi have written about it.

A number of dialogue participants with whom I spoke expressed their conviction that the very process of entering into conversation with Christians or members of other faith traditions is helpful for Muslims themselves to understand their own differences and to learn how better to relate to each other. These differences may be ideological, cultural, sectarian or racial-ethnic. "The roots of pluralism are so deep within the Islamic tradition that there is a kind of un-Islamic reaction against pluralism," says Ali Asani. "Muslims are often tempted to look at other Muslims as kafirs." While relations between Sunnis and Shiites are reported to be generally good in this country, there are still pockets of misunderstanding that may usefully be addressed (or at least better understood) within the context of interfaith dialogue.

Who Initiates the Dialogue?

In talking with Muslims who have been involved in Christian-Muslim conversations, I specifically asked where the initiative generally lies for bringing people together. While there is general agreement that it is Christians who usually extend the invitation, I encountered a range of responses in terms of whether that is a good thing. Zahid Bukhari, the codirector of the MAPS project, feels that most Muslims still consider themselves to be guests in America and that they are therefore in a "response" rather than an "initiation" mode.[30] "There is an imbalance because Christians are the majority in America, so naturally it is up to them to invite Muslims into the conversation," says Leila Ahmed of Harvard.[31] Some, however, see clear disadvantages to having the Christians always be the organizers. "Generally it is a Christian table set with some Muslim guests who are trying to figure out why they have been invited to dinner," commented Amina McCloud of De Paul University.[32] Many Muslims feel that until they get their own act together and determine who will be invited, what the agenda will be, and on whose terms, there will always be an imbalance in the conversation.

In fact, some initiatives are beginning from the Muslim side. The Quran enjoins Muslims to initiate dialogue with others, insists Imam Sayed Hassan Qazwini of the Islamic Center of America, and it is incumbent on Muslims to do this. Qazwini believes that Muslims have less problem in initiating dialogue with non-Muslims than they have initiating it with each other.[33] While many feel that the situation may change somewhat, it will be a long time before Muslims are active in getting dialogue conversations going. Others cite growing efforts on the part of Muslims to take such initiatives. Amir al-Islam of Medgar Evers College, formerly with the World Conference on Religion and Peace, reports that Muslims in the Western world are now taking a major role in expanding the dialogue and are really pushing the agenda.[34]

Major national organizations are getting involved and do sponsor some events, says Sulayman Nyang, especially with interfaith groups. Christians are now being invited to national Muslim conventions, which he sees as representing a new trend in interfaith relations. Increasing numbers of Muslims, he says, see the benefits of the dialogue and are developing what he calls "a kind of interfaith savvy," especially those who have been active in multifaith encounters. The Muslim Public Affairs Council (MPAC) has been a leader in organizing interfaith exchanges. MPAC has invited members of the National Council of Churches, the National Conference of Catholic Bishops (NCCB), and local and national Jewish organizations to engage in dialogue efforts.[35] Notable among mosque communities that have led in dialogue initiatives are such groups as the Islamic Center of Long Island (under the leadership of al-Hajj Ghazi Khankan) and the Islamic Center of Southern California (under the leadership of Maher and Hassan Hathout). Changes are clearly under way in some quarters, although the jury is still out as to how much active initiative the Muslim community in the United States will take.

Meanwhile, there are things that Christians who have invited Muslims into their "space" can do to make them more comfortable, says Kirmani. Many Muslims prefer not to enter a church sanctuary unaccompanied by someone from the host congregation, and they should be met at the door. It is also a good idea, he says, to make sure that two people, a man and a woman, should be designated as official hosts. And if there is to be prayer, it should be oriented toward God rather than Jesus.[36]

Benefits of the Dialogue

There is no question that most Muslims who have chosen to participate in Muslim-Christian dialogue have found it beneficial, for a variety of reasons. Among them are the following:

- *It builds trust, respect, and friendship.* Particularly with groups that are able to develop continuity, the process of getting to know one another lays the basis for seeing the "other" as a real person and not just "a Muslim" or "a Christian." Participants stress that sometimes it takes years before a genuine level of trust, or what some of them call "safe space," can be established. "It is because of groups like this," said ISNA Secretary General Sayyid Saeed about the NCCB-sponsored Midwest dialogue, "that we have established the trust that helps us get past events such as the pope's recent statement about other religions. The more we understand one another, the more we respect one another." From trust comes a raising of the comfort level to the point where some have learned how to laugh together, even at their own expense. Trust also comes into play in terms of individual communities. Several Muslims commented that it is necessary to involve people in the dialogue who are already well trusted in order to bring others along, given the fact that there is already a high level of mistrust of the dialogue process.

- *It provides a balance to the negative image America has in the minds of many Muslims.* Just as many Americans tend to see Muslims in the image of the terrorists portrayed in the media, so many immigrant Muslims bring with them the picture of the United States as imperialist and a supporter of dictatorship and oppression in the Muslim world. Or, as Imam Mohammad Ali Elahi of the Islamic House of Wisdom in Dearborn, put it, "Muslims see Christianity as a weapon in the hands of colonizers. Dialogue is a blessing and a source of great education, allowing Muslims [to] get past the bitter memories of tragedies that have happened in the Middle East."[37] It has been through the process of dialogue that many Muslims have come to realize and appreciate the openness to and appreciation of Islam and themselves as members of the Muslim community that are exhibited by many Christian participants.
- *It helps change American attitudes toward Islam.* Muslims are keenly aware of the negative impression many Christians have of them and their faith, and many believe that by engaging in face-to-face conversation a whole new appreciation can be fostered. As a result of dialogue encounters, increasing numbers of Christians are working together with Muslims to combat prejudice, misunderstanding, and so-called disinformation in schools, the workplace, and other public arenas.
- *It helps foster unity as believers, people of faith.* This "benefit" was mentioned to me primarily by African American Muslims, and it seems to be part of their strong attempt to stress faith over race as a source of identity. "The basis of our coming together *is* faith. We come together to establish God in our lives. Most of the social problems come about because people have let God out of their lives."[38] Increasingly, other Muslims are recognizing and articulating the importance of coming together as people with a basis in a common heritage and a shared monotheistic faith who are struggling to live conscientiously in a society that often does not reward such attempts. Some affirm the dialogue because it helps them in their own understanding of Islam. "Because of . . . an interfaith retreat last summer," says Dr. Shahid Athar of Indiana University's School of Medicine, "I am now a better human and a better Muslim."[39] Imam Hamad Ahmad Chebli of the Islamic Society of Central New Jersey said that imams are often called on to interact with American Christian culture and society and are ill informed. Chebli comes to the dialogue because it makes him a better Imam.[40]
- *It provides a mechanism for social reform.* Many Muslims are very enthusiastic about this possibility. "Other religious leaders may well be facing the same problems Muslims are," said Imam Talib Abdur-Rashid of the Muslim Alliance in North America at a recent MAPS meeting of national organization leaders. "Dialogue may help us understand that and work together on solutions." Muhammad Yunus of ICNA agreed,

saying, "We need to work hand in hand with brothers and sisters of other faiths in helping solve problems of American society." Some go so far as to see that the dialogue is primarily driven now by the social process and the recognition of the power of religious communities collaborating for social action. "We don't have the luxury or the time to spend talking theology," says Amir al-Islam. "We are committed to our faiths, but our faiths inform us that we have not thanked God and served God unless we serve the people. We must shift the way we look at each other and see if we can't work collaboratively."[41]

Such collaboration is not always easy for Muslims, however. Dr. Moein Butt of the Islamic Society of Greater Houston observes that while the sixty-nine mosques and Islamic centers in Houston are increasingly getting involved in community activities, Christians and Jews have taken the lead on the civic front and Muslims are often very resistant to associating and working with them.[42]

Problems with the Dialogue

Enthusiasm over the good things that have come out of Christian-Muslim dialogue does not deter Muslims from active identification of many problems that they believe need to be addressed for real progress to be made in interfaith understanding. Among them are the following:

- *The playing field is not level.* Christians (and Jews) have been dialoguing in the American context for a long time. They know the rules, while Muslims, who are generally new to the process, often do not. As a result of their inexperience, says Marcia Hermanesen of Loyola University, Muslims sometimes present their ideas in a traditional way that is neither appealing nor fully comprehensible to Western Christians.[43] "Muslims are a little behind in the dialogue compared with Christians," says Irfan Ahmad Khan. "We have to give them time to catch up." Some immigrant Muslims who experience a sudden displacement and cultural shock at coming to the United States find it extremely difficult to live up to the demands and goals of interfaith exchange. It is therefore a great challenge to get them involved so that there can be a true cross section of Muslims represented in the dialogue.[44] On a somewhat different note, one Muslim commented to me that he thinks that Muslims are often underrepresented in "official" dialogues because Christians who attend as representatives of church organizations get their way paid while Muslims do not have such resources and must donate both time and money.[45]

  An unequal relationship sometimes exists when Christians know more about Islam than Muslims do about Christianity. Or, sometimes the Muslims involved in the dialogue are invited because there are not many in the community from which to choose, and they may actually not know a great deal about Islam. This is exacerbated when the Christians involved are scholars of Islam and may know more about elements of Islamic theology than the Muslims do. "What we are doing now in the dialogue is nice stuff, promoting friendly relations, et cetera," says Ghulam Hader Asi of the American Islamic College. "But we will never have effective dialogue until Muslims are better trained in their own tradition and especially in the Christian tradition." We need better knowledge of those we are dialoguing with, he says, and how sects and denominations differ.[46] From another perspective, Akin Akintunde of the University of North Carolina feels that many Muslims think that Christians don't have an adequate knowledge of Islam. "Thus, Muslims are always ready to react, sometimes belligerently, to what they perceive as an unjustifiable arrogance *cum* ignorance on the part of Christians."[47]

- *Muslims have not developed a conceptual framework for dialogue.* "Up to today we do not have any by-laws or constitution or guidelines for dialogue. We just come together and decide to talk about this or that. We need to have a structured format and know where we are going."[48] One of the problems for immigrant Muslims is that they usually have not participated in interfaith dialogue in their home countries and thus rely on Christians to set the agenda. They have not yet developed a language of dialogue.[49] "We should lay the foundations of dialogue as a discipline—with rules, regulations, premises, methodology, and guidelines—so that emotions don't take over. We need more intellectual work from both Muslims and Christians on the *how* of it," says Imam Ibrahim Negm,[50] who sees this as an important mutual project for Christians and Muslims as well as an individual project for each. It is crucial that we bridge simplistic comments about better understanding and move toward arguments about what is crucial for holding the dialogue, he says. "Muslim Student Association president Altaf Husein worries that young Muslims will get discouraged with the dialogue because it is often too free-wheeling with no rules or guidelines. He urges an agenda of more issue-based conversation focused on specific topics of mutual interest to Muslim and Christian students."[51] According to Amir al-Islam, Muslims are less actively participating in the National Council (formerly the National Council of Christians and Jews) precisely because of the lack of a clearly defined agenda.[52]

- *Muslims and Christians often approach the dialogue with different issues and concerns.* It has already been noted that the theological dialogue, a favorite with many Christians, is generally of less interest to Muslims. The latter often prefer to talk about issues that sound political to Christians and therefore divisive, as a result of which Christians try to go back to the theological discussions that many Muslims do not find helpful.[53] This is further complicated when the theological discussion is formulated in what are basically Christian categories.[54] Dialogues sponsored by Western Christians are usually dominated by Christian concepts and categories such as salvation and redemption, reflects Riffat Hassan of the University of Louisville, so that the Muslim is forced to dialogue in terms alien to his or her religious ethos or may even be hostile to it.[55] Political discussions, of course, pose their own problems and in fact *are* often divisive, particularly if they detail problem areas of the world in the analysis of which Christians and Muslims may not agree or where American political inclinations may be very distasteful to Muslims. It is often frustrating for Muslims, says Muzammil Siddiqi, when Christians do not seem to understand how Muslims view things even after they have been told many times, as, for example, concerning the issue of Israel/ Palestine.

- *Many Muslims continue to suspect that Christians have an (often not so hidden) agenda of converting them away from their faith.* In general, it seems to be the case that Muslims who have had experience in Christian-Muslim dialogue are less concerned about this point, either having been reassured that such intent is not the case or having acquired the degree of sophistication to be able to respond appropriately if they do encounter it. The real problem is that many Muslims who have not had experience with dialogue keep their distance, and urge others to do so, out of fear that their faith will be challenged or compromised.[56] This is of particular concern when it comes to encouraging the youth of the Muslim community to participate. "To educated Muslims there are no dangers but to ignorant conservatives there are many," says Shahid Athar. "They see the interfaith process as compromising on faith . . . creating doubts in the minds of young Muslims."[57]

Imam Muhammad Nur Abdullah of Dar-ul-Islam Masjid in St. Louis worries that young people may not be able to be discriminating: "While those who have been about the business of dialogue for a long time have perspective and understanding that there are serious and significant differences between Christians and Muslims, younger people may be tempted to see the commonalities to the point of making the differences insignificant, moving toward a kind of blending of the faiths."[58] In a kind of reversal of this concern, but also reflecting a certain suspicion that many Muslims have about the dialogue, Amir al-Islam notes that in any conversation between Christians and Muslims it is hard to avoid what he calls "the East-West thing." Muslims see that the West has taken everything from them, he says, and now they want to talk faith. And they wonder why.

- *Muslims and Christians often come from different ideological perspectives.* Muslims know that the dialogue is often initiated by Protestant Christians who tend to be more "liberal," both socially and theologically, than the Muslims with whom they are in conversation. This not only puts the theological discussion on an uneven basis, but it also presents problems when certain social and ethical issues are introduced. More than one Muslim-Protestant dialogue has faltered when it becomes clear that there is no commonality between the groups on matters of abortion or homosexuality; Muslims generally find themselves more comfortable in this arena when they are talking with Roman Catholics. Plemon al-Amin feels that as non-Muslims come to know more about Islam and thus don't need so much education about it, Muslims need to counter by being a bit more flexible and "giving," even if it means stepping temporarily outside their own set rituals and practices for the sake of the conversation. This stance does not mean compromising on ethical and moral issues about which Islam has clear prohibitions, he says, but encourages Muslims to understand that the Quranic insistence that all people are free to practice what they believe in their own way should encourage greater flexibility.
- *Many Muslims are concerned that the dialogue is dominated by particular groups of Muslims.* It seems to be a fact that Muslim participation in interfaith dialogues is most evident on the part of immigrants from South Asia. For some others, particularly Arabs and African Americans, this is problematic insofar as they feel that the perspectives of Indians and Pakistanis may not reflect their own or those of many other Muslims in the United States. In the same way, some Shiites worry that their voices are not being adequately represented in dialogues in which Sunnis almost always predominate. For the most part Shii representation in dialogue sessions is minimal, often with only one alongside a number of Sunnis, and does not reflect the size of the Shii community in the United States. And African Americans are often upset because they feel that they are inadequately represented in many dialogue sessions and that generally they are not taken seriously by immigrant colleagues when they do participate.

African American Muslims and the Dialogue

Estimates of the number of African Americans in the Muslim community range from about 30 to 35 percent. African Americans are visible in all aspects of Muslim public life, and certainly they play an active part in Christian-Muslim dialogue. When I asked members of both African American and immigrant groups who they thought was more open to involvement in interfaith exchange, I found consistency in the responses: Immigrants think that immigrants are more receptive and interested, and African Americans think the same of themselves. Primarily because African Americans either were themselves once Christian or have Christians in their families, many feel that it is easier for them to relate to Christians and to know "where they are coming from." In general, African Americans are better at dialogue with Christians than immigrants, says Plemon Amin, because it is part of their own heritage and they understand Christianity better.[59] As Sulayman Nyang observes, "It is like a family affair."[60] Also true of many families, however, is the reality that tensions can be high and can lead to what might be called a love-hate relationship.[61]

Imam Warith Deen Mohammed, the leader of the Muslim American Society (now more generally known as the Ministry of W. D. Mohammed), strongly encourages African Americans to rebuild their family ties and to reaffirm their connection with their Christian heritage. This, says Ayesha Mustafa, editor of the *Muslim Journal,* tends to make them more eager to participate in interfaith conversations, observing that the involvement of African American Muslims in dialogue has picked up considerably.[62] The imam himself for the last several years has become deeply involved with the Roman Catholic Focolare Movement headed by the Blessed Lady Chiara Lubich. He has traveled to Rome to meet with her, and together they have hosted a series of public events in the United States. "The key for this kind of relationship is respect for God, respect for His Word and respect for each other," says the *Journal.*[63] Mustafa thinks that this association will be longstanding, based on what she sees as a spiritual kinship between the imam and Lubich. In general, the imam has expressed his desire that interfaith dialogues will serve the purpose of presenting a better understanding of Islam, providing a context in which to work on social issues, and creating a more responsive environment for the Muslim American Society (MAS).[64]

Collaboration between MAS and Focolare represents an unusual blend of African American and White along with Muslim and Christian. In general, the involvement of African Americans in the dialogue is either Black on Black (Muslims and Christians) or African American Muslims together with immigrant Muslims talking with Christians (usually White). Black-on-Black dialogue, while recognized by Muslims as an important endeavor, is not a common occurrence. Muslims attest to what they believe to be a deep concern in the Black Christian community, often rising to fear, about the fact that so many Black Christian youth (especially males) are choosing to become Muslim. Imam E. Abdulmalik Muhammad of MAS has said that the only time he is invited to Black churches is to discuss social problems impacting the larger Black community. "White churches are more open to dialogue with Muslims than are black churches," he said, "The black churches are still afraid of us."[65] Several members of the MAS indicated their impression that Imam Warith Deen himself is not particularly interested in

Black-on-Black dialogue, feeling that most Black Christians are primarily interested in identifying White racism as a common bond, while he does not
want to be concerned with that matter. He himself wants theological dialogue that does not haggle over points of belief but provides opportunities
for exchange so as to enhance the mutual understanding of God.

Amir al-Islam agrees that there is very little Black-on-Black dialogue and
that it needs some serious attention. Talking with Focolare is fine, he says,
but his own wish is that the MAS would work to initiate dialogue "within
the family." He thinks that perhaps it will be necessary to have facilitation
from the outside, probably by White Christians.[66] The National Council of
Churches Commission on Interfaith Relations has been trying for years to
initiate such a dialogue, but thus far these efforts have netted little result. Al-
Islam's own preference is that the context for Black-on-Black dialogue be
the concern for what he calls "a crisis of monumental proportions" within
the African American community, including guns, AIDS, and teen suicide.[67]

Other issues come to fore in the consideration of African American Muslims and immigrants participating together in Muslim-Christian dialogue.
Some immigrants, for example, feel that while it is crucial to have the participation of all Muslims it is frustrating when African Americans want
everyone to listen to their own problems before people can talk together.
Immigrants, says Imam Muhammad Nur Abdullah, are generally more
open than their Black coreligionists and are less obviously concerned
about racism. Sheikh Ibrahim Nejm notes that when immigrant and African
American Muslims participate together in a dialogue session, it often turns
into a debate rather than a dialogue, or more specifically a subdebate
within the overall conversation.

Concerns expressed by African Americans, not surprisingly, reflect another
perspective. Acknowledging that local dialogues seldom include both African
American and immigrant Muslims, they suspect that this is because immigrants, with Christian initiators, generally control the agenda and the list of
invitees. This, they feel, is because immigrants want Christians to talk with
"authentic" Muslims rather than "newcomers on the scene." The African
Americans, of course, tend to feel that they themselves are the truly authentic Muslims in the American context because of their indigenous identity. At
a deeper level than these kinds of judgments, however, African American
Muslims do recognize that serious problems sometimes impede their own
participation in dialogue. Among the problems that I have heard identified
are the continuing struggle with identity issues, the lack of much serious intellectual leadership, and the general inexperience of African Americans with
what has been called the "diplomacy of dialogue." Many express the frustration of constantly feeling that they need to "prove themselves" in relation to
immigrants; bluntly, they feel caught among the triple pressures of American
racism, lack of appreciation by immigrant brothers and sisters, and American

anti-Muslim attitudes. "I am very concerned that there is a distorted image of Islam in America," says Sheikh 'Abd Allah Latif 'Ali, the chair of the Imams Council of New York, "meaning an immigrant image that does not understand prejudice against indigenous Muslims here in America."[68]

Participation of Women in the Dialogue

While women are slowly becoming more active and visible participants in Muslim-Christian dialogue, they still remain very sparsely represented. A number of reasons were cited by the Muslim women with whom I spoke: Women are less visible in the community than men and thus are not known individually by those who are initiating and organizing dialogues. Muslim men neither encourage their participation nor give the names of possible female participants to conference organizers. Women are interested in different issues than men and generally do not want to join the conversation if it is about theological or doctrinal matters. Dialogues are almost always dominated by male "authority figures" such as imams, and most women do not feel comfortable speaking up in such situations. In traditional cultures, women do not usually engage in open conversation with men at all, let alone men of other religious traditions. Many Muslim women prefer to listen rather than to talk, and they are embarrassed when they are strongly encouraged by their Christian hosts to participate more actively. When women do speak, they are not really listened to by either Muslim or Christian men.

Female interfaith dialogue groups seem to be gaining in popularity with some Muslim women, particularly sessions that involve women from the three Abrahamic religions (Islam, Christianity, and Judaism) or from a range of traditions. In some cases, Muslim women are moving into leadership positions in ongoing interfaith forums. (In Wichita, Kansas, for example, the next president of Interfaith Ministries is Ramzieh Azmeh.[69]) African American women, who until recently have not been involved in many such sessions, are now beginning to get interested in women's interfaith conversations.[70] Several women expressed their frustration that dialogues among women always seem to focus on questions about wearing Islamic dress; non-Muslim women participants find it hard to hide their opinion that anyone who chooses to wear the *hijab* (loose-fitting dress with headscarf) is somehow backward or oppressed. One Muslim expressed her annoyance that Christian women insist on pushing a more "liberal" agenda; she reports that they seem to feel that women should be more open than men to moving forward on matters of gender equality, sexual openness, and so forth. Muslims, she said, can be easily turned off by such expectations.

Several observations can be made in relation to women and the dialogue. Some Muslim women in the United States who *are* interested in serious textual and theological study, both immigrant and indigenous, understand that they are engaged in *ijtihad* (individual interpretation). They tend to see Islam as a dynamic evolving entity (often because of the initiative of women)[71] and to view themselves as having moved beyond the more static understanding of Islam held by many Muslims (especially males) who are currently involved in the dialogue. Given the obstacles in the way of their being heard clearly in such sessions anyway, they are not interested in fighting the same battles over and over again. In effect, they have already "moved on."

A second observation is that a few women, tired of the usual talk, are using the dialogue as an opportunity to press agendas for action. Dialogue veteran Riffat Hassan of the University of Louisville, for example, has taken the occasion of interfaith conversation as another forum for advocating the liberation of women from male dominance.[72] She claims the right of women to participate in inter- and intrareligious dialogue not passively but actively setting the agenda. Hassan has long believed in the necessity of continuing to carry on doctrinal discussions between Christians and Muslims.[73] Nonetheless, more recently she has turned her attention away from the dialogical model to work more actively for an end to the violation of women in her native Pakistan. Muslim women in general are becoming more interested in interfaith activity as the agenda seems to be shifting away from conversation, theological or otherwise, and more toward practical or "problem-solving" kinds of engagement. Many are looking for new venues of discussion and cooperation in which to move agendas of social action or of providing assistance to members of the broader community.

Aminah Carroll, the lone Muslim member of the Women's Interfaith Institute in the Berkshires, identifies gender prejudice and sexual abuse as common problems faced by women. "Inviting Muslim women to become a part of the solution to these socially ubiquitous problems is an act of inclusivity generous women of other faiths may take, she says.[74] One might note, for example, the interfaith context in which Najeeba Syeed-Miller uses the tools of mediation, facilitation, and reconciliation in her work on conflict intervention and resolution in California.[75] Amina Wadud of Virginia Commonwealth University, long active in Muslim-Christian encounters, says that, in her opinion, traditional dialogue "isn't really going anywhere," and she is therefore moving more directly into an interfaith context in which she works for causes of justice and peace. Wadud is currently active in the World Conference on Religion and Peace (WCRP).[76]

Participation of Youth in the Dialogue

American Muslims are acknowledging that if serious attempts are not made immediately to involve younger Muslims in the internal activities of the community as well as in formalized Muslim relations with others in American society, serious consequences may incur. A number of those with whom I spoke, therefore, expressed their concern with the reality that few young people are actively involved in Christian-Muslim dialogue or express any interest in such involvement. Several noted that it does not work to simply add them to the mix of participants already in place because their issues are different, and they get easily discouraged when the agenda reverts to the interests of those who have been at it for a long time. "Youth are not involved in the dialogue because they are concentrating on different issues," says Nihal Hassan, a young Muslim from Indianapolis. "They are at an age when their personality is forming, and it would be very important to instill in them ideas of openness and understanding. But it is best to have them working together on projects."[77] Yahya Hendi, the chaplain at Georgetown University, agrees. It is crucial to get the youth involved, he insists, but they aren't interested in theological issues. "They are constantly changing in terms of their interests, backgrounds and the things they are concerned about. The old issues don't do anymore."[78]

As is true for many Muslim women and others, it seems clear that today's young people are more interested in multifaith than in bilateral Christian-Muslim conversations and are more interested in action than in talk. MSA president Altaf Husein talks about his activities with young representatives of a variety of faith traditions in which they engaged in such activities as building a house for Habitat for Humanity. "Youth want more community dialogue through interfaith engagement," says Muzammil Siddiqi. "They want activities and projects."

As is always the case, youth bring challenges to the established religious community. Precious Muhammad, recent graduate of Harvard Divinity School, describes a situation in Georgia where two lesbian Christian women adopted four Muslim children. Honoring their religious affiliation, the women brought the children to Friday prayers, themselves sitting in the back wearing headscarves. "So what do you do in this pluralistic society where certain things are clearly not acceptable in Islam," she asks, "and then you have a new definition of family?"[79]

Interfaith/Multifaith Dialogue

It has been noted several times in this chapter that many Muslims prefer to be involved in conversation groups with a range of partners beyond the two-way Muslim Christian dialogue. Some are willing to term this "interfaith" exchange, while others feel that "multifaith" is a safer term insofar as it tends to safeguard the integrity of the participating traditions and does not lead to a blurring of distinctions. Partly at the initiative of Christian ecumenical groups that find themselves drawn into an acknowledgment of the growing religious plurality of America, and are therefore inviting members of other religions to meet and talk with them, Muslims are finding themselves increasingly involved in inter-/multifaith dialogue. "Many Islamic centers around the country are members of local and regional interfaith groups," says Mohammed Nimer of CAIR. "These groups exchange speakers who introduce their faith to other groups and send delegations to attend religious celebrations of other faith communities."[80]

While such initiatives often make more conservative Muslims uneasy, particularly when it comes to the participation in the celebrations of others that Nimer notes, they are reported in an increasing number of arenas. Ghazi Khankan of the Islamic Center of Long Island (one of the few mosques that has a specific concentration on interfaith activities) participates in many different kinds of programs with rabbis, ministers, and priests. It is very useful for the American public to see this kind of exchange, Khankan says.[81] The Chautaqua Institution in New York is beginning an Abrahamic initiative whose purpose is to educate about the three Abrahamic faiths and to define a common purpose and seek a common mind, particularly on the issues of science and ethics, the arts, and the common ethical premises of a civil society.[82] The Rumi Forum located in Washington, D.C., professes in its website to have an open-door policy to bring together scholars of every faith in the spirit of mutual respect. The forum has an ongoing Christian-Muslim dialogue with Catholic University. Muzammil Siddiqi's ongoing participation in a three-way traveling dialogue is featured in a volume entitled *The Abrahamic Connection: A Jew, Christian and Muslim Dialogue.*[83]

Often the interfaith involvement is more for action than for talk. Imam Khalid Abdul Fattah Griggs of Masjid Winston-Salem in North Carolina reports that he is involved in an interfaith group called Interfaith Partnership for Advocacy and Reconciliation (IPAR), a social action group of Christians, Muslims, and Jews that engages in such activities as sponsoring feeding programs in schools, recreation centers for kids, and the like.[84] Coalitions take a different form from dialogues, says Salam al-Marayati of MPAC in Los Angeles, tending to focus on social concerns that groups have in common. Such conversations are drawing increasing numbers of young couples or people in their twenties and thirties to engage in what al-Marayati calls "religious progressive politics." Members of a range of different religious traditions are involved.[85] California is the home of a variety of multifaith initiatives, including United Muslims of America (UMA) in Fremont, the Interfaith Group for the Homeless, the Interfaith Alliance of Northern California, and United Religious Initiative, whose stated purpose on its website is to promote enduring interfaith cooperation and to end religiously motivated violence.

One of the most complex issues facing Muslims and others who are engaged in inter-/multifaith exchange is whether and how to attempt any kind of common worship. Most Muslims are opposed to such attempts, and at best are willing only to allow others to "observe" them when they are performing *salat* (obligatory Islamic prayer). Sometimes they will themselves "observe" Christians or others during their own services of prayer and worship. At a kind of next level, some Muslims are willing to participate in interfaith services by reading from the Quran (most commonly the Fatiha) or giving a prayer. This kind of shared worship is perhaps most common on college and university campuses. Georgetown University chaplain Hehya Hendi says that Christians and Jews regularly participate in his Friday services. Shamshad Sheikh, chaplain at Mount Holyoke College, reports that students design services with a theme and have each faith group do a reading that relates to it. "But when it comes to prayer," she insists, "we always have separate groups. We welcome another faith to join the group, but it is strictly one faith only."[86] In a few instances, local dialogue groups report that they have attempted common prayer, being careful not to use language that could be offensive to any of the participants. Some feel that the benefits of a common experience outweigh the risks, while others are concerned that such a "watered-down" version of the liturgy of any of the participants serves to dilute rather than to enrich.

Again, California can be cited as the locus of some more visible experiences in "common worship." On September 10, 2000, "more than 3,000 Muslims and Christians viewed 9:30 and 11 A.M. services in which Dr. Robert Schuller and Sheikh Salah Kuftaro, son of the Syrian grand mufti, discussed shared belief in Jesus Christ." Further discussions are taking place between Christians and Muslims in the Crystal Cathedral, and the two groups are trying to establish a chapter of CAMP (Christians and Muslims for Peace) to work with inmates of California State Prison in Lancaster.[87]

REFLECTIONS ON MUSLIM-CHRISTIAN DIALOGUE

In this concluding section, I turn to four American Muslim academics who have given serious reflection to, and have written substantively about, the nature of Muslim-Christian exchange. They are the late Isma'il al Faruqi of Temple University, Mahmoud Ayoub of Temple University, Abdulaziz Sachedina of the University of Virginia, and Seyyed Hossein Nasr of the George Washington University.[88] This is not to suggest that these Muslim scholars are the only ones who have pondered and written about interfaith dialogue, but to argue that their reflections provide important resources for the future of philosophical and theological exchange between the faiths of Islam and Christianity. They have, to use the MAPS rubric, been highly active and visible in the American public square both in person and through the written word.

Isma'il al Faruqi

Before his untimely death in 1986, Isma'il al Faruqi was one of the most active Muslim personalities in interfaith work, and one of the very few Muslims who has engaged in a thorough study of Christian theology and ethics. Much of his writing proceeds from the deep textual understanding of the two religions, on the basis of which he was a major contributor to dialogue between Christians and Muslims. This is not to say, certainly, that al Faruqi's analysis of Christianity has been satisfactory to most Christians, despite his genuine efforts to find what he wanted to describe as authentic Christianity free from false accretions and the influence of Greek thought. He remained persuaded that despite such aberrations, and despite the distortions that Christians have always visited upon Islam, it should be possible to find some kind of rapprochement.

Basic to al Faruqi's approach is a deep commitment to dawah. Rather than the dawah of proselytism, however, he advocates that of invitation or what he calls the mutual search for truth. If conversion *is* involved, it is the conversion of both sides to the truth. "Both religions assert that they have *the* truth," he says, which is logically impossible. . . . Conversion to *the* truth is the aim of dialogue."[89] Christian analysts of his writings have understood this to mean he was convinced that if Christians and Muslims were serious in the mutual pursuit of truth they would arrive at the essence of what is contained in the Quran.[90] Al Faruqi was no fan of deep theological engagement, however, persuaded that primacy should be given to ethical rather than theological issues, based on the common effort to follow God's commandments. He called dialogue a "dimension of the human consciousness . . . a category of the ethical sense,"[91] the only kind of human interrelationship that is of real value.

Al Faruqi was involved in dialogue that also included Judaism. As the title of his *Trialogue of the Abrahamic Faiths*[92] indicates, he was one of the first to advocate the tripartite conversation among the descendents of Abraham. In *Trialogue,* he argues that there must be basic principles that guide the conversation; these he enumerates as coherence that is internal to traditions, accords with cumulative human knowledge, reflects the religious experience of humankind, corresponds with reality, and serves the achievement of ethically higher values.[93] Muslims as well as Christians have raised serious critique about al Faruqi's methodology as well as his assumptions. He remains, however, a kind of "Muslim father of the dialogue" insofar as he was among the first on the American scene to seriously frame the challenge and pursue the goal of arriving at "truth" with vigor and commitment.

Mahmoud Ayoub

Isma'il al Faruqi, a Palestinian, was succeeded at Temple University by Mahmoud Ayoub, one of the most faithful and active participants in Muslim-Christian (and Abrahamic) dialogue in the United States over the course of many years. Ayoub was born in Lebanon, and by virtue of an unusual "interfaith" background, he brings a very deep understanding of both Islam and Christianity to the table.

Ayoub has been consistent in his assertion that dialogue is not about conversion or "scoring points," but working together for better mutual understanding while maintaining the distinctness of each of the participant faiths. Dawah, he says, is not necessarily a call to join a religious community but a call to God. Ayoub has written at length about Quranic Christology, what he calls the Christology of the human rather than the divine Jesus.[94] Jesus, he reflects, has provided a bridge of piety and spirituality between Christianity and Islam but unfortunately has also been a great theological barrier.[95]

Ayoub is convinced that the Quran contains justification of the attitudes of both pluralism and exclusivism, depending on the context of the revelation. He himself stresses the former such that he regards the People of the Book (Jews and Christians) "as a large family of faith, speaking different languages, but worshipping the One God."[96] While he consistently denies the divinity of Christ, he is convinced that Islam has not brought any understanding of God that differs from what is inherent in Christianity and that the revealed word of God must be the common bond uniting all people of faith. Like al Faruqi, he stresses the importance of ethics over theology, although he describes it more as the opportunity to work together for justice than the academic pursuit of an ethical consensus.

One of the main benefits of dialogue for Ayoub is the possibility of developing and deepening friendships.[97] He fears that dialogue in the American context has become "fashionable," sometimes with "touchy-feely" dimensions that he and most Muslims want strongly to avoid, and is thus in danger of losing its meaning. Dialogue as a concept, he says, is beginning to "wear out." Recognizing that there are deep divisions in the Muslim community itself, including those between Sunnis and Shiites, he urges more consistent intrafaith dialogue, perhaps even before much creative interfaith or multifaith conversation can take place. In the best of worlds, the dialogue should be between or among people who have the skills and interests to delve deeply together into the scripture, history, and theology, Ayoub says, but he worries that such an endeavor would be confined to a very few scholars and leave most participants from each community behind.

In the end, both Muslims and Christians engaged in the dialogue must make a basic decision either to allow the claim to truth for the other or not. If the decision is not to allow such claims, he believes, then the dialogue is neither genuine nor does it have any point. "God speaks many languages, and truth does not lie in what theologians have come up with. Truth lies in the *living religions.*"[98]

Recognizing that the current mosque-/church-level dialogue is mainly restricted to the older generation and needs the infusion of younger thinking, Ayoub worries that the youth are drifting away from an interest in religion in any form, let alone dialogue. Perhaps a more hopeful venue than the religious institution for instilling such interest, he says, is the college or university classroom, where some students are showing a deep interest in learning about the other faiths. In any case, he is unwilling to give up on the dialogue, persuaded that it will take continuing struggle to make it worthwhile but that the effort is valid, important, and perhaps even essential.

Abdulaziz Sachedina

Like the other scholars described here, Abdulaziz Sachedina has been a frequent participant in and contributor to interfaith dialogue sessions, especially Muslim-Christian, over the course of many years. Also like the others, he brings a sharp critical edge to the discussion and encourages participants to work seriously with the sources of their traditions to better understand the scriptural grounds for interfaith engagement. In Sachedina's most recent work, entitled *The Islamic Roots of Democratic Pluralism,*[99] for example, he argues that the Quran tacitly endorses what he calls "the salvific efficacy of the other religions of the Book."[100] A state philosophy of "antipluralism," however, has characterized fundamentalist Muslims leading Islamic governments in modern nation-states. Such leaders in turn often criticize the efforts of Muslims in the West to discourse on the subject of pluralism, accusing them of giving in to secular Western critique of Islam as inadequate to running a modern state. Sachedina defends himself by saying that his task has been to present a theology of interreligious relations in Islam that may depart from earlier interpretations, but not from the Quran itself. He also argues that one way in which it is possible for religious people to work together for the common good without having to share religious doctrine is to articulate and proceed from each tradition's ethical imperative. Ethical discourse must be the major component of interfaith relations. "The challenge for Muslims today," he says, "as ever, is to tap the tradition of Koranic pluralism to develop a culture of restoration, of just intrareligious and interreligious relationships in a world of cultural and religious diversity."[101]

Responding to questions I put to him about his 1997 article "Islamic Theology of Christian-Muslim Relations,"[102] Sachedina drew more directly the implications of his position for interfaith dialogue. Dialogue presupposes what he calls the equality of two sides. No Christians or Muslims can sit in dialogue when in the depth of their hearts, because of a prejudicial attitude, they fail to accept the salvific efficacy of the other's religious tradition. Essential to dialogue is what he calls "internal purity of intention and mutual acceptance." Acknowledging that most Muslims today do consider Christians to be kafirs, he insists that for them it is the end of dialogue. When I asked whether he considers one outcome of interfaith exchange to be the possibility of learning from the other so as to enhance one's own understanding of faith, he said that humans must first learn to discover that understanding each other is for mutual and reciprocal coexistence.

Seyyed Hossein Nasr

Active in Muslim-Christian dialogue in the United States since he left his native Iran in 1979 at the time of the Iranian revolution, Seyyed Hossein Nasr is one of the most prolific Muslim authors on the subject. A scholar who is trained in the Islamic sciences, philosophy, theology, and esoteric Sufism, Nasr is also extremely well grounded in Christian history and theology. He is a traditional Muslim who values theological dialogue when it is carried out by well-prepared, solidly trained, and genuinely inquisitive scholarly participants who can talk together about the pursuit of truth. Nasr believes deeply that modernity has led people of faith, both Muslims and Christians, away from a realization of the role of the sacred in human lives. He is interested in looking at theological issues, not with the end of finding truth in one version over another, or for the purpose of persuading one side to accept the tenets of the other. Rather, he advocates an epistemology in which a single reality, most basically the oneness of God, might be seen in several different ways, or from different perspectives.[103] Such an approach is difficult to reconcile with modern philosophical categories and fits better with the perennialist philosophy of such thinkers as Rene Guenon and Frithjof Schuon, of which he is an advocate.

Nasr's latest contribution to a critique of the dialogue is entitled "Islamic-Christian Dialogue: Problems and Obstacles to be Pondered and Overcome."[104] I took the opportunity of posing a number of questions to Nasr on the basis of that article. Following is a brief presentation of questions and responses,[105] presented as a summary of his thoughts about Christian-Muslim conversation.

Q: Why has dialogue not been initiated by Muslims in America as it has in the Middle East and other Muslim lands?
A: Muslims are not much interested in initiating religious dialogue because they first want to consolidate their situation as part of the religious mainstream in America. But, at the same time, they are very anxious to participate when invited.
Q: You discuss the importance of Muslims and Christians discovering the esoteric and metaphysical dimensions of their respective faiths. Is this a process in which they can work together in a mutually beneficial way?
A: This is a task that Muslims and Christians should, first of all, carry out by themselves. But there can certainly be many benefits of mutual action in this domain (as, for example, I had with Henry Corbin).

Q: Given the impossibility of most groups reaching the level of theological thought and exchange for which you are calling, should they skip the theological conversation and go on to talk about other things?

A: Those who have theological and metaphysical qualifications should certainly attempt theological conversation. But others should simply settle for respect. It does not help the cause of Muslim-Christian dialogue if the people participating in theological debates are without the qualifications necessary to do so as, unfortunately, has taken place often during the last few decades.

Q: If, as you say, it is important to bring the question of who is saved to the center of the dialogue, should it be discussed by each side "privately" first?

A: Each faith community must first discuss this issue within its own confines. Only later is it fruitful to face this issue in dialogue. . . . In the long run, I believe that it is only members of the two communities who believe that salvation is *not* limited to members of their own faith who can carry on fruitful dialogue with each other.

Q: To what extent is dawah/evangelism an essential part of the dialogue?

A: Dawah/evangelism cannot but be an important and even positive part of the dialogue. If the power structures underlying such a dialogue were not there I would consider such activities as quite legitimate for both sides. But such a situation would be *totally* different from what you actually have today, namely, Western evangelists making use of all of the power of the Western civilization and modern science to propagate the mission of Christ with the result that modern Christian missionary activities in the non-Christian world go hand in hand with further secularization of those worlds.

Q: You warn those in interfaith conversation to make sure that the third partner to the dialogue is not secularism. But isn't there some concern that the third partner might rather be traditionalism? This is particularly problematic to both Muslim and Christian women, for many of whom traditionalism often has carried negative connotations.

A: I do believe that Muslim men and women can join Christian men and women in dialogue concerning the nature of God on the level of the Essence which transcends all dualism and polarity including gender categories. But I disagree strongly with you when you equate the third partner as secularism with the third partner as traditionalism as I use the word *tradition*. If by traditionalism you mean simply accumulated customs, then there is something to your assertion. But I use the word *tradition* as the transmission of sacred norms from the revealed origin of religion through the centuries and believe that both Christianity and Islam should carry out this dialogue precisely on the basis of that traditional structure which goes back to the Sacred revealed by God.

Here, then, are some of the thoughts, concerns, frustrations, and hopes raised by Muslims who have been involved in interfaith dialogue in the United States. It remains to be seen whether such involvement will continue to be, as Sulayman Nyang puts it, an index of acculturation and visibility in the American public square.

NOTES

1. See, for example, Jane I. Smith, "Islam and Christendom," in *The Oxford History of Islam*, ed. John L. Esposito (New York: Columbia University Press), 305–45.

2. "Christian-Muslim Dialogue: A Survey of Recent Developments," Msgr. Michael L. Fitzgerald, M.Afr., Pontifical Council for Interreligious Dialogue, available on Internet.

3. See, for example, Jacques Waardenburg, *Muslim-Christian Perceptions of Dialogue Today* (Leuven: Peeters, 2000), the last of three volumes based on the proceedings of three international symposia on Muslim-Christian dialogue.

4. "Another pressing reason for a dialogue in the 1960s and 1970s was the western obsession, American in particular, to establish a grand alliance against the communist bloc." Zafarul-Islam Khan, "Some Reflections on the Question of Christian-Muslim 'Dialogue,'" *Muslim & Arab Perspectives* 3, nos. 1–6 (1996): 55.

5. Part of the "Faith Communities Today" study project of the Hartford Institute for Religious Research at Hartford Seminary. The survey sampled 631 mosques, of which 416 interviews were completed, with a 4 percent margin of error.

6. Conversation with the author, October 2000.

7. Walid Saif, "An Assessment of Christian-Muslim Dialogue," paper delivered at a Christian-Muslim Consultation sponsored by the WCC in Amersfoort, Netherlands, November 8, 2000.

8. Saif, "An Assessment of Christian-Muslim Dialogue"

9. Some Muslims attribute this kind of confrontation model to followers of Ahmad Deedat.

10. *Da'wah through Dialogue* (Leicester, England: Foundation for Islamic Knowledge, 1999), 164.

11. "Interfaith Dialogue: A Muslim Perspective," shared with the author in April 2001. Kirmani reflects that this kind of dialogue has been used effectively by the Washington Interfaith Conference.

12. A sample of this kind of exchange is found in the ninety-minute video entitled *Christian Muslim Dialogue*, in which Aminah Asselmi, the associate editor of American Trust Publication in Plainfield, Indiana, and Floyd Clark, retired from Johnson Bible College in Knoxville, Tennessee, each speak for thirty-five minutes and then participate in a question-and-answer session. The video can be ordered under the web category entitled "Shopping: Buy Christian-Muslim dialogue products" on www.Yahoo.com.

13. Laila Jawad, conversation with the author, October 10, 2000.

14. Conversation with the author, March 9, 2001.

15. Conversation with the author, February 2, 2001.

16. "A regional dialogue is a dialogue that is constructed in such a way to encourage Muslim-Catholic participation," says Borelli. "A hub city is chosen. There are local hosts and there are national sponsors. Catholic and Muslim partners, usually the diocesan officer and the local imam, come together by car or other means. An agenda is chosen and we meet annually. This is how we maintain an ongoing relationship with ISNA, ICNA and now the *shurah* councils of N. and S. California." E-mail communication with the author, March 27, 2000.

17. Siddiqi did his doctoral work at Harvard's Center for the Study of World Religions on Muslim theologian Ibn Taymiyya's views of Christianity. The author talked with him about this issue in May 2001.

18. Conversation with the author, October 24, 2000.

19. See the last section of this chapter for an explication of al Faruqi's views on this subject.

20. Conversation with the author, March 16, 2001.

21. "Interfaith Cooperation for Social Action: Together in Community," February 26, 1998.

22. Conversation with the author, October 26, 2000. Khan has been called the "Mawlana of Interfaith Dialogue," Midwest Region Dialogue of Catholics and Muslims in Indianapolis, November 8–9, 2000.

23. Personal communication with the author, February 16, 2001.

24. Communication with the author, June 9, 2001.

25. E-mail communication to the author, November 21, 2000.

26. Conversation with the author, February 10, 2001.

27. This view was expressed, for example, by Imam Fawaz Damra of the Islamic Center of Cleveland in an interview with the author, March 31, 2001. He indicated that Muslims who have been influenced by thinkers such as Yusuf Qaradawi, however, are leaders in interfaith understanding.

28. "Bridgebuilding between Christian and Muslim," available at http://islam.org/Mosque/Bridge.htm.

29. Conversation with the author, March 30, 2001.

30. Conversation with the author, November 2000.

31. Conversation with the author, December 2000.

32. Conversation with the author, January 12, 2001.

33. Conversation with the author, May 9, 2001.

34. Conversation with the author, May 9, 2001.

35. Mohammed Nimer, "Muslims in American Public Life," in *Muslims in the West: From Sojourners to Citizens*, ed. Yvonne Haddad (New York: Oxford University Press, 2002). In light of current conditions in Israel/Palestine, the senior adviser to MPAC, Maher Hathout, on May 25, 2001, sent a letter to the Jewish members of the dialogue saying that conversations will need to be suspended. "In times of hot situations . . . we need to protect the dialogue by slowing the speed until there is a better environment to optimize the process."

36. Kirmani, "Interfaith Dialogue."

37. Conversation with the author, November 2000.

38. Conversation with an African American imam in New York, October 12, 2000.

39. Athar, "Lessons from an Interfaith Retreat," *Indianapolis Star,* July 16, 2000, p. D3.

40. Conversation with the author, March 15, 2001.

41. Amir al-Islam, Christian-Muslim dialogue at ITC, conversation with the author, March 15, 2001.

42. MAPS Focus Group 1.

43. Conversation with the author, May 2, 2001.

44. Rula Abi Saab, conversation with the author, May 2, 2001.

45. Imam Chebli, conversation with the author, May 2, 2001.

46. Conversation with author, November 2000.

47. E-mail communication with the author, February 16, 2001.

48. Imam Ahmad Chebli, e-mail to the author, February 16, 2001.

49. Liyakat Takim, e-mail to the author, February 16, 2001.

50. Interview with Negm.

51. Altaf Husein's conversation with the author, May 10, 2001.

52. The council does hold annual meetings of "Seminarians Interacting," including Christian, Jewish, and Muslim students, that have received excellent reviews from Muslim student participants.

53. Amina McCloud says that some Christian initiators of dialogue are "conflict avoiders." They set the agenda with items that should engender conflict, then try to avoid it.

54. Ghulam Asi notes that sometimes the same words are used with a common meaning, but it is important (but often difficult) to recognize that many times meanings and connotations differ.

55. "Women in the Context of Change and Confrontation within Muslim Communities," in *Women of Faith in Dialogue,* ed. Virginia Mollenkott (New York: Crossroad, 1987), 96–109.

56. Irfan Ahmad Khan's October 26, 2000, interview with the author.

57. Letter to the author, October 23, 2000.

58. Conversation with the author, January 9, 2001.

59. Conversation with the author.

60. Conversation with Sulayman Nyang.

61. Amina McCloud.

62. Conversation with the author, March 10, 2001.

63. "Encounters in the Spirit of Universal Brotherhood," *Muslim Journal* (March 16, 2001): 1.

64. Imam Alfred Muhammad of New Jersey, consultant with Advent Funding Company, conversation with the author, December 12, 2000.

65. Laila al-Marayati, "Christian Muslim Relations," Religious News Service 1999; available at www.islamamerica.org/articles.cfm?article_id=7 (accessed in 1999).

66. Conversation with the author.

67. Christian-Muslim dialogue at ITC.

68. June 10, 2000, MAPS regional seminar.

69. Altaf Husein.

70. Ayesha Muhammad.

71. See, for example, Hibba Abugideiri, "The Renewed Woman of American Islam: Shifting Lenses toward Gender *Jihad?*" *Muslim World* 91, nos. 1 and 2 (Spring 2001): 1–18.

72. She says, for example, that while Jews and Christians have been fighting sexism for a long time it is new for Muslim women who have been kept "in physical, mental and emotional bondage." *Women in the Context of Change and Confrontation,* 97.

73. Lecture on Jesus and Mary in the Islamic tradition at Hartford Seminary, December 1990.

74. Interview with Aminah Carroll.

75. Syeed-Miller presented a synopsis of her work at the "Muslims in America"

conference, Cambridge, Massachusetts, March 10, 2001. In an e-mail communication with the author, June 11, 2001, she expressed her interest in continuing to work "in the area of inter-ethnic dialogue."

76. Conversation with the author, March 11, 2001.

77. E-mail to the author, January 21, 2001.

78. Conversation with the author, March 30, 2001.

79. MAPS regional seminar, June 10, 2000.

80. MAPS regional seminar, June 10, 2000.

81. MAPS regional seminar, June 10, 2000.

82. From the foundation's website.

83. Edited by Benjamin J. Hubbard and George Grose (Notre Dame, Ind.: Cross-Cultural Publications, 1994).

84. Comment made at MAPS Regional Seminar 1.

85. Conversation with the author, May 10, 2001. Al-Marayati has observed that while Los Angeles has long been a leader in local dialogue, nothing is happening on a consistent basis with individual churches. "It's just here or there. It's insufficient and neglected." The way to proceed, he feels, is to talk about shared concerns. "You can always get a book to learn about basic Islam. Talking about shared concerns, about life as it is on a daily basis, makes people real to each other." Laila al-Marayati, "Christian Muslim Relations," *Religious News Service 1999.*

86. E-mail communication to author, April 2, 2001.

87. *Washington Report on Middle East Affairs* (April 2001): 52.

88. All of these scholars have written extensively, and have been written about, for many years. Space does not permit more than a brief reference to their respective approaches to interfaith dialogue, with little indication of the personal factors that inevitably come into play in the formulation of these approaches.

89. Isma'il al Faruqi, *Islam and Other Faiths* (Leicester, England: Islamic Foundation, 1998), 241.

90. "Thus, while allegedly offering a neutral foundation for Muslim-Christian relations," says Peter Ford, "based on mutual respect and on reason, what emerged in al-Faruqi's argument is that such a foundation is none other than Islam itself." "Isma'il al-Faruqi on Muslim-Christian Dialogue: An Analysis from a Christian Perspective," *I.C.M.R.* 4, no. 2 (December 1993): 241.

91. Al-Faruqi, "Isma'il al-Faruqi on Muslim-Christian Dialogue," 248.

92. Published by Al Sa'dawi Publications, in Alexandria, Virginia, 1991. He described Judaism as the first and Christianity the second moment of Arab consciousness among religions of the book. The term *trialogue* has since been both adopted and criticized on the grounds that *dialogue* can include more than two parties.

93. Ataullah Siddiqui, *Christian-Muslim Dialogue in the Twentieth Century* (Leicester, England: Islamic Foundation, 1997), 86–87.

94. See, for example, his Macdonald Center Lecture, "The Miracle of Jesus: Reflections on the Divine Word," delivered at Hartford Seminary in December 1991.

95. Siddiqui, *Christian-Muslim Dialogue,* 107–9.

96. Mahmoud Ayoub, "Islam and Christianity between Tolerance and Acceptance," *ICMR* 2, no. 2 (December 1991): 179.

97. This and the following are taken generally from years of interaction between the author and Ayoub, and specifically from a conversation held February 12, 2001.

98. Conversation with author, February 12, 2001.

99. Abdulaziz Sachedina, *The Islamic Roots of Democratic Pluralism* (New York: Oxford University Press, 2001).

100. Sachedina, *The Islamic Roots of Democratic Pluralism*, 48.

101. Sachedina, *The Islamic Roots of Democratic Pluralism*, 139.

102. *Islam and Christian-Muslim Relations* 8, no. 1 (1997): 27–38. Communication with the author was through e-mail, March 2001.

103. Adnan Aslan, *Religious Pluralism in Christian and Islamic Philosophy* (New York: Curzon, 1998), 203–5.

104. *Islam and Christian-Muslim Relations* 11, no. 2 (July 2000): 213–27.

105. From a letter written to the author by Hossein Nasr, February 23, 2001.

III

ISLAM AND THE BLACK EXPERIENCE IN AMERICA

8

Preliminary Reflections on Islam and Black Religion

Sherman A. Jackson

There are upward of six million Muslims in America today. Of these, unofficial estimates hold at least 42 percent to be Black Americans. The second largest group, the Indo-Pakistanis, number around 29 percent, followed by the Arabs, who make up between 12 and 15 percent. The remaining 14 to 17 percent represent a cross section of races and ethnicities, including a growing number of White and Hispanic Americans. Of these numbers, Black Americans are clearly the largest single block of Muslims in America. Equally important, however, if not always recognized in these terms, Muslims constitute the largest block of non-Christians within the Black American community. Indeed, in numerical terms at least, the relationship between Black American Muslims and the Black American community at large is rapidly approaching the relationship between Black Americans and the rest of America.

This apparent attraction between Islam and Black Americans has been the subject of numerous speculations, some explicit, others implied. A recent body of literature has sought to explain it in terms of the success of the early propaganda attributed to the Nation of Islam in which the latter attempted to shame black Americans away from Christianity by declaring the latter to be "the White man's religion."[1] Islam, by contrast, at least on this depiction, was proclaimed to be the Black man's religion, complete with deep and verifiable roots in the African motherland. In a far more sinister but clearly cognate thesis, the nineteenth-century German orientalist Carl Becker pointed to the attraction between Blacks and Islam as a sign of the latter's inferiority. Christianity being too sophisticated and civilized for primitive, simple-minded folk, Islam was the most that one could expect of Blacks. In other words, on Becker's logic, only an inferior religion could hold such attraction for such a clearly inferior people.[2] A third commonly heard explanation, albeit in more tacit terms, begins with the image of Islam as the friend and liberator of the oppressed. Blacks being the quintessential oppressed people of the world, it is only natural, or so this explanation goes, that Black Americans should gravitate toward Islam.

In all of these explanations, Blackness, like oppression, is essentially stripped of its historical specificity and treated as an abstract universal, a veritable supercategory at the center of which lies some putative essence in which all people with black skin (however we define and measure that) are presumed to participate. As such, whether we are talking about Black Americans, black Nigerians or Blacks in Surinam, the relationship to Islam is essentially the same: Blacks relate to Islam as Blacks or "oppressed people." As such, there is nothing special or unique in the relationship between *Black Americans* and Islam.

To be sure, this view is significantly indebted to the widespread tendency (among both politically correct Whites and ideologically driven Blacks) to play down if not obliterate the distinctions between Blacks or Africans, on the one hand, and Black Americans, on the other. This in turn is predicated on a certain refusal (or inability) to recognize that it is neither blood nor biology but history that makes "a people" and that it matters little whether that history is subjectively chosen or imposed by some other from without. On this refusal, Black Americans continue to be viewed (and indeed to view themselves in many instances) as displaced Africans rather than as a distinct and genuine people whose "peopleness" was fired in their centuries-long crucible in North America. The Western, or what Ali Mazrui once referred to as the "Afro-Saxon," identity of Black Americans continues to be treated as a fact to be either overcome or explained away rather than acknowledged, embraced, and probed for meaningful insights. This persists despite the fact that, as Charles H. Long so eloquently puts it:

> It would be difficult, if not impossible, to make the case for the non-Western identity of the black community in America, though several make this claim. The element of truth in this claim is that though we [Black Americans] are Westerners, we are not Westerners in the same way as our compatriots, and thus we afford within America an entree to the *otherness* of humankind.[3]

While this view has been reiterated in one or another form by several scholars of Black American studies,[4] it remains marginal to public and even academic discourse on the history of Black Americans. Whereas Copts, Phoenicians, Assyrians, and other groups in Egypt and Syria, for example, could *become* Arabs in a matter of a few centuries,[5] and Swedes, Francs, Brits, and countless Europeans could become "Americans" in a similar amount of time, nearly half a millennium of American history has failed to gain recognition as having exerted a similar effect on Blacks. This entrenched myopia has tended to promote a sustained marginalization if not discounting of important aspects of American history. As a result, America is often the last place one looks in attempting to explain any number of tendencies and phenomena among Black Americans.

Over the remainder of this chapter, I shall challenge this tendency and argue that the past, present, and future of Islam among Black Americans can only be understood in the context of the relationship between Islam and Black religion. By "Black religion," however, I am referring neither to the Black church nor to what scholars generally identify as the primordial religious orientation of Africans prior to their induction into the transatlantic slave trade.[6] Instead, I am referring to a very specific, and one might say *sui generis,* religious orientation that develops among Black Americans *in America.* Indeed, as I use the term, Black religion might be more accurately referred to as Black American religion.

I begin with a brief (but I hope adequate) refutation of the notion of the universal Black/oppressed and his or her relationship to Islam. From here I move to a description of Black religion and its essential characteristics as a religious orientation. I then trace the early relationship between Black religion and Islam (or Islamically inspired movements) in the early part of the twentieth century and then look at some of the positive and negative aspects of this relationship as manifested among contemporary Black American Muslims. Finally, I offer some thoughts on the future of Islam and Black religion, including the question of whether Black religion remains inextricably woven into the fabric and future of Black American Islam and the extent to which it has had and continues to negotiate its place alongside other sources of Islamic religious authority.

THE BLACK/OPPRESSED VERSUS THE BLACK AMERICAN

In one of her essays recollecting her experience as a foreign student in the United States in the 1970s, the Moroccan Muslim feminist Fatima Mernissi recalls her surprise to find that Islam was spreading among Black Americans. This was strange, according to Mernissi, because while Black Americans seemed to be finding in Islam a message of equality, liberation, and social justice, *inequality* and *exploitation* of the disenfranchised had always functioned in her experience as accepted norms.[7] Having lived and traveled throughout the Muslim, and especially the Arab, world, Mernissi was well acquainted with some of the rigid class divisions and social stratification that characterized Muslim societies. This, in fact, constituted the source of her amazement. For if societies that held up Islam as the ideal could see no contradiction between that ideal and sustained inequities and exploitation, how was one to explain the tendency among Black Americans to turn precisely to that ideal as a basis for alleviating their sociopolitical woes?

Of course, as a feminist, the inequity uppermost in Mernissi's mind was that affecting women. Color discrimination, while alive and well in the Muslim world, has not produced a "discreet and insular" class that identifies itself as "a people." And even if such a class did exist, they would not likely go under the designation "Blacks." For the Black–White dichotomy so central to Western social discourse has little to no functionality in Middle Eastern and Asian Muslim contexts.[8]

The same cannot be said, however, of other parts of the world where Islam has had a significant presence. And, indeed, when we turn to at least one of these communities, we find that not only have oppression and inequity been tolerated in the name of Islam but that this has taken place in contexts where Black people bore the brunt of such injustices. The example I have in mind is that of South Africa, where a Muslim community, first Malay and then Indian, existed from the middle of the seventeenth century. This community, however, was lamentably—indeed, defiantly—slow in coming to condemn anti-Black apartheid. In fact, for the better part of its history the Muslim community in South Africa saw no contradiction at all between apartheid and the faithful practice of Islam. Thus, as late as 1964, the South African Muslim Judicial Council (MJC) could defend its de facto collaborationist position in the following terms:

> Has the [apartheid] government forbidden the worship of Allah? Has the government closed down or ordered the demolition of any mosque in a declared white area? If our government has ordered our Muslims to desert the faith of our forefathers, then our *ulema* [religious scholars] would have been the first to urge us to resist, even to the death.[9]

While this was not the position of all non-Black Muslims in South Africa, it was by all appearances the dominant view up until the 1970s.[10] This view, no doubt, goes a long way in explaining the extremely slow and limited spread of Islam among Black South Africans. More important, however, it raises, as does the experience of Mernissi cited earlier, serious questions about the presumed affinity among Islam, Blackness, and oppression. For if oppression and Blackness are supposed to promote conversion to Islam, why has this not occurred among oppressed Blacks in South Africa, where, incidentally, they had far greater and direct exposure to Islam?[11] Stated differently, why have oppressed Blacks in South Africa failed to locate in Islam what their Black American brothers and sisters across the Atlantic would come to identify as the very essence of the religion?

Of course, the easy answer to this question would be that the Indian and Malay monopoly over the meaning of Islam in South Africa prevented South African Blacks from coming to see in Islam the ultimate solution to their problems. Under Indian and Malay authority, in other words, Islam was not presented—and thus could not be seen—as holding any meanings that rendered it an effective antidote to the apartheid system. While there is much of value in this view, it cannot serve as a full response. For, the truth be told, a similar, if not identical, situation obtains in the United States today, where immigrant Muslims claim superior if not ultimate authority to define Islam and the Muslim agenda.[12] Indeed, the major Muslim political organizations in America, all run by immigrants, tend more often than not to support the Republican Party, despite the latter's antiaffirmative action, antisocial program stance. In fact, during the 2000 presidential campaign, these organizations went so far as to issue a public endorsement of Republican candidate George W. Bush without so much as attempting to secure a mandate from the Black American Muslim majority![13] Yet, there is no evidence to suggest that this has slowed, let alone stopped, the spread of Islam among Black Americans.

To my mind, the real difference between South African—and other—Blacks, on the one hand, and Black Americans, on the other, lies in the absence among the former of two things: (1) an indigenously rooted vehicle via which they could successfully *appropriate* Islam and (2) charismatic figures who could harness and make effective use of that vehicle. The vehicle to which I am referring in the case of Black Americans is Black religion. The charismatic figures I have in mind are none other than the early-twentieth-century "Islamizers," such as Noble Drew Ali and, especially, Elijah Muhammad.

It is important to note in this context the meaning and function of *appropriation* as I use the term. By *appropriation,* I am referring to the act of enlisting the aid of a set of nonindigenous ideas or doctrines in one's own existential or ideological struggle. What renders an act one of appropriation rather than one of simple borrowing is that the appropriator does not recognize any "property rights" of the original owners. Instead, the whole point of appropriation is both to claim the idea or doctrine for oneself and to assume the right to define, interpret, and tailor it in accordance with one's own needs, with little to no interest in how the original owners or their heirs might have gone about these tasks. It is here, in fact, that the importance of the *vehicle* via which appropriation is made possible comes to the fore. For the function of this vehicle is essentially to enable the appropriator to make believable the claim that he or she is neither surrendering to any "other" nor attempting to plagiarize or "piggyback" on the latter's identity. Rather, the new idea is adopted, or so goes the unspoken claim, for the purpose of enabling the appropriator to become a truer and more authentic self. In other words, a Black adopts Islam or Christianity not to become an honorary Arab or White but to become a truer, more authentic "Black man"! To be able to do this, however, he must first be able to claim Islam or Christianity as his own. This is ultimately what the vehicle of appropriation enables him to do.

The importance of these vehicles of appropriation is often overlooked in analyzing the process of religious conversion. This is probably because religious conversion is most often viewed from the perspective of the proselytizer or missionary. That is, most of the time religious conversion is seen in terms of the success of the proselytizer in getting the convert to "come over" to the new religion rather than in terms of the success of the convert at getting the new religion to validate his or her past and inspire in him or her a vision of a new tomorrow. This is precisely the advantage that Black religion conferred first on Black American Christians in the eighteenth and nineteenth centuries and then on the Black American Islamizers at the beginning of the twentieth century, as a result of which they were able to appropriate Islam. By finding in Islam, in other words, the means to an ostensibly more perfect expression of Black religion, the Black American Islamizers were able to co-opt, legitimize, and indeed popularize Islam among the Black American masses. In fact, had it not been for this historical act of appropriation, it is doubtful that Islam would have ever come to enjoy the success that it has come to enjoy among Black Americans.

BLACK RELIGION

There is no scholarly consensus on the definition of Black religion, nor is there complete uniformity in the use of the term.[14] There is, however, unanimous agreement that the central and most enduring feature of Black religion is its sustained and radical opposition to racial oppression. At bottom, Black religion is an instrument of holy protest against racism. Its point of departure is American slavery, and, as C. Eric Lincoln once noted, had it not been for American slavery, there would have been no Black religion.[15] In its sustained attempt to proscribe Black consciousness and restrict it to a universe of meanings that promoted the internalization of feelings of inferiority and the concomitant propriety of Black servitude to Whites, American slavery engendered in Black Americans what Charles H. Long refers to as a "lithic consciousness"—that is, a state of mind and being that in confronting reality invokes *a will in opposition,* a veritable cosmic no.[16] At bottom, this is largely a reactionary no, and there is in the protest sentiment of Black religion a distinctly negative element, being more committed from a certain perspective to a *refusal* to do than it is to any *insistence* on doing.

That this protest sentiment or "will in opposition" should find expression in religion rather than in some other construct is partially a function of Black Americans' African past. As the noted African scholar John Mbiti points out, Africans are notoriously religious![17] But the American experience would contribute in at least two important ways. First, the onerous restrictions on Black Americans, most notably in the area of education, resulted in an effective barrier between them and the intellectual zeitgeist of the day. As a result, the masses of Black Americans were effectively passed over by the rationalizing forces of the European Enlightenment as these swept across the American plain en route to the ultimate dethronement of religion as the final arbiter in public and private life. To use the (now-passé) antireligious depiction of the nineteenth-century European philosopher and putative founder of sociology, August Comte, the masses of Black Americans remained in a *religious* state of consciousness, while White Americans "moved on" to a rational and then a scientific one. Second, the American experience introduced the erstwhile Africans to Christianity—more specifically, Protestantism. This led to a number of important transformations in their religious orientation. Equally important, it provided a vehicle via which a distinctly Black American religious orientation could be expressed.

America during the seventeenth and eighteenth centuries was, if anything, increasingly a Protestant country, still living in the echo of the Protestant Reformation and producing its own First and Second Great Awakenings. Traditional African religion, with its magic and conjuring, its multiple gods and intermediaries, its spirit world and attachment to the "living dead," was too alien and, especially in a staunchly Protestant context like America's, too easily dismissed as primitive, pagan heathenism. As such, it stood little chance of gaining public accommodation and still less of a chance of jarring the moral conscience of White Protestant Christians who supported the American system of race-based slavery. In the latter part of the eighteenth century, however, Black Americans began to enter into Christianity in significant numbers. And it was here that Black religion would undergo its first important metamorphosis and achieve its first feat of appropriation. From this point on, Black Americans would no longer be limited to yelling and screaming in tongues at the horrors of American slavery. Rather, in Christianity they found both a coherent voice and a recognizable righteous indignation. By enlisting the authority and imprimatur of Christianity, Black religion's holy protest acquired both an effective mode of expression and a modicum of legitimacy.

Having said this much, however, it should be noted that this was a "marriage" between Black religion and Christianity, not a dissolution of the former into the latter. As such, while Christianity may have been taken as the last name (and thus we speak of the Black *church*), Black religion retained its original character and identity, including the spirit of protest and palpable vestiges of the affective and frenzied traits of African religion. Black Christianity consisted, in other words, of both a core and an outer shell. The core was essentially Black religion. The shell was the theological and liturgical teachings of White Christianity. This is not at all to suggest any lack of sincerity on the part of Black Americans who professed Christianity. The point, however, is that Black Americans had a patently differ-ent appreciation of and agenda for Christianity. As such, their approach to and practice of the religion was, to say the least, patently unique. And White missionaries and church leaders were relentless in voicing their frus-tration at what they deemed to be the superficiality of Negro conversion. As one such writer put it, "Most of the time the Negro outwardly accepts the doctrines of Christianity and goes on living according to his own con-flicting secular mores."[18]

Nevertheless, the marriage between Black religion and Christianity con-tinued into the nineteenth century. In fact, the first decades of the nine-teenth century saw Black religion reach the apogee of its success in ap-propriating Christianity. Contrary to the view still popular in many circles, that Christianity functioned invariably as an opiate that lulled Black Amer-icans into accepting their condition of subjugation, the nineteenth century was a watershed of protest by Black American Christians who used both the pen and the sword to prosecute their cause. In 1802, Gabriel Prosser mounted his violent revolt in Virginia. This was followed by the bloody as-sault of Denmark Vessey in South Carolina in 1822. In 1829, Robert Alexan-der Young published his pamphlet *The Ethiopian Manifesto, Issued in De-fense of the Blackman's Rights, in the Scale of Universal Freedom,* in which he called for militant action and revolution. That same year saw the publi-cation of David Walker's scathing *Appeal to the Colored Citizens of the World,* in which he spoke of the innate devilishness of Whites and their sta-tus as the "natural enemies" of Blacks. Meanwhile, in 1831, Nat Turner's "vi-sions" led him to unleash holy terror on the White citizens of Southamp-ton, Virginia, in the largest and most significant slave revolt in American history. All of this activity was carried out in the name of Christianity. This was a Christianity, however, emboldened by the spirit of Black religion.[19]

Revolution, however, was not the only contribution that Black religion made to Black Christianity. At least two other features figured prominently in this amalgamation. The first of these was Black religion's notoriously atheological approach to religion. This was manifested in the almost com-plete neglect of the theological intricacies of White Christology. Rather than focus on the divinity, sonship, or vicarious substitution of Christ, most Black American Christians tended to identify with Jesus as a "fellow sufferer . . . the little child . . . the companion . . . the man who understands."[20] Indeed, Jesus for most Black American Christians was not so much the God of heaven—though that he was too—as he was the more immanent—and more intimate—"Lord who befriends us and is concerned about our prob-lems."[21] White churchmen were constant in criticizing their Black brethren for their confused and vague understandings of Christ. Meanwhile, even learned leaders of the Black church, men like Richard Allen, would devote little to no effort to developing a Christology of their own. Rather, they would simply go along—or at least apparently so—with the catechism handed down by the White mother-church.

To be sure, this combination of theological apathy and conservatism was not merely a function of Black religion. It was also connected to what I said earlier about the rationalizing forces of the European Enlightenment having bypassed the masses of Black Americans. Black American Christians appear to be almost oblivious to the liberalizing forces that produced the Fundamentalist backlash among White American Christians in the late nineteenth and early twentieth centuries. They remained staunchly literalist in their scriptural interpretations; and they produced nothing of the likes of such liberal theologians as Harry Emerson Fosdick or Shailer Matthews, until the rise of Black theology in the 1960s. This entrenched theological conservatism would reappear in the thinking of both Noble Drew Ali and Elijah Muhammad, whose theologies may appear as radical innovations in the context of Muslim orthodoxy but reveal themselves to be pale imitations of Christianity when viewed in the context of American religion.[22] Not only would Black American obliviousness to European/American liberalism promote theological conservatism; it would also sustain a palpably conservative social ethic, according to which "men were men," and "women were women," "right was right," and "wrong was wrong," an ethic whose status among the masses of Black Americans has only been obscured by the stated views and tendencies of Black American political leaders, tendencies born in large part of the marriage between liberalism and the civil rights movement in the 1960s. In fact, in a survey taken as recently as 1985, the majority of Black Americans were shown to favor the death penalty and school prayer, while most Black American politicians opposed these; most Black Americans opposed school busing, while most Black elected officials favored it; and three times as many Black Americans opposed abortion as did their leaders.[23]

The second contribution of Black religion is reflected in Black Christianity's focus on Africa as the locus of its longing and belonging. Not America but Africa was home to the Black American. And there was a deep and abiding sense that the image of Africa had to be guarded, clung to, and zealously preserved. For to lose Africa would be to suffer the ultimate defeat. It would mean being rendered a stepchild of history, a creature of men—White men!—rather than a creature of God. This obsession with the image of Africa is reflected in the names of many of the independent Black churches that emerge from the latter part of the eighteenth century—such as the African Methodist Church, or the African Methodist Zion Church. It would also influence quasi-secular and religious movements in the twentieth century, including Marcus Garvey's back-to-Africa enterprise or Maulana Karenga's Kwanzaa. Like all romanticisms, this particular feature of Black religion was especially given to excess. But this should not seduce one into dismissing its importance or influence. For no religious movement that hoped to gain a following among Black Americans could afford to ignore the image of Africa. Indeed, even Islam would benefit from its perceived "African connection," which would enable it to appeal to Black Americans in a way that, say, Buddhism or even Judaism never could.

These, then, for our purposes, are the main features of Black religion. Taken as a whole, Black religion might be thought of as a form of "radical conservatism": radical in its rejection of racial subjugation, conservative in its theology and its social ethic. Probably from the early decades of the nineteenth century, Black religion came to be esteemed as the most authentic and genuine form of religious expression for and among Black Americans. Hailed as the religion of the masses,[24] it would become *the* religious orientation—indeed, *the* orientation, period—to which any successful movement among Black Americans would have to pay homage.[25]

ISLAM AND BLACK RELIGION

As we move into our discussion of the relationship between Islam and Black religion, four key facts must be born in mind. First, the spread of Islam among Black Americans was a twentieth-century phenomenon. Second, it was a northern phenomenon. Third, it was an urban phenomenon. And, finally, it was largely a working-class and underclass phenomenon.

That there were African Muslims among America's slave population is widely known and well documented.[26] My point in limiting the spread of Islam among Black Americans to the twentieth century is to emphasize the fact that prior to that time Islam was unable to sustain and perpetuate itself on North American soil. The reasons for this, if one thinks about it, are quite simple. While non-Muslim slaves had to contend with the stigma of color, Muslim slaves had to weather the much older and more deeply rooted stigma of religion. Whereas, according to scholars like Theodore Allen, Whiteness as a racial category united first landed and than all Europeans (particularly against Blacks) was not invented until the late seventeenth century,[27] the negative image of the Moor and the Muslim went back more than half a millennium. The first Crusade began in 1095. Dante's *Divine Comedy,* with its horrific portrayal of the Prophet Muhammad, was completed in 1321. Indeed, even the very discovery of America itself owed a debt to Islam. For contrary to many a grade school textbook, Christopher Columbus was prompted to seek his alternate route to India not by a spirit of discovery but by fear of the Muslim masters of the Red and Mediterranean Seas. As Norman Daniel[28] and others have so clearly demonstrated in their works, fear and hatred of Islam existed in the West long before the transatlantic slave trade began. And when these sentiments joined forces with White supremacy and the dehumanizing brutalities of American slavery, it became virtually impossible for African Muslim slaves to perpetuate their faith. Metaphorically, this is poignantly reflected in the complete absence, prior to the very eve of the twentieth century, of a single standing mosque in all of North America, the mosque, along with the Call to Prayer (*adhân*), being the quintessential public symbol of Islam.

To all intents and purposes, then, Islam begins its relationship with Black Americans in the early decades of the twentieth century. Africa and African Islam play virtually no role whatever in this process. Instead, it was the Black church's de facto estrangement from Black religion that forced the latter to search for a new vehicle via which to promote its cause. Through personalities and channels, the identities of which remain to this day shrouded in veils of mystery, Islam—or what was imagined to be Islam—was co-opted to fill that role. This was the beginning of the marriage between Islam and Black religion.

The marriage between Christianity and Black religion had been a southern-dominated affair. While a number of Black churches flourished in the North, the overwhelming majority of Black Americans lived in the South. The South, moreover, was home to Black American folk culture. After slavery, the evils of segregation dominated Black life in both the North and the South. But because Black southerners shared with their White counterparts many features of a common *culture* (e.g., food, language, "southern pride"), integration (as the antidote to segregation) did not necessarily imply assimilation or adopting the ways of an *alien* dominant culture. As long as the majority of Black Americans remained in the South, Black religion, with its spirit of cultural pride and defiance of subjugation, could function, *mutatis mutandis,* pretty much as it always had. At least it could express itself, to the extent that circumstances allowed, in a voice and in cultural patterns genuinely felt to be its own. But when, on the eve of World War I, massive industrialization and job opportunities led Black Americans to migrate en masse to the North, the Black church found itself in a new *cultural* milieu where it confronted problems and opportunities that forced it out of its traditional posture. Here, in what I would characterize, following the lead of H. Richard Niebuhr, as a classic pattern of "bourgeoisification,"[29] the fine line between integration and assimilation became blurred. In its effort to come to terms with this new and overwhelming reality, the Black church found itself helplessly drifting away from its Black religion roots.

Psychologically and culturally displaced, masses of Black Americans became increasingly alienated from the Black church. But this alienation did not extend—at least not to the same degree—to Black religion. In fact, if anything, the mission of Black religion became more rather than less meaningful to Black Americans. As E. Franklin Frazier implies in his treatment of the "secular rebellion" of the early gospel singers, even where the Black church was no longer felt to be the place where one could express one-self, the themes, moorings, and sentiments of Black religion remained an important part of what one wanted to express.[30] This was the context out of which men like Timothy Drew (later Noble Drew Ali) and Elijah Poole (later Elijah Muhammad) would ultimately emerge. Both originally south-erners who had migrated North, they stepped into a vacuum created by the misfortunes of the Black church. The disembodied spirit of Black religion now floating about in search of new accommodations, "Islam," at this point more imagined than real, was appealed to for sanctuary.

The detailed histories of these early pioneers have been treated by nu-merous scholars, and I will not rehearse them here.[31] For my present pur-poses, however, it is important to recognize that these men were not so much *interpreting* Islam as they were *appropriating* it. There was little to no attention devoted to the manner in which previous Muslim communities had understood or practiced Islam. And there was only the most perfunctory at-tempt to integrate even the most basic Islamic doctrines and rituals into the religious life of the community. From the very Testimony of Faith (*shahâ-dah*) to the finality of prophethood with the Prophet Muhammad to Five Pil-lars of Islam, almost nothing was translated into practice. In fact, there is lit-tle evidence that Noble Drew Ali or Elijah Muhammad knew much at all about Islamic doctrine. And what little they did know they seem not to have taken very seriously. Rather, these men were appealing to Islam as a means of raising the concerns and spirit of Black religion to a new level of re-spectability within the Black American community, just as Christianity had facilitated the appeal to White America in earlier times. As in the latter case, Black religion functioned as the core with the trappings (namely vocabu-lary) of Islam serving as the outer shell. Also as in the case of Black Chris-tianity, it was Islam that was being appropriated by Black religion rather than the other way around. For it was Black religion that needed the legiti-mation and historical weight that a great world movement like Islam could confer. And it was ultimately Islam at this stage that would go to work for Black religion rather than the other way around. Yet, even as the early "Is-lamizers" ignored and supplemented the substance of Islam while manipu-lating its image, without their efforts it seems that Islam would have had a difficult time finding its way into the hearts and minds of Black Americans.

To be sure, the early Islamizers were aided in their mission by the fact that they could present Islam as possessing several qualities and character-istics that rendered it well suited to the vision and character of Black reli-gion. First, Islam was "African," or at least "Eastern," complete with its own non-European language, language being perhaps the most important and deeply missed of all the casualties of the American slave experience. Sec-ond, White people (or at least Europeans) had no authority to define its ethos or substance. Third, it had a well-established reputation for revolution and armed struggle. Fourth, it was tied to a grand and glorious civilization in which people of color stood center stage. Fifth, it had a deep fraternal spirit—all Muslims are brothers. Sixth, it had clear atheological tendencies, its basic creed, "There is no god but God," being so simple that it bordered on a tautology. Even Islam's apparent disadvantages (e.g., being the object of Western hatred and fear) now translated into positive attractions, as the disillusionment of displaced and now more radicalized, lower-class Blacks in the North evolved into an unabashed separatist movement. Finally, Islam had no organized ecclesiastical hierarchy capable of imposing restrictions on who could speak in its name. This feature sat well with the proletarian origins of the early pioneers, neither of whom had gone beyond a secondary education. Indeed, this absence of institutional hierarchy facilitated their claim of having the authority to interpret and define Islam according to their own lights and priorities.

Muslim observers have often been shocked and dismayed by the theological and doctrinal excesses, omissions, and outright blasphemies of the early Black American Islamizers: God is a man; God is black; Elijah Muhammad is a prophet; Noble Drew Ali is the author of another revelation; the White man is the devil; and so forth. While certainly condemnable from the standpoint of Islamic orthodoxy, these infelicities are actually no more outlandish than some of what we encounter in the early history of the Muslim world, where, incidentally, the people knew Arabic and had direct access to Muslim scripture (Quran *and* hadith) and Muslim scholarship. This is clearly demonstrated in the famous heresiographical work, *Maqâlât al-islâmîyîn*, by the renowned Abû al-Hasan al-Ash'arî (d. 324/935), eponymous founder of the Ash'arite school of Muslim theology. Here al-Ash'arî records the views of numerous early groups who associated themselves with Islam. While al-Ash'arî clearly does not consider all of these views to be orthodox, he does seem to see in them a reflection of the efforts of various early groups to "find themselves" in Islam. This is why he entitles his work *Doctrines of Those Who Associate Themselves with Islam (Maqâlât al-islâmîyîn)* rather than *Doctrines of the Muslims (Maqâlât al-muslimîn)*. The following is but a tiny sample among the hundreds contained in this two-volume work:

    1. A group called the Bayânîyah held that God existed in the image of a man, and that He would perish in His entirety, except for His face.[32]
    2. A group called the Mughîrîyah held that a man named al-Mughîrah b. Sa'îd was a prophet and that he knew the Greatest Name of God (*ism Allâh al-a'zam*) and that the one they worshipped was a man made of light who wore a crown on his head and had all the limbs and organs of a man.[33]
    3. A group called the Khattâbîyah held that all of the [Shiite] Imams were prophets and messengers of God and that there would always exist two of them, one vocal, the other silent. The vocal one was Muhammad (upon him be peace) and the silent one was 'Alî b. Abî Tâlib.[34]

The point in all of this is not to try to vindicate any of the doctrines of the early Black American *Islâmîyîn*. Rather, my point is simply to place these doctrinal infelicities in the context of what I said earlier about the enterprise of religious conversion—namely, that it entails a process via which the convert seeks to get the new religion to validate his past and speak effectively to his future. This is often a very messy process that entails numerous misses (at least from the standpoint of orthodoxy) en route to complete assimilation. Yet, it is perhaps a necessary process if the religion is to be successfully integrated into the life of the convert community. It is also necessary if the convert community is not to end up in virtual paralysis because of a process of being force-fed *theological*[35] and other doctrines it neither understands nor deeply feels, finding itself in the meantime alienated from its historical self and thus incapable of tapping into its own historical legacy for tools and insights via which it can effectively confront and redirect reality on the ground.

This is precisely the pitfall the Black Islamizers of the early twentieth century were able to avoid. Because they assumed ownership over what they perceived and presented to be Islam, they were able not only to turn it to the existential needs of the Black American community but to earn Islam a place of legitimacy in the collective psyche of Black Americans as a whole. Moreover, because their manner of appropriation did not rupture their relationship with traditional Black American culture, they were able—and this is especially true of the Nation of Islam—to redefine both that culture and its relationship to the dominant culture, forging thereby a new modality of Blackness that was both identifiably "Islamic"[36] *and* American. With their bow ties and two-piece suits, their clean-cut and soldierlike demeanor, the Nation of Islam was able to create a deeply felt and publicly recognized "Muslim" identity without importing a single material feature of this identity from outside the United States. Indeed, their success at connecting Islam with a new modality of American Blackness can be seen in their influence among non-Muslim Black Americans. For example, the spread of Arabic names (including those bastardized versions of the *a-ee-a* pattern— e.g., Tameeka, Shameeka, Lakeesha) is a direct result of this cultural redefinition. Indeed, though seldom recognized as such, the Nation of Islam achieved a most masterful feat of dual appropriation.

Having said all of this, it should be noted that contrary to the impression one generally draws from scholarly literature on Islam in America, the Nation of Islam and the Moorish Science Temple have constituted minorities among Black American Muslims, at least for the past quarter century, the majority of Black American Muslims being Sunnis (referred to in earlier times as "orthodox Muslims") of various creedal and ideological commitments. Nevertheless, the impact of the early Islamizers on the spread of Islam in Black America goes far beyond their numbers. Indeed, their ignorance and excesses notwithstanding, through their marriage of Islam with Black religion, men like Noble Drew Ali and Elijah Muhammad succeeded in creating a psychological space through which millions of Black Americans would subsequently enter Islam. This is what Blacks in places like South Africa failed to produce or avail themselves of. Meanwhile, had immigrant Muslims, with their orthodox Islam rather than Black religion, been the conduit through which Islam was first introduced to Black Americans, it is doubtful that it would have ever enjoyed the success that it has come to enjoy in the Black American community.

ISLAM AND THE LIMITATIONS OF BLACK RELIGION

Like all human constructs, however, Black religion embodies a number of deficiencies, false obsession, and drawbacks. Being grounded in "Negro folk culture," it tends to reflect certain fears, prejudices, and limitations born of its folk roots. Thus, for example, it tends to be anti-intellectual and to place far too much hope and energy in fraternalism and separatism. It tends also to be deistic rather than theistic, relying more on vague notions of God rather than on God's Revelation. Perhaps, most important, however, Black religion tends to be far too parochial in its obsession with issues of race, having little to nothing to offer non-Blacks or to say on issues unconnected to race. As one Black critic of Black religion, Joseph R. Washington Jr., has noted, Black religion "exists without any meaningful goals, with the sole exception of providing refuge for the disinherited."[37] "Born in slavery, weaned in segregation and reared in discrimination, the religion of the Negro folk was chosen to bear the roles of both protest and relief. Thus, the uniqueness of black religion is the racial bond which seeks to risk its life for the elusive but ultimate goal of freedom and equality by means of protest and action."[38]

Like the Calvinist revivalists of yesteryear, the socioreligious ethic of Black religion is largely negative. The "will in opposition" aims almost exclusively at resisting or removing evil from the world rather than contributing good to it. This in turn leads Black religion to its most serious and inextricable paradox: Black religion remains relevant almost entirely to the extent that the evil it seeks to remove from the world remains in the world. In other words, to the extent that it succeeds in removing the evils associated with racism, Black religion threatens to render itself obsolete.

All of this has serious implications for Black American Islam, given, on the one hand, its historical relationship with Black religion and, on the other hand, the enormous gains made in the area of race relations since the rise of the civil rights movement. To the extent that improved race relations diminishes the relevance of Black religion, one can only wonder about the extent to which Black American Islam has been or will be similarly affected. What, if any, adjustments can we expect in the relationship between Islam and Black religion? What, if any, other factors are likely to affect this process?

At present, Black American Muslim communities continue to display many if not most of the false obsessions and drawbacks associated with Black religion. For example, they appear to be far more comfortable with protest and social critique than they are with identifying and capitalizing on opportunity. Similarly, they display a latent anti-intellectualism that has resulted in their being grossly underrepresented in Black American intellectual life. There is also a perduring separatist impulse, which, while most often justified in terms of preserving religious identity and avoiding the influence of a hegemonic secular worldview, tends to manifest itself in the rather curious desire to separate from White non-Muslims but not from Black ones, even when this means remaining in crime-ridden, crack-infested neighborhoods with failing schools and depleted infrastructures. Even the term *kafir,* which should mean non-Muslim, is commonly used as a veiled reference to "the White man." Finally, the socioreligious ethic of the Black American Muslim remains largely negative, with little attention to developing and promoting a positive vision for the future, one that includes not only moral and religious concerns but also aesthetic, cultural, and economic ones, via which life can be lived not only righteously but fully as well.

To be fair, however, Black religion alone cannot be made solely responsible for these tendencies among Black American Muslims. Over the last twenty-five years, massive immigration from the Muslim world has produced a fundamental shift in the basis of authority in American Islam. Whereas prior to 1975 American Islam had been dominated by Black Americans, by the early 1980s immigrants had moved into a position of political, economic, and intellectual dominance. This resulted in Black American Muslims losing their interpretive voice and their effective monopoly over what had functioned as a bona fide, indigenous tradition of "Muslim" thought and exegesis. The pragmatic, folk-oriented approach of Elijah Muhammad, Noble Drew Ali, Dâ'ûd Faysal, and others was displaced by the supertradition from the Muslim world, which was not only much more dependent on Arabic and the so-called *ulûm shar'îyah* (knowledge of Shariah) but was grounded in social and historical realities significantly removed from those of Black Americans. In this encounter, Black American Muslims lost confidence in their ability to formulate an agenda and articulate solutions to their problems in terms that were likely to be recognized and accepted as Islamic. This has thwarted their ability to tap into their indigenous heritage and develop a positive vision for Islam in the United States. This, no less than the residual influence of Black religion, has contributed to many of the aforementioned tendencies found in Black American Islam.

Yet, rather than retreat into the comfort and safety of classical Black religion, Black American Muslims have chosen to face the challenge of mastering the new criterion head on. Today, almost every major city in America has a contingent of Black American Muslims studying traditional Islamic sciences in the Muslim world. And there is a growing number of Black American Muslim Ph.D.s who hold positions in Islamic studies and related areas in major U.S. institutions: Aminah Wadud at Virginia Commonwealth, Akel Kahera at the University of Texas at Austin, Akbar Muhammad at SUNY–Binghamton, Ihsan Bagby at Shaw University, Samory Rashid at Indiana State, and Aminah B. McCloud at De Paul, not to mention scholars like Antar Stanford and R. Mukhtar Curtis who hold nonacademic positions in prison chaplaincy and community service. Over the coming decades, as more and more Black American Muslims master Arabic and the traditional Islamic religious sciences, alongside what they deem useful of the critical Western tradition, Black American Muslims are bound to re-devote their attention, with renewed vigor, to both the old concerns of Black religion and the changed realities of post–civil rights America. This is bound to be an exciting time, one that will likely see Black American Muslims return to a position of ownership in the intellectual life of American Islam. This will be an American Islam, however, whose basis will no longer be classical Black religion but an amalgamation of a radically altered Black religion, the traditional Islamic religious sciences, and aspects of the critical Western tradition.

In the meantime, Black religion is likely to continue to inform and influence Black American Islam. This has both positive and negative implications. On the negative side, Black religion will likely continue to sustain an essentially negative predisposition among Black American Muslims, one that is more concerned with avoiding and ridding the world of evil than it is with promoting and filling the world with good. Moreover, the almost single-minded and exclusivist obsession with issues of race, however much this may be disguised, is likely to continue. For, as Joseph R. Washington Jr. puts it, "Race is everything to black religion; nothing else really counts. And on issues other than race the followers of black religion have little time to think. In fact, on every issue besides race, they are dependent upon their white brethren."[39]

The danger in all of this is, of course, that it is likely to limit the scope of Black American Muslim intellectual and activist activity to matters related to race, leaving other matters from culture to aesthetics to economics to politics to their immigrant brethren. To paraphrase Washington in this regard, on every issue other than that of race, Black American Muslims are likely to remain in a state of abject dependency on their immigrant brethren.

As for the positive contributions of Black religion, there are potentially two. First, the "will to opposition" is likely to sustain what James Baldwin once described as a deep and abiding distrust of the dominant Western intellectual tradition. This is likely to promote a more critical stance on the part of Black American Muslims vis-à-vis the secularizing tendencies of

Western thought. On this skepticism, Black American Muslims may be more likely to develop into more authentic "Muslim intellectuals" rather than secularized Western intellectuals with Muslim names.

Second, for better or worse, Black religion maintains a tremendous amount of esteem among Black Americans at large, and, as such, it remains an important source of legitimacy. Moreover, the raison d'être of Black religion, namely racism, or more specifically White supremacy, is still alive and well in America. As such, there is still a place, albeit different from the past, for the holy protest of Black religion. As C. Eric Lincoln says, "any religion of Blacks in America which did not in some fundamental way address the prevailing issues of racialism would be improbable if not grotesque."[40]

In conclusion, then, we may say that for all the benefit and vigor that Black religion has brought to Black American Islam, the relationship between the two remains problematic. While Black American Islam may still have Black religion by the tail, it seems that it can neither safely cling to it nor simply let it go. Clearly, the relationship between the two will have to be renegotiated. And whatever the future of Black American Islam might be, the process and dynamic of this renegotiation are certain to be at the heart of it.

NOTES

1. See, for example, G. Usry and C. Keener, *Black Man's Religion: Can Christianity Be Afrocentric?* (Downer's Grove, Ill.: Intervarsity Press, 1996), 21–44 and passim. Usry and Keener's thesis is not without basis, as Elijah Muhammad's *Message to the Black Man* and numerous editions of the Nation's newspaper, *Muhammad Speaks,* plainly demonstrate. But Usry and Keener are clearly ideologically driven, a fact that delivers them into some fairly stark anachronisms. For example, neither Elijah Muhammad nor any of the early Islamically oriented groups (e.g., Moorish Science Temple) were the originators of this view. Indeed, it goes back almost two hundred years to Black American Christians. For example, as early as 1829, a full century before the Nation of Islam came into being, David Walker would repeatedly refer to Whites as "the Americans," "the Christians," and the "natural enemies" of Blacks. In fact, he would even allude to the tyrannical slaveholders as "devils." See his *Appeal to the Coloured Citizens of the World, but in Particular, and Very Expressly, to Those of the United States of America,* ed. S. Wilentz (New York: Hill & Wang, 1995), especially 71 for the reference to devils. Decades later, Bishop Henry McNeil Turner would also insist that Whites had commandeered Christianity and infected it with their racial biases. Even C. Eric Lincoln repeatedly refers to Christianity as "the white man's religion." See his *Race, Religion and the Continuing American Dilemma* (New York: Hill & Wang, 1999), 31, 52, 59, and passim. It might be noted, incidentally, that all of these views run the risk of buying into the reification of Whiteness (and Blackness) as transcendent and permanent realities, failing to appreciate, for example, that Christianity was on the scene long before Whiteness as a racial category had even been invented. On this point

see, T. Allen, *The Invention of the White Race,* 2 vols. (New York: Verso, 1994), 1:1–51.

2. See J. van Ess, "From Wellhausen to Becker: The Emergence of *Kulturgeschichte* in Islamic Studies," in *Islamic Studies: A Tradition and Its Problems,* ed. M. Kerr (Malibu, Calif.: Undena, 1980), 48–49.

3. "Interpretations of Black Religion in America," in *Significations: Signs, Symbols, and Images in the Interpretation of Religion* (Aurora, Colo.: Davies, 1995), 152–53.

4. See, for example, A. Raboteau, *Slave Religion: The "Invisible Institution" in the Antebellum South* (Oxford: Oxford University Press, 1978), 47ff.; E. F. Frazier, *The Negro Church in America* (New York: Schocken, 1974), 9–14; C. Eric Lincoln, *Race, Religion and the Continuing American Dilemma* (New York: Hill & Wang, 1999), 23–59.

5. Contrary to the popular stereotype that Islam spread so quickly because it was imposed by the sword, it took literally centuries for places like Egypt, Syria, greater Iraq, and Iran to become majority Muslim. On this point, see R. Bulliet, *Conversion to Islam in the Medieval Period: An Essay in Quantitative History* (Cambridge, Mass.: Harvard University Press, 1977). Interestingly, some of these early communities "became" Arabs along with becoming Muslim (e.g., Egypt, Syria, parts of Iraq), while others did not (e.g., Iran, parts of North Africa).

6. On this orientation, see the informative and authoritative work of J. S. Mbiti, *African Religions and Philosophy,* 2d ed. (Oxford: Heinemann, 1989).

7. F. Mernissi, *Islam and Democracy: Fear of the Modern World* (New York: Addison-Wesley, 1992), 111.

8. In places like England, black is not simply a color but implies as well a social standing or political alliance. As such, it may apply not only to Africans but to all nonwhites, including such groups as Indians and Pakistanis. See Satya P. Mohanty, *Literary Theory and the Claims of History: Postmodernism, Objectivity, Multicultural Politics* (Ithaca, N.Y.: Cornell University Press, 1997), 17. On a recent trip to Australia, I learned of a similar phenomenon there.

9. See F. Esack, *Qur'ân, Liberation and Pluralism: An Islamic Perspective of Interreligious Solidarity against Oppression* (Oxford: Oneworld, 1997), 31.

10. Esack, *Qur'ân,* 32ff.

11. South Africa boasted standing mosques, religious scholars, schools of law (*madhhabs*), the public practice of Islamic liturgies, Muslim educational institutions, and so forth. In North America, meanwhile, prior to the twentieth century, all of these were either eradicated or forced underground.

12. For more on this point, see my "Islam and Affirmative Action," *Journal of Law and Religion* 14, no. 2 (1999–2000): 406–10.

13. These organizations include, inter alia, CAIR (Council for American-Islamic Relations), AMC (American Muslim Council), and MPAC (Muslim Public Affairs Council). My point here is simply that these organizations acted in apparent defiance of the wishes of the Black American Muslim community, not that it is un-Islamic or even against the interests of the Muslims to support the Republican Party or that the Democratic platform is in the best interest of Black American Muslims. Indeed, my own view is that the marriage between liberalism and the civil rights establishment has had a devastating effect on Black Americans, including Muslims, over the past quarter century.

14. See, for example, C. H. Long, "Perspectives for the Study of African-American Religion in the United States," in *African-American Religion: Interpretive Essays in History and Culture,* ed. T. Fulop and A. Raboteau (New York: Routledge, 1997), 21–35; Lincoln, *Race,* xviii–xxv, 52–59 and passim; J. R. Washington Jr., *Black Religion: The Negro and Christianity in the United States* (Lanham, Md.: University Press of America, 1984). I should add that while it is perhaps the most widespread and powerful religious orientation among Black Americans, Black religion is not the only religious orientation among Black Americans, as demonstrated, for example, in the thought of Howard Thurman. See also Frazier, *Negro Church,* 80–85, on middle-class Blacks who reject the folk tradition.

15. Lincoln, *Race,* 31.

16. "Freedom, Otherness and Religion: Theologies Opaque," in *Significations,* 212.

17. Mbiti, *African Religions and Philosophy,* 1.

18. Wilmore, *Black Religion,* 26.

19. It is true that not all those who revolted against American slavery in the name of Christianity were Black Americans. The names John Brown and Elijah Lovejoy come immediately to mind as White Americans who mounted violent protests. Yet, inasmuch as American slavery in particular was the raison d'être behind these revolts, they can be considered products of Black religion, in the same way that Blacks embraced and practiced aspects of White Christianity.

20. See Charles Long, "Perspectives for the Study of African-American Religion in the United States," in *African American Religion: Interpretive Essays in History and Culture,* ed. T. E. Fulop and A. J. Raboteau (New York: Routledge, 1997), 32.

21. Wilmore, *Black Religion,* 30.

22. On this point, see, for example, Z. I. Ansari, "Aspects of Black Muslim Theology," *Studia Islamica* 53 (1981): 1–53.

23. See Henry Louis Gates Jr. and Cornel West, *The Future of the Race* (New York: Vintage, 1997), 35.

24. Gayraud Wilmore, for instance, refers to it as "black folk religion." See his *Black Religion and Black Radicalism: An Interpretation of the Religious History of African Americans,* 3d ed. (Maryknoll, N.Y.: Orbis, 1998), 48, 258, and passim.

25. Wilmore, *Black Religion,* 276.

26. See, for example, Allan D. Austin, *African Muslims in Antebellum America* (New York: Garland, 1984); and Sylviane A. Diouf, *Servants of Allah: African Muslims Enslaved in the Americas* (New York: New York University Press, 1998).

27. See Allen, *The Invention of the White Race,* 1:14. Meanwhile, scholars such as Oscar Handlin imply that many peoples now thought of as White (e.g., Jews, Italians, Armenians, and even Swedes and Germans) were not included into Whiteness until the middle of the twentieth century! See his *Fire-Ball in the Night: The Crisis in Civil Rights* (Boston: Beacon, 1964), 24–25.

28. See, for example, his *Islam and the West: The Making of an Image* (Oxford: Oneworld, 1997).

29. Niebuhr does not use the term *bourgeoisification,* but he describes a process that suits that designation. See his *The Social Origins of Denominationalism* (Glouchester, Mass.: Smith, 1984).

30. See, for example, Frazier, *Negro Church,* 77–78.

31. See C. Eric Lincoln, *The Black Muslims in America,* 3d ed. (Grand Rapids,

Mich.: Eerdmans, 1994); Aminah B. McCloud, *African American Islam* (New York: Routledge, 1995); Richard B. Turner, *Islam in the African American Experience* (Bloomington: Indiana University Press, 1997).

32. Abû al-Hasan 'Alî b. Ismâ'îl al-Ash'arî, *Maqâlât al-Islâmîyîn wa ikhtilâf al-musallîn*, 2 vols., ed. M. M. 'Abd al-Hamîd (Cairo: Maktabat al-Nahdah al-Misrîyah, 1389/1969), 66–67.

33. Al-Ash'arî, *Maqâlât*, 69–72.

34. Al-Ash'arî, *Maqâlât*, 76–77.

35. I assume a fundamental distinction between theology, on the one hand, and religion, on the other. *Religion* (from the Latin *religio*) is simply the activity of sustaining a conscientious commitment to a set of rituals and obligations based on the recognition that one is bound or indebted to a divine or supernatural power outside oneself. *Theology*, on the other hand (from the Greek *logos*, reasoning, and *theos*, God or divinity), is the act of systematically thinking about God. On these definitions, it is clear that religion does not have to have theology and may in fact be antitheological. As such, one can reject a particular group's theology without rejecting their religion per se. For more on this point, see my *The Boundaries of Tolerance* (New York: Oxford University Press, 2002).

36. I do not mean hereby to legitimize the Nation of Islam's theology. My point is simply that when they walked down the street, they both felt and were immediately recognized as "Black Muslims."

37. Wilmore, *Black Religion*, 161.

38. *Black Religion: The Negro and Christianity in the United States* (New York: University Press of America, 1984), 33. This was a reissue of Washington's book, which was first published in 1964.

39. Washington, *Black Religion*, 229.

40. Lincoln, *Race*, xxiii.

9

Islam among African Americans

An Overview

Zafar Ishaq Ansari

The realization that Muslims have become a significant, and permanent, part of the American mosaic has been slow to come. Of late, however, a number of works have been published, notably those written or edited by Yvonne Haddad, highlighting the Islamic presence in the United States (see especially Haddad and Lummis 1987; Haddad 1991; Haddad and Smith 1994). Despite these and other useful works, few people are aware that today there are more than 200,000 Muslim businesses, 1,200 mosques, 165 Islamic schools, 425 Muslim associations, and 85 Islamic publications in the United States. Nor are many people aware that Muslims, who number between five and six million, are poised to outnumber Jews and become the second largest religious group in the United States (Haddad and Lummis 1987:3).

African American Muslims constitute a very large segment of the Muslim population of the United States—according to some estimates, as much as 42 percent (Barboza 1993:4). Also, African American Muslims have been the first Muslims to have settled in the New World and have been present there for close to five centuries. This long period of their history and their prolonged struggle to maintain their faith in extremely difficult circumstances are subjects that have just begun to be explored.

This chapter studies essentially the contemporary revival of Islam among African Americans. This necessitated casting a cursory look at the history of African American Muslims in the New World, especially the United States, to provide the necessary background for this study. My colleagues and I have surveyed the rise of some of the movements that arose in the name of Islam, both sectarian and orthodox, in the course of the present century and have attempted to see how orthodox Islam has been able to consolidate itself among African Americans. This development seems undeniable, notwithstanding the persistence of fairly important heterodox groups such as the Nation of Islam under Lonis Farrakhan and the Five Percenters.

Africans began to arrive in the New World in the fifteenth century. Some of the earliest ones to arrive came with the explorers; some possibly came even before the so-called discovery of America. Originally, as one would expect, their number was small but gradually increased owing to the need of the American economy for slave labor. By 1863, when the Emancipation was proclaimed, their number had risen to 4.5 million. Since then, their number has been steadily rising mainly through procreation. Their population in 1990 was 30.6 million out of the total U.S. population of 249 million; it was projected to be 31.6 million out of 254.6 million for 1992 and 32.9 million out of 260 million for 1995 (U.S. Department of Commerce 1993: tables 19 and 20). Thus, their percentage in the total population, which has been on the rise, stands today at 12.6 percent, and it is estimated that it will continue to rise in the coming decades, reaching the high figure of 16.2 percent in 2050 (U.S. Department of Commerce 1993: tables 19 and 20).

Although African Americans have always been a minority in the United States and its different states and regions, they have traditionally been concentrated in the rural South. Since around the beginning of the twentieth century, however, they have been moving northward—a movement that perceptibly increased during the Great Depression and gained further momentum since World War II. As a result, while a majority of the African Americans still live in the South, their presence in the urban North is also quite conspicuous. Among the southern states, they constitute 35 percent of the total population of Mississippi, 30 percent of South Carolina, 29 percent of Louisiana, 27 percent of Georgia, 26 percent of Alabama, and 22 percent of North Carolina. In one of the states of the North, Maryland, they constitute 23 percent of the population.

A major demographic feature of the African American population is its conspicuous presence in major U.S. cities. During the recent past, African Americans have virtually been taking over the metropolitan cities, while Whites have been moving out to the suburban areas. In New York, their number is around 2.1 million; in Chicago, 1.4 million; in Detroit, over 800,000; in Philadelphia, about 700,000; and in Los Angeles 600,000 (*Encyclopedia of World Cultures* 1991, I:10–11).

The influence of African Americans in the political life of their country, however, is much less than warranted by their numbers. They are the most disenfranchised among the ethnic minorities of the United States. The voter turnout rate among them has been the lowest in the national, state, and local elections. This is due, in part, to their low level of education, their poverty, their political alienation and apathy, and, in the southern states, the remnants of Jim Crow laws. Although the legal barriers to the political participation of African Americans have been removed—thanks mainly to the civil rights legislation of the 1960s and 1970s and to the proactive role of the federal courts—social and economic barriers still inhibit their fuller participation in the political process.

In recent years, however, the political participation, representation, and clout of African Americans have increased. This is for several reasons. First, at the level of neighborhoods, school boards, counties, and local governments, the representation of African Americans has increased substantially in recent years—thanks to the Voting Rights Act and the proactive intervention of the federal courts. Second, the redistribution of several constituencies and voting districts in the South has helped create African American majority districts and has thus increased the number of African American elected officials in the U.S. Congress as well as in state legislatures. Third, the minority alliance of African Americans, Hispanics, the poor, and the underprivileged—what Jesse Jackson calls "the rainbow coalition"—has proven a successful strategy for African American candidates in urban areas. Coalition politics in urban areas and centrist political ideology have also helped African Americans capture political offices; for the first time, an African American became the governor of Virginia, and for the first time an African American woman became senator from Illinois. Fourth, the flight of the Whites from the inner cities to the suburbs has led the central cities to become predominantly African American and Hispanic. It is because of this phenomenon that in several large metropolitan areas—New York, Chicago, Atlanta, Philadelphia, Detroit, Los Angeles, Washington, D.C.—African American mayors have been elected. Fifth, Jesse Jackson's bids for the Democratic presidential nomination in 1984 and 1988 also helped mobilize a large number of African American voters both in the urban North and in the rural South. This paved the way for a substantial increase in the number of elected African American officials at the local, state, and national levels.

Another significant development at the political level also deserves mention. Since the civil rights movement—and even earlier—African Americans have by far and large voted for Democratic candidates in presidential and congressional elections. Recently, however, as a result of frustration with Democratic liberalism, a section of the middle-class African American electorate concerned about crimes, drugs, rising taxes, and the escalating costs of social spending has turned to a more conservative, Republican alternative.

EARLY HISTORY OF AFRICAN AMERICAN MUSLIMS
IN THE UNITED STATES

The estimate of the total number of African American Muslims in the United States varies from 1.2 million to about 1.7 million out of the total American Muslim population of more than 4 million. (Barboza [1993:9] mentions a report of the American Muslim Council that estimates the total number of Muslims in the United States between five and eight million. Haddad [1991:28] estimates their number at four million.) The estimates about the proportion of African American Muslims to the total Muslim population of America vary from 30 to 42 percent. (According to Barboza [1993:9], African American Muslims constitute 42 percent of the total Muslim population of the United States, versus over 30 percent, according to Haddad [1991:28].) Even if we were to calculate on the basis of the higher figure of 1.7 million African American Muslims out of a total of 30.6 million African Americans, African American Muslims constitute about 5 percent of the total African American population of the United States.

This percentage is strikingly lower than the percentage of Muslims in the total African American population in the New World during the early period of their history in the United States, which, according to recent research, was presumably no less than 30 percent (Moore 1994:226) and possibly as high as 50 percent.

The history of African Americans shows a continued presence of Muslims of African origin in the New World beginning with the discovery of America late in the fifteenth century; perhaps it even predates, as mentioned earlier, the discovery of America. Be that as it may, the mass influx of Africans—of whom a good proportion was Muslim—began early in the seventeenth century. For it is then that the well-known Atlantic slave trade began and remained in full operation for about two centuries.

During the course of centuries, about ten million Africans landed in the Western Hemisphere in chains. A great majority of them settled in Brazil and the Caribbean. However, about one out of every twenty slaves was brought to North America. (This makes the number of Africans who came to the United States close to half a million.) A vast majority of them (i.e., about 90 percent) remained up until the first decade of the twentieth century in the southern states, especially in Georgia and South Carolina. For a variety of reasons, perhaps the most important of which was the policy of the slave masters to ensure that the slave families did not remain integrated, the African slaves could not maintain any vital links with their past or retain any strong sense of collective identity. Indeed, many African Americans today consider themselves to have virtually no collective memory of their past, no knowledge of their roots.

African slaves came to America from a wide variety of regions in the African continent and represent almost all ethnic stocks. It has not been possible so far to accurately estimate the proportion of Muslims in the early period of American history among them. In general, however, the earlier perceptions about the proportion of Muslims that had leaned on the conservative side have now been shown to be incorrect. Scholars specializing in the early history of African Americans are presently inclined to the view that there was a very high percentage of Muslims among the Africans who came to the New World or to the United States.

Clyde-Ahmad Winters, for instance, has shown that in both South and North America, the proportion of the Muslims among the Africans brought to the Americas was quite high. He has contended that a majority of the earliest and latest slaves to arrive in the Americas came from those African regions where the Muslims were in majority. According to Winters, the first mention of African Muslims in the New World began with the discovery of the New World. Estevanico, who, as we know, served as a guide in the exploration of Arizona, was a Negro Arab from Morocco. We also learn of several other Muslim slaves and adventurers who were used by the Spaniards to help them in exploration and as interpreters (Winters 1978:188).

Considerable evidence indicates uninterrupted Islamic presence in America from the earliest times after the discovery. It is known, for instance, that in 1518, the Spaniards were upset about the Islamic activities of many slaves. This seems understandable in view of the fact that Granada had fallen only in 1492 so that it was not unnatural for the Spaniards to fear Muslim political ambitions. This fear also explains the effort of the Spaniards to prevent African-Indian marriages. The Spaniards also feared the rise of a Muslim empire in the New World under African imams, which resulted in the removal of African and native Indian Muslim activities from America. It was again the same fear that made the Spaniards decide subsequently not to purchase any more slaves from northwest Africa, especially Berbers and Wolof. It is also noteworthy that the early revolts in South America were led mainly by Muslims, as were the fearsome series of uprisings in Brazil in the nineteenth century (Winters 1978:188–90).

The slave traders specialized in the sale and recruitment of children and teenage slaves, for more slaves could be bought for the same amount since they were smaller and their price was less. Some of these Muslim slaves had learned the entire Quran by heart and also knew, by the time they reached their teens, how to pray. It seems that on average the Muslim slaves were better educated and generally more civilized than their non-Muslim counterparts, and there is much evidence to suggest that they tried hard to cling to Islamic beliefs and practices (Winters 1978:191; Kly 1989:152–60, passim).

Scholars have brought to light a fair number of African Muslim slaves who impressed the people around them for one reason or the other, but especially for their intelligence, higher education, and piety, as we shall see. We find occasional references to them in the contemporary writings covering a very wide geographic area of North America and different periods of American history. This, again, points to a continuity of Islamic presence in the New World.

Among these African slaves we learn about Ayub Sulaiman Ibrahim Diallo, who became known as Job Ben Solomon in Maryland. He went to England and wrote two Qurans from his memory while he was there. In the late eighteenth century we encounter "Prince" Abdul Rahman Ibrahima of Mississippi and Lamine Kebe (better known as "Old Paul"). We also encounter Salih Bilali. He read and wrote Arabic and was a deeply religious person who abstained from liquors and kept various fasts, especially of Ramadan. He was a Fulani, born in 1770, and held in bondage in Georgia. Again, we come across Omar ibn Said, called Moro, who was held as a slave in North Carolina. He studied Islam up to the age of twenty-five, performed *hajj* (pilgrimage), and took part in holy wars. Above all, we now know a great deal about Kunta Kinte who came from Juffure, Gambia, and landed in America in 1767. He was the ancestor of the famous African American litterateur, Alex Haley (1976), whose desire to learn about him led him to a fascinating voyage of discovery to the village of his ancestors. (For some of these early Muslims, see Nyang 1990:214–17; Nyang 1992:6–7; Kly 1989:153–55; Winters 1978:191–95.)

Even though the number of African American Muslims in this early period was quite high, Islam could not strike roots in the United States as an organized religion. In fact, gradually the proportion of Muslims significantly decreased. This was for a variety of reasons, including the fact that Muslim slaves were occasionally forced to renounce their religion and names on pain of death (Kly 1989:158; Moore 1994:226). The result was that many of them sublimated their true religion, and many others gave it up altogether; some even accepted the religion of their masters, whereas some secretly clung to Islamic belief and practice and occasionally played a leading role in revolts and insurrections.

Apart from the pressure of the slave masters on the slaves to renounce Islam, a number of other factors also prevented organized Islam from striking roots. One of these was the large-scale transportation of African slaves. During the years 1790–1860, over two million slaves were moved from one part of America to another owing to interstate slave trade. In most cases the husband and the wife lived on different plantations. Additionally, each slave witnessed about eleven sales of his family of origin and of his own immediate family. In the South, when the mother was sold, the children were kept by the slave master. Even otherwise, at about the age of eight, children were separated from their mother. The transmission of Islamic values was thus rendered extremely difficult, owing to the destruction of the family and the traditional work schedule of the slaves—from "sun up to sun down" (Winters 1978:193–94).

This early period of African American history seems to be of crucial importance and presents us with intriguing questions. Adequate answers to these questions will illuminate an important aspect of African American history covering more than two hundred years and will reveal how and why Islam among a very high proportion of African Americans was reduced, by the turn of the twentieth century, to insignificance. But apart from that matter, adequate answers to these questions will probably also contribute to explaining why, after Islam had been almost obliterated from African Americans, they have recently begun to turn to Islam en masse.

Kly (1989) has attempted to answer some of these questions in a perceptive paper entitled "African American Muslim Minority: 1776–1900." Kly shows that the African American Muslim slaves have passed through very hard times precisely because they were Muslims. "They were tortured, burnt alive, hung or shot unless they renounced their religion and their names and accepted to be called by the name of the one who claimed to own them" (153). Kly has also shown that despite terror, small pockets of Muslims and some isolated individual Muslims managed to survive in their faith through the period of enslavement (193).

The first Muslim slaves seem to have landed on the coasts of South Carolina and Georgia. In a great many writings of the eighteenth, nineteenth, and even early twentieth centuries, we find useful information about the presence in this region of practicing Muslims who were descendants of these African Muslim slaves.

It is also significant that it is in the South Carolina and Georgia coastal region, from which 95 percent of all African Americans began their sojourn in the United States, that we find traces of an uninterrupted presence of Muslims. However, the African Muslims, especially those of the South Carolina–Georgia region, were subjected to excessive persecution. The Muslims responded by constantly rising in revolt against slavery and oppression. Kly (1989) speaks of some such Muslims in these words:

> They often lived as marauders on small islands on the coast of South Carolina and Georgia. When they were captured, they were either killed, or tortured, and forced to forsake their Islamic practices and accept the Christian teachings of that period (one of which was that they were created by God to be the slaves of the colonists). Eventually most of this community was exterminated or converted to a hybrid form of Christianity (Afro-Christianity) that was taught and developed by those Africans who had submitted to the practice of slavery with the hope of developing African-Christianity as a way of submitting to the practice of slavery while promoting Christianization and Anglo Americanization as the means to achieve freedom. (157)

The earliest Muslim community of African origin thus lived under quite inhospitable conditions. The destruction of the family deprived them of a major source for the transmission of Islamic belief and practice. Also, the prevalent conditions were not propitious for the establishment of institutions that might have sustained Islamic life—*masjid* (the mosque), *madrasah* (Muslim schools), and so forth. Still, these African Muslims made a brave attempt to adhere to Islam and deserve to be remembered for their strong devotion to their faith. Whenever possible, they prayed five times a day and selected imams from among themselves such as those known to the Anglo-

Americans as "African Tom" and Bilali. These early Muslims in South Carolina and Georgia, as well as elsewhere, could not survive as Muslim communities, and a very vast majority of their descendants became Christians. Many cultural vestiges of these communities did survive. While Islamic belief and practice might have disappeared or greatly weakened, a vague consciousness that they were originally Muslims seems to have lingered on. This vague consciousness seems to be a major factor in the contemporary revival of African Americans' interest in Islam. In the words of Morroe Berger (1964), "It is quite possible that some of the various American Muslim groups of the past half century or so had their roots in these vestiges, that the tradition was handed down in a weak chain from generation to generation" (64). There also seems much sense in the statement that a seminary student made to the *Wall Street Journal:* "I believe that the religion of Islam is part of the genetic memory of African Americans" (Barboza 1993:195).

It is understandable, therefore, why the claim of African American leaders from Noble Drew Ali to Fard Muhammad to Elijah Muhammad that Islam is the true original religion of the African Americans struck a familiar chord in the hearts of a very large number of African Americans.

ISLAM IN THE INTERWAR YEARS

During the second half of the nineteenth century, the Islamic presence in the United States seemed on the verge of extinction. Muslims in large numbers had eventually been assimilated, and those who were left with any Islamic consciousness found no external means to sustain it.

It was precisely at this stage—the last decades of the nineteenth century—when immigration brought Muslims from overseas, a development that replenished the Islamic presence in the United States. Muslim immigrants came from Syria, Iraq, Egypt, India, Eastern Europe, and Turkey and settled in different parts of the United States, especially in and near the commercial centers in New York, Pennsylvania, New Jersey, Massachusetts, Ohio, Michigan, and California. The early immigrants were usually men with low education and low proficiency in English and who remained occupied, in the main, with their economic pursuits. However, soon they also concerned themselves with building small prayer places or mosques for the preservation of their religion and culture. The predominant impulse that one can notice in them was to maintain Islam and transmit it to their descendants. There hardly seems to have been any aspiration to convey the teachings of Islam to their non-Muslim neighbors.

With passage of time, however, better-educated Muslims arrived in greater numbers and the interaction between the immigrant and indigenous Muslims, especially African Americans Muslims, increased. Also, gradually some of the immigrant Muslims began to get active about Islam and even began to teach Islamic belief and practice. Thus, during the first decades of the present century, it is mainly some of these new immigrant Muslims who carried the message of Islam to the indigenous population, including the African Americans. At times these were from Arab countries, the Caribbean, or the South Asian subcontinent.

The story of Islam among African Americans during the twentieth century is largely one of initiatives taken by the immigrants to spread their different versions of Islam and the responses of African Americans to those initiatives. These initiatives occasionally led to the spread and reinvigoration of mainstream Islam. But often it also gave rise to a number of cults, movements, and institutions of a heterodox and heretical character. All this, however, caused a large number of African Americans to identify themselves with Islam, and this development ultimately led a great number of them to the Islamic mainstream.

THE RISE OF ISLAMIC ORTHODOXY AMONG AFRO-AMERICANS

The studies on Islam in the United States have been generally focused on the heterodox groups, a fact that has relegated to the background the fact of the existence of a sizable number of orthodox Muslims. Consequently, the efforts of these Muslims to maintain and promote orthodox Islamic belief and practice have not been much highlighted. The presence of such orthodox individuals and groups, among both the immigrants and African Americans, has not been fully appreciated possibly because human beings have a propensity to feel excited about things that are bizarre and exotic and out of the ordinary, whereas there is little excitement for things with which one is familiar.

Before we embark on a study of the different movements that arose among African Americans in the name of Islam from the second decade of the present century, it seems necessary to point out that several significant orthodox Islamic groups arose late in the nineteenth and in the early twentieth century.

One of these earlier groups arose in New York City. This should not be astonishing, because there have been for long a fair number of Muslims of both African and non-African origins in New York City. This city, which presently has three hundred thousand to six hundred thousand Muslims (Ferris 1994:210), had known Islam since the era of the discovery from the Africans who brought it to the city, and probably the Muslim seamen and other temporary Muslim migrants introduced the observance of Islam that left its mark on New York City.

One of the earliest orthodox Islamic groups known to us was formed by a White American convert to Islam, Alexander Russell Webb (d. 1916). Webb was an educated person and an able journalist who was interested, at the intellectual level, in oriental philosophy. He accepted Islam while he was American consul-general in the Philippines, presumably as a result of his contacts with some Muslims in Bombay, India. Webb was a zealous missionary who established the American Moslem Brotherhood in 1893 in New York. He also founded the Moslem World Publishing Company, which published the journals *Voice of Islam* and *Moslem World* between 1893 and 1895. By the end of the century, the Brotherhood had virtually disintegrated as a result of inner dissensions.

In 1907, Polish, Russian, and Lithuanian Muslim immigrants to Brooklyn, New York, founded another group presumably of the same kind—the American Mohammadan Society, the first society around a mosque. It remained the main Islamic outpost in New York for more than a generation, claiming an average of four hundred members through the 1950s.

It is again in New York City that still another, and a powerful, orthodox Islamic group was established in the 1920s by the Moroccan-born Sheikh Daoud Ahmad Faisal, who came to the United States via Grenada. He organized the second bona fide mosque, the Islamic Mission of America. In 1939, he rented a building in Brooklyn Heights that he was able to buy in 1947. Apart from holding congregational prayers, this organization was interested in spreading the teachings of Islam in America. Conversion, the improvement of the image of Islam, and the dissemination of the message of a just and compassionate God remained central to Faisal's goals for the Islamic Mission.

Faisal also established an Islamic school called the Institute of Islam. The school's main period of activity was between 1950 and 1965 when it offered daily, two-hour-long, year-round Islamic and Arabic classes for children and adults.

From the late 1950s through the mid-1960s, the Islamic Mission was one of the city's only immigrant mosques, and Faisal administered to a three-hundred-member congregation, including diplomats, businessman, and university students. There was also a Muslim Ladies Cultural Society.

The Islamic Mission brought African American and immigrant Muslims together. It served as a forum where African Americans received exposure to the mainstream Islam. Faisal tried to promote harmony and interaction within New York's Islamic community. For a variety of reasons, however, there occurred serious splits in the Islamic Mission, and a significantly large chunk of African American Muslims separated from it and established a movement of their own.

The relatively large number of Muslims in New York City, with a large proportion of immigrant Muslims and their relatively higher intellectual level, enabled the mainstream Islam to strike roots there. In smaller cities where Muslims were fewer in number, or in places that were somewhat remote from metropolitan cities and had a significant proportion of educated immigrant Muslims, the story of Islam was different.

It would be pertinent to note that alongside the aforementioned orthodox groups, a heretical movement also established itself in the United States in the early years of the twentieth century. A small number of immigrants from the South Asian subcontinent started the Ahmadiyyah movement in the United States. The Ahmadiyyah believe that the founder of their sect, Mirza Ghulam Ahmad (d. 1908), was a prophet. Since this was fundamentally opposed to the finality of the prophethood of Muhammad (peace be on him), the Ahmadiyyah faced opposition from the outset, especially from the immigrant Muslims. The members of the group, however, always insisted that they were the exponents of true Islam and that their version of Islam alone was authentic. The leader of this group, Mufti Muhammad Sadiq, started a magazine, *The Muslim Sunrise,* to spread the teachings of the sect.

The Ahmadiyyah have had a significant impact during the first half of the twentieth century on the African Americans. Given the fact that authentic knowledge about Islam was scarcely available at this period, and given the relatively low level of education among African Americans, the Ahmadiyyah were able to win a good number of converts among them. (For the Ahmadiyyah in the United States, see Nyang 1992:8–11. See also Haddad and Smith 1994:xvii.)

This was, among other things, because of the proselytizing zeal for which the Ahmadiyyah have been known. A majority of these converts, however, gradually became aware of the falsity of the Ahmadiyyah doctrines. As the number of immigrant Muslims increased, many African Americans who had converted to the Ahmadiyyah gradually became better aware of the authentic teachings of Islam, which prompted many of them to renounce the Ahmadiyyah. This development does not detract from the fact that for quite some time in the first half of the twentieth century, the Ahmadiyyah fired the imagination of quite a number of African Americans and, for some odd reason, especially of jazz musicians (see Barboza 1993:14). It is also quite possible that they had influenced, even if indirectly, the rise of the heterodox, sectarian cults, such as the Moorish Science Temple and the Nation of Islam, a subject that remains to be carefully studied.

Against the background of the developments described here, we shall now proceed to study the major developments during the twentieth century among the African Americans, specifically vis-à-vis Islam.

ISLAM, MUSLIM IMMIGRANTS, AND BLACKS
IN THE UNITED STATES

To appreciate the predicament of the African Americans in the early 1900s, which provides the background against which the African American movements of this period should be viewed, certain important facts ought to be borne in mind. Perhaps the most important of all is the fact that although the African Americans were able, after considerable struggle and suffering, to obtain freedom in 1863 when slavery was formally abolished, raising the expectations of African Americans, the relief ensuing from freedom was not very substantial. However, one important consequence of the emancipation for African Americans was their freedom to migrate. The African slaves had remained overwhelmingly concentrated, as pointed out earlier, in the South right until the early years of the twentieth century. There they had supplied for long the manual labor needed for the cultivation of cotton, tobacco, rice, sugarcane, and indigo, on which the prosperity of the South rested. Sick and tired of their lot in the South, the African Americans developed a romantic notion of the state of affairs in the North. This led to a continual series of migration of the African Americans to the northern states commencing from the early years of the twentieth century on. During the first three decades of the century alone, two and a quarter million African Americans migrated to the North.

It did not take long for the African Americans to realize, however, that their dreams had remained far from realization. Many of them had looked forward not only to material prosperity but also to freedom, equality, and justice, only to discover that their lot had hardly improved. The Great Depression of 1929 and subsequent years aggravated their problems by creating large-scale unemployment, causing them indescribable suffering and agony. All this was in addition to the not infrequent acts of lynching of the African Americans and their continual subjection to discrimination in ways altogether offensive to human dignity.

The situation in which the African Americans found themselves during the early years of the twentieth century gave rise to two seemingly different responses. We might term the first of these responses to be the rise of movements of a secular, nationalist character, and the second, to the rise of religious movements and personalities.

The most potent manifestation of the secular nationalist response to the contemporary predicament of the African Americans was the movement founded by a Jamaican Black called Marcus Garvey (d. 1940). Garvey emphasized the African identity of the Negroes, as they were then called, and urged them to seek their destiny independent of the Whites. His ardent enthusiasm for African heritage and for the black color characteristic of the Africans is epitomized in a slogan that was to gain considerable popularity among African Americans: "Black is beautiful."

Garveyism was primarily a nationalist movement and was quite secular in spirit. Garvey identified the problem of African Americans with that of colonialism. In 1914, he envisioned uniting the Negro peoples of the world into one great body, to establish a country and government absolutely their own. The Negroes in diaspora were required to go back to their native land—Africa. To bring about awakening among them and to mobilize them for the achievement of their national objectives, Garvey established the Universal Negro Improvement Association (UNIA). He also established the Black Star Lines that would transport the Negroes to Africa.

Garvey advocated racial purity, racial integrity, and racial hegemony. He sought to organize Negroes in the United States into a vanguard for Africans' redemption from colonialism and hoped to lead them back to Africa. One of the major instruments that he wished to use was economic cooperation through racial solidarity. He believed that if the Negroes of the world could be united together by the consciousness of race and nationality, they could became a great and powerful people.

His movement and philosophy are reflected in the following statement of objectives:

> To establish a universal confraternity among the race; to promote the spirit of pride and love; to reclaim the fallen; to administer to and assist the needy; to assist in civilizing the backward tribes of Africa; to assist in the development of independent Negro nations and communities; to establish a central nation for the race; to establish commissaries or agencies in the principal countries and cities of the world for the representation of all Negroes; to promote a conscientious spirit of worship among the native tribes of Africa; to establish universities, colleges, academies and schools for the racial education and culture of the people; to work for better conditions among Negroes everywhere. (Cited by Essien-Udom 1971:38)

Garvey's movement gave a very large number of African Americans a new consciousness of their worth and a fresh confidence in their future. His movement fired the imagination of a people who were desperate for a new hope and a new purpose. However unrealistic its programs might be, Garvey's assertion of racial pride evoked the sympathy and support of thousands of African Americans.

Even though Garvey had created great popular stir, he encountered serious practical problems. Influential sections of the African American community bitterly pitted themselves in opposition to him. This was in addition to his arousing the hostility of the American establishment. His economic projects, especially the Black Star Lines, also did not prove successful. In fact, he got embroiled in a succession of court cases in which he was indicted for resorting to fraudulent practices. Eventually, he was convicted and deported to his native country, Jamaica, in 1925. Gradually, Garveyism lost its appeal.

Apart from this predominantly secular movement, several movements also arose among African Americans that, even if they were activated by nationalist objectives, expressed themselves in religious terms. The racial segregation that characterized American life was so pervasive that it even embraced their religious life. Thus, there were exclusively Negro churches for African Americans since White churches were disinclined to open their doors to them. To many African Americans, the Negro church was merely a fact of life, it being exclusively among the several undesirable things that they had gotten used to. Moved by counterracism, however, some African Americans began to glorify the religious dimension of their Black identity. In fact, Black identity became the foundation and the moving force of several millenarian movements led by such charismatic African American leaders as Daddy Grace and Father Divine. (For Father Divine, see Harris 1953; for the millenarian movements during the earlier part of the century, see Bontemps and Conroy 1945.)

It is significant that during the early decades of the last century a large number of African Americans, especially those in some of the northeastern states, began to identify themselves with Islam. This was more evident in the case of those African Americans who had only recently migrated from the South. It is not insignificant, as Kly (1989:155) has pointed out, that Noble Drew Ali and Elijah Muhammad, the two most prominent figures who emphasized Islam as the central fact of African American identity, had migrated from Georgia—the region that had had a long, uninterrupted Islamic presence of significant proportions, in fact up until the 1940s.

It is in this context that we shall now examine two extremely important African American religious cults that arose in the name of Islam: the Moorish Science Temple and the Nation of Islam. Both these represent the first stirrings of Islamic revival among a people who had presumably never quite forgotten that their ancestors were Muslims and who had begun to look upon Islam as a possible means to achieve their liberation and retrieve their dignity.

Moorish Science Temples

The Moorish Science Temple was established by Timothy Drew (1866–1929) in Newark, New Jersey. Later the Moorish temples were established in Detroit, New York, Chicago, Pittsburgh, Philadelphia, and many cities across the South. The membership during the life of Timothy Drew, who decided to call himself Noble Drew Ali, reached as high as between twenty thousand and thirty thousand. Noble Drew Ali scarcely had any formal education but had some conversance with oriental philosophy. He was much concerned with the identity problem of his people and considered this to be one of central importance. It was only when his people would have a clear consciousness of their identity, he thought, that the African Americans would be able to develop self-respect and dignity. He declared, therefore, that they were to be known as Asiatic or Moorish: "They must henceforth call themselves Asiatic, to use the generic term, or more specifically the Moors or Moorish Americans" (Lincoln 1973:53).

Consistent with this line of thinking, Noble Drew Ali issued nationality and identification cards, each card bearing a star and crescent, a known Islamic symbol. He honored Jesus, Muhammad, Buddha, and Confucius as Divine Prophets.

Noble Drew Ali identified himself with Islam, called himself and his followers "Moslems," and had a book that he called the "Holy Koran" (which, incidentally, was quite different from the Quran). He was openly anti-White, treated Whites with open contempt, and believed that the Whites would be destroyed and the Asiatics would soon be in control. While the cult considered itself "Moslem," it emphasized the question of collective identity more than anything else. Noble Drew Ali believed that before a people can have a God, they must have a nationality (Essien-Udom 1971:34). "You can have a God; you must have a nation." Noble Drew Ali declared the North African state of Morocco to be their nation. He also emphasized the importance of name as an indicator of one's identity. Strict morality was the keynote of the movement. The role of the husband as protector and provider for his family was stressed. Hence, the so-called Negroes should call themselves Asiatics, Moors, or Moorish Americans (Essien-Udom 1971:34; Lincoln 1973:53). Women, on the other hand, were required to be good homemakers and to obey their husbands. Several of these characteristics were to feature prominently in the Nation of Islam, which arose after the decline of the Moorish Science Temple, and, according to some, the Nation was in fact a wing of the Moorish Temple after its split from within.

Noble Drew Ali also claimed himself to be the reincarnation of Muhammad and called himself a prophet (Lincoln 1973:56; Essien-Udom 1971:35). He was acquainted with certain aspects of Islamic teachings and became convinced that Islam was the only instrument for Negro unity and advancement.

According to legend, Noble Drew visited North Africa, where he received commission from the king of Morocco. He also claimed to have met the U.S. president to receive a charter for the propagation of Islam. His teachings are embodied in his Holy Koran, which, strangely enough, bore a photograph of King Abdul Aziz Ibn Saud of Arabia. So far as Noble Drew Ali's Holy Koran is concerned, we might quote from Bontemps and Conroy (1945):

Drew Ali had written and published his Koran, a slim pamphlet consisting of a curious mixture of the Mohammadan holy book of the same name, the Christian Bible, and the words of Marcus Garvey, and anecdotes of the life of Jesus—the whole bound together with the prophet's own pronouncements and interpretations. (175)

Noble Drew Ali died or was killed in 1929 at a time when severe splits arose among the Moors. Gradually, the movement weakened, and it seems many of its members gradually joined the Nation of Islam. It is even contended that the founder of the Nation of Islam, Fard Muhammad, was a member of the Moorish Science Temple who established a movement of his own when the Moors were caught in the vortex of decline.

START OF THE NATION OF ISLAM

The Moorish Science Temple was the direct forerunner of a very powerful movement that arose soon after the death of Noble Drew Ali. It arose around the name of a mysterious silk peddler, whose complexion and features were almost those of a White man and who began to preach in 1930 a set of doctrines to the African Americans in Detroit. This man—who was called by many names—is generally known as Wallace D. Fard or Fard Muhammad, and the movement is known as the Nation of Islam. (For the Nation of Islam, see Lincoln 1973; Essien-Udom 1971; see Ansari 1981 for its religious doctrines.)

Hardly anything can be said with certainty about Fard's racial and geographic origins or about his life prior to his appearance in Detroit in 1930. (For the earliest account of the movement initiated by Fard, see Benyon 1938:894–907.) A number of divergent opinions have been expressed about him: that he was a Jamaican, a Palestinian, an Arab from Mecca belonging to the Quraysh tribe, a Turk, an Indian, and even a Jew.

A few things are certain in regard to Fard's teachings, however. He called the group that he organized in Detroit the "Allah Temple of Islam." He designated his own religious doctrine as Islam and sought to convert the African Americans to it, claiming that it would liberate them from the dominance of the White race. He denounced the Whites as "blue-eyed devils," "cave men," and "Satan." As for himself, he seems to have claimed to be the Mahdi, and probably he either himself made the claim or was subsequently declared by his followers to be a prophet. Whether he called himself God or an incarnation of God is not quite clear; perhaps he did not. But it is certain that before the 1940s had run out, the Nation of Islam believed that he was God-in-Person.

In 1934, Fard disappeared as mysteriously from the American scene as he had appeared on it. There was some rift and feuding in the Nation of Islam, but eventually one of Fard's followers, Elijah Muhammad, was able to establish himself as its leader. He retained that position from 1934 until the very end of his life in February 1975. Elijah Muhammad bolstered his authority by claiming himself to be the Messenger of Allah.

Despite the great emphasis placed on Islam, the religious doctrines of the Nation of Islam have very little to do with the religious doctrines characteristic of Islam, the doctrines explicitly embodied in the Quran. A comparative study of the basic doctrines espoused by the Nation of Islam conclusively establishes that.

Let us first consider the concept of God in the Nation of Islam. During the long period (1934–1975) when Elijah Muhammad was the leader of the Nation, its concept of God was quite divergent from the Islamic one. The Nation emphasized that God is man and that he is Black, denouncing the concept of a nonmaterial God as a deception of the devils.

The God of the Nation of Islam is so human that he even dies, a notion that is seemingly closer to Christianity than to Islam. Not only that, Elijah Muhammad also frequently employed the characteristically Christian expression "God-in-Person" with regard to Fard, who is claimed to have come to North America for the redemption of his people, and who endured suffering and courted imprisonment to show his love to them. All these are reminiscent of Christian concepts such as those of incarnation and redemption by suffering. Presumably these ideas were derived from the Christian milieu of North America where the movement arose.

The Nation identified God with W. D. Fard and called him "God-in-Person." Whose incarnation is or was he?

This brings us to another aspect of Elijah Muhammad's concept of God—its corporateness. Allah, as conceived by him, to borrow the words of Eric Lincoln (1973:75), "is not a godhead complete in himself." Allah seems to be identified with the collective entity of the Original People, the Black People, the Righteous. The Quranic statement about God that he is the first and the last (57:3) has been interpreted by the Nation of Islam to mean that the Black Man is the first and the last, that he is the maker and owner of the universe. Similarly, the Quranic verse that orthodox Muslims take as the affirmation of Divine transcendence was racialized. Instead of saying God is neither begotten nor did he beget (Quran 112:3), the Nation of Islam taught that Blacks were the descendants of this God in a purely biological sense, and hence they are Originals; they are righteous and partake of divinity. "All Blacks are God (Allah), and one of them is the Supreme Being." (For the Nation of Islam's concept of God, see Ansari 1981:142–46.)

The divergence of such a concept of God from that entertained by the Muslims all over the world is too evident even to need any elaboration.

The same divergence from Islam characterizes the Nation's doctrines regarding prophethood and especially their belief relating to the Prophet Muhammad (peace be on him). (For the Nation of Islam's concept of prophethood and belief about the Prophet Muhammad, see Ansari 1981: 147–55.)

The Nation of Islam shares with Muslims the belief in the prophethood of the earlier prophets such as Noah, Abraham, and others. They also consider Muhammad ibn 'Abd Allah (peace be on him) to be one of them and also acknowledge that the Quran was revealed to him.

It is striking, however, that reference to the Holy Prophet in the writings of Elijah Muhammad is scarce, is couched in a highly matter-of-fact phraseology, and lacks the warmth and love and devotion that characterize a Muslim's attitude toward him. It is also significant that quite often when Elijah Muhammad or his spokesmen enumerate prophets and messengers, the name of Muhammad either is missing or is not mentioned in unmistakably clear terms. What is much more significant is that occasionally when Muhammad (peace be on him) is mentioned, the one meant is Elijah Muhammad rather than the Prophet (peace be on him).

What, then, was the standpoint of Elijah Muhammad regarding the status of Muhammad ibn 'Abd Allah (peace be on him)? It is obvious that Elijah Muhammad, like the Qadiyanis, does not believe that Muhammad ibn 'Abd Allah (peace be on him) was the last prophet and Messenger of Allah. Almost ever since Fard's disappearance, Elijah Muhammad consistently claimed that he was the Messenger of Allah and at least since 1960 that he was the last Messenger of Allah. Perhaps the official doctrine of the Nation of Islam relating to Muhammad ibn 'Abd Allah (peace be on him) was adequately expressed by Elijah Muhammad when he said that the former was "a sign of the real Muhammad." (Elijah Muhammad's statement in *Muhammad Speaks* is cited in Ansari 1981:150.) At least in the 1970s, the Nation of Islam seems to have been of the view that the Prophet Muhammad (peace be on him) was indeed not a prophet or messenger in his own right but that his prophethood was merely a reflection of the prophethood of the real Muhammad (i.e., Elijah Muhammad) (Ansari 1981:150).

This tendency led the Nation of Islam, again and again, to compare Elijah Muhammad with prophets, including Muhammad ibn 'Abd Allah (peace be on him), and to claim that the former was incomparably superior to all of them. His alleged superiority is claimed on several grounds. The knowledge of truth given to the prophets, according to Bernard Cusheer (1971, cited in Ansari 1981:151), was inferior, since it was a mixture of facts, imagination, and so forth, and their grasp of the truth was limited. On the contrary, Elijah Muhammad's understanding of the truth was indeed perfect because of the former's direct contact with Allah (i.e., Fard), since Fard was Elijah Muhammad's teacher (let alone his guest). No prophet, including Muhammad ibn 'Abd Allah (peace be on him), had ever enjoyed that privilege (Ansari 1981:151).

Thus, no prophet, including the Prophet Muhammad, was considered by the Nation of Islam, especially during the last years of Elijah Muhammad's life, to be on the same level as the latter. The former, in their opinion, did not understand "the full reality of God" and "the depths of the sum of the teachings of the Qur'an" and "had nowhere near the knowledge of such subjects as astronomy as Messenger Elijah Muhammad has." The Holy Prophet, according to Elijah Muhammad, did not receive from Allah all the truth . . . that Muhammad of Arabia never saw his teacher" (Ansari 1981: 151–52).

Functionally speaking, in the Islamic tradition, prophethood is the vehicle for the communication of God's guidance. Muslims believe that this guidance is embodied in the Quran and the Sunnah, the latter being the authoritative explanation, elaboration, and exemplification of the Quran by the Prophet (peace be on him). Laying claim to full-fledged prophethood, Elijah Muhammad invested himself with all the authority which, in the Islamic tradition, belongs only to the prophets and messengers of God, and which was conferred finally by God on Muhammad (peace be on him) since in him prophethood reached its apogee and came to an end.

As for Elijah Muhammad, a natural corollary of his claim to prophethood was the belief that his interpretations of the Scriptures are authoritative. Among the Scriptures, Elijah Muhammad assigns a special position to the Quran and evinces for it a large measure of respect. This attitude to the Quran—which was revealed, after all, to someone other than Elijah Muhammad—would seem somewhat strange in the context of Elijah Muhammad's claims about his own unique status. This paradox is perhaps resolved were we to keep in mind Elijah Muhammad's claim to be the only authoritative interpreter of all Scriptures, including the Quran, to be the real Muhammad. It is obviously on the basis of this authority that Elijah Muhammad had changed the form of the ordained prayer and replaced the lunar month of Ramadan for fasting by the solar month of December. In fact, despite what the Quran has to say on this point, Elijah Muhammad remained unconvinced about the way fasting is traditionally observed by Muslims on the ground of Quranic prescription.

In like manner, the Nation's concept of the Hereafter varies fundamentally from the Islamic concept. (For the Nation of Islam's concept of the Hereafter, see Ansari 1981:155–61.) Stated succinctly, the Islamic doctrine of the Hereafter signifies that following the destruction of the present cosmic order at an appointed time in the future, all men will be resurrected and will be judged by the all-knowing, all-powerful, absolutely just and highly merciful God who will reward the righteous with eternal bliss and happiness in Heaven and punish the unrighteous with suffering in Hell.

The Nation of Islam also believes in the Hereafter. However, the actual content of their doctrine is vitally linked with the characteristic assumptions and concerns of the Nation of Islam and totally vary from the Islamic doctrine of the Hereafter.

To grasp the Nation's doctrine concerning the Hereafter, one must keep in mind that the White man (who is also called the man of sin, the devil, etc.) is considered to have been "made" about six thousand years ago and to have been granted a term of six thousand years to rule over the world. The period of White rule is characterized by the prevalence of evil and corruption. This period of history is termed by the "Nation of Islam" as "this world" or "this world of sin." By contrast, the "Hereafter" is the period that will follow the end of the dominance of the White man and the destruction of his "world of sin," a period that would inaugurate the never-ending rule of the Original or Righteous man.

The "Hereafter" will be preceded by the judgment of "Allah." This judgment, too, will take place on the Earth. The coming of "Allah" (Fard), which coincides with the lapse of the term of six thousand years granted to the White man to dominate the Earth, is seen to be the major event that will lead to the Hereafter. "Allah" in the person of Fard came to rescue His people, the Black men, to resurrect them from their deathlike state, and to punish and destroy the Whites.

The Nation's concept of resurrection can be better grasped if we bear in mind that they conceive of no life beyond the grave. According to Elijah Muhammad, the so-called Negroes of America are at present a dead people; and resurrection means nothing else but the mental resurrection of those dead people, their attaining to the consciousness that the time had come for them to get justice.

Quite consistent with these ideas is the concept of Heaven and Hell. These signify conditions of earthly life rather than states of supraterrestrial and postterrestrial existence. Also, to experience Heaven and Hell, one need not wait until one's death. Heaven and Hell are the conditions that exist on this Earth and that human beings experience during their lives.

Heaven, as described by Elijah Muhammad, is enjoyment of peace of mind and contentment with the God of the righteous and the Nation of the righteous. It consists of "enjoyment and unlimited progress in the new world of universal peace and happiness unlike anything seen, heard or imagined since the creation of the universe." The full flowering of this Heaven, however, will take place after the end of the era of White dominance. In that state, the righteous will enjoy the spirit of gladness and happiness forever in the presence of Allah. It will be a condition of absolute peace and brotherhood that will exclude even the possibility of disagreement. It will be a new life wherein even those who are a thousand years old will remain young and look like teenagers of sixteen (Ansari 1981:158–59).

Muslims who look at these religious doctrines from their perspective are prone to be scandalized by them, especially by statements claiming that W. D. Fard was Allah and Elijah Muhammad. Were such statements to be seen in the context of the African American cults of the time, however, they would make some sense. For esoteric claims such as these had already become a well-established tradition among the African American cults. It would be illuminating to look at some of these doctrines in the context of the Black cults of the time to explore their possible sources. The belief that Fard was God's incarnation is, in any case, not as outlandish in a Christian society as it is in a Muslim society. Moreover, claims of divinity had been made and accepted in the United States in the period that concerns us. Two best-known examples are those of Father Divine and Daddy Grace. Likewise, the claim to be a prophet or messenger of God was also not unprecedented. In fact, the same spirit evident in the claims for divinity was implicit in the claims of prophethood. A little before the appearance of Fard, Noble Drew Ali had been accepted by his followers as a prophet. Another religious preacher named Cherry was also considered a prophet and claimed to have received his mantle directly from God. Likewise, Bishop Ida Robinson claimed to have been ordained by God.

The Nation's denial of afterlife in the generally understood sense of the term also appears highly shocking to Muslims. It should, however, be viewed in the background of the excessive otherworldliness of the Christian church in twentieth-century America. It was not uncommon to look upon this excessive emphasis on the afterworld as a means to divert the attention of African Americans from their sordid state of existence. The emphatic promise of a pie in the heaven implied that the African Americans should be satisfied with their raw, unbuttered bread on Earth.

Whatever be the actual sources of the religious doctrines of the Nation of Islam, the success of the movement seemed to lie in its capacity to satisfy some of the most deeply felt urges of a considerable segment of the African Americans of the urban North. These doctrines and their identification with Islam only show that a good number of African Americans had then begun their quest for salvation beyond the confines of the formal Christian Church and the accepted value structure of American society.

The demonization, in quite a literal sense, of the White man by the Black Muslims might be crude, and their view of God unsophisticated and, on the whole, unconvincing. Yet those doctrines served a major purpose: they created a new sense of belonging and enabled the converts to look toward the future with serene self-confidence.

The Nation of Islam could also feel justifiably proud of having given thousands of African Americans a higher purpose of life. It reformed the lives of a very large number of persons, changing habitual criminals into law-abiding citizens. It promoted what was in the United States a different concept of womanhood. It was able to bring stability in the family life of its followers. And it brought about significant economic improvement in the lives of its followers by encouraging them to become active and productive as individuals and to cooperate in constructive economic ventures.

During the last ten years of Elijah Muhammad's life, the Nation faced several serious problems, some of which were of an intellectual character. Elijah Muhammad seems to have been seized by a dilemma. For he was at once drawn to two different poles, was pulled in two different directions. On the one hand, he stressed his identification with the Muslims and called upon his people to embrace Islam. He made it a point to publicize his relations with Muslim dignitaries abroad. The letters or cables sent to Elijah Muhammad by Muslim heads of states or distinguished religious leaders of the Muslim countries were greatly publicized. All this enhanced the position and prestige of Elijah Muhammad among African Americans. At the same time, it also created among his followers a sense of belonging to the Muslim *ummah* (community), even though it was not as clear and strong as their sense of belonging to the Nation of Islam.

On the other hand, Elijah Muhammad was exceedingly eager to retain the separate entity of his group, an entity separate even from the "Muslims of the East," as he called them. It is obvious that had his doctrines been exactly identical with Islam, it would have been impossible for him to retain this distinct entity. To ensure this distinctness, Elijah Muhammad stressed the unique position of African Americans and also took great pains to keep his followers insulated from all extraneous influences, especially from the influence of the "Muslims of the East."

It became quite evident within weeks after his death in 1975 that he did not quite succeed in that. His own son and successor, Wallace Muhammad, took a radically different line from that of his father. The Nation had identified itself with the name of Islam. Wallace Muhammad carried this nominal identification with Islam to its logical conclusion—to a conscious acceptance of the teachings of Islam.

THE RISE OF MALCOLM X

The late 1950s and the early 1960s saw the Nation of Islam rise to great heights of popularity. This was the period when African Americans were actively struggling for achieving equality of status, integration, and an amelioration of their economic condition. The major issue was that of integration—integration of educational institutions and public facilities, especially public transport. A group of White liberals and larger numbers of African Americans were engaged in this struggle under the banner of such organizations as the National Association for the Advancement of Colored People (NAACP) and under such leaders as the Southern Baptist pastor Martin Luther King Jr.

The Nation of Islam offered an alternative to the integrationist ideal; it offered the ideal of separation. Rather than try to become integrated with Whites, they emphasized that the interests and the dignity of African Americans could only be ensured by separating from Whites—religiously, socially, economically, and even politically. (The idea of separation was pushed by Elijah Muhammad so far as to demand sufficient land in the South for the establishment of a state exclusively for African Americans.) But it was his second-in-command, the charismatic Malcolm X, who mainly carried the message of separation with great vigor to the teeming masses of African Americans. He was able to electrify and mobilize many of them by his extraordinary oratorial skill, his defiant posture, and his remarkable courage. As we know, early in April 1964, Malcolm X disavowed this position and embraced Islamic universalism.

There are some specific reasons for Malcolm X's conversion, to which we shall refer shortly. However, it would also be useful to bear in mind some changes of a broad character that were taking place since the early 1950s in the United States, including in the Nation of Islam, for they also contributed to the change in the intellectual orientation of those who eventually opted in favor of the Islamic mainstream.

In the 1950s, the number of Muslim immigrants considerably increased, and they became active in Islamic affairs. The Federation of Islamic Association, formed in 1952, held its annual conventions, which drew a good number of Muslims from different parts of the United States and Canada. This created a greater sense of unity among Muslims and also gave fresh impetus to Islamic activity.

The establishment of the Muslim Students Association (MSA) in 1963 was an even more significant event. MSA organized Muslim students on the campuses and initiated activities that strove to heighten awareness of Islam in American society as a whole. Thus, the teachings of Islam—the teachings of orthodox Islam—were becoming increasingly known. The result was that an increasing number of people began to feel that the doctrines espoused by the Nation of Islam had scarcely anything to do with the true Islam.

Elijah Muhammad had himself been in touch with and had made use of some of these immigrant Muslims (e.g., Jamil Diab, Abdul Basit Naeem, Zaiul Hasan, etc.) as friends and as teachers of Arabic and Islam to his followers, or as his spokesmen to other Muslims. This naturally made them come into contact with the members of the Nation of Islam, especially with those in the higher echelon of the movement, and especially with the members of Elijah Muhammad's family. Moreover, some members of his family and Malcolm X had visited Saudi Arabia and other countries in the Middle East. It was presumably this kind of exposure to the "Muslims of the East" that sowed the first seeds of doubt. This doubt was the outcome of discovering that virtually a billion Muslims of the world had nothing to do with much of what Elijah Muhammad taught his followers as "Islam." Also, when these followers studied the Quran, they discovered that there was no sanction for several of Elijah Muhammad's teachings.

It was because of the discontent thus created that some members of the Nation of Islam broke off from the Nation and joined the mainstream Islam. Toward the end of the 1950s, the national secretary of the Nation of Islam, who renamed himself Hammas Abdul Khalis, left the Nation and formed a parallel group of his own. A few years later, in the 1960s, three persons of major significance—two of the sons of Elijah Muhammad—Akbar Muhammad and Wallace Muhammad—and above all, his main spokesman, Malcolm X, also converted to orthodox Islam. (For the early period of Wallace Muhammad's life, when he was a zealous follower of the Nation of Islam, see Ansari 1985a.) Of these, the departure of Malcolm X from the Nation of Islam proved to be a great catalyst, prompting many African Americans to identify with Islamic orthodoxy.

Malcolm X has himself narrated in great detail how he was led away, step by step, from his leader in whom his faith for well over a decade had been total; from one whom he quite literally believed to be the Messenger of Allah. In 1963, a series of incidents shook Malcolm X's faith in Elijah Muhammad, especially since those incidents revealed that the latter did not care to practice the morality he preached. Elijah Muhammad took a stern disciplinary action against Malcolm X in November 1963, prohibiting him to make any public speech or issue any public statement. This came as a rude shock to Malcolm X, who became convinced that the action was part of a conspiracy, which had been hatched in concert with his opponents and aimed at destroying his position. Initially, it was not Malcolm X's discontent with the religious doctrines of Elijah Muhammad but his unhappiness with, what seemed to him, the compromising sexual behavior of Elijah Muhammad, and then his adoption of a posture that appeared unjustifiably hostile, that drove him to leave the Nation of Islam early in 1964.

Once Malcolm X was out of the Nation of Islam, he felt no compulsion to adhere literally to its religious doctrines. The opportunity to read more extensively about Islam, to exchange views with other dissidents in the Nation, especially Wallace Muhammad and Akbar Muhammad, and to contact Muslims outside his original group pushed him in a different direction. All this culminated with his *hajj* in April 1964. During the hajj, Malcolm X became acutely conscious of the "color-blindness" of Islam, and quite soon he was led to believe that the doctrines he had learned from the Nation of Islam had no *locus standi* in Islam. This was apart from the moving experience of universal human brotherhood during the hajj that demolished the very kernel of the racist doctrine (or, shall we say, the counterracist doctrine) espoused by Elijah Muhammad. The letters Malcolm X wrote from Saudi Arabia vividly articulate this moving experience and its impact on him:

> Never have I witnessed such sincere hospitality and the overwhelming spirit of true brotherhood as is practiced by people of all colors and races here in this ancient Holy Land, the home of Abraham, Muhammad, and all the other prophets of the Holy Scriptures. For the past week I have been utterly speechless and spellbound by the graciousness I see displayed all around me by people of *all colors*.
>
> I have been blessed to visit the Holy City of Mecca. . . . There were tens of thousands of pilgrims from all over the world. They were of all colors, from

blue-eyed blonds to black-skinned Africans. But we were all participating in the same ritual, displaying a spirit of unity and brotherhood that my experiences in America had led me to believe never could exist between the white and the non-white. . . . I have never before seen *sincere* and *true* brotherhood practiced by all colors together, irrespective of their color. . . .

[O]n this pilgrimage, what I have seen, and experienced, has forced me to *rearrange* much of my thought-patterns previously held, and to *toss aside* some of my previous conclusions. . . .

During the past eleven days here in the Muslim world, I have eaten from the same plate, drunk from the same glass, and slept in the same bed (or on the same rug)—while praying to the *same* God—with fellow Muslims, whose eyes were the bluest of blue; whose hair was the blondest of blond; and whose skin was the whitest of white. And in the *words* and in the *actions* and in the *deeds* of the "white" Muslims, I felt the same sincerity that I felt among the black African Muslims of Nigeria, Sudan, and Ghana.

We were truly all the same (brothers)—because their belief in one God had removed the "white" from their *minds,* the "white" from their *behavior,* the "white" from their *attitude.* (Malcolm X 1966:340–41)

On returning to the United States after this soul-shaking event, Malcolm X—who renamed himself Al-Hajj Malik Shabazz—became and remained occupied until the very end of his life in February 1965 with *rearranging* his ideas. While his ideas remained in a constant state of flux, he gave vent to two different, though not necessarily contradictory, sets of ideas.

First, although he discarded the concept of the inherent and incorrigible perversity of Whites, he remained as ardent and as uncompromising as ever before in his struggle to put an end to the degradation to which the African Americans were subjected. He tried to close the ranks of African Americans and even made an effort to unite with all African American leaders, including the leaders of the civil rights movement such as Martin Luther King Jr., whom he had earlier ridiculed.

As for the common African Americans, his message to them was not to be intimidated by the violence that might be unleashed against them. Contrary to the philosophy of nonviolence preached by King, he urged African Americans to have recourse to the gun in self-defense. Moreover, he attempted to develop contacts with the leaders of African and Muslim countries with the intent of internationalizing their question.

Malcolm X established one organization each to institutionalize the two of his major concerns. The Muslim Mosque, Inc., embodied his commitment to spread that version of Islam which he had embraced after his hajj. The second organization was the League of African American Unity, which was to concern itself with the liberation of African Americans, *by any means necessary.*

Thus, the last year of Malcolm X's life, which was full of hectic activity, had a twofold impact on African Americans. On the one hand, his work provided a powerful impetus to such radical movements as Black Power of the mid-1960s and to the emergence of militant groups such as the Black Panthers.

No less consequential was the impact of Malcolm X's espousal of "orthodox Islam," with the result that he became, in the eyes of a large number of Muslims of his country, and to some extent, even outside, the symbol of Sunni Islam in America. (The expression "Sunni Islam" was used in contradistinction to the Nation of Islam rather than in opposition to the Shiah.)

From 1965 onward, a number of Sunni African American groups arose or were strengthened. Malcolm X had provided a very powerful impetus for this development and became their main inspiration in their journey to orthodox Islam. Despite their mutual disagreements, the African American Sunni groups revered Malcolm X as their hero, their ideal, as one who had become dearer to them after his brutal assassination. But even those who might not fully agree with Malcolm X's ideas still recognized his role as a watershed in the present century's history of Islam in the United States. (Significantly enough, Steven Barboza's [1993] recent work is entitled *American Jihad: Islam after Malcolm X*.) To what extent the phenomenon is causally related to Malcolm X's espousal of the Islamic mainstream, the fact remains that the 1960s witnessed a conspicuous growth of Sunni Islam among African Americans, a development to which we shall turn now.

THE RISE OF SUNNI ISLAM IN THE 1960S

One of these Sunni groups that arose in the 1960s, acquired considerable prominence, and remained occasionally in the news was the Hanafi Madhab Center. This group acquired special importance during the 1970s. With its headquarters in Washington, D.C., it was headed by Hammas Abdul Khalis, who was at one time the national secretary of the Nation of Islam but had subsequently left it in 1958. Abdul Khalis was under the influence of a scholar from what is now Bangladesh but was then part of Pakistan, and it was from him that he learned the fundamentals of orthodox Islam.

Abdul Khalis was a very zealous and energetic person, and after leaving the Nation of Islam, he focused his efforts on converting his former comrades to orthodox Islam. He wrote letters to the members of the Nation of Islam, vociferously pleading that they part company with the Nation of Islam, for its doctrines were wrong and its leader, Elijah Muhammad, was a false prophet. The group formed by Abdul Khalis called itself Hanafi Madhab Center, presumably because his mentor, like most Muslims of the subcontinent, belonged to the Hanafi School and regarded it as the most authentic form of Islam.

The group was strengthened circa 1970 when a star basketball player, Kareem Abdul-Jabbar, joined it and, according to popular belief, bought for it its headquarters in Washington, D.C. This further boosted the importance of the Hanafis. Around the some time, Abdul Khalis launched the drive to convert the members of the Nation of Islam by writing letters to them. The letters were full of vehement denunciation of Elijah Muhammad and of his teachings and actions. This brought Abdul Khalis a very sharp reprisal. Some of his opponents, who were later identified as belonging to the Nation's temple in Philadelphia, entered Abdul Khalis's home. They shot his wife and his daughter, and they drowned three of his other children and his nine-day-old granddaughter (Abdul-Jabbar 1993:214).

In March 1977, the Hanafis again made headlines. Abdul Khalis with some of his followers took over Washington, D.C.'s, City Hall, the Islamic Center, and the office of B'nai Brith. Holding hostages, Abdul Khalis demanded that the movie *The Messenger,* which offended his religious sensibilities, be withdrawn from theaters and that the men convicted of killing his family members, as well as those convicted of assassinating Malcolm X, be delivered to him. Abdul Khalis finally surrendered as a result of the persuading efforts of Muslim ambassadors. He was ultimately sent to prison to serve a long sentence.

Over the years, however, the group seems to have declined. The best-known supporter of the Hanafi Madhab Center, Kareem Abdul-Jabbar, himself became disenchanted. According to him, Abdul Khalis "got into a personality cult featuring him. It got bad" (quoted in Barboza 1993:214). What is important to remember is that while those who had been attracted to the group, and a good example is Kareem Abdul-Jabbar, might have quit the Hanafi Madhab Center, they retained their association with orthodox Islam.

At the doctrinal level, the Hanafis emphasize that they are Sunnis, that they are guided by the Quran and the *hadith* (oral form of the Prohetic tradition), and that they believe in Muhammad (peace be on him) as the last prophet of God.

The Hanafis also took special interest in presenting the teachings of Islam to African Americans and informing them that Islam does not recognize distinctions of race and color. While membership figures are not available, they were estimated to be several hundred. Their mosques are located in Washington, D.C., New York City, Chicago, and Los Angeles. In recent years, the Hanafis are not much in the limelight, although a great many of them presumably remain associated with the Islamic mainstream.

Dar ul-Islam

Another Sunni African American organization, and the most powerful one in that category, was Dar ul-Islam. (For this important movement, see

Curtis 1994.) It took its formal shape in the early 1960s, and the most prominent figure that emerged in the group was Imam Yahya Abdul Kareem. In 1962, the members pledged to follow the last Prophet Muhammad (peace be on him) and to keep to the Shariah. In 1963, all forty to fifty members repledged themselves. It did not take long for their members to increase to 150. However, internal conflicts soon developed.

In 1967, the idea of Black Power had caught the imagination of many African Americans. The pith of the idea was that African Americans should control their own affairs and destiny, that they should protect themselves and, when needed, fight their enemies. The summer of 1967 witnessed no fewer than forty racial riots. Subsequently, several self-defense groups arose among the African Americans. These were largely patterned after the Fruit of Islam organization of the Nation of Islam.

All available evidence suggests that the impetus to build an independent Dar ul-Islam came not only from the concerned persons' commitment to Islam but also from an African American nationalist consciousness popular at the time. In other words, the Dar ul-Islam members were not only concerned with translating the vision of an ideal Islamic life into practice but were also concerned to defend and promote the interests of African Americans.

Dar ul-Islam gradually grew into a popular and influential movement. While it remained headquartered in New York City, its influence spread to several states. By 1975, it had become the largest indigenous Sunni group in the country, and its main area of influence extended mainly to the cities along the Eastern Seaboard and all of its larger metropolitan towns. It became one of the main groups that challenged the Nation of Islam at almost every level.

Dar ul-Islam resembled some of the strict, albeit activist orthodox Muslim groups in the Muslim world. They emphasized strict adherence to the Shariah. They stressed that men should have beards, and women should cover their head. They emphasized that Muslims should not resemble non-Muslims in their appearance, a view they supported by reference to a well-known hadith on the subject: "He who makes himself resemble a people, is one of them." The Muslims who wore Western dresses and followed the Western lifestyle were considered deviant and looked down upon.

In the early part of his life, Imam Yahya Abdul Kareem had been under the influence of Maqbool Elahi, a scholar from Pakistan who held classes on Islam in New York, and then studied under the late Fazlur Rahman Ansari in Pakistan, who was at once a theologian and a Sufi. It so happened that in 1982, the Sufi seeds that perhaps lay largely dormant in Yahya Abdul Kareem's soul were activated and sprouted forth. Yahya declared that Dar ul-Islam had ceased to exist and that the group had become a part of an international Jamaat al-Ghuraba with a Pakistani called Shaykh Mubarak Ali Jamil al-Hashmi as their leader. A part of the movement, headed by Imam Jamil Abdullah al-Amin (formerly H. Rap Brown, the former chairman of

SNCC after Stokey Carmichael), broke away from the main group and called itself Dar ul-Islam. But the movement soon lost its appeal and strength.

Wherein lay the strength of Dar ul-Islam? Why did it attract a large number of African Americans? What was its main contribution? Mukhtar Curtis (1994) has attempted to answer these questions in his study on Dar ul-Islam:

> Islam offered to Dar members a lucid, divinely ordained value system with a promise of rewards and punishments in this life and the hereafter. It included a set of daily behaviors that distinguished a practicing Muslim from others. The believer required no skills in deconstructionism to understand Islamic monotheism nor was one's worry that the divine text, the Qur'an, was subject to alteration. . . . The second Islamic criterion, the Prophet's behavior, was also not subject to revision, was made available in hadith translations. The simplicity of the basic tenets of Islam and its consonance with certain aspirations of blacks, particularly those who desired a culture and polity separate from and not dominated by white America, made Islam and Dar attractive. The converts personified many of the individual attributes associated with Malcolm X, such as a readiness for self-defense, a disciplined traditional morality, and an exemplary strong African American manhood. . . .
>
> On a societal scale the hope was that the Muslim communities would become independent and self-contained with their own political, economic and defense systems. The ultimate earthly hope was that the Dar faithful would form a sovereign state. (66)

Ansarullah

Still another African American religious group stands somewhere in between a group such as Dar ul-Islam, which is a fully Sunni group, and the groups considered sectarian and heterodox. That group is Ansarullah.

Ansarullah emerged in the convulsive period of the 1960s, and like some other groups, its ideology is an amalgam of Islam and Black Nationalism. This group was established by an African American who had an occasion to visit Sudan. On return to the United States, he claimed to be a descendant of the great Mahdi of Sudan, Muhammad ibn Abd Allah (d. 1885). He gave himself the name of Al-Hajj Al-Iman Isa Abd Allah Muhammad Al-Hadi Al-Mahdi. He claimed that Al-Hadi Al-Mahdi, who had been killed in 1969, had come to the United States long ago, married an African American woman, and then had returned to Sudan. He claimed to have been born of that marriage and was thus the grandson of the great Mahdi.

The Ansar emphasized dress worn by the Ansar in Sudan—a long, loose garment for men and an Arabian-like garment for women. They also emphasized the importance of learning Arabic and urged the Ansar to speak to their children in that language.

The Ansar, who later adopted the appellation "Nubian Islamic Hebrew Mission," firmly believe in the unity of God and insist that no other word but *Allah* may be used for him. Likewise, they believe in Muhammad (peace be on him) as the final prophet. They believe, in addition to the Quran, in other Scriptures—the Old Testament, the Psalms of David, and the New Testament.

The Ansar believe in certain doctrines that are peculiar to them alone. They believe, for instance, that after the Flood, Ham desired to commit sodomy while looking at his father's nakedness, which led to the curse of leprosy on Ham's fourth son, Canaan, making his skin pale. It was thus that pale races came into being. The Amorites, the Hittites, the Jebusites, and the Sidovites are sons of Canaan and their descendants. Mixing blood with these "subraces" is not lawful for the Nubians. This seems to bear some resemblance to the myth popularized by the Nation of Islam that the Whites came into being as a result of the genetic experimentation of a Black scientist, Mr. Yakub, which led to the creation of a totally perverse race of the Whites.

The Ansar have not been as severely opposed by orthodox Muslims as were the Nation of Islam. This seems to be because they broadly subscribe to some of the fundamental tenets of Islam. It is presumably for this reason that the Ansar were invited to the First Islamic conference of North America (Nyang 1992:11). On the other hand, there has been considerable uneasiness among orthodox Muslims about them because of several of their exotic doctrines, a sample of which has been mentioned. One of the major objections to the Ansar is their acceptance of the Bible as a source of religious teachings as authoritative as the Quran (Gutbi 1991:21–22). The group seems inclined to cling to these exotic doctrines, for they serve the purpose of preventing its full assimilation into mainstream Islam. The change of the name of the group to Nubian Hebrew Islamic Association, among other things, seems to represent this desire to maintain a district entity of the group.

AFRICAN AMERICAN SUNNIS

As described here, Sunni or orthodox Islam began to gain popularity among African Americans during the 1960s and 1970s. Apart from the two major Sunni African American organizations mentioned earlier, there were several others. Moreover, a large number of African Americans converted to Sunni Islam and identified themselves with both local mosques and Islamic centers, or at least they tried to remain faithful to the tenets of the faith they had embraced. But it was 1975 that marked the greatest moment of triumph for orthodox Islam. For it is then that Wallace D. Muhammad (who later renamed himself Warith Deen Muhammad), one of the sons of Elijah Muhammad, succeeded his father to the leadership of the Nation of Islam. W. D. Muhammad had in fact renounced, as far back as 1963, many of the doctrines of his father that were opposed to the teachings of Islam. Both he and his brother, Akbar Muhammad (at that time a student at al-Azhar in Egypt), formed a rebellious trio with Malcolm X.

Thus, no sooner had W. D. Muhammad assumed the reins of leadership than he embarked on purging the Nation of Islam of its teachings to which the orthodox had long been objecting and bringing it in harmony with orthodox Islam. The entire operation was executed with great skill, with the result that a very good proportion of the rank and file of the Nation of Islam smoothly went along with the transition. W. D. Muhammad termed this transition the "Second Resurrection," indicating thereby that while the content of his message was different, it was essentially a continuation and culmination of the First Resurrection of the African Americans brought about by his father at the instance of Fard Muhammad.

W. D. Muhammad did not lose much time in pointing out the errors of his father's doctrines, although he did so with circumspection and dexterity. He attributed the doctrinal errors of his father mainly to the fact that it was part of a strategy that Fard Muhammad and his father had adopted to introduce the true teachings of Islam gradually to the African Americans. Since people at that time would not have been receptive to the true teachings of Islam, several incorrect ideas were inducted so as to make Islam palatable. Gradually, W. D. Muhammad was able to persuade his followers that his father was not even aware of the true teachings of Islam and that his claim to be a prophet was not correct. Likewise, the Black-centeredness of the Nation of Islam was cleverly discarded in favor of Islamic universalism, and again this was accomplished by resorting to very ingenuous arguments. (For the change brought about by W. D. Muhammad in the Nation of Islam, see Mamiya 1992. See also Ansari 1985b for a brief account of the doctrinal changes and for an effort to find the roots of these changes in the early life of W. D. Muhammad.)

Several milestones mark this epic journey. First, W. D. Muhammad threw open the doors of his movement to men of all racial origins, including Whites. This was done just a few months after his assumption of leadership. How revolutionary this step was can be gauged by the fact that for a full forty-five years, the members of the Nation of Islam had taught that Whites were, quite literally, devils. W. D. Muhammad justified the change by reinterpreting the racial doctrines of the Nation of Islam, contending that they had a symbolic rather than literal meaning. The word *white,* said W. D. Muhammad, was a symbol of evil, and *black* was a symbol of goodness. Hence, anyone who is born White is not ipso facto evil. In fact, depending on his attitude of mind, a White man might in fact be Black (i.e., good), and vice versa.

Second, in the very first year of his leadership, W. D. Muhammad introduced the proper Islamic rituals of worship, discarding the distorted forms in which they had been practiced earlier. Likewise, he did not take long to discard the idea that his father was the Messenger of Allah. This, apart from the notion that Fard Muhammad was God-in-Person, was the major barrier between the Nation of Islam and orthodox Muslims. Within a matter of two to three years, W. D. Muhammad had fully convinced a majority of the members of the Nation of Islam that they ought to accept the teachings of Islam in the manner understood by the "world community of Islam."

In 1976, W. D. Muhammad also changed the name of the Nation of Islam to the "World Community of al-Islam in the West." This was a clever move on his part so as to disengage the minds of his followers from the past and to foster the universalism of Islam. In 1980, he renamed his organization American Islamic Mission, Inc., which was dissolved in 1986 in order that his followers might become fully integrated with the Muslim *ummah*.

The doctrinal reorientation that took place under Warith Deen Muhammad is well illustrated by the case of the Masjid ul-Mutkabir in Poughkeepsie in the Hudson River Valley of New York state. This group has been competently studied by Christine Kolars (1994:475–99), and the profile of the community around Masjid ul-Mutkabir that is described here is essentially based on the information provided by this essay.

The small city of Poughkeepsie had its branch of the Nation of Islam when the mantle of its leadership fell on Warith Deen Muhammad in 1975. At that time, the Poughkeepsie branch of the Nation of Islam was headed by Minister Mark X, and it was he who led this group through the transition, in Kolars's words, "from proto-Islam to Islam," one early manifestation of the change being the change of Mark X's name to that of Sabir al-Hajji.

Masjid ul-Mutkabir is headquartered in a rented building and has a small membership, with twenty to thirty families who are active in the community on a regular basis. These families are African American, and a number of the older members were associated with the Nation of Islam until 1975. The adult members are mostly married, and family life is strongly emphasized by the society and its imam. Abstinence from premarital and extramarital sex, alcohol, and drugs are crucial elements in the doctrine of the community, and these topics are addressed on a regular basis in the *khutbah* (sermon) of the Friday prayer. The members have adopted Arabic first names, and many have retained their former first names along with the new Arabic-Muslim names. The children all have Arabic first names.

The Friday prayer is regularly observed. The majority of the worshipers are men, but a small number of women also attend the service. Islam is emphasized as the key element in determining the manner in which they should conduct their lives.

The interpretation of Islam adopted by the Masjid ul-Mutkabir community has had a great effect on male–female relations within the group. Although the doctrine encourages women to devote themselves to the raising of their children, it also supports their education and stresses their participation, as often as possible, in community activities. The education of women is emphasized as a Quranic imperative.

Although this mixture, which encourages a woman to be both a mother and a community activist, may seem contradictory, the movement interprets these aspects as two divisions of the woman's primary role as a teacher of children. This role is considered intrinsic to the community's existence and perhaps the most important task in the structure of the African American Muslim community. The task of good upbringing of children is emphasized. The remarks of the present Imam Shamsideen are significant: "I'm the head of the family. My wife takes care of our children. That's her duty. But if a decision needs to be made, I consult my wife. We are together; we can't make decisions without talking to the other person" (Kolars 1994:485).

The members of Masjid ul-Mutkabir have made a sincere effort to construct their own new Muslim identity, rejecting their Christian origins. Although they maintain contacts with the African American community through their extended families, their main organized contact is through the other African American masjids. Although the members of Masjid ul-Mutkabir are devoutly religious and claim to have completely rejected their Christian upbringing, they maintain contacts with their non-Muslim family members despite religious differences. A frequent topic of the Friday *khutbah* (sermon) is the rejection of Christian beliefs and the resistance of American culture. The doctrine of trinity is refuted as a doctrine inconsistent with the Islamic monotheism. The imam stresses that while Jesus is recognized as a prophet, the idea that he was of divine origin is held as unacceptable.

One of the consistent themes of the Friday khutbahs is the importance of maintaining a strong Muslim identity. In December 1991, when Warith Deen Muhammad visited the Hudson Valley, he addressed an audience of three thousand Muslims, the majority of whom traveled from the area around the Hudson Valley to attend. This attendance is indicative of the powerful leadership role that W. D. Muhammad continues to play as the mentor and symbolic leader of a large number of African American Muslims despite his resignation as the leader of the African American Islamic Mission in 1978.

In addition to the mosque, the group also has two major institutions to serve their objectives. One of these is the educational institution, called the Sister Clara Muhammad School, established in 1987. (For the importance of Sister Clara Muhammad Schools, see Cooper 1993.) Run as an uncertified home-study program, it comes under the jurisdiction of the Poughkeepsie school district and is subject to review by its board. The school is designed to serve the children of the Poughkeepsie Muslim community, but its primary efforts are directed toward the African American children.

The Sister Clara Muhammad School represents a long tradition of emphasis on education, since the earliest period of the Nation of Islam. African American children should be educated in schools of their own. These schools were, in the days of the Nation of Islam, an instrument for fostering the Black identity and Black pride. They also helped create an institutional basis for the emphasis on self-awareness and self-help by the Nation of Islam. This feature continues to be dominant in the orthodox African American Muslim community. The founding of the Sister Clara Muhammad School serves as a proof of the continuing perceived need for special-interest schools within the African American community. Imam Shamsideen states, "The main reason for having the kids out of public school . . . is because in public school they're not teaching the name of God. . . . Education and all we do are to support our faith, that Allah is God, and that Muhammad is His Messenger" (Kolars 1994:489). For more on the importance of Clara Muhammad Schools, see Webb (1994:307–8).

Another institution of considerable importance is Baitul Nasr, which is a rehabilitative community program in which members of the masjid are involved. It includes a therapeutic program to counsel clients on drug abuse, a violent behavior awareness program, and a program to provide shelter and resources for women and children in need. Baitul Nasr is also geared to helping former offenders to orient themselves to life outside the correctional facility. It must be pointed out that the Nation of Islam has a long record of playing an effective rehabilitating role, which continues today. Moreover, the prisons have also been a major recruitment ground for proselytization. Both in the past and in the present, many African Americans serving prison terms have been converting to Islam.

One of the major effects of the transition of the Poughkeepsie branch of the Nation of Islam to orthodox Islam is that the degree of interaction between the African American Muslims and the community of immigrant Muslims in the Hudson Valley area has increased. However, several differences exist between the immigrant and the African American Muslims here as elsewhere in America, and these contribute to the maintenance, by each group, of its particular mosque and organizational structure. Apart from the obvious ethnic difference, there is considerable disparity in their income levels, educational standards, and occupations. Thus, while there is a certain amount of interaction between the Poughkeepsie masjid (which, despite its theoretical openness to all, is practically an African group) and the Mid-Hudson Islamic Association (which is essentially an immigrant group), the activities of each group are internally focused. Thanks to the acceptance of the orthodox Islamic doctrines by the members of Masjid ul-Mutkabir, however, a number of immigrant Muslims also attend its services, although the majority of the worshipers are African Americans. The two communities cooperate in various projects, and it is not unusual for the neighboring Muslim community to ask the members of Masjid ul-Mutkabir for help in local projects. Any request is reciprocal in nature, and it is not unusual for the leading members of the immigrant community to attend the functions sponsored by the African American Muslims community.

The cooperation between the communities, however, is not highly developed and there is no great overlap between membership and participation of the two groups. Significant differences such as language skills, vastly different cultural traditions, and, above all, the wide disparity in the economic circumstances of the members of the two communities still stand in the way of close interaction between the two communities.

THE FIRST MUSLIM MOSQUE

Another example of how Muslim communities have developed during the last half century is provided by the organization called the First Muslim Mosque of Pittsburgh, Pennsylvania, an interesting historical account of which is provided by Jameela A. Hakim (1992). The present section is based on that account.

The starting point here, unlike the case of Poughkeepsie, was the establishment of the Moorish Science Temple rather than the Nation of Islam. While the Moors declined as a whole after the death of Noble Drew Ali in 1929, they remained strong in Pittsburgh during the 1930s, having a membership of over one thousand.

The group consisted of African American converts, some of whom were the sons and daughters of converts. However, a few Muslims from the East, or "from across the water," to use the jargon of the group, were also associated with it. Owing to the low standard of Islamic knowledge among the members, it became possible for Yusuf Khan, one of the immigrants from the South Asian subcontinent, to assume full charge of teaching Islam. Yusuf Khan introduced the Quran and the *hadith* to the group, taught them the five daily prayers, and urged them to accept Muslim names. Khan not only carried out instruction in Islam and Arabic but also gave books and reading material. Before that, very few persons had seen a copy of the Quran.

Gradually it became known that Yusuf Khan's teachings were not in harmony with the teachings of the Moorish Science Temple. This led to a split in the congregation, and those who did not agree with the teachings of Yusuf Khan left.

For a while, all went well with the community. It kept attracting new members, and the teaching program also proceeded smoothly. Then sometime in 1935, a section of the community began to oppose a doctrine taught by Khan, namely that Mirza Ghulam Ahmad (d. 1908) was a prophet. After heated discussion and debate, it became clear that the majority of the members would not "compromise on the finality of Muhammad's (peace be upon him) prophethood." This led to the second split in the group. Some of the members left and formed an Ahmadiyyah group that continued to operate in the city parallel to the original group.

While the main body remained intact, it had no leader. Eventually they found their leader in Saeed Akmal, who embarked on a drive to spread the teachings of Islam in Pittsburgh as well as in the outlying districts.

This is how there came into being in Pittsburgh a community and organization largely purged of the heterodox doctrines of both the Moorish Service Temple and the Ahmadiyyah. Thus, from a heterodox, sectarian beginning, the group moved toward identifying itself with the Islamic mainstream.

ISLAM IN THE UNITED STATES TODAY

Were we to compare the American scene toward the closing years of the present century with what it was at its outset, it would be evident that Islam has come a long way. In numbers, it is on its way to becoming the second largest religion in the United States after Christianity. So far as the African Americans are concerned, we find that Islam has progressed among them both horizontally and vertically. The tenets of Islam are today better known to a much larger number of African Americans than ever before, and this knowledge is accompanied with an enhanced commitment to accept and follow those tenets. Moreover, although the revival of Islam among African Americans in its early phase was of a sectarian and heretical character, in the course of time a large proportion of them has identified itself with the Islamic mainstream.

Notwithstanding these developments, one ought to be cautious against entertaining any romantic notions. For these developments, which have strengthened Islam among the African Americans, do not detract from the fact that the gains made by Islam so far can be consolidated only after much effort, or from the fact that many powerful forces at work in the American society have a constantly de-Islamizing effect on all Muslims living in the United States, including African American Muslims. Additionally, while orthodox Islam has made some considerable headway, fairly powerful pockets of sectarianism and heterodoxy remain that offer stiff resistance to assimilation in the Islamic mainstream.

We have seen in this chapter how under Warith Deen Muhammad, the Nation of Islam underwent a significant doctrinal transformation. In fact, for a few years it seemed that things were moving so smoothly and effectively in the direction of Islamic orthodoxy that it would gain a pervasive and decisive victory and will be able to overcome the schisms in the American Muslim community. Such expectations have been only partially fulfilled. While the majority of the Nation of Islam welcomed the reformist ideas of

Warith Deen Muhammad, the change for many of them was just too much
to take. For some time these malcontents simply showed apathy. In 1978,
however, Louis Farrakhan, who had been very prominent in the leadership
of the Nation of Islam during the last years of Elijah Muhammad's life, revived that movement with almost all its characteristic features. The only
change that has been effected under Farrakhan is in respect of religious rituals (prayers, fasting, etc.).

As for the religious teachings of the Nation of Islam—that Fard is Allah,
that Elijah Muhammad was the Messenger of Allah, that the Blacks are the
Originals and the Whites are an inherently evil people who are destined to
be utterly destroyed by Allah in the near future, that the Judgment means
the restoration of the supremacy of the Original and the Righteous Blacks,
and that the Hereafter is the period of history that will follow the destruction of the Whites and the establishment of the supremacy of the Blacks—
all of these have been retained.

Farrakhan has not only tenaciously clung to these teachings but has
come forth with an impressive array of arguments that are quite appealing
to those who were familiar with, and favorably disposed to, the rhetoric of
the Nation of Islam. Also, W. D. Muhammad seems to have been so seized
with the zeal to purge the Nation of Islam of all racist notions and to introduce Islamic universalism to such an extent that he showed little concern to voice the socioeconomic grievances of the African Americans who
continue to be subjected to gross discrimination, injustice, and indignity in
present-day American society. Furthermore, W. D. Muhammad emphasized
his identification with the United States with great zeal, with the result that
his detractors began to accuse him of having struck a deal with the establishment. In such circumstances, when Louis Farrakhan began to speak out
vehemently for the rights of the African Americans, he received a warm response not only from those who had a sympathetic predisposition toward
Elijah Muhammad's doctrines but also a wide cross section of African Americans. All this proved advantageous to Farrakhan, who was able to win over
the loyalties of many African Americans, quite a few of whom had been associated with the Nation of Islam in the days of Elijah Muhammad.

Farrakhan has often been severely criticized for being anti-Semitic. His
strong statements against the Jews, let alone White Americans, might have
antagonized large sections of American society, including an influential section of the middle-class African Americans. But judging from a purely pragmatic perspective, these statements have served one of Farrakhan's purposes: to win the support of the radically disposed and underprivileged
African American, many of whom have indeed begun to regard him as a
possible redeemer.

Farrakhan has been playing his role as the leader of the revived Nation
of Islam quite effectively. He does not seem inclined to strike any signifi-

cant compromise with the Islamic mainstream or to modify any of those teachings of his mentor that Muslims find totally unacceptable. His uncompromising posture seems to stem, at least partially, from the desire to maintain the distinct entity of the flock that he shepherds. Such an objective certainly requires that Farrakhan should not abandon the characteristic doctrinal positions of the Nation of Islam. (For the Nation of Islam under Louis Farrakhan, see Gardell 1994 and Mamiya 1992.)

Another group that broke away from the Nation of Islam as far back as 1964 under the leadership of Clarence "Pudding" 13X calls itself "The Five Percenters," or "The Nation of Gods and Earths." The center of this movement is New York City, especially the Bronx. In New York City alone, they are said to number in the thousands, perhaps even tens of thousands.

To grasp the doctrinal position of the group, it would be instructive to cast a glance at the nine points listed under its banner, "What We Teach":

1. We teach that Black People are the Original People of the Planet Earth.

2. We teach that Black People are the Mothers and Fathers of Civilization.

3. We teach that the Science of Supreme Mathematic is the key to understanding man's relationship to the universe.

4. We teach Islam as a natural way of life; not a religion.

5. We teach that education should be fashioned to enable us to be self-sufficient as a people.

6. We teach that each one should teach one according to their knowledge.

7. We teach that the Blackman is God and his proper name is Allah (Arm Leg Leg Arm Head).

8. We teach that our children are our link to the future and they must be nurtured, respected, loved, protected and educated.

9. We teach that the unified Black Family is the vital building block of the Nation.

Clarence Pudding 13X began to have doubts about the Nation of Islam in the early 1960s. The Nation had taught that the Black Man was God. Since Fard Muhammad was not Black in appearance, how could he be God? In 1964, there was turmoil in the Nation of Islam chiefly because of the differences between Malcolm X and the leadership of the Nation of Islam. A disciplinary action was taken against Clarence in the manner it had been taken against Malcolm X. The result in this case was the same. Clarence left the Nation, although he has clung to most of its basic doctrines, one important exception being the doctrine that Fard is God. (For more on the Five Percenters, or the Nation of Gods and Earths, see Nuruddin 1994.)

A recognition of the fact that both those movements, in addition to several minor splinter groups of the original Nation of Islam, exist and that some of these enjoy considerable following among African Americans, enables one to have a more realistic picture of the situation.

CONCLUSION

Important demographic changes are taking place in the United States, changes that are likely to be very consequential. We have noted earlier that the proportion of African Americans in the total population of the United States is likely to rise from an estimated 12.6 percent in 1995 to 16.2 percent in 2050. The same is true of Hispanics, whose growth rate is quite high, and, according to projections, their proportion in the total population of the United States will rise from 9.5 percent in 1992 to 21.1 percent in 2050 (U.S. Department of Commerce 1993: table 20). Thus, the ethnic profile of the United States seems poised for a substantial change with the result that the present predominance of Whites, which has been supported, to a large extent, by their numerical preponderance, is likely to be substantially diluted. The American society of the future clearly will become increasingly multiethnic.

Significant similarities are apparent between the situation of African Americans in the early decades of the twentieth century and that of Hispanics at the present. The latter, like African Americans, are also an underprivileged minority, and it is a minority that is becoming increasingly conscious of being discriminated against and subjected to wrong and injustice by the White majority. In short, some of the conditions that had prompted a good number of African Americans during the early 1900s to look up to Islam as a means for achieving self-betterment and dignity are also present for Hispanics. Although it is difficult to document this situation, our initial inquiries indicate that Hispanics have begun to convert to Islam in significant numbers. (Their present number, according to Barboza [1993:9], is five thousand.) In view of the altered cultural landscape, it can be reasonably predicted that in the changed context, American Muslims will be in a better position to reinforce their Islamic identity and contribute to the enrichment of American society.

The effectiveness of American Muslims in playing the dual role of strengthening their identity and constructively participating, like all other citizens of the United States, in the national enterprise of America—ceaseless striving for a better tomorrow—will largely depend on the extent to which American Muslims are able to develop a sound vision of their role in the United States and to close their ranks and create greater cohesiveness. Up until now, there seems to have been a divide between the indigenous, largely African American Muslims and immigrant Muslims, with the result that people of each of these two categories have, to a large extent, lived and functioned in separate orbits. The immigrants themselves have not been a unified entity. Instead, they have remained divided among themselves along linguistic, ethnic, cultural, and regional lines.

There are reasonable grounds to believe that, notwithstanding their state of affairs up until now, cohesiveness among American Muslims will increase in the course of time. In our view, the factors that were responsible in the past for the prevalent state of affairs will, in all likelihood, increasingly lose their strength and effectiveness. In fact, the operation of that process can already be noticed. In the melting pot of the United States, the edge of ethnic, linguistic, and cultural particularities of immigrant Muslims has already begun to be blunted. This is especially true concerning a good number of immigrant Muslims who have entered the second or the third generation of their residence here. There is nothing strange about this development, as would be evident from the experience of the Catholic and Jewish immigrants from European countries—that by the third generation, the narrower ethnic or national identities of immigrant Catholics and Jews were replaced by their broader religious identities. The Jews from different European countries who immigrated to the United States ceased to be, in the third generation, German Jews or Polish Jews, for example. They became simply Jews. Likewise, Italian Catholics or French Catholics also became simply Catholics.

Thus, there are strong reasons to expect an enhanced cohesiveness among American Muslims in the future. Ironically enough, this development will, to a considerable degree, be a function of Americanization. The process already seems to be at work. For instance, we find that English has become the first language of the children and grandchildren of those immigrants who were initially not at all fluent in it. This development will be instrumental in solidifying Muslim ranks, since it enables them to have effective communication and hence better understanding with their brethren-in-faith of other ethnic backgrounds. Likewise, although a kind of gap between the immigrant and indigenous Muslims continues to exist, it is becoming reduced, and the trend is likely to continue.

A factor contributing to this development is the increased upward mobility of the indigenous Muslims, including the African American Muslims, especially during the last few decades. Likewise, Muslims of diverse backgrounds are coming closer because of the shared features of what is called the American way of life—from such trivialities as Kentucky Fried Chicken and Dunkin' Donuts to the nation's more profound aspects. Likewise, a major factor that had kept the immigrant Muslims and the African American Muslims apart in the past was the vogue of sectarianism and heterodoxy among a section of African Americans. As we know, a great deal of change has already taken place in this regard, which has demolished some of the barriers between the two groups, and interaction and cooperation have been steadily on the increase.

It also seems pertinent to highlight some of the external factors that are affecting the attitudes of Muslims in America. Since the Iranian revolution of 1979 and the subsequent hostage taking of American consular staff, both the print and electronic media in the United States have focused on the phenomenon of militant Islam. The stance of the media toward Muslims and the policies pursued by the United States and the governments of other Western nations have had a significant impact on the Muslims living in all Western countries, including the United States. The constant demonization of Islam as a violence-prone religion and the ceaseless stereotyping of Muslims virtually as a bunch of blood-thirsty terrorists have developed in some Americans an almost irrational hatred and contempt for Islam and Muslims. This has occasionally led (such as during the Gulf War or after the blowing up of the federal building in Oklahoma City) to violent attacks on mosques and Islamic centers and on stores owned by Muslims or Arabs, let alone to ominous threats that Muslims occasionally receive from extremists.

All this seems to have had an adverse effect on the outward expansion of Islam in the United States, which has apparently slowed down for the moment. It is understandable that many of those who would think of converting to Islam would feel hesitant to do so in view of the possible consequence that they might be stigmatized by their friends and neighbors.

That is, however, one aspect of the impact. It is also important to take note of the Muslim perceptions of Western policies and the effect they have had on their attitudes. The Western military intervention in the Persian Gulf and the Western posture on a host of problems, from the Rushdie affair to the Bosnian tragedy to the brutality of Chechnya, let alone the unreserved support of Israel, "right or wrong," have been perceived by a large number of American Muslims as indicators of deeply rooted Western feelings of antagonism toward Islam and Muslims. This has created in many Muslims a siege mentality, with the result that they are constantly haunted by the phantom of Western hostility. This extraneous factor supplements the factors mentioned earlier and is contributing to the inner cohesiveness among the diverse Muslim elements in the United States.

Thus, many portents are betokening a more potent role for American Muslims in the future. It goes without saying that like the rest of the American Muslims, African American Muslims are likely to have a greater opportunity than ever before to affect the course of events in the United States.

How well are American Muslims, especially African American Muslims, equipped to avail of the opportunities that are likely to open up in the future? What kind of life will they live in the United States, and what kind of contribution will they make to American life and culture?

To answer these questions, it would be necessary to examine the institutions that American Muslims have established so far and to examine their efficacy. The most important institutions are the large number of mosques/Islamic centers spread across the United States. These provide not only a place to hold congregational prayers but also a social center for the Muslims living in a city or neighborhood. Above all, these mosques/Islamic centers are instrumental in holding public lectures as well as classes for instruction in Islam, especially in holding Sunday school classes.

In addition, we also find a growing number of Muslim schools that have been established to provide a more substantial Islamic education to Muslim children alongside general education. What is more, these schools attempt to impart education in an Islamic atmosphere, with an accent on developing Islamic attitude and character in the younger generation.

The activities of the mosques/Islamic centers are mainly aimed at creating a better understanding of Islam, chiefly among the members of the Muslim community, and reinforcing their loyalty to Islam. A major objective of these activities is to transmit Islamic knowledge and Islamic norms to Muslim children and youngsters so as to enable them to live in the United States as good, practicing Muslims. Special camps are also held for this purpose by these mosques/Islamic centers or the local Muslim associations that oversee the mosques. These institutions seem to be only peripherally concerned with improving the common American's awareness of Islam. Whatever serious activity takes place in this field consists of *dawah* (Muslim propagation of Islam) work among people serving terms of imprisonment. This is a continuation of the activity in which the Nation of Islam was known to have engaged with great success.

New Islamic institutions on the national level have also been established. The Federation of Islamic Associations, established in the early 1950s, has almost petered out and has been replaced by several other national organizations. Likewise, although MSA has maintained its existence, it is now a much less active organization than it used to be about two decades ago. These have been replaced by new organizations. The most important of these organizations is the Islamic Society of North America (ISNA), which has its headquarters in Plainfield, Indiana. Another organization on the national level is the Islamic Circle of North America (ICNA), which has maintained itself as an almost exclusively Indo-Pakistani group and which has largely been inspired by the ideology of Jama'at-i Islami. Both these organizations, but especially ISNA, have been concerned with building institutions that would support and strengthen the foundations of Muslim identity in the United States. ISNA had made a very promising start, but for quite some years it had showed much less rigor in its activities than in the late 1970s and early 1980s. Of late, however, it has begun to show signs of fresh energy under the inspiring leadership of its new secretary-general, S. M. Sayeed.

It is noteworthy that there is a serious lacuna in the efforts of American Muslims insofar as they have failed to establish academic institutions that would give rise to an indigenous Islamic scholarly tradition. Hence, a majority of scholars who are working as imams of mosques/directors of Islamic centers, are imparting instruction in Islam, or are lecturing on Islam or making use of the media to improve the American awareness of Islam are mostly immigrants. (This point applies, with hardly any exceptions, to immigrant Muslims.) This seems an odd arrangement. For these scholars, who have certainly contributed to the cause of Islam, are not quite equipped to operate effectively in a country like the United States. More often than not, they lack the requisite proficiency in English. Also, their educational background is not quite adequate for communicating with Muslim children and youngsters who were born and brought up in the United States, let alone for becoming effective spokesmen of Islam. Moreover, many of them come with their baggage from their home country—often a narrow, sectarian outlook, and a fairly rigid attitude toward the detailed questions of law. Without doubt, these religious teachers from overseas have so far made a very important contribution to the cause of Islam in the United States. Despite due deference for this role, the time has come for American Muslims to develop resources within the United States to cater to the American Muslim community's need for religious leadership.

As African American Muslims are concerned, to our knowledge they have scarcely brought imams and religious leaders from abroad, although occasionally they have benefited from the foreigners who are locally available. Instead, they have appointed local persons from among themselves to look after the religious needs of the community. Some of these imams have shown their potential and have conclusively proved their competence as leaders. The academic grounding of a majority of them in Islamics, and schooling as such, however, is not very sound. On the other hand, American Muslims require not only a large number of scholars and thinkers of average caliber in Islamics. Rather, they need *outstanding* scholars and thinkers who would combine Islamic erudition with intellectual brilliance and would be capable of spelling out the Islamic worldview in an idiom comprehensible to their fellow citizens, as well as articulating the Islamic vision of life in terms that would be relevant for, and meaningful in, a religiously pluralistic society such as the United States. In short, one of the most urgent tasks facing American Muslims is to produce Islamic scholarship of the highest order.

It may be recalled that in the 1950s and in subsequent years, the Muslim world provided America with three of the most outstanding scholars of the twentieth century: Fazlur Rahman (d. 1988; from Pakistan), Ismail al-Faruqi (d. 1986; from Palestine), and Seyyed Hossein Nasr (from Iran). It is time that Islamic scholars of that stature begin to emerge from the ranks of American Muslims.

African Americans have long been living under conditions that had prevented them from bringing out their full scholastic potential. But it is also well known that their forefathers in Africa had made rich scholastic contributions, including contributions specifically to Islamic thought and learning. In recent decades, African Americans have begun to make their presence felt in academia, and their latent academic talents have begun to flower. The time seems ripe for dedicated African American Muslims to contribute their share to the enrichment of contemporary Islamic thought.

African Americans have lived long in a country that can justifiably be proud of being the most advanced in science and technology, of being in the vanguard of contemporary human thought and civilization. Those African American Muslims who might be able to combine their awareness of contemporary learning with a profound knowledge of Islam, and add their vivid awareness of both the sordid and positive aspects of contemporary civilization owing to their presence in America for several centuries, would be eminently qualified to take up the challenge to enrich the intellectual tradition of Islam.

REFERENCES

Abdul-Jabbar, Kareem. 1993. "Leap of Faith." In *American Jihad: Islam after Malcolm X,* ed. S. Barboza. New York: Doubleday, 213–20.

Adele, Younis L. 1983–1984. "The First Muslims of America: Impressions and Reminiscences." *Journal: Institute of Muslim Minority Affairs* 5, no. 1: 17–28.

Ansari, Zafar Ishaq. 1981. "Aspects of Black Muslim Theology." *Studia Islamica* 53: 137–76.

———.1985a. "The Religious Doctrines of the Black Muslims of America, 1934–74." *Islamic Order* 7, no. 2: 17–47.

———.1985b. "W. D. Muhammad: The Making of a Black Muslim Leader." *American Journal of Islamic Social Sciences* 2, no. 2: 245–62.

Barboza, Steven, ed. 1993. *American Jihad: Islam after Malcolm X.* New York: Doubleday.

Benyon, E. D. 1938. "The Voodoo among Negro Migrants in Detroit." *American Journal of Sociology* 43, no. 6 (May): 894–97.

Bontemps, A., and J. Conroy. 1945. *They Seek a City.* Garden City, N.Y.: Doubleday.

Cooper, Mary H. 1993. "Muslims in America," *C.Q. Researcher* 3, no. 16 (April 30): 363–67, 369–70, 372–78.

Curtis, M. M. 1994. "Urban Muslims: The Formation of the Dar ul-Islam Movement." In *Muslim Communities in North America,* ed. Y. Y. Haddad and J. I. Smith. Albany: State University of New York, 51–73.

Encyclopedia of American Religions. 1989. 3d ed. Detroit: Gale Research.

Encyclopedia of World Cultures. 1991. 10 vols. David Levinson, editor in chief. Boston: Hall.

Essien-Udom, E. U. 1971. *Black Nationalism: A Search for an Identity in America.* Chicago: University of Chicago Press.

Ferris, Marc. 1994. "To Achieve the Pleasure of Allah: Immigrant Muslim Community in New York City, 1891–1991." In *Muslim Communities in North America,* ed. Y. Y. Haddad and J. I. Smith. Albany: State University of New York, 209–30.

Gardell, M. 1994. "The Sun of Islam Will Rise in the West: Minister Farrakhan and the Nation of Islam in the Latter Days." In *Muslim Communities in North America*, ed. Y. Y. Haddad and J. I. Smith. Albany: State University of New York, 15–49.

Goldman, Peter. 1973. *The Death and Life of Malcolm X*. New York: Harper & Row.

Gutbi, M. A. 1991. "Muslim Organizations in the United States." In *The Muslims of America*, ed. Y. Y. Haddad. New York: Oxford University Press, 11–24.

Haddad, Y. Y. 1991. *The Muslims of America*. New York: Oxford University Press.

Haddad, Y. Y., and A. T. Lummis. 1987. *Islamic Values in the United States: A Compensative Study*. New York: Oxford University Press.

Haddad, Y. Y., and J. I. Smith, eds. 1994. *Muslim Communities in North America*. Albany: State University of New York.

Hakim, Jameela A. 1992. "History of the First Muslim Mosque of Pittsburgh, Pennsylvania." In *Islam in North America: A Sourcebook*, ed. M. Koszegi and J. G. Melton. New York: Garland, 153–63.

Haley, Alex. 1976. *Roots*. Boston: Hall.

Harris, Sara. 1953. *Father Divine, Holy Husband*. New York: Doubleday.

Holt, T. C. 1980. "Afro-Americans." In *Harvard Encyclopedia of American Ethnic Groups*, ed. Stephan Thernateni. Cambridge, Mass.: Harvard University Press, 5–23.

Kly, Y. N. 1989. "The African American Muslim Minority: 1776–1900." *Journal: Institute of Muslim Minority Affairs* 10, no. 1: 152–60.

Kolars, Christine. 1994. "Masjid ul-Mutkabir: The Portrait of an Orthodox Muslim Community." In *Muslim Communities in North America*, ed. Y. Y. Haddad and J. I. Smith. Albany: State University of New York, 475–99.

Koszegi, M., and J. G. Melton, eds. 1992. *Islam in North America: A Sourcebook*. New York: Garland.

Lincoln, C. E. 1973. *The Black Muslims in America*. Rev. ed. Boston: Beacon.

Malcolm X. 1966. *The Autobiography of Malcolm X*. With the assistance of Alex Haley. New York: Ballantine.

Mamiya, L. 1992. "From Black Muslim to Bilalian: The Evolution of a Movement." In *Islam in North America: A Sourcebook*, ed. M. Koszegi and J. G. Melton. New York: Garland, 164–80.

Moore, Kathleen. 1994. "Muslim Commitment in North America: Assimilation or Transformation?" *American Journal of Islamic Social Sciences* 11, no. 2: 223–44.

Nuruddin, Y. 1994. "The Five Percenters: A Teenage Nation of Gods and Earths." In *Muslim Communities in North America*, ed. Y. Y. Haddad and J. I. Smith. Albany: State University of New York, 109–32.

Nyang, S. S. 1990. "Islam in North America." In *The World's Religions: Islam*, ed. Peter Clarke. London: Routledge, 214–23.

———.1992. "Islam in the United States of America: A Review of the Sources." In *Islam in North America: A Sourcebook*, ed. M. Koszegi and J. G. Melton. New York: Garland.

Perry, Bruce. 1991. *Malcolm X: The Life of a Man Who Changed Black America*. New York: Staton Hill.

Simpson, Frank. 1947. "The Moorish Science Temple and Its 'Koran.'" *Muslim World* 37: 56–61.

Sloan, J. 1977. *The Blacks in America, 1492–1977: A Chronology and Fact Book*. 4th rev. ed. Dobbs Ferry, N.Y.: Oceana.

Smythe, Mabel M., ed. 1976. *The Black American Reference Book.* Englewood Cliffs, N.J.: Prentice Hall.

U.S. Department of Commerce. 1993. *Statistical Abstract of the United States, 1993.* Washington, D.C.: Author.

Walker, Dennis. 1990. "The Black Muslims in American Society: From Millenarian Protest to Trans-Continental Relationships." In *Cargo Cults and Millenarian Movements: Transoceanic Comparisons of Recent New Religious Movements,* ed. G. R. Trompf. Berlin: Mouton de Gruyter.

Webb, Gisela. 1994. "Islam and Muslims in America." In *Islam, Muslims and the Modern State,* ed. Hussin Mutalib and Taj-Hashmi. New York: St. Martin's.

Winters, Clyde-Ahmad. 1978. "Afro-American Muslims: From Slavery to Freedom." *Islamic Studies* 7, no. 1: 187–203.

10

The West African Paradox

Sylviane A. Diouf

For almost four hundred years, West Africans represented 100 percent of the Muslims living in the Americas. Men, women, and children from Senegal, Gambia, Mali, Guinea, Sierra Leone, Côte d'Ivoire, Ghana, and Nigeria practiced their faith under the most brutal type of servitude. In the United States, their highly visible presence has been seen, heard, written about, and remembered from the early 1700s to the 1940s.[1] But, paradoxically, the general public and academia soon forgot them, and few contemporary Americans are aware of their story and contributions.

Today, sub-Saharan African Muslims (including East Africans) have become a small minority. According to the American Muslim Poll conducted in 2001, they represent 7 percent of the approximately six million Muslims living in the United States.[2] Their modest size notwithstanding, they are a steadfastly growing and dynamic group that, within a few years, has had a visible impact on the American public square. In fact, more Africans and perhaps twice as many Muslims arrived in the United States within the past forty years than during the entire era of the slave trade.[3]

The story of the West African Muslims in the United States continues to revolve around a paradox. The first to preserve Islam in the United States, they are among the latest immigrants to join the American *ummah* (community) and are *historically* invisible. They are the second largest Muslim population after the Asians but are usually overlooked when American authorities, media, or academia examine the Islamic world, or ponder about worldwide Muslims, making them *politically* invisible. Highly noticeable because some of their niche occupations put them right in the middle of the public square, they are also *physically* invisible, in part because, according to stereotypical criteria, they generally do not "look" Muslim. Moreover, they are also often forgotten within the larger Muslim community, for demo-graphic or other reasons, and are in consequence *culturally* invisible.

Their lack of visibility in the general public is paralleled by academic oversight. Africans who have migrated to the United States have generated few studies.[4] In addition, books on new immigrant communities seldom mention them. African Muslims have not fared better, and publications fo-cused on Muslim communities in North America have generally ignored them. Media coverage has been better at shedding some light on the com-munity. Since 1994, newspapers and magazines have sporadically covered West Africans, the Senegalese in particular.

This chapter explores the history of the West African Muslims in the United States, their professional presence and institutions in the public square, and issues of gender, age, and identity. It is based on fieldwork conducted in 1996 and 2000 among men, women, and children from Sene-gal, Gambia, Sierra Leone, Ghana, Mali, Guinea, Côte d'Ivoire, and Nigeria living in New York City, home to the largest West African Muslim commu-nity in the country. It is to be noted that the past decade has seen a small but steady movement toward other areas. African Muslims who have set-tled in Washington, D.C., Cincinnati, Columbus, Philadelphia, Los Angeles, Houston, and Atlanta have set up their communities along lines similar to what can be observed in New York. Empirical observation seems to indi-cate that they are more middle-class than their counterparts in New York, the first stop for many on the migration trajectory. With the exception of the Nigerians, whose immigration preceded the others, few West African Muslims have established formal institutions such as "African mosques" out-side New York City, most likely because of their small numbers and more recent arrival.

THE PRECURSORS

As noted earlier, the story of the West African Muslims in America hardly starts with contemporary immigrants. It reaches back to the very first days of European presence in the continents or, according to some scholars, even earlier.[5] When the Atlantic slave trade started about 1502 in the Caribbean, Islam had already been present in some parts of West Africa for five hundred years. It is estimated that the Muslims represented between 15 and 20 percent of the twelve to fifteen million Africans shipped away be-tween the 1500s and the 1860s.

There were among them well-educated, well-traveled, multilingual peo-ple who had frequented Quranic schools and could read and write in Ara-bic and in their own languages written in the Arabic script. Some had trav-eled across the region, as well as to North Africa, Egypt, and Arabia for the pilgrimage to Mecca. Far from being absorbed into the dominant Christian world, the West African Muslims made tremendous efforts to keep their faith alive and to respect the Five Pillars of Islam, as attested by numerous planters, travelers, chroniclers, court records, fellow slaves, and the Muslims themselves. Many continued to pray, to give alms, to fast, to refuse pork and alcohol, and to wear turbans, skullcaps, and veils.[6] In Rio de Janeiro and Bahia, they operated Quranic schools and makeshift mosques,[7] and there, as well as in the United States, Trinidad, and Jamaica, they managed to procure chaplets and Qurans in Arabic.[8]

Muslims have left significant marks in several African-derived religions practiced today by people of African descent, such as Palo Mayombe in Cuba, Candomble in Brazil, and Voodoo in Haiti.[9] The tradition of giving *saraka* (a corruption of the Arabic *sadaqa,* or freewill offerings) lives on in the American South and in several Caribbean countries.[10]

They also have left Islamic-inspired music[11] and some Arabic vocabulary.[12] But Islam disappeared, in its orthodox form, after the death of African-born Muslims and their children, which occurred in the United States, in the 1920s or 1930s, and later in Brazil, Cuba, and some French- and English-speaking Caribbean islands where indentured Africans were introduced between the 1840s and 1870s.[13]

WEST AFRICAN MUSLIMS TODAY

The second chapter in the story of the West African Muslims in North America opened in the 1960s with the arrival of a few students. At Hampton Institute (now Hampton University) in Virginia, for example, they were instrumental in the conversion of some African American students. They also pressured the administration to give them a space for prayer.[14] The West African presence expanded in the 1970s and 1980s with the influx of Nigerians (they represented 17 percent of all African immigrants between 1974 and 1995), Ghanaians (7 percent), Liberians (4 percent), and Sierra Leoneans (2 percent), a minority of whom was Muslim.[15] While Nigerians sought better economic opportunities in the United States, Liberians and Sierra Leoneans were mostly fleeing the civil war in their respective countries. Finally, in the 1980s and 1990s as they were hit by structural adjustment policies, a 50 percent devaluation of their currency, and restrictive immigration procedures in Europe, men and women from French-speaking West Africa—a majority of them Muslims—made their way to the United States.

According to the 2000 census, an estimated 511,000 to 746,000 foreign-born sub-Saharan Africans live in this country.[16] These figures, however, do not reflect the great number of undocumented people who shy away from contact with authorities, nor do they include, evidently, American-born

Africans. There may be close to a million sub-Saharan Africans and their children in the United States.

ISLAM, MIGRATION, AND ENTREPRENEURSHIP

There is a tradition of emigration in Islam, starting with the *hijra* (the Prophet's migration) from Mecca to Medina and continuing with his Companions taking refuge in Ethiopia. Islam also has a long tradition of trade, there again starting with the Prophet Muhammad. To West Africans, their own traditions, as well as Islam, Islamic schooling, and the Muslim confraternities, represent another impetus for migration and entrepreneurship.

The Juula of Côte d'Ivoire—like their cousins the Mandinka and Malinke of Senegal, Gambia, and Guinea—are part of the "Muslim diaspora" of traders. They had been long-distance traders before the advent of Islam, but the expansion of the religion opened up vast opportunities for them to serve as intermediaries between the Arabo-Berbers of the North and the people of the South.[17] They converted to Islam early on and opened the way to the religion in the southern reaches of West Africa. Going to the United States is only another step in their migration story. The Fulani or Halpulaaren (people who speak Pulaar) are also early Muslims. Traditionally pastoralists, they are scattered throughout West Africa. Involved in the main *jihad* (armed struggle) of the eighteenth and nineteenth centuries, from Senegal to Nigeria, the Halpulaaren have extended the borders of *dar al-Islam* (world of Islam) in West Africa.[18] They are also early emigrants to Central Africa and Europe. The Soninke (also known as Sarakole and Maraka) of Senegal, Gambia, Mauritania, and Mali, founders of the Ghana Empire, have been involved in trade for centuries. The demise of the trans-Saharan and transatlantic trades doomed their area, a commercial crossroads that was never agriculturally developed.[19] Young men became migrant laborers and went in search of work to neighboring countries. The most adventurous left for Central Africa and Europe, France in particular, and lately for the United States. To the Murids, migrating emulates the hijra of the founder of their *tariqa* (Sufi orders), the Senegalese sheikh Ahmadou Bamba, also called Serigne Touba (1850–1927), who was deported to Gabon and Mauritania by the French.[20] The *talibs* (disciples) must relive the pain of the sheikh by going through their own exile. Moreover, following the injunction of their founder, they must learn what is useful in the Europeans' ways. During their stay in the West, they have to contribute financially to the development of the holy city of Touba and to the reinforcement of the brotherhood. Thus, while the French used Serigne Touba's exile as a tool to destroy the *muridiyya*, the Murids' self-imposed exile strengthens its power and influence.

Another element that acts as a push factor for emigration is Islamic schooling. In Gambia, Senegal, and Mali about 69 percent of the children go to Western-type secular schools, and the rest—mostly rural children—enroll in Quranic schools that provide, exclusively, a religious education.[21] As a result, youngsters may be able to read and write in Arabic and in their own language written in the Arabic script but are often illiterate or barely literate in French or English; nor do they have knowledge of other subjects necessary to work in the formal sector.[22] With a lifetime of farming or petty trade to contemplate, many do not hesitate to emigrate. For the older generation, the literacy rate is even much lower, with about 30 percent of the adults in Senegal, Mali, and Guinea who can speak, read, and write in French. Their rate of Quranic schooling, on the other hand, is higher than that of today's youngsters. According to Saite Sall, the president of the African Islamic Center and himself a product of Quranic schools, "People who have been to Quranic schools are disciplined, they can endure privations and hard work. They are focused, resilient, and are used to sharing and helping one another. You see them land in New York on Sunday, and Monday morning, you find them on the street, selling, making a living." Many street vendors and cab drivers echo this view. Quranic education, they stressed in numerous conversations, prepared them for a tough life in America. Used to austerity, self-control, and self-sacrifice, they usually care little for entertainment and comfort.[23] They often work long hours and live with several other men in one-bedroom apartments. Even with low wages, this frugality enables them to save up a large part of their earnings and send money to their family back home. After a few months or years, they are often able to open up a business in the United States and/or at home.

INVISIBILITY/VISIBILITY: THE PARADOX

Despite their long presence in the Americas, African Muslims' lack of religious visibility is striking. Various elements contribute to this particularity. To start with, few Americans know of the African history of Islam. There is little awareness that it has been a local religion, in sub-Saharan Africa, for a thousand years. Another reason is that Islam and its followers are often perceived through the prism of terrorism and fundamentalism. Sub-Saharan Muslims, who have not been associated with either one, are not seen as being part of "the Islamic problem." Therefore, there is a tendency to not include them in the Islamic community either.

Another contributing factor to the African's invisibility is that, according to popular perception, they do not "look" Muslim. People have come to identify Islam with veils, headscarves, drab long dresses, and skullcaps. But most West African Muslim women do not sport veils outside prayer, nor do they wear long dark dresses. Therefore, they do not seem to be wearing any "Islamic attire," and men do not routinely wear skullcaps, fez, or turbans.[24]

Paradoxically, for all their invisibility, West African Muslims may also be among the most noticeable Muslims in the country. They are often seen wearing *grands boubous,* large, embroidered, flowing robes; but people, outside Africa, generally do not realize that the clothes they consider "traditional African garb" are in fact African Muslim attire. In Africa, the baggy pants and the boubou were introduced by the Muslims and have been the visible sign of their religious identity for centuries. Today, however, what was the badge of the Muslims has been widely adopted by non-Muslim Africans, including in parts of Africa where Islam is virtually absent. In the United States and Europe, these clothes have come to symbolize the Africans, not the Muslims. Ironically, Afrocentrists who rail against the Muslims as "not authentic" Africans are also the ones who have propagated African Islamic fashion in the United States.

The Murids may be the most visible Muslims in the United States. A day dedicated to their founder has been declared in New York, Cincinnati, Atlanta, Chicago, and East Orange, New Jersey. On July 27, "Cheikh Ahmadou Bamba Day" in Manhattan, they walk several hundred strong—men and women in grand boubous, children in jeans and T-shirts—down 7th Avenue in Harlem from 125th Street to Central Park. They chant *La-ilaha ill-Allah* (there is no god but God) all the way, before holding a short prayer in Central Park.

But, more generally, it is some of the West Africans' lines of work, as street vendors, delivery men, store owners, hair braiders, restaurateurs, and taxi drivers, that heighten their visibility by putting them in close contact with the public, even though the majority is employed in "American jobs" and is therefore much less noticeable.

WEST AFRICANS IN THE PUBLIC SQUARE

In big cities, West African street vendors have become a fixture, just like they are in Dakar or Lagos. They began to appear on the busy avenues of midtown Manhattan in the early 1980s. Most were Murids with a Quranic education. Murids are traditionally farmers and traders, and in the United States, they capitalized on the experience acquired back home. According to Djibril Mbaye, a former president of the Association of the Senegalese in America, "It's about tradition but also pragmatism. Most of [them] are illiterate, do not speak English, at least when they arrive, and are undocumented aliens. The American working world is closed to them. They have to be self-employed. Because of their Senegalese experience, they know how to sell. All they need to do is adapt their products to an America clientele."[25] Today, as more Senegalese are moving to market stalls, stores, restaurants, and wholesale companies, freshly arrived Malians, Guineans, and Ivorians are re-placing them.

Street peddling is often a stepping-stone for undocumented people who aspire to have their own stores or rent stalls and booths in markets and fairs. Saving money, pooling resources in the traditional African form of the *tontine* (community-organized savings association) or *esusu*, many West Africans have been able to open stores and have revitalized sections of Harlem and Brooklyn.[26] On 116th Street and vicinity, called Little Africa, they own several restaurants, grocery stores, a *halal* butcher shop, photo-copy centers, tailor shops, wholesale stores, braiding salons, and telecom-munication centers. Others sell electronic equipment, cosmetics, household goods, and Islamic items. There is a balance between the selling of African cultural and religious creations (clothes, hairstyles, food, pictures of reli-gious leaders, prayer beads, Murid literature); the trade in the necessities of life in New York (photocopies, electronic equipment, cosmetics, tax prepa-ration, computer classes); and the tools of modernity that link both the *here* and the *there* (telecommunication centers, international calling cards). This mix creates an almost self-sufficient enclave. It is an apt reflection of a West African community that, in other ways, claims its attachment to its cultural and religious values, is quick to take advantage of what modernity can of-fer, and plays a major role in familial, communal, and national develop-ment at home.

Their businesses securely established, the Africans have asserted their presence by entering existing trade structures, and creating their own. A measure of their strength could be seen in July 2000, when the Merchants Association of the area of 116th Street in Harlem elected its board: the pres-ident and the treasurer both were Senegalese. Moreover, Africans repre-sented more than two-thirds of the merchants present at the meeting. A few years ago, this stretch of Harlem was burned out, boarded up, and unsafe. Today, city officials, the police, and community leaders credit the West Africans for turning it around. With its successful stores and two African mosques—Aksa and Salam—116th Street has become the showcase of the West Africans' business savvy.

On a smaller scale, Fulton Street in Brooklyn has a number of West African restaurants, braiding salons, and tailor shops. The Halpulaaren, nu-merous in the area, call it Futatown, from Futa Toro (Senegal) and Futa Jal-lon (Guinea), the areas many of them originally came from. Broadway has become another West African enclave. It is the territory of travel agents, shipping brokers, and wholesalers who provide African merchants—retail-ers in the United States, and other wholesalers in Africa—with electronics, luggage, clothes, cosmetics, custom jewelry, and solar energy products.

In Harlem, Brooklyn, and on Broadway, religion is often an integral and visible part of the storeowners' and businesspeople's professional world. The Murids have the habit of giving names linked to their tariqa to their places of business. Along 116th Street and inside Mart 125 on 125th Street, stores with names like Touba (the holy city), Lamp Fall (from Sheikh Ibra Fall, a close companion of Sheikh Bamba), Kara (a Murid town), Touba Khassayitt (religious poems written by Sheikh Bamba), Touba Mathlaboul Fawzani (title of a book of poetry by the Sheikh), Mbacké (last name of Serigne Touba), and Mame Diarra (mother of Sheikh Ahmadou Bamba) signal their owners' religious affiliation. Non-Murids may be more discreet; nevertheless, religion is often overtly displayed in their stores and offices, in the form of pictures of the Kabbah, portraits of religious leaders, Quranic verses, and Muslim calendars.

Another niche for the West Africans has been transportation. According to 1991 estimates—the latest available—more than 11 percent of New York's forty thousand taxi drivers are Africans; they represent the second largest group after South Asians.[27] These numbers are quite high since Africans are—officially—about 1 percent of the total population of the five boroughs. For some, it is a traditional occupation: the Juula, for example, have a quasi-monopoly on transportation in Côte d'Ivoire. But for others, driving a cab is often an entry point. Many people who have a formal education, sometimes a college degree, but have been unable to get an "American job" because of limited linguistic skills or dubious immigrant status start their social ascent in the taxi business and leave when they are proficient in English or have saved enough money to finish their studies or open a business. Some continue in the same line of work for themselves. In the early 1990s, several West African drivers pooled their resources and opened car services in underserved areas of Harlem and the Bronx.

Most Nigerians, Sierra Leoneans, and Ghanaians are much less visible than their francophone counterparts because, thanks to their knowledge of English and higher studies, they have been able to integrate the American marketplace and are not grouped in a specific ethnic niche. As a group, Africans have the highest educational attainment of any community in the country, native or foreign born. Twenty-four percent have a bachelor's degree, and more than 21 percent have a graduate degree or higher.[28] The majority of educated Africans are Nigerians. From 1970 to 1985, the oil-rich country sent thousands of students to American colleges, and many remained, especially after the collapse of the economy.[29] The bulk of the community is professional, solidly middle-class and higher, works at all levels of American businesses, and counts numerous college professors.[30] However, as already stressed, there are few Muslims among them, and the same is true of Sierra Leoneans, Ghanaians, and Liberians.

WOMEN: CHANGE AND CONTINUITY

Women well illustrate the paradox of visibility/invisibility. Their number has consistently increased in recent years, as men have married and sent for them or as economic and social factors at home have pushed them to emigrate on their own. They also have invested the public square, noticeably wearing their traditional dress that mark them as Africans, but no veil that could signal them as Muslims.

The question of the veil has generated some discussion among West African Muslims. A few African imams in Harlem and the Bronx have preached for its adoption. In the United States, veiled women are associated with piety and devotion to their religion; they are often considered "good Muslims" on sight. How does this categorization affect equally devout women whose tradition is markedly different? In West Africa, one thousand years after the introduction of Islam, the *hijab* (loose-fitting dress and veil) has very few followers. A few African women interviewed for this study mentioned that they were favorable to the veil. However, none was wearing one. A young Nigerian girl with a headscarf stressed that if she were asked to take it off in school, she would rather forgo her education. But many men and women see it as more of an Arab tradition than an Islamic one. Nigerian Yoruba, for example, who are members of the Nigerian Immigrant Mosques, "think that the Arabs want them to dress like Arabs before they can be recognized as practical Muslims. Nigerian Muslims reject this idea completely."[31] Among both sexes, the general feeling seems to be that if, in specific cultures, the sight of a nonveiled female does not provoke prohibited effects, there is no need for a veil. For most women, their entry into the American ummah, as a minority, has not meant conforming to what is often cited as an imperative of the religion.

Although they live in patriarchal societies, African women have been involved in all types of work outside the home. Following indigenous and Islamic traditions, they are free to keep their own income and are not required to participate in the household's expenditures. Home confinement has never been a tradition, except in northern Nigeria. But in the United States, a new trend is appearing in some West African families where men forbid their wives to work. This attitude is part of a larger issue that pits traditions, a certain idea of Americanization, and the Islamic model of marriage, one against the other.

When asked about gender relations in the United States, most people interviewed for this study labeled them "very difficult." A consensus on the root cause clearly emerged. It is linked to the type of marriage people contract and to the proximity of other models of matrimony and personal life. Marriage is a costly process for an African man, especially for an emigrant. Arranged marriages are still the norm throughout the continent; and for the émigré, it is often the only way to find a wife. As most stress, because they have been away, they don't know who "the good women" are; therefore, they rely on their families to select them. Once a young woman has been chosen, a dowry has to be offered, the marriage has to be celebrated with all the expenses such ceremonies entail, and in-laws are supposed to be taken care of on a regular basis. In addition, the husband has to pay for his wife to come: passport, visa, clothes, and airfare. Having spent a lot, some men feel entitled to full control not only of the household but also of the wife.

However, several examples have shown that women do not always accept this scenario passively. West Africans, one after the other, tell the same story of rural youngsters who unexpectedly find themselves living in their own apartment, making money in New York or Atlanta, and "changing." Some earn as much or more than their husbands, braiding American women's hair. The braiding salon continuously comes up in conversations with both men and women, and it seems to be the main culprit, a place of both opportunity and perdition. There, young women come into contact with more savvy elders and with American clients who have different views of marriage, family life, gender roles, divorce, female independence, and male prerogatives. With new perspectives and opportunities, some women have left their husbands to live on their own.

According to several informants, the issue is not necessarily that women want more freedom but rather the excessiveness of what they term freedom the American way, which is seen as "anything goes." Young rural women who may have little experience with autonomy sometimes go overboard, they say, while their husbands become excessively rigid and authoritarian. Some women, pointing to their long hours at work and the money they contribute to the household, demand more rights within the family. This sometimes creates tensions with husbands whose authority has been reinforced by the women's isolation from kin. As a response, some men simply forbid their wives to work, leaving them particularly isolated. The freedom of movement they enjoyed at home, where everyone knows everyone, is often restricted by husbands who realize no one will monitor them, as relatives and neighbors may do back home.

Imams acknowledge there has been an explosion of divorce within the West African community in the early years and that they are often called upon to mediate between spouses. But couples are now trying to tinker about with elements borrowed from here and there. The traditional/Islamic model that requires the man to be solely responsible for the household still has its devotees. However, some husbands whose wives make money and keep it to themselves resent their lack of participation and often decry their spending habits, what they call their American materialism. This change in attitude may be due to the fact that in the United States, women earn much more than what they would have gained at home, which makes their contribution to the household more desirable. The women who are not allowed to work are often resentful for the solitude and the lost opportunities, not only for themselves but also for their parents and siblings in Africa who would have benefited from their income.

Some households have adopted a team model. Many religiously devout couples emphasize that they have come to the conclusion that women's work in the American public square is not a threat, especially for religious women who, wherever they are and whatever the situation, are supposed to know "how to behave." They also stress that contrary to what they had been doing or would have done in Africa, they share the household's expenditures and therefore take decisions in common. They see their couple as a partnership evolving in the particular situation of migration that requires adaptation, flexibility, but not, they stress, imitation of the mainstream model.

Gender relations are certainly changing, as can be seen by the fact that some husbands have returned home, while their wives and children elected to stay. Some years ago, such a situation would have resulted in divorce, but today, these households remain unified, with a redefinition of roles and responsibilities. Women have taken on new positions that were previously considered the males' domain. Many support their extended families by sending regular contributions and buying houses back home, for rent while in emigration and for their own use when they go back.

As they are confronted with a novel situation that offers unique opportunities, but puts additional demands on them and can also lead to familial disruption, women are negotiating new terms within their households. Tellingly, Islam is often called upon to regulate women's behavior. Those who are seen as too Americanized or who rebel against their traditional role are said to have been "bad Muslims" to begin with. Some women who pay part of the household's bills sometimes seem apologetic, explaining that as Muslim wives they know they are not supposed to pay for shelter, food, and dress but do it as a gift to their husband.

West African Muslim couples—especially those from a rural background—are going through a transition after the shock and disruption that characterized the 1990s. They are trying to reach a balance between traditional and Islamic models, and accrued autonomy and new roles for women. In the past few years, women, who have the most to gain from this redefinition, have been the agents of change within their families; ultimately, because of their influence on the children, they will also introduce some degree of transformation within their communities.

QUESTIONS OF IDENTITY

West Africans are Muslims, immigrants, and Blacks, in a society that assigns specific spaces and roles to each one of these layers of identity. These identity markers in turn define the type of interaction that people have with the rest of society. But West African Muslims have more identities than those three. They can also define themselves according to nationality, ethnicity, gender, age group, occupation, caste, class, religion, brotherhood, and continent. Self-identification is not fixed; it is fluid, inclusive, and depends on the context. Identification by others, on the other hand, is generally rigid. In a society obsessed with color, that specific criterion has become the most significant, and in the United States, race is the master status and often substitutes for real identity. Africans are Black. This truism is not as banal as it seems; it contains a number of reductions, misconceptions, and misunderstandings. It also makes their religious identity invisible. When people are described as Arabs, for example, the link with Islam immediately comes to mind, but there is no reason to associate a color with this religion. Black defines how Africans are generally perceived but obscures how they self-identify and are identified by other Blacks, two elements that are essential in understanding the place and specificity of the African Muslim in American society.

In spite of the ambient definitions they find in the United States, West Africans have forged their own, as multidimensional peoples who came with their history, culture, and religion. How they identify themselves here is markedly different from their definition at home. Many Muslims come from societies where they represent the immense majority: Senegal, Gambia, and Mali are between 90 and 94 percent Muslim, and Guinea has an 85 percent Muslim population. In these countries, although religion is an integral and very substantial part of people's identity, they do not have to define themselves vis-à-vis the "others" along religious lines. There are few "others," no power struggle based on religion, and inclusion of the religious minorities. In countries such as Côte d'Ivoire (from 40 to 60 percent Muslims), Sierra Leone (60 percent), Nigeria and Burkina Faso (50 percent), and Ghana (30 percent), being Muslim sometimes has political and social connotations.[32] In Côte d'Ivoire and Nigeria, in particular, Islam and Christianity have become political tools used to gain influence and power. When West African Muslims enter the United States, they all become part of a small minority. This new reality may be expected to require adjustments. But they stress repeatedly that they *know* they are a minority but do not *feel* it. Most African Muslims emphasize that they can fulfill their religious obligations without restriction and that their religious identity is not threatened. Because of their high rate of self-employment, West Africans enjoy more flexibility for practice. Some who hold American jobs mention that they did not ask for and probably would not get the breaks that would enable them to pray during the day, but they are quick to point out that even at home, arrangements are not always possible for certain types of work.

Because they are not visible Muslims, West Africans are usually not the victims of anti-Islamic remarks or attitudes, although a few mosques recorded some post–September 11 hostility. Africans are evidently aware of the problems faced by other Muslims in the United States and of the negative image their religion has in the media and the general public. African Muslims often stress that they are the brothers and sisters of all Muslims, but they also acknowledge that there is little contact with Arabs, Indo-Pakistani, or Iranians. Racial and ethnic prejudices are far from absent in the Muslim world and have been transported to America. Interaction is often based on ethnic and cultural differences—not to mention religious schools, brotherhoods, and a myriad other differences—rather than on religious unity.

As much as their religious identity matters, when asked how they define themselves, all the West Africans interviewed mentioned that they are Africans first. This, of course, represents a novel way of defining themselves. Prior to their migration, they normally claimed, depending on the context, a national, ethnic caste, or—especially in countries where religion is a point of contention—religious affiliation. Africanness had little relevance. Asked why they do not define themselves as Blacks, they give a religious and a cultural angle to their answer. To do so, they stress, is contrary to Islam, which does not make references to and distinctions based on color. In addition, they assert, for Africans being Black has no importance. To be African, on the other hand, has substance. It means to have a continent, a specific country, a culture, a language, a history, and particular values. It also means a commonality, beyond certain differences, with other Africans. And it is this sum total they feel is what really defines them. Their Africanness, they say, is the primordial difference between them and the people they are now in contact with in America, including African Americans. The fact that many have been in the country long enough to understand that Blackness is a relevant mode of identification within the specific American context could lead to questioning the underlying reasons why so many still do not define themselves as such.

A look at the history of Caribbean immigration may be instructive. As numerous studies have shown, West Indian immigrants often believe that integration in the African American community would result in a diminution in status, and they are also conscious of real differences in cultures, and histories between themselves and African Americans. In consequence, they often stress their particular ethnicity, not necessarily their Blackness.[33] Africans, too, generally elect not to "become Blacks"; in other words, they choose to remain a specific group defined by geographic and cultural criteria, not racial ones. Given the pervasive stereotypes that surround African Americans in media and the general population, the Africans, like the Caribbeans, may want to emphasize "We are not like them." This attitude is certainly exacerbated by the fact that many live in the inner city, among a population often plagued by alcohol and drug addiction, unemployment, single motherhood, teenage pregnancy, and delinquency. People for whom family, respect for the elders, marriage, entrepreneurship, frugality, adhesion to strict religious principles, abstinence from drug and alcohol, and social conformity are essential tend to resent any amalgam between themselves and a group with whom, they feel, they only share one superficial trait: color.

So, there is certainly some of the "not like them" syndrome at work, but it is not the only explanation. Affirming Africanness is not valorizing in the American context. On the contrary, Africa is still widely perceived—including by many African Americans—as a savage, backward wasteland. Because they have so little to gain, the Africans' self-identification may have deeper meaning than just a dissociation from a marginalized group; it also seems to stem from a genuine sense of difference and a pride in Africa—whatever its image—that make them regroup around an African identity rather than a more encompassing racial one.

The killing by the New York police in 1999 of Amadou Diallo, a young unarmed Guinean street vendor, has been instrumental in revealing how difficult it is to reconcile self-identification and identification by others. Few people doubt that the young man was shot because he was Black; the fact that he was also an African, an immigrant, and a Muslim was irrelevant to his fate. Logically, after Diallo's death and during the trial of the police officers, African Americans were the most vocal, organized, and tenacious and demonstrated the most concern. The Muslim community, by contrast, was silent; not much was heard from the Pulaar-Speaking Association (Diallo was a Fulani) or other West African groups. To many Africans, this tragedy brought the point home that whatever else they may be, and how else they want to define themselves, in the United States they are indeed, first and foremost, Blacks.

But just as Africans and Caribbeans insist on their national or ethnic identity, so, too, do African Americans, who often make a point of marking their difference from the other Black communities. Tensions have been noted between Africans and African Americans, and it is sometimes the difference in religions that is at the core of the problem, but more generally it is the immigrant status of the newcomers, and the very fact that they are Africans. Problems appeared in New York when Africans began investing what some African Americans consider their own public square. The emergence of African businesses in the inner city has not been widely accepted by the African American community.[34] Some African Americans voice resentment at what they see as just another wave of immigrants settling in the neighborhood, keeping to themselves, and unwilling to adapt to the locals' ways.[35] However, in contrast to the Jewish, Arab, and Asian store owners who preceded them, the West Africans not only work in these areas; they live and shop there, and they send their children to the local schools. They have also built their mosques, at great cost for small communities. The presence of their religious institutions may be seen as a sign that they are not just a transient group, aiming to make money out of a community that has few choices, but that they consider themselves an integral part of the neighborhood.

In the area of identification by African Americans, Africans have to deal with a unique situation that no other immigrant group has to confront. One accusation almost all the interviewees mentioned having heard hurled at them is the powerful "you sold us." A deeply erroneous reading of the slave trade, transmitted by school, media, and academia, has led some to accuse all Africans—including those living today—of widespread complicity and collective culpability in this tragedy. The African Muslims who shared their experience for this study stressed how shocked they were at the reception they received in some African American neighborhoods.[36] They mentioned derision, insults, stereotypes, and verbal aggressions, usually concluding with references to the slave trade. Most believed that African Americans were expressing genuine sentiments. However, a few questioned their motives. It is apparent that for some African Americans this accusation may be no more than a facade. People who are resentful of the immigrants' success and/or do not want to be associated with Africans because of rampant stereotypes of primitivism and poverty cling to this myth—used by others to deflect the reparations movement—that gives a moral justification to their anti-immigrant feelings and/or shame at being linked with Africa and Africans. By placing themselves on the higher moral ground of history and victimization, they can legitimize their antagonism.

Islam can also be part of the equation. Afrocentrists have repeatedly denounced the Muslims as the original slave dealers. They point to contemporary Mauritania and Sudan to bolster their claim that Islam and the Muslims are anti-Black and proslavery.[37] They propagate the myth that Islam was imposed on West Africans by the sword and that most Africans were sold to the Europeans by Muslims, conveniently forgetting, for example, that more than half the Africans shipped to the Americas and the Caribbean originated from countries where Muslims were not present. Thus, as Africans are often told they are guilty for the deportation and enslavement of African Americans, African Muslims are seen by some as doubly culpable.

NEW MOSQUES, NEW ROLES

According to the Islamic Circle of North America, there are at least 153 mosques in New York, and West Africans pray and participate in the activities of many of them, as they do in other American cities. But they also have founded more than twenty mosques that cater primarily to their own community, just as other mosques often regroup believers on the basis of common language and national or ethnic origin.

The development of most West African mosques started about 1997. Their implantation reflects not only an increase in the African demography but also an anchoring of the community in American society. When people are willing to invest hundreds of thousands of dollars in buying and refurbishing a building to turn it into a place of worship, it indicates an understanding that the community—if not the individual believer—is there to stay. At least a dozen mosques are located in the Bronx, four in Harlem, two on Staten Island, one in Yonkers, and the rest in Brooklyn; but as their numbers increase annually, it is problematic to give an accurate count. They are at different levels of development, with some housed in small buildings and offering few activities, while others are on the way to becoming religious complexes with schools and cultural centers. They are also different in their "recruitment" and generally follow one or the other of the models described here.

Masjid Aksa in Harlem is an international, multiethnic, and transbrotherhood mosque. It was founded in 1997 by mostly Ivorian nationals led by Arabists, men who went to Quranic or franco-Arabic schools in Africa and/or studied in the Arab world. Turned off by what some perceived as a cool reception by Masjid Malcolm Shabazz—Malcolm X's former mosque on 116th Street—they started collecting $50 a month from African believers and rented a large two-story building on Frederick Douglass Boulevard and 116th Street.

Aksa is one of the few mosques with a full-time imam, Souleimane Konaté, an Arabist from Côte d'Ivoire who studied journalism in Saudi Arabia. From its base of Ivorian Juula, the mosque has expanded and has become thoroughly international. Its members are Gambians, Senegalese, Guineans, Burkinabes, Malians, Sierra Leoneans, African Americans, and there are some Asian and Middle Eastern regulars. One theme the imam often emphasizes is African unity. "We are a minority, but if we act as Africans, not as Ivorians, Burkinabes, or Nigerians, we will get things done. We can learn from the Latinos. They are made of several nationalities, but they present a united front." This insistence on African solidarity is on the agenda of a number of African imams. They have formed an association and meet twice a month to discuss issues affecting their communities. To further the link between groups, they regularly lead the prayer and deliver sermons at each other's mosques. Those who can, do it in as many languages as possible, in order to reach a maximum of believers. Souleimane Konaté, for example, gives his sermons in Arabic, Juula,[38] English, and French.

Another multinational mosque, but more limited in its geographic scope, is Masjid Darul Hijra, home to Senegalese, Gambians, and Guineans. It is strictly brotherhood-neutral and enforces a code of nonproselytism for one brotherhood or the other. A few Senegalese with a limited objective—to help compatriots in need—founded the association that runs the mosque several years ago. It has grown tremendously over time, not only in size and diversity but also in objectives and activities.

What prompted the creation of the association was the wave of murders of West African livery cab drivers that swept the city in the early 1990s. Their compatriots and coreligionists organized themselves to help the families of the deceased and to give a hand to those left handicapped. Within a few years, the African Islamic Center, Inc., had gathered enough money not only to help Muslims and non-Muslims alike but also to buy two buildings in the Bronx.

Some mosques are geared almost exclusively to groups that choose to define themselves according to national, ethnic, or tariqa lines. Gallé Cheikh Tidiani is a case in point. It is monoethnic, monobrotherhood, but at the same time multinational. Its members are Halpulaaren, irrespective of their country of origin. The mosque and the Pulaar-speaking association that founded it group Fulani from Gambia, Senegal, Mali, Mauritania, Guinea, Cameroon, Sierra Leone, Liberia, Burkina Faso, Niger, and Nigeria. They share a language and a culture across political boundaries. The Fulani are overwhelmingly *tijani* (a Sufi order). Thirty men who pooled resources to repatriate the bodies of Fulani who had died, some by homicide, established the association in 1988. Today, it has more than eight hundred members—including women—across the country and has bought two buildings on Fulton Street. The association also broadcasts a one-hour weekly radio program in Pulaar. Most members are traders, vendors, cab drivers, and store owners. The association continues to repatriate the dead and help their families, but its main objective is to preserve Fulani culture. The card-carrying members stress that they are not an isolationist group and that many also belong to national associations. They view these groups as complementary and explain that their nationality and ethnicity are not in opposition but are equally important in the definition of their identity, and so is their tijani affiliation.

Masjid Dii-Nul Haqqi, run by the Nigerian-American Muslim Integrated Community, Inc. (NAMIC), whose members are also to be found in several states, represents a particular case. As the leadership declined repeatedly to provide any information for this study, the information presented is based on a visit of the mosque during Friday prayer and discussions with Nigerian nonmembers. One of the largest mosques in the city, and by far the biggest West African mosque, Masjid Dii-Nul Haqqi is an imposing former armory located in an industrial area of Brooklyn. NAMIC bought it in 1997, with the pooled resources of its members, and it has been in renovation ever since. Pointing to a monoethnicity that is not apparent in the name of the association, sermons are delivered in Yoruba and sometimes English. Like its counterparts in Philadelphia, Chicago, Cedar Rapids, St. Louis,

Washington, Houston, and Dallas, Dii-Nul Haqqi functions as a Yoruba mosque. These Nigerian mosques are different from other monoethnic mosques in that they are not multinational. For example, there are at least two Soninke mosques in New York, but as the Soninke come from Senegal, Gambia, Mauritania, and Mali, even though these mosques are monoethnic, they are still multinational. So is the Halpulaaren's mosque, Gallé Cheikh Tidiani.

Given the international reach of most West African mosques, the Nigerian-American association represents a unique case of monoethnic and mononational community. Many Hausa and Fulani Nigerians are not aware of its existence, and, according to other imams, it has no relations with the rest of the West African mosques. The Nigerian mosques, in New York and other states, have cordial relations with Nigerian churches and other Muslim organizations. Nevertheless:

> Many members of the Nigerian Immigrant Mosque have less acquaintance with other Muslim groups in their locales despite the fact that their leaders often participate in the social and religious functions of other Muslim groups. Of course, they pray in other mosques and attend Friday prayers at any mosque, but they do not socialize with them. Members of the NAMIC complain that other Muslim organizations in the U.S.A. pay no attention to African issues; they consider non-Arabs as less religious.[39]

NAMIC and its sister mosques are particular in the Islamic landscape in that they do claim a national and ethnic composition. Even though many mosques cater to specific groups, they painstakingly stress that they are "Muslim mosques," not Pakistani, Turkish, or Albanian. Their names usually do not reflect the origin of their members. NAMIC and the other Nigerian mosques, on the contrary, position themselves overtly as national mosques that in addition are also monoethnic.

The first tariqa-centered West African mosque in New York, with a truly international following, was established in the Bronx in 1995 by the Niassene, a tijani brotherhood founded by Sheikh Ibrahima Niasse (1900–1975.) The Senegalese sheikh has numerous disciples in Mauritania, Nigeria, and Ghana; and in the Bronx, the believers come from a variety of West African countries. His grandson, Sheikh Hassan Cissé, a former doctoral student at Northwestern University, is the founder of the African American Islamic Institute, which has consultative status with the United Nations Economic and Social Council. Cissé has pursued his grandfather's mission by reaching out to African Americans. Several dozens send their children to the Quranic school he runs in Madina Kaolack, Senegal.

For years, the Murids have been pooling monthly contributions of up to $100 with the objective of establishing a mosque and religious center. The building, located on 137th Street in Harlem, finally opened in 2001 and is the largest (in terms of membership) exclusively tariqa-centered West African mosque. The vast majority of Murids are Senegalese, and the appeal of the brotherhood among other Africans is almost zero, but it has recruited among African Americans. Exhibiting a will to broaden their base in the United States, they organize events—including an annual Islamic lecture at the United Nations—open to all during the week leading to Cheikh Bamba Day, when the last surviving son of Serigne Touba, Cheikh Mouhamadou Mourtada M'Backé, comes to town.

As varied as they are, almost all the mosques surveyed shared a common trait: they were often too small. Come Friday, the West African Muslims become highly noticeable, not only because many choose to wear their traditional clothes to go to mosque but also because some remain on the street for the duration of the service. Several hundred men and women generally fill the large first-floor room of Aksa, while others pray in the equally large basement or outside, on the sidewalk. At Al-Noor and Salam, rugs are often laid in front of the mosque to accommodate the overflow of believers, which can number more than a hundred. On 145th Street and Convent Avenue in Harlem, young men make *salat* (obligatory prayer) on the stoop of Masjid Rouchd and on the sidewalk in front of the building where 150 of them live and worship. One of the reasons—besides piety—mosques can overflow is that a large number of worshipers are self-employed and are thus able to arrange their own schedules. Even for those who work in American companies, accommodation is still possible. Some workers take Fridays off instead of Saturdays or Sundays. Others ask for and generally obtain a few hours off on Friday. When needed, imams provide letters to employers stating that the employee's religion demands worship on that particular day and that a believer is not supposed to spend a month without going to mosque.

Women are often quite numerous in the mosques. Of the locales surveyed, only one did not have a space for the women. The imam explained that in a congregation being exclusively made of young single men, a women's area would be useless. Some mosques have a special room, or a moving partition, while others do not put up a physical separation between men and women. Women may make up more than a third of the believers, and the majority are in their twenties and thirties. Mothers often come with their babies and preschool-age children. In most places, African food is served. People chat over rice, *attieke* (a food made from manioc seeds), or millet couscous. For the women who do not work and seldom go out, the mosque fills an essential social need. Although recent in the city landscape, as well as in the geography of Islam in America, the West African mosques have been developing and multiplying at a steady pace. They perform the same functions as in Africa, but they are increasingly assuming new roles. They have become conference halls, community centers, schools, and even counseling centers, as imams are increasingly solicited to intervene in the domestic sphere. Mosques also serve as orientation focal points for recent immigrants who need advice on how to navigate their new world. They are social aid societies, helping the newcomers pay their rent and offering money to the men and women who decide to go back home. They have become job referral centers: companies sometimes ask imams to send them prospective employees. In addition, some imams have had to master new skills to assist the believers' special needs. They act as intermediaries between men and women who are often undocumented and the authorities. Imams frequently negotiate with the police for the release of peddlers who have been arrested for illegal vending and sometimes arrange for the cancellation of tickets given to taxi drivers.

The mosques are still at an early stage of development, but some already operate at a sophisticated level. Having observed that the city provides assistance to religious bodies, some position themselves to take advantage of these programs. Imam Konaté of Aksa is probably the leading advocate for assertiveness. "Whatever priests get for their church," he emphasizes, "we ought to ask for the same. We, African Muslims, have rights that we sometimes are not aware of, or are too timid to demand. By knowing and working with the system, Aksa has gotten quite a bit, from bags of potatoes to computers." The mosques are thus starting to operate as multidimensional, multitask entities that touch all aspects of the believers' life. They have become conduits through which individuals, who are often undocumented and sometimes illiterate, can nevertheless benefit from the opportunities the country has to offer.

The West African mosques are truly an American phenomenon. As Yvonne Haddad has stressed, "Some Muslims find the development of the ethnic mosque an objectionable and unhealthy development, part of the Americanization process which has historically divided the various immigrants into their constituent national identities on the path of assimilation."[40] The African mosques may appear to be the expression of a monocultural movement. However, the fact that these mosques exist as African mosques already positions them as multinational bodies, since Africa is neither a country nor a state. The African mosques cross, from the start, national and ethnic boundaries. The drawing together of different nationalities into one sphere shows a surpassing of the frames of reference valid at home. West Africans, through their mosques, have adapted to the local reality, not because they divide themselves into national and/or ethnic entities but because, like the West Indians and the Latinos, they tend to regroup, regardless of nationality and ethnicity.

THE QURANIC SCHOOLS

One theme constantly comes up in conversations with African imams and believers: the need for Islamic schools that would cater to African children. Imam Mohammed Masurur—a Ghanaian who studied in Saudi Arabia—of

Masjid Al-Huda in the Bronx sums up the general feeling: "We are young communities, and until recently we could not compete with the system. We had no qualified personnel, but now we do. We need full-time African Muslim schools." Presently, very few African children are enrolled in Islamic schools. For some parents, these establishments are not an option, as they prefer the secular system. But others mention that they would rather have their children attend Islamic schools, if they were available in their neighborhood. They stress that good Islamic schools are generally located in the areas where wealthy Asian and Middle Eastern Muslims live and are therefore out of their geographic and financial reach. Many are wary of the influence that American youngsters, who have different cultural, social, religious, and educational values, may have on their own children. Stereotypes seen on television and encounters with neighborhood delinquents have convinced many that the frequentation of American children, at school or on the street, put the young Africans at risk.

Some mosques have made the opening of schools their priority, and Masjid Darul-Hijra opened the first Islamic school run by Africans in New York, in September 2001. It is coed and has enrolled several dozen children who study the regular American curriculum, as well as Arabic and Islamic topics. Several mosques offer Quranic education on a limited basis. With only two afternoons of study a week and imams who are not always very knowledgeable, the results are mixed.

One Quranic school, however, stands out from the rest. Located in the Bronx, it is operated by the Sheikh Ibrahim Niass (or Niasse) Islamic Institute and is the creation of Safietou, a daughter of the sheikh. A memorizer of the Quran since she was twelve, she is a Rutgers University graduate. In 1993, the young woman convinced several coreligionists to contribute $5 a week toward buying a locale that could accommodate a Quranic school that would double as a prayer room for the Niassene brotherhood. In January 1995, the school opened its door in a Bronx house bought for $200,000, with seven children in attendance. Today, fifty uniformed youngsters, aged four to eighteen, take classes on Saturday and Sunday. Most children are born in the United States from parents who immigrated from Nigeria, Gambia, Togo, Senegal, Guinea, Ghana, Tunisia, Morocco, and Puerto Rico. The methods are traditional, and besides exercise books, the children use *aliwa,* the wooden slates typical of African *madrasa* (Muslim schools). The teenagers who spend their weekends at school and were interviewed for this study stressed that they do so voluntarily and enjoy being there. Expressing an often-heard remark, a fifteen-year-old New York–born Senegalese boy mentioned that he enjoyed the fraternity of youngsters from different national origins. The youngsters emphatically stressed that they did not miss what most youth their age do on weekends and that they had learned a lot about discipline, focus, unity, loyalty, and how to interact with people. Others noted that the discipline and methods of learning they have acquired at the Quranic school help them achieve in their secular school.

THE NEW GENERATION: AFRICAN MUSLIMS OR AMERICAN MUSLIMS?

The saying "It takes a village to raise a child" has been so used and misused that one hesitates to bring it up again, but for African immigrants, ironically, what was once a living reality has become elusive. In the United States, the basic unit is no longer the extended family, the village, or the neighborhood but the nuclear family. In the context of migration, fathers often become the only authoritative figure, whereas in Africa uncles share this responsibility. Conflicts cannot be resolved through elders' intervention, and corporal punishments, which are routinely used back home, can lead parents to jail, as has already happened in a few cases. Television, school, and the street offer a subculture that is often in contradiction with the cultural and religious principles that parents try to teach. They therefore often see Quranic schools not only as a religious necessity but also as a rampart against what some perceive as too much Americanization. They mention that besides wanting to raise Muslim children, they are concerned with raising African children; they insist that their offspring must not lose their Africanness, defined in terms of language, modes of behavior, moral values, and manners.

The solution, for those who can afford it, is to have the children spend the summer in their country. Other parents have chosen just the opposite way. They do not want their children to be raised in a culture they find alien and have sent them back home. They visit only during summer vacations. These various efforts seem to be working for the first generation of youngsters born in the United States. Most of those interviewed had a good knowledge of their parents' culture, spoke their language, and participated in community events. Showing the continued resonance of models of identity first defined by their parents, they present themselves as Africans (to outsiders) or as members of a specific national group (to other Africans.) Their Muslim identity generally comes in second, and they generally do not refer to themselves as "Blacks" or African Americans. For the time being, most children are part of the first generation raised entirely or partially here, and it is too early to assess what will happen with the second generation. Some parents state they are conscious that their descendants may be "American Muslims," not African Muslims, or may become "Americans," no longer Africans.

There is ambiguity about this scenario. They view positively their children's economic and political integration, but attachment to their own culture—and an often expressed rejection of the American ways—make them dread its dilution or eventual disappearance. Other parents exhibit no such fears. They point to the Chinese, Italian, or Caribbean neighborhoods to emphasize that it is possible to maintain a viable African community with its own identity. The African Islamic schools of the future will play the most decisive part, they say, in the sustaining of a distinctive community. In addition, they assert that steady immigration will continuously inject African-ness into the group. Some go farther and state that African fashions, crafts, arts, hairstyles, music, and dance have already influenced the larger society and are an indication that their descendants may live in a world where some degree of Africanness will be part of the mainstream.

CONCLUSION

West African Muslims have just started their social, cultural, economic, and religious—but not yet political—anchoring into the American public square. Where it is going is an open question. An observation of the situation in Europe where the same populations have been living for ten years longer is of little help due to substantial historical, social, cultural, and political differences between the host countries. Likewise, the directions taken by other Muslim communities in the United States are no indication because of great dissimilarities in many respects between African and Arab or South Asian immigrants.

What readily appears from conversations with people from various backgrounds and countries of origin is that as much as they appreciate the economic and educational opportunities offered by the host country, they insist on distancing themselves from its culture, perceived as valuing and promoting individualism, promiscuity, greed, and violence. Assimilation is therefore usually rejected, but some type of accommodation is deemed indispensable. As exemplified by the problems that transpired within some households as to the place and role of women, this adaptation is sometimes difficult. Many see their religion as a rampart against American mores: Islam and African cultural and social values provide them with a road map to navigate their new world with a sense of control.

A close reading of the community shows that age and education fissures are becoming apparent. Just as it happened in Europe, the Arabist group has been the driving force in the establishment and running of Islamic institutions. Intellectuals from the secular system, on the other hand, have been involved in organizing national associations within which Arabists, intellectuals, and illiterate share responsibilities. But, in some groups, intellectuals and the younger generations appear to want a more active role in religious matters. The older, more traditional leadership who came out of Quranic schools has showed some resistance to the trend, based on age prerogatives and type of education. However, their lack of English proficiency and knowledge of the workings of the host country represents a serious obstacle to bringing the mosques to the next level.

The regional regrouping of the West African Muslims in African mosques means they have avoided the pitfalls of narrow ethnic identification. The consensus is neatly on building not only religious but also social, economic, and political organizations and institutions, first at the regional level and later at the continental level. In that, they are helped by the fact that African ethnic groups are often scattered among countries, and by the absence of major political problems between their respective nations, which is often not the case in the Arab world or in South Asia.

West African Muslims occupy a unique space, due to their mode of self-identification and also, if they pay attention to it, due to the way they are identified in this country. As Africans, they have the opportunity of forming alliances with the rest of the African population: Christian West Africans, Muslim East Africans, and Africans *tout court*. As Muslims, they can solidify their links with the Muslim community and benefit from a stronger Islamic representation in the political arena. As immigrants—and for many, specifically as undocumented aliens—they can also look for support in the vast and diverse immigrant group. As Blacks, West African Muslims can work in conjunction with a large, organized African American community whose numbers and political clout are much stronger than that of any other group they can identify with.

In short, West African Muslims must draw on their own internal resources to address issues of identity, education, gender, age, and what they want for the future and how to achieve it. They must fight invisibility and oversight by making their voice heard and listened to in the Islamic community as it engages a conversation on Islam and Muslims in and of America. They also have to avoid insularity by reaching out and cooperating with other groups and organizations in the wider society. The West African Muslim community is still in its infancy, which makes any assessment of what social, political, cultural, and, to a certain degree, religious path it will take premature. But, as a conversation on remaining an African Muslim in America today and tomorrow grows within its ranks, the community clearly indicates that it is not too early to start thinking about it.

NOTES

1. For West African Muslims in early America, see Allan D. Austin, *African Muslims in Antebellum America: Transatlantic Stories and Spiritual Struggles* (New York: Routledge, 1997); Sylviane A. Diouf, *Servants of Allah: African Muslims Enslaved in the Americas* (New York: New York University Press, 1998); Michael Gomez, *Exchanging Our Country Marks: The Transformation of African Identities*

in the Colonial and Antebellum South (Chapel Hill: University of North Carolina Press, 1998), 59–87.

2. Zogby International, *American Muslim Poll,* November–December 2001, 4.

3. The estimated global number for Africans brought to the United States through the slave trade is about six hundred thousand.

4. Kofi Apraku, *African Émigrés in the United States: A Missing Link in Africa's Socioeconomic Development* (New York: Praeger, 1991); Agyemang Attah-Poku, *The Socio-Cultural Adjustment Question: The Role of Ghanaian Immigrant Ethnic Association in America* (Brookfield, Vt.: Avebury, 1996); Arthur A. Johnson, *Invisible Sojourners: African Immigrant Diaspora in the United States* (Westport, Conn.: Praeger, 2000); April Gordon, "The New Diaspora: African Immigration to the United States," *Journal of Third World Studies* 15, no. 1 (1998): 79–103; Chike Alex Anigbo, "The African Neo-Diaspora: Dynamics of Prospects for Afrocentrism and Counterpenetration: A Case Study of the Nigerian Community in the United States," Ph.D. diss., Howard University, 1994; Hugo Athanasius Kamya, "The Interrelationship of Stress, Self-esteem, Spiritual Well-Being and Coping Resources among African Immigrants," Ph.D. diss., Boston University, 1994; Charles Kofi Amissah, "The Socio-Economic Achievement of Sub-Saharan African Immigrants in the United States," Ph.D. diss., University of Illinois–Chicago, 1994.

5. Ivan Van Sertima, *They Came before Columbus: The African Presence in Ancient America* (New York: Random House, 1976).

6. For prayers: Works Progress Administration (WPA), *Drums and Shadows: Survival Studies among the Georgia Coastal Negroes* (1942; reprint: Athens: University of Georgia Press, 1986): 141, 161–66, 179; Philip D. Curtin, "Ayuba Suleiman Diallo of Bundu," in *Africa Remembered: Narratives by West Africans from the Era of the Slave Trade,* ed. Philip D. Curtin (Madison: University of Wisconsin Press, 1967), 41; Diet: William Brown Hodgson, *Notes on Northern Africa* (New York: Wiley & Putnam, 1844), 69; Thomas Teas, "A Trading Trip to Natchez and New Orleans in 1822," *Journal of Southern History* 7 (August 1941): 388; Gabriel Debien, *Les esclaves aux Antilles françaises* (Pointe-à-Pitre: Société d'histoire de la Guadeloupe, 1974), 388. For dress: WPA, *Drums and Shadows,* 162, 179–81; Georgia Bryan Conrad, "Reminiscences of a Southern Woman," *Southern Workman* 30, no. 5 (May 1901): 252; George Callcott, "Omar ibn Seid, a Slave Who Wrote an Autobiography in Arabic," *Journal of Negro History* 39, no. 1 (January 1954): 62; Carl Campbell, "John Mohammed Bath and the Free Mandingos in Trinidad: The Question of Their Repatriation to Africa 1831–38," *Journal of African Studies* 2, no. 4 (1975–1976): 467; Gilberto Freyre, *The Masters and the Slaves* (Berkeley: University of California Press, 1986), 319.

7. Raymundo Nina Rodrigues, *Os Africanos no Brasil* (Sao Paulo: Companhia Editora Nacional, 1976), 53–56; Joao Jose Reis, *Slave Rebellion in Bahia: The Muslim Uprising of 1835 in Bahia* (Baltimore: Johns Hopkins University Press, 1993), 96–100.

8. George Raeders, *Le Comte de Gobineau au Brésil* (Paris: Nouvelles Editions Latines, 1934), 75; Edward Bean Underhill, *The West Indies* (London: Jackson, Walford & Hodder, 1862), 46.

9. Diouf, *Servants of Allah,* 189–90.

10. Sylviane A. Diouf, "Sadaqa among African Muslims Enslaved in the Americas," *Journal of Islamic Studies* 10, no. 1 (January 1999): 22–32; Maureen Warner

Lewis, *Guinea's Other Suns: The African Dynamic in Trinidad Culture* (Dover, Mass.: Majority, 1991).

11. Alan Lomax, *The Land Where the Blues Began* (New York: Bantam Doubleday, 1993), 233–34; John Storm Roberts, *Black Music of Two Worlds* (New York: Praeger, 1972), 167, 197, 213.

12. The priests and assembly in Palo Mayombe (a Kongo religion) and in certain Voodoo *houngans* (places of worship) greet one another by saying, "Salam ualeikum, ualeikum salam." Some songs recorded in Peru and Trinidad in the twentieth century still contain Arabic words; see Fernando Romero, *Quimba, Fa, Malambo, Neque: Afronegrismos en el Peru* (Lima: IEP, 1988), 188, 236; J. D. Elder, "The Yoruba Ancestor Cult in Gasparillo," *Caribbean Quarterly* 16, no. 3 (September 1970): 9; Maureen Warner Lewis, *Trinidad Yoruba: From Mother Tongue to Memory* (Tuscaloosa: University of Alabama Press, 1996), 36.

13. Djibirilu, the man considered the last African orthodox Muslim, died in 1959 in Bahia, Brazil. He was the son of a Yoruba religious leader. See Vincent Monteil, "Analyse des 25 documents arabes des Malês de Bahia (1835)," *Bulletin de l'IFAN* 29, nos. 1–2 (1967): 88–98.

14. For early twentieth-century immigrants, see Suleyman S. Nyang, "The African Immigrant Family in the United States of America: Challenges and Opportunities," paper presented at the Annual Conference on Africa and the Diaspora, California State University, May 1998.

15. Gordon, *The New Diaspora*, 93.

16. They represent 2.5 percent of the total foreign-born population.

17. M. Brett, "Islam and Trade in the *Bilad al-Sudan,* Tenth–Eleventh Century a.d.," *Journal of African History* 24 (1983): 431–40; Lamin Sanneh, *The Jakhanke Muslim Clerics* (Lanham, Md.: University Press of America, 1989); Ivor Wilks, *Forests of Gold* (Athens: Ohio University Press, 1993).

18. For Fulani jihad in Senegal and Mali, see David Robinson, *The Holy War of Umar Tal* (Oxford: Clarendon, 1985); Madina Ly-Tall, *Un islam militant en Afrique de l'ouest au XIXe siècle: La Tijaniyya de Saiku Umar Futiyu contre les pouvoirs traditionnels et la puissance coloniale* (Paris: L'Harmattan, 1991); Boubacar Barry, *Senegambia and the Atlantic Slave Trade* (Cambridge: Cambridge University Press, 1998). For Guinea: Walter Rodney, *"Jihad and Social Revolution in Futa Jalon in the Eighteenth Century," Journal of the Historical Society of Nigeria* 4 (1968): 269–84. For Nigeria: A. Bivar "The Watthiqat ahl al-Sudan: A Manifesto of the Fulani Jihad," *Journal of African History* 4, no. 2 (1961): 235–43; Melvin Hiskett, *The Sword of Truth: The Life and Times of the Shehu Usuman dan Fodio* (New York: Oxford University Press, 1973).

19. For Soninke migrations: Mahamet Timera, *Les Soninke en France: D'une histoire à l'autre* (Paris: L'Harmattan, 1996); François Manchuelle, *Willing Migrants: Soninke Labor Diasporas, 1848–1960* (Athens: Ohio University Press, 1997).

20. Donald B. Cruise O'Brien, *The Mourides of Senegal: The Political and Economic Organization of an Islamic Brotherhood* (Oxford: Clarendon, 1971); Mark Karp, "The 'Protestant Ethic' of the Mourids of Senegal," in *African Dimensions: Essays in Honor of William O. Brown,* ed. Mark Karp (Brookline, Mass.: African Studies Center, Boston University, 1975); Jean Copans, *Les Marabouts de l'arachide: La confrérie mouride et les paysans du Sénégal* (Paris: Sycomore, 1980); David Robinson, "Beyond Resistance

and Collaboration: Amadu Bamba and the Murids of Senegal," *Journal of Religion in Africa* 21, no. 2 (1991): 149–71; Sylviane A. Diouf, "Senegalese in New York: A Model Minority?" *Black Renaissance* 1, no. 2 (1997): 92–115; Sophie Bava, "Reconversions et nouveaux mondes commerciaux des mourides à Marseille," *Hommes & Migrations* 1224 (March–April 2000): 46–55.

21. For Islamic education in West Africa, see Stefan Reichmuth, "Islamic Education and Scholarship in Sub-Saharan Africa," in *The History of Islam in Africa,* ed. Nehemia Levtzion and Randall L. Pouwels (Athens: Ohio University Press, 2000): 419–40.

22. On the link between Quranic schools and migration, see Sylviane A. Diouf, "Islam, mendicité et migration au Sénégal," *Hommes & Migrations* 1186 (April 1995): 37–40; and "Senegal Upgrades Its Koranic Schools," *UNICEF Features* (April 1995).

23. The novel *Jaguar: A Story of Africans in America* by Paul Stoller (Chicago: University of Chicago Press, 1999), a work of fiction based on anthropological research that aims at presenting "a story of Africans in America," is in fact about the life in New York of Muslim Songhai street peddlers from Niger (who represent an infinitesimal part of the West Africans in the United States), and it gives a very inaccurate picture—among many other flaws—of these men as being obsessed with sex, polygamy, and food.

24. In West Africa, turbans are reserved to high-ranking clerics. Saharan people, on the other hand, wear them routinely.

25. Diouf, *Servants,* 102.

26. The *tontine* (*esusu* in Yoruba, *susu* in the West Indies) is a savings association operating outside of the banking system. Every week or month, its members deposit a fixed amount with the treasurer, and the entire savings account is paid to one of them every month.

27. Bruce Schaller, *The New York City Taxicab Fact Book,* 3d ed. (New York: Schaller Consulting, 1994). By comparison, U.S.-born drivers are about 10 percent.

28. U.S. Bureau of the Census, *Educational Attainment of the Foreign-born Population 24 to 54, 1997* (Washington, D.C.: U.S. Government Printing Office, 1997). As a comparison, of all persons living in the United States, 20 percent have a bachelor's degree and 7 percent a graduate degree or higher. According to the U.S. Bureau of the Census, *Selected Characteristics by Ancestry Group 1990:* among the 52,388 Nigerians adults, 87.6 percent have a high school diploma, 52.9 percent have a bachelor's degree or higher, and 26.3 percent have a graduate degree or higher.

29. During the school year 1999–2000, there were only 3,602 Nigerians in U.S. universities. See *Open Doors 1999/2000: Report on International Educational Exchange,* available at www.opendoorsweb.org; accessed in 2000. The percentage of Muslims among Nigerian students is low. Muslims often continue their studies in the Arab world, instead of England or the United States.

30. The median household income of Africans is $31,300, the same as the median income of European immigrants. For comparison: The median is $30,000 for all foreigners and $36,100 for native-born people (U.S. Bureau of the Census, *Median Household Income by Nativity, 1996*).

31. Yushau Sodiq, "The Nigerian Immigrant Mosques in America," unpublished manuscript, pp. 9–10.

32. Percentages are often disputed. Côte d'Ivoire, for example, has officially

about 40 percent Muslims. The figures cited here are those of the Central Intelligence Agency.

33. Nancy Foner, "Race and Color: Jamaican Migrants in London and New York," *International Migration Review* 19 (1987): 708–22; Philip Kasinitz, *Caribbean New York: Black Immigrants and the Politics of Race* (Ithaca, N.Y.: Cornell University Press, 1992); Flore Zéphir, *Haitian Immigrants in Black America: A Sociological and Sociolinguistic Portrait* (Westport, Conn.: Bergin & Garvey, 1996).

34. In 1992–1993, a feud between West African (and some African American) street vendors and African American, White, and Asian storeowners on 125th Street in Harlem escalated to the point that the issue became part of a hearing and a report of the New York City Commission on Human Rights, along with police brutality and harassment. The problems ended with the vendors being regrouped against their will in an open-air market on 116th Street. They are now lodged in small stores at the African Market. Another point of contention has been the fact that African hair braiders charge much less for the same service than their American colleagues. The latter have fought their competition by pushing for regulations forcing the braiders to take classes in hair care and styling and to be licensed. The campaign has worked, resulting in heavy fines for many African women.

35. See Tracie Rozhon, "Grit and Glory in South Harlem," *New York Times*, March 16, 2000.

36. For a discussion of this issue, see Arthur, *Invisible Sojourners*, 77–86. In this regard, too, Stoller's book, *Jaguar*, is naïve at best, as it stresses how African street peddlers feel very much embraced by African Americans.

37. For Afrocentrism and Islam, see Yusuf Nuruddin, "African-American Muslims and the Question of Identity between Traditional Islam, African Heritage, and the American Way," in *Muslims on the Americanization Path?* ed. Yvonne Yazbeck Haddad and John L. Esposito (Atlanta: Scholars, 1998), 267–330.

38. A dialect of the Mande language, it is understood by the Mande people of Senegal, Gambia, Guinea, Mali, Sierra-Leone, Liberia, and Burkina Faso.

39. Sodiq, "The Nigerian," 9.

40. Yvonne Yazbeck Haddad, "The Dynamics of Islamic Identity in North America," in *Muslims on the Americanization Path?* ed. Haddad and Esposito, 41.

IV

ON LOCATING MUSLIMS IN
THE AMERICAN LANDSCAPE:
DEMOGRAPHIC AND
BEHAVIORAL ASPECTS

11

Muslim Americans

A Demographic Report

Ilyas Ba-Yunus and Kassim Kone

In searching the literature on Islam in the United States, one is struck by the great interest that social scientists as well as others have lately shown in estimating the rather rapidly growing Muslim population in this country. It has been a matter of curiosity for some, a matter of pride for others, and, seemingly, a matter of concern for still others. However, Muslims are no strangers to American shores. There is speculation these days that the Muslim presence might have predated Columbus (Wiener 1922; Davidson 1959; Sertima 1976; Quick 1996; Nyang 1999). What is more certain is that Muslim names started appearing in slave records as early as the seventeenth century (Austin 1984; Mehdi 1978; Poston 1992). Indeed, it is quite plausible that by the end of the eighteenth century, there could have been more Muslims than Catholics and Jews in America. Alex Haley's (1976) *Roots* is based on a similar folklore, especially among African Americans living in the big-city ghettos.

This chapter describes a survey of the American Muslim communities conducted during the spring and summer of 2001 and the summer of 2002, but it also draws on other research, surveys, and summaries. Some of these studies have been extremely sketchy and speculative. They belie difficulties involved in estimating a population not covered by the U.S. Census. Others have focused on the Muslim population only tangentially while pursuing interests in some other populations. Still others used more complex research designs in order to obtain information from immigration and birth statistics.

Because these studies were conducted with designs of varying rigor, their estimates of the Muslim population in the United States also vary greatly— from around ten million (American Muslim Council [AMC] 2001) to about three million (Smith 2001). Muslims are a unique religious population in that in addition to two major factors of growth (natural growth and migration), they are also experiencing growth, not inconspicuously, due to net conversion to Islam. Because of a convergence of these three factors, it is hard not to arrive at overly ambitious estimations. On the other hand, this very convergence may explain why the estimation of the Muslim population in the United States cannot be too conservative. Apart from this polarizing tendency, what most of these studies lack from a demographic point of view is a focus on the structure of the Muslim population. Educational, income, and professional compositions are demographic factors that have generally been ignored. Without these, no demographic picture would ever be complete. This report intends to address these considerations in the study of the Muslim population in the United States.

ESTIMATIONS OF SIZE

Federation of Islamic Associations in America

How many Muslims are living in the United States at present has been a very difficult question to answer. As mentioned, because the U.S. Census Bureau does not touch anything even remotely resembling religion, estimation of the Muslim population is left to nongovernmental organizations, which, for understandable reasons, lack reliability.

The first such attempt was made in 1959 by the Federation of Islamic Associations in America (FIAA). This study consisted of an enumeration of the number of households in each community affiliated with the FIAA. This count yielded a total of 187,112 households. Because of a possibility of under-enumeration, this figure was upgraded to 200,000. Multiplying this number by 6, an estimate of the then-average Muslim family size, the FIAA announced an estimate of the Muslim population in 1960 at about 1.2 million (Alam 1968). However, this study lacked scientific rigor. Moreover, it ignored most communities not affiliated with the FIAA. These were small but numerous communities, mostly of non-Arab origin (Turkish, Albanian, African American, Bosnian, and the Punjabi communities of Pakistani origin). Though this estimate deserved serious upgrading, unfortunately such revision was not done.

Ba-Yunus and Siddiqui (1998) estimate that this FIAA population had a natural growth rate (not considering immigration) of 2 percent, with a capacity to double itself in thirty years. This means that FIAA's targeted population alone was around 2.5 million in 1990.

Weeks and Siddiqui

In 1993, John Weeks and M. Moin Siddiqui presented a summary of the most notable studies aimed at measuring the extent of the Muslim population. First on their list is an article by Thomas Phillip (1980) published in the *Harvard Encyclopedia of American Ethnic Groups*. Phillip estimated the American Muslim population to be between two hundred thousand and three hundred thousand.

Phillip's study was deficient on several counts. It did not consider the African Americans swelling the ranks of Sunni Islam after the demise of Elijah Muhammad in 1975. It did not take into account the population of Muslim students on American campuses. Also, Phillip did not refer to any authentic sources or methodology, although the FIAA study was already fifteen years old by the time the *Harvard Encyclopedia of American Ethnic Groups* was published.

In 1981, Arif Ghayur estimated the Muslim population to be at 1.2 million. His method was based on immigration from predominantly Muslim countries since 1960. To this he added, somewhat arbitrarily, seventy-five thousand as his estimate of the African American Muslim population in 1980. Indeed, this study was an improvement over previous similar efforts in that it at least tried to reach some authentic sources of information. However, it has its own shortcomings. For instance, Ghayur's estimation of the African American Muslim population was without any foundation. He did not or could not reach any local, regional African American Muslim organizations for information. Moreover, many non-Muslims have migrated to the United States from Muslim countries. In fact, until lately, Christian Arabs used to predominate among immigrants from Arab countries (Haddad 1986; *The Economist* 2002). Similarly, Ghayur could not reconcile the fact that the Indian Muslims, who are easily identifiable among Muslims in the United States, are from a predominantly non-Muslim country. Also, Ghayur did not consider the existence of a pre-1960 Muslim population. Even if we assume that the FIAA targeted population did not experience substantial change in its growth rate, it must have stood in the neighborhood of two million in 1980. If we add this figure to Ghayur's estimate, as faulty as it may be, it may be concluded that in 1980 the Muslim population in the United States was not less than 3.2 million.

In 1984, John Weeks replicated Ghayur and gave the figure of 1.5 million Muslims in the United States as of 1980 (Weeks and Siddiqui 1993). The difference between their estimates is due to Weeks's larger figure of African Americans. Evidently, this study also suffers from the same difficulties as that of Ghayur. By updating the FIAA targeted population, Weeks's estimate may be enlarged to 3.5 million for 1980.

Stone

In a conference on Muslims of America held in the spring of 1989 at the University of Massachusetts, Carol Stone (1991) presented a report on the

"Estimate of Muslims Living in America." The design of her study was aimed at discovering total numbers in 1980 of the first- and second-generation immigrants from Muslim countries. Dividing this number into the proportion of Muslim in these countries, she arrived at the 1980 estimate of the Muslim immigrant population of 2.3 million. To this Stone added, somewhat arbitrarily, a figure of one million to represent the size of the African American Muslim population, for a total of 3.3 million Muslims in the United States in 1980. (It is remarkable how close the estimates made by Ghayur, Weeks and Siddiqui, and Stone are for the same period of time.)

Then, adding the number of new immigrants (applying the same method as earlier) and a crude birthrate of sixteen per thousand, Stone concluded that there were 4.3 million Muslims in the United States in 1986. Using Stone's data, *Time* magazine updated the figure to 4.6 million for 1988 (Oatling 1988), showing an average growth of 150,000 per year.

Ba-Yunus and Siddiqui

Ba-Yunus and Siddiqui (1998:24) continued with the same procedure to arrive at the figure of just about 7 million in 2000, or 2.6 percent of the overall U.S. population; about 8 million in 2005; about 9.5 million in 2010 (i.e., 3 percent of the American national population); and more than 13 million in 2020 (3.4 percent of the national population). Their projections show that provided this growth rate (slightly higher than 3 percent per year) continues, the Muslim population in the United States has a capacity to double itself in somewhat less than twenty-two years. This means that one could expect the number of Muslim Americans to reach in the neighborhood of fourteen to fifteen million before the year 2025.

However, although Stone's method shows substantial improvement over previous studies, it is full of discrepancies. For one, it suffers from the ever-present problem of not being able to ascertain the number of African American Muslims in the Muslim American population in general. Likewise, her use of a crude American birthrate (sixteen per thousand) for Muslims does not sound realistic. Given the background of most Muslims (third world and relatively low-income African Americans), one might be inclined to use a higher figure. Moreover, as Smith (2001) has pointed out, Stone computed the Muslim growth rate on the basis of only birth migration. She totally ignored the factor of the death rate, which should not be the least consideration in any computation of growth rates. The same could be said about Ba-Yunus and Siddiqui (1998), who also take a risk in making long-term projections that may be seriously disturbed by unforeseen demographic changes in, say, immigration. There are already unconfirmed reports circulating that immigration to the United States from Muslim countries is down by 14 percent since September 2001.

Kosmin

An important alternative to the census in estimating religious populations in the United States has been survey methodology (for earliest such efforts, see, e.g., Herberg 1955). However, this methodology has only yielded inconsistent results. In 1989, for instance, a Gallup Poll found that 4 percent of respondents in a national sample (eighteen and older) listed their religion as "other." Taking a clue from the 1991 *Statistical Abstracts of the United States*—namely, that Muslims may account for about half of those whose religious affiliation is given as "other"—Weeks and Siddiqui (1993) concluded that 2 percent of the Gallup Poll's "others" ought to be Muslims, assuming that this percentage is applicable to Muslim minors as well. This estimation sets the Muslim population of 1989 at 4.94 million (compare it to ISNA's 5 million in 1987).

In 1989, Kosmin presented the findings of a survey he and associates did on religious distribution in the United States. Their survey, primarily aimed at estimating the size of the Jewish American population, was carried out by a consumer research agency, ICR. The survey results received publicity in the press (e.g., Goldman 1991). This survey, though aimed mainly at the Jewish population, also yielded rich information on various other religions. Kosmins's finding regarding the Muslim population is a surprising contrast to Stone's and the Gallup's in that, according to it, the Muslim population in the United States was only 1.4 million in 1991.

Because of this sharp difference, others gave a second look at Kosmin's design and method. Weeks and Siddiqui (1993), for instance, point out that Kosmin's survey must have been flawed for a number of reasons.

For instance, Kosmin's sample consisted of 125,000 households, but only 113,000 of them responded to ICR's calls. According to Weeks and Siddiqui (1993:8), a disproportionate share of those who chose not to respond must be Muslims, most of whom are relative newcomers to the United States. Although many of them are very successful economically, they are not fully assimilated socially and culturally. They often show a great deal of timidity when it comes to responding to a stranger asking personal questions. Then, there are new Muslims, mostly African Americans but also Hispanics in increasing numbers, living mostly in inner-city neighborhoods. Few of these people, like many poor Whites, may be described as being in the mainstream of American life. In short, immigrant as well as indigenous Muslims comprise a subculture that does not place a high value on anonymous surveys conducted by telephone. Plausibly, those who are still at the margins of the melting pot are not expected to behave like the ones who are melting in the pot.

Bagby, Perl, and Froehle

One of the latest estimates pertaining to the Muslim population in the United States is the Mosque Study Project by Ihsan Bagby, Paul Perl, and

Bryan Froehle (2001). Bagby and his associates show a great deal of sensitivity to the pitfalls in taking the country-of-origin route and using survey methodology. They decided to reach the mosques directly and count their number (i.e., 1,209) and try to estimate the total number of regular mosque goers nationally (i.e., almost two million). On that basis, they concluded that claims of six or seven million Muslims in the United States are not unreasonable.

Bagby was not new to this kind of venture. In 1994, he had directed a similar project with great care and industry to produce a report on a survey of Masajid in North America, which was published by the Islamic Research Institute. However, in his latest project, he and his associates decided to take a sample rather than cover all the mosques. Why? Rather than looking into their mailing lists, why did they decide to estimate their weekly Friday (Juma) congregations and the number of regular users? There is no doubt, as Smith (2001) pointed out, that the number of the users, even if estimated by the size of the Juma congregation, does not inform us as to who else is in the community but not coming to the mosque.

Smith

The most recent estimate of the Muslim population in the United States is by Tom Smith (2001) in a report prepared for the American Jewish Committee. After a critical review of some selected researches, he came to the conclusion that the Muslim population in the United States could only be between 1.9 and 2.8 million in 2001. Because Smith has been with the prestigious National Opinion Research Center at the University of Chicago, his estimation received a great deal of attention, especially in the media, because it clearly deviates from earlier estimates. For this reason alone, let us look into some of the critiques and assumptions that Smith made before giving his estimate.

First, it is surprising that Smith had access to so few previous works on the subject at hand. Of the four reports that he considered, two were unpublished. One of these unpublished reports, the one by Ba-Yunus, was, in fact, thoroughly revised and published in 1997. Somehow this published report escaped Smith. Nonetheless, his observation that "it is practically impossible to translate these estimates for Illinois into national figures" is valid.

Second, in criticizing Stone, Smith points out that immigrant flows to the United States often differ greatly from the ethnic profiles of the country of origin. In support of his claim, he shows that Russian immigrants in the late 1800s and early 1900s were heavily Jewish rather than Orthodox, which most Russians are. Likewise, most Lebanese were Christians rather than Muslims when they migrated to the United States in the nineteenth and early twentieth centuries. Smith is right but only so far as the "first massive wave" of migration (of the late nineteenth and early twentieth centuries) is concerned. The "second massive wave," starting in the second half of the twentieth century and still not abating, seems to be very different from the first one. The second wave is overwhelmingly non-European, originating in third world countries including, quite significantly, the Muslim countries. The first wave consisted of people who were mostly escaping the potato famine in Ireland, the anti-Jewish programs in Russia, and the continuous decline of Ottoman rule resulting in bloody anti-Muslim "ethnic cleansing" episodes in the Balkans.

On the other hand, the immigrants of the "second wave" were, with few exceptions, not escaping from anything (major exceptions being refugees from Palestine, Afghanistan, Somalia, Bosnia, and Kosovo, all of them Muslim countries). Rather than being "pushed," they were mostly being "pulled" by the lure of America. According to Isbister (1996), immigrants come to the United States mainly "to improve their prospects, to get better jobs, to earn more income, to raise their standard of living, to provide more promising opportunities for their children." The very first beneficiaries of a new immigration policy initiated under the Johnson administration in 1965, therefore, were a few thousand undergraduate and graduate students mainly from the developing countries studying in American and Canadian universities. Contrary to what the makers of this immigration bill expected, it opened the floodgates for the well-informed, skilled, and experienced professionals in developing countries to head for the greener pastures of America. This movement is what in part started the "brain drain" debate. Of late, Muslim countries are deeply involved in such cross-border movements. Newland (1979) calls them "economic refugees."

This second wave of immigration to the United States does not seem to be ethnically selective on the part of the sending countries. However, about 80 percent of immigrants to the United States of Arab descent used to be non-Muslims, mostly Christians, until 1970. Presently, about as many Muslims of Arab descent are entering the United States, according to the Center for Immigration Studies (*The Economist* 2002:30).

Third, Smith looks at the mosques and the Islamic Centers from an American perspective when he says, "[D]enominations and congregations in general frequently overestimate their membership." We know of no mosques that are competing against one another for membership or making false claims to attract more people. On the other hand, over the years one gets a good idea as to how many people a mosque could contain in its limited space when filled to capacity, especially at the time of weekly Friday congregation and other special occasions—a matter of great concern and discussion in every mosque as the space seems to be shrinking as more worshipers appear every year.

As to the membership, it is relatively small and is routinely recorded, but most, if not all, Islamic institutions are known to also maintain correspondence or a mailing list, which is relatively large—much larger—because, maybe apart from the membership, it invariably contains names and addresses also of those who come to pray, if at all, only twice a year—at the time of two celebrations of Eid al-Fitr (at the end of Ramadan, the month of fasting, and Eid al-Adha, the Abrahamic tradition of Sacrifice). Most mosque administrators take pains to maintain such mailing lists because this is how they get donations to their mosques. An unupdated mailing list tends quickly to become an unnecessary liability and a source of revenue loss that the mosques can hardly afford. These lists are, therefore, updated periodically if not regularly each year.

Fourth, Smith seems to be only guessing when he says that Bagby's (2001) estimate of 1,629 Muslims per mosque is very high. Why is it "2.4 times greater than a similar figure from 1994"? Exactly which figure Smith is referring to is not clear. Moreover, his assertion that individuals may be associated with more than one mosque and therefore be doubly counted is not plausible. This is so because most mosques or Islamic centers in the United States, strange as it may sound, are ethnically divided. Thus we see individual mosques run and attended almost exclusively by African Americans, Arabs, Pakistanis, Indians, Turks, and even Bosnians. For instance, Majid Taqwa in Brooklyn, New York, is almost 100 percent African American in administration as well as membership; Mosque Foundation outside Chicago is almost exclusively Arab in character; while the Islamic Society of Orange County is nearly 100 percent South Asian. Some people may occasionally go to a mosque run by Muslims of ethnic groups other than their own. But in most cases they are members of their own ethnic mosque. Exceptions to this rule are downtown Musallas (discussed later) and mosques owned and/or run by Muslim Students Associations (MSAs) near colleges or the universities. Mosques outside the metropolitan areas are also multiethnic, but whether the MSAs or those outside of the metropolitan areas, these places of Islamic worship are so far apart (eighty miles, on average, as calculated from Bagby's mosque address list) that little overlap in membership among them is possible.

Lastly, and more important, although Smith is not the only one at fault, is the myth in American culture about the scientific validity of surveys based on national polling. Starting with George Gallup, who rightly predicted the presidential election outcome in the 1930s, agencies conducting surveys based on national samples are mushrooming these days. One of the more prestigious of them is the National Opinion Research Center of the University of Chicago. Tom Smith is the main supervisor of this agency.

However, surveys have failed dismally in the past. For instance, Prime Minister Harold Wilson of England was wrongly predicted as the winner in the British elections of 1970. Also, in the 2000 presidential election in the

United States, Vice President Al Gore was twice declared a winner and candidate George Bush was once declared as the winner in Florida—both wrongly at the time.

Prestige aside, surveys are based on scientific methodology that is open to public scrutiny. In theory, the validity of a survey is based on how representative the sample is of the population from which it is drawn. Over the years, techniques designed to increase the randomness of the sample have become increasingly sophisticated. Still, what is difficult to control in practice is eliciting responses from the prospective respondents in the sample. If all respondents respond, the survey may be deemed valid. But, with each case in the sample remaining absent or giving a meaningless or spurious response, the measurement rod of the survey is distorted. In social science research, as a matter of convention, more than 5 percent of nonresponding cases is often considered to be invalid research. But when the nonresponse rate exceeds 10, 15, 25, or even close to 50 percent, the survey results are deemed extremely problematic. Although national surveys do not disclose this flaw (because no one asks them), at the time of this writing most such surveys are suffering from this shortcoming. The prestigious General Social Survey (GSS) of the University of Chicago is no exception unless the way it manages the nonresponse rate is clearly explained.

Thus, to reject every other finding as being out of hand merely because it does not conform with the survey findings is open to serious questions. We would expect Tom Smith, an accomplished surveyor, to try to search for techniques that would encourage those who generally do not respond to heed the survey caller's request. To believe that Muslims do respond to the surveys like most others, because most of the Muslims are educated, highly trained professionals and quite successful in life, is to forget that most of these relatively newcomers to America are, to recall Robert Park's (1908) descriptor, "marginal men" and probably will remain so despite their success in the United States. Most Muslims, like most other very successful immigrants, belong to their own subculture; that is, they interact mostly with other Muslims, mostly marry within their own religious community, and remain most interested in happenings in the Muslim world. Most have very specialized and relatively limited vocabularies. Lastly, like most other immigrants to the United States, they are timid to a degree and "do not know the ropes."

METHODOLOGY

Our point of departure was the list of the mosques prepared by Bagby, Perl, and Froehle (2001). Additionally, mailing lists of a number of local, metropolitan, regional, and national Muslim organizations—including the

Islamic Society of North America (ISNA), the Islamic Circle of North America (ICNA), the American Islamic Mission (AIM), the Muslim American Society (MAS), and the Islamic Association of North America (IANA)—were used to locate different Islamic centers and communities, mosques, and other educational and worshiping facilities across the United States and Canada, especially to estimate the size of their respective constituencies. Annual community reports, historical records, and interviews with the old-timers, if and when available, provided further insight. Overall, sixteen small and large listings consisting of the names and addresses of institutions of Islamic worship were available for this study. An effort was made to compare, verify, and update these listings outside as well as inside major metropolitan areas by seeking help from informants randomly picked from those active in Islamic work in different regions.

Originally, the number of informants used in this study was 1,550, or 31 informants per state, a number that was in the end reduced to 1,315, or fewer than 26 informants per state. Quite significantly, a number of Muslim taxi owners/drivers were used as informants in large metropolitan areas (Boston, New York, Philadelphia, Washington, D.C., Atlanta, Detroit, Chicago, Houston, and Los Angeles) to locate otherwise difficult-to-find local *masajid* (mosque). They also helped us in collecting data from more than one local masjid, thus compensating for the loss of more than two hundred informants.

The main task of the informant was to check correspondence or mailing lists from each Islamic institution and update it with the help of the administration or other interested parties at that place, thus providing us with correct data while, at the same time, providing that institution a crucial service. Moreover, these informants were requested to randomly pick only two names from the lists and, after checking these individuals for their age, sex, and ethnicity, ask them the following questions:

1. Are you on the mailing list of any other mosque and/or school?
2. How many people are actually living at this address?
3. How many of them are males?
4. What is the age of each male in your household?
5. What is the age of each female in your household?
6. How many people were in the household five years ago and ten years ago?
7. Please specify the professions that you and others in your household are in.
8. How many of you in your house identify yourselves as (a) African American, (b) White American, (c) Hispanic, (d) Arab, (e) Pakistani, (f) Indian, (g) Turkish, (h) Iranian, (i) African, or (j) other?

For the purpose of this study, we distinguished among several types of Islamic activity. First, an Islamic center or a Muslim community center was defined as a place that generates various activities other than the five daily prayers and the Juma congregation. Most Islamic centers hold weekly Quranic study sessions, regular community dinners, women's programs, weekend schools, picnics and other outdoor and indoor activities, besides symposia and speeches by Muslim as well as non-Muslim speakers. These centers, especially in large cities, could be old community houses, church or school buildings bought by the Muslims, or even homes or apartments converted into Islamic facilities. Or, they are newly built multipurpose mosques in the suburbs. A large number of them, especially outside large metropolitan areas, are now newly built structures often reflecting Islamic architecture, featuring a dome or a minaret, for instance. Whatever the case, each center is supported by and betrays the existence of an expanding and relatively prosperous Muslim community in the surrounding territory. There is no doubt that the Islamic center has now become an integral part of mainstream religious culture in the United States as well as in Canada, showing that Islam has taken root and is prospering here.

Excluded from this definition are what may be called the masjid or neighborhood mosque, which holds five daily prayers in addition to the Juma prayers. There are numerous such neighborhood *masajid* (plural of *masjid*), or mosques, especially in large cities. They are mostly unregistered and unlisted in telephone directories. These smaller grassroots institutions generally serve those, who because of age, sickness, part-time jobs, or new arrivals, stay home or do not live in the close vicinity of an Islamic center. Additionally, those who take advantage of such facilities could be transients, day laborers, or taxi drivers who need and want to have a convenient place to congregate at prayer times. These could be in the basements of large apartment buildings, abandoned stores, and other unclaimed structures the city is happy to see being used. Most researchers in the past have ignored the existence of such neighborhood masajid (an exception being *The Center Finder*, a now-suspended publication of the Chicago chapter of ICNA), thus underestimating presumably the fastest-growing number of places of Islamic congregation.

Because most of them do not have any published addresses, these neighborhood mosques are difficult to locate. They are much less expensive to establish and maintain. Besides, they are more convenient than the much larger Islamic centers. Muslim taxi owners/drivers, as mentioned earlier, played an important role as informants in locating these centers of worship.

Also, large cities have facilities established for the expressed purpose of holding Friday congregation. Let us call them part-time *musallas*, because such facilities usually come to life only once a week for Juma congregations, at given times, usually 12:30 to 2 p.m. Almost exclusively they serve those who are working in the neighboring district in their jobs as professionals. Many, if not most of them, may otherwise be members of or benefit from major Islamic centers in the city. These part-time musallas are relatively much easier to locate because, in most cases, they are registered organizations raising funds besides having their addresses published.

Additionally, there are recently emergent educational organizations that offer nearly all those activities seen in an Islamic center but with a main focus on full-time education of Muslim children. Thus, while the Islamic centers run part- or full-time schools among their various functions, educational organizations focus mainly on schooling while at the same time providing for the functions of full-time Islamic centers.

Last but not least in importance are MSAs on several campuses. The largest of such MSAs, such as the one at the University of Michigan at Ann Arbor or the University of Illinois at Urbana-Champaign, may have a few thousand Muslim students each. In general, on a campus where you may have fewer than ten Muslim students on average, you may still find an MSA (though not necessarily using the name MSA), which, often in cooperation with the Muslim families in the neighboring area, if they are available, maintains a facility or a place where Muslim students as well as the families can get together in at least Friday congregation. In fact, the Muslim Students Association of the United States and Canada, registered in Illinois in 1963, is a national organization that has been in the forefront of most patterns of organized Islamic activity in North America since the early 1960s. Because there are no mosques on most campuses, Muslim students conduct their activity in houses that they rent or purchase near the campus, in interfaith chapels, in reserved rooms in student unions, or in the basements of nearby churches.

What is important about these Islamic centers, the neighborhood masajid, or mosques, the musallas, the schools, and the MSAs, is that most of them maintain a mailing or correspondence list mainly to inform people of important events, raise funds for running the facility, give salaries to its employees (the imam being one of them), pay bills, keep records, and so forth. The correspondence or the mailing list is not to be confused with the membership list, which most often is very small. Correspondence lists, on the other hand, are relatively huge. For instance, the Islamic Center of Central New York at Syracuse has only eighty-five households as members, but it has a mailing list consisting of more than six hundred addresses. The Islamic Center of Missouri at St. Louis has a membership list of only about eight hundred but a mailing list exceeding eight thousand. These lists are updated periodically by each organization. For the purpose of this study, names appearing on these lists with the same address and telephone number were defined as a household—a family or a few individuals living at the same address.

The method adopted appears to be quite simple but proved to be quite cumbersome. Responsible persons (the president of the board, the imam or the secretary, and even some old-timers) of the Islamic centers, the neighborhood masajid, the musallas, full-time schools, and MSAs were requested to provide to the informants their correspondence lists and also the membership records, which later proved to be quite irrelevant. This was so because the membership list is only a fraction of the total population living in the surrounding areas. Additionally, they were requested to provide us past listings (for any number of years) if possible. Informants and the administrators then worked together to find names with the same addresses in order to lump them together as households.

In short, the method used in this research was to bypass survey techniques based on drawing random samples and generalizing from them. The method was aimed at 100 percent coverage—more like the use of the short form by the U.S. Bureau of Census.

FINDINGS

Muslim Demographic History in the United States

As mentioned earlier, there is growing speculation that the Muslims, especially those from Africa, discovered America before Columbus. After scanning several fragmented records and claims, Nyang (1999) concludes, "[R]egardless of how one may feel about the evidence, the fact remains that Muslims or persons believed to be Muslims visited this part of the world in the pre-Columbian past" (p. 12).

Whatever the nature of these speculations, historical records show that the very first Muslims who came to North America were Africans who came involuntarily as slaves imported from West Africa. Muslim names start appearing in slave documents as early as 1717 (Austin 1984; Mehdi 1978; Poston 1992). Because most of them were trapped in the Senegambia region where Islam had already made deep inroads, many of these slaves were Muslims. According to some estimates (Austin 1984), at least 10 percent of them came from established Muslim communities in Africa. Haley's (1976) *Roots* is based on a similar folklore among African Americans in the United States.

However, voluntary migration of Muslims to the United States started in the latter half of the nineteenth century, coinciding with the largest (so far) and longest migratory episode in America, mostly from Europe. It continued for almost fifty years, from the early 1870s to 1920, the year it was canceled by an act of Congress. According to Weeks and Siddiqui (1993), this chain migration yielded some thirty-five million immigrants in the United States.

How many of these immigrants were Muslims is anybody's guess. There must have been quite a few. Mosques and Islamic centers erected by these late-nineteenth-century immigrants still exist in and around large metropolitan areas such as New York, Philadelphia, Boston, Detroit, Chicago, Los Angeles, and San Francisco, to name just a few. Such Islamic centers also existed in such medium-sized cities as Jersey City, New Jersey; Springfield, Massachusetts; Manchester, New Hampshire; Indiana City, Michigan; Gary, Indiana; Decatur, Illinois; Cedar Rapids, Iowa; Joplin, Missouri; Omaha, Nebraska; Tucson, Arizona; and Sacramento, California, in addition to a number of smaller mosques that were abandoned and, therefore, disappeared as a very mobile Muslim population shifted locations.

A relatively unnoticed group of Muslims dating back to this time has been that of the indentured laborers of Punjabi origin (from what is now Pakistan), who were imported in British Columbia mostly as farmhands in the middle of the nineteenth century. According to Alam (1968), toward the beginning of the twentieth century many of these workers had already moved southward to settle in the Stockton valley of California. The descendants of these laborers are still found in large numbers in Stockton, Sacramento, and the San Francisco Bay area, where they are mostly self-employed as middlemen, restaurant owners, and hotel and innkeepers.

The second wave of massive migration comparable to that in the nineteenth century started almost one hundred years ago and is still in progress. At this writing, it has already been going on for over fifty years. Starting in the 1950s, it became a deluge under the Johnson administration's open immigration policy in 1965. What distinguishes it is that this massive immigration, contrary to all expectations among American legislators, hit a responsive chord in the third world countries, while Western Europeans, curiously enough, remained by and large unresponsive. For instance, during the 1980s, close to seven million immigrants came from Asia, Latin America, and southeastern Europe, compared with just about half a million from Western Europe (Rumbaut 1994: table 1). This illustrates the immigration explosion of non-European populations in the United States this time around.

It is evident (Weeks 1989:261) that this migration, open-ended so far, yielded more than twenty-five million immigrants between 1970 and 2000. How many of these are Muslims is only a part of the picture that our report presents.

Where in the United States Do They Live?

Immigration to the United States in the latter half of the twentieth century has not been exclusively due to the open immigration policy (short-lived as it was) of the Johnson administration. Concurrently, the asylum seekers and the refugees from nearly all over the world have been and are being allowed entry into the United States. Although 650,000 immigrants are allowed entry each year, additionally a total of 600,000 refugees were also allowed to enter during the latter half of the twentieth century (Weeks 1989:252). A majority of these refugees, as mentioned earlier, could have originated in Muslim-majority countries. Besides, there has also been a substantial rise in work visas (in most cases changeable to immigrant status and eventually to citizenship) granted, especially to the high-tech specialists mostly from third world countries—overwhelmingly from India, with a huge absolute volume of the Muslim population (almost 150 million).

However, more than half a million immigrants who are granted entry visas in this country are directly or indirectly related to the Johnson administration's open immigration policy during the latter half of the 1960s. In the five years before the decade was out, this policy yielded slightly more than three million immigrants (Weeks 1989:205) before it was rather hastily withdrawn in 1970 under the Nixon administration.

The 1960s, then, could be taken as a turning point in the demographic history of Muslims in North America. Never before have Muslims been allowed to immigrate to the United States as well as Canada in such large numbers, in such a continuous fashion and over such a long time (almost four decades by the time of this writing and still continuing).

Consequently, the Muslim presence in the United States and Canada is quickly becoming visible. In 1960, for example, there were only 150 Muslim students at the University of Minnesota in the Minneapolis and St. Paul areas, and the number of nonstudent Muslims was unknown. In 2000, there were over three hundred Muslim students at the same university, with about two thousand Muslim families living in the Twin Cities and surrounding suburbs. Like most other new immigrants and many African Americans, most Muslims prefer to live in or close to large metropolitan areas such as Los Angeles, New York, Chicago, Detroit, Philadelphia, Houston, Boston, Dallas, St. Louis, Atlanta, and Washington, D.C., and their suburbs. Furthermore, a quick telephone survey of fifteen randomly picked cities with populations over one hundred thousand, conducted in August 2002, shows that each one of them has at least one Islamic center and two neighborhood mosques. This shows an overwhelmingly urban character of Muslims—immigrants or indigenous—in the United States.

Moreover, Muslims are spilling over into smaller towns in growing numbers lately. Utica, New York (population: fifty thousand), had less than ten Muslim families in 1970. Their number grew to around 250 families in 2002 (interview with Dr. M. Omar, Utica, New York, 2002). Besides, in 2000, according to the Mohawk Valley Resource Center for Refugees, there were more than four thousand people of Bosnian origin living in Utica (Hassett 2002).

A quick check of the membership lists of the ISNA as well as the Muslim American Society (MAS), the largest body of African American Muslims, shows that Muslims as professionals—doctors, educators, engineers, computer scientists, and small businessmen—have begun to move and are now living in relatively smaller cities and towns such as Muncie, Indiana; Cortland, New York; Winona, Minnesota; Edmund, Oklahoma; Waco, Texas;

Pullman, Washington; and Panama City, Florida. This spilling over of the Muslim population from major metropolitan areas into smaller cities and townships not only shows the ease with which Muslim individuals and families are able to move into small-town America. It also reflects the growing demand for Muslim talent across the board on this continent.

Not all of these Muslims moving in smaller towns are new immigrants or their offspring. Towns such as Lakhwana, New York; Dearborn, Michigan; Gary, Indiana; and Cedar Rapids, Iowa, have second- and even third-generation Muslims whose parents or grandparents worked in steel factories, farming, import/export, real state, and the food industry.

Likewise, African American Muslims, who were concentrated mainly in large cities, have more recently fanned out to relatively smaller places like Peoria, Illinois; York, Pennsylvania; Ponca City, Oklahoma; Joplin, Missouri; Tustin, California; and Gary, Indiana, among others. They have established their own mosques either in cooperation with or in addition to other mosques or Islamic centers in their respective cities or towns.

How Many and Where?

In our estimation in this project, there are 5,745,100 Muslim men and women of all ages living in the United States today. Of these, only 3,953,651, or about 69 percent, were born as naturalized citizens. Of the rest, a total of 1,321,011, or 23 percent, were legal immigrants. Of the rest, there were foreign students as well as those on professional and business visas. We were able to locate a total of 1,751 Islamic institutions. However, because of nonavailability or disarray with respect to mailing lists, we were able to receive information from only 1,510 (87 percent). Of these, 801 (53 percent) were Islamic centers; 194 (13 percent) were neighborhood masajid, or mosques; 101 (7 percent) were musallas; 199 (13 percent) were full-time schools; and 215 (14 percent) were MSAs. Of these, 437, or 29 percent, were run by people of Arab background; 392 (almost 26 percent) were run mainly by African American Muslims; and 379 (about 25 percent) were administered by South Asian Muslims. The mosques or the musallas run by the MSAs, composed of 187,015 college students (including foreign students), constitute a little more than 3 percent of the total Muslim population. They were typically multiethnic. The rest of the institutions were run by Turks, Bosnians, Malaysians, and Somalis, among others.

Overall, there was an overlap of 14,487 names that we addressed. Most of this overlap was detected in the listings of the musallas where people mostly go for the Juma or Friday congregation only. The total number of households attached with all Islamic institutions in this study was 1,149,100, yielding an average of close to 766 households per institution.

Table 11.1. Concentration of the Muslim Population

State	Number of Islamic Institutions	Population
New York	126	579,152
Illinois	112	381,155
California	143	310,538*
New Jersey	105	208,210
Pennsylvania	61	281,455
Michigan	51	272,380
Massachusetts	48	272,273
Maryland	25	251,185
Texas	63	211,031
Georgia	25	121,379
Florida	15	105,101
Total	774	2,993,859

*Data from two Islamic centers and eleven mosques were lost.
This figure was computed by the missing-data technique.

Furthermore, our informants collected data from 2,852 households picked randomly from the correspondence lists. From these, we randomly selected a subsample of 1,000 households. Our computations show that the average size of Muslim households, attached to these institutions, is a little over five individuals.

The distribution of the Muslim population in the United States is far from uniform. We found that 774, or slightly more than 50 percent of the institutions of Islamic worship, comprising almost three million Muslims, live in only eleven states (see table 11.1), with an average of about 260,000 Muslims in each of these eleven states. Therefore, the rest of the forty-one states have only about seventy thousand Muslims each. A majority of these eleven states of relatively higher Muslim density (New York, New Jersey, Pennsylvania, Massachusetts, Maryland, Georgia, and Florida) are on the East Coast. Three of them (Illinois, Texas, and Michigan) are in the Midwest. All of them except two (Texas and California) are to the east of the Mississippi River. Only California, with the largest number of Islamic institutions, is on the West Coast.

Household Size and Structure

Out of a total of close to 1 million, our informants were able to collect most information requested of them from 2,852 households. Because of time constraints, we drew a sample of one thousand from these for further analysis, as mentioned earlier. We found that the overall average size of the Muslim household was about 5.5, including all adults as well as minors of both sexes using the same address and the telephone number (710, or about 70 percent, had more than one telephone or at least one cellular telephone).

Table 11.2. Age/Sex Structure in the Sample

Age	Male		Female		Total		
	N	Percentage	N	Percentage	N	Percentage	Sex Ratio*
1–20	658	51	630	49	1,288	25	104
21–40	532	48	585	52	1,117	22	92
41–60	739	50	746	50	1,485	29	100
61–80	562	50	558	50	1,120	22	101
80+	64	58	46	42	110	2	152
Total	2,555	50	2,565	50	5,120	100	100

*Rounded to the nearest whole number.

Because many of our subjects did not remember or were reluctant to reveal the real ages of their dependents, we used broader (twenty-year) age categories than usual (table 11.2). Table 11.2, presenting the Muslim population in the United States as a whole, shows the pattern of a newly immigrant population with the largest concentration (54 percent) in working-age categories (twenty-one to sixty). However, it seems to be assuming a youthful character with an expanding base (25 percent under age twenty). Table 11.2 also shows substantial numbers (20 percent) in preretirement- and retired-age categories. This seems to be a bias due to the broader than usual age categories that we used. A fine-tuning could have shown that a majority of those in these categories would be closer to sixty than eighty years old.

Table 11.2 also shows that the males and the females among Muslim in the United States are almost equally divided with a total rounded sex ratio (number of males per one hundred females) at 100, although a closer look shows that overall females outnumber males by a slight margin. Although males conspicuously outnumber females in the youngest-age category (one to twenty), in the next two age categories, when combined together, females seem to outnumber males (a combined sex ratio of 96). However, when you combine the next two age categories, you may find that there are conspicuously more grandfathers than grandmothers in the Muslim households, with a sex ratio of 126, meaning that there are 126 males for every 100 females in this late age.

ETHNICITY

Muslims in the United States are ethnically a highly diverse population. Indeed, the ethnic composition of this population shows the extent to which Islam spread in the world during the past fourteen centuries.

The largest single group in our sample (close to 32 percent) comprise people of Arabic origin. On the whole, it may translate to 1.8 million Arabs and their first- and second-generation descendants. They are followed by the American Muslims (mostly African American) with 29 percent in the sample, or 1.7 million on the whole. A close third are South Asians (from Pakistan, India, Bangladesh, Ceylon, Afghanistan, and Maldives) with 28.9 percent, or 1.6 million. Then, there are 5 percent (close to 290,000) Turks and 2 percent (115,000) Iranians and Bosnians. The rest are Kosovars, Malays, Indonesians, and others.

PROFESSION

According to table 11.2, 2,602, or about 51 percent in our sample, are in the middle of working age. Some must have been left unaccounted for because of the age category 61–80, which includes more than mere retired persons. Likewise, some who are working full-time do not appear in the age category 1–20, either. If this is the case, we think we located these invisible data, for in our subsample we found that a total of 3,100 of our respondents were working full-time (see table 11.3).

As is evident, the professional distribution of Muslims betrays their high level of education and income. Most of them (86 percent) are concentrated in three professions: engineering and electronics, computer science and data processing, and medical doctors and various related professions.

Table 11.3. Muslim Males and Females in Professions*

Profession	Male		Female		Total	
	N	Percentage	N	Percentage	N	Percentage
Engineering/electronics	866	28	744	24	1,610	52
Computer science/data processing	435	14	371	12	806	26
Medicine/doctors and others	122	4	126	4	248	8
Business/Finance	125	4	92	3	217	7
Self-employed	94	3	60	2	154	5
Professor Teacher, imam	19	0.6	12	0.4	31	1
Lawyer/police/politics	13	0.4	6	0.2	19	0.6
Other	9	0.3	6	0.2	15	0.5
Total	1,683	54	1,417	46	3,100	100

*Percentages are rounded to the nearest whole.

Teaching and law are not the most favored professions. Substantial numbers work in business and finance professions (7 percent), and a few are self-employed (5 percent). The "other" category includes such professions as journalism, social work, taxi driver, and auto sales.

What is significant is the relative visibility of females in the full-time workforce, especially in elite professions (40 percent). Still, the workforce sex ratio (119 males for every 100 females) favors the male worker. Presumably, then, quite a few Muslim females are housewives.

GROWTH

Our efforts to find correspondence lists from several Islamic centers proved to be unreliable or too few to generalize from. Also, because we did not have specific data on birth-, death, migration, and conversion rates, we had to estimate the growth of the Muslim population mainly through the respondents in our sample. However, in our sample, we could not get reliable information on these households beyond five years in the past. Table 11.4 shows that 32 of these 1,000 households in 2000 did not exist in 1999. Likewise, there were only 855 households in 1995, giving us an overall 30 percent increase in the five-year period.

It is also evident from this table that as the number of the Muslim households increased, so did their population. The 855 households that existed in 1995 had a total population of 4,260, with about 5 members per household. Their number has been growing at an overall rate of 3 percent per year, giving us a total of 4,936 for 1,000 homes in the sample in 2000. At this rate, this population promises to double itself in less than twenty-five years. Thus, although it may be risky to do so, and barring any serious interruptions, one could expect that soon after 2020, the American Muslim population would be substantially in excess of 11.5 million, or more than 3 percent of the projected national population.

Table 11.4.   Growth Rate of the American Muslim Population

Year	Number of Households	Total Population	Growth Rate*
1995	855	4,260	—
1996	877	4,385	3
1997	883	4,416	3
1998	929	4,646	4
1999	968	4,836	2
2000	1,000	4,936	3

*Rounded to the nearest whole number.

CONCLUSION

Perhaps one day the U.S. Census will start asking questions regarding religious affiliation, for the American religious landscape has changed drastically, especially since the beginning of the 1970s. A population once used to having immigrants mainly from European countries is now facing a huge influx of people migrating from the third world. In just about two decades after new immigration policy was instituted in 1965, the Asians came to dominate immigration rates with 48 percent, followed by Latin Americans with 35 percent—together totaling, then, more than 80 percent of the immigrants to the United States (Bouvier and Gardner 1986:17).

These new immigrants have contributed to religious diversity as never experienced before in the United States. Nowadays we find Americans who pursue, in addition to the traditional Protestant, Catholic, and Jewish denominations, religions such as Islam, Buddhism, Hinduism, Sikhism, Taoism, Bahaism, and a score of other previously rather unknown faiths. In addition to attracting purely academic curiosity, this new religious mosaic has attained great political and economic significance as well.

Among these new American religions, it seems that Islam stands out as being the object of exceeding scrutiny and scholarly pursuits. However, above all what this chapter highlights is that, while the census is not perfect itself, a population not covered by the census is difficult, if not impossible, to estimate with accuracy. None of the alternative methods is perfect, either. While "guesstimates" may often be beset with the subjective biases and selective perceptions of their authors, the census, the most rigorous of all attempts at estimating a population, seems to undershoot the target. Even the U.S. Census cannot claim to be an exception to this rule.

Thus, while the estimates of the Muslim population in the United States of about 10 million cannot be substantiated, the claim of the best estimates that put it between 1.9 and 2.8 million seems to be equally untenable. Simple calculations support this opinion. Let us take the higher of these two figures and round it out to the nearest whole: three million. Should this number be accurate, how many of these individuals are foreign-born? If we assume that of these three million Muslims, native-born people (indigenous as well as children born to immigrant Muslims) constitute only one million (which seems to be a gross underestimation), then we are left with only two million foreign-born Muslims. Considering that, since the 1960s, the United States has admitted about thirty million immigrants, this figure, amounting to less than 7 percent of total immigration since the 1960s, looks awfully low, especially in view of the fact that Asia, with the largest concentration of the Muslim population in the world, has seen the most people emigrate to the United States. If we assume that of these 3 million Muslims, one-half, or 1.5 million, are native-born, then the proportion of immigrant Muslims is reduced to only 5 percent of the total migratory volume in the United States during the period under consideration. Such a claim is like saying that while the people of the whole underdeveloped world in general are seeking an opportunity to migrate to the United States, the Muslim people of the world remain tied to their homelands. The push-pull hypothesis would not support this assumption. Most Muslims in the world are living under some of the most dictatorial or oppressive regimes; and, contrary to what many might believe, Muslims are some of the most literate people in the third world and may, therefore, be relatively more knowledgeable about and more prone to the lure of better prospects in the United States.

Our data show that there may not be fewer than 5,745,100 Muslim men and women of all ages in the United States today. However, not surprisingly, this figure seems to be an underestimation, although we cannot say by how much. As mentioned earlier, we received information from 1,510, or only 86 percent, of 1,751 Islamic institutions due mainly to disarray or absence of mailing lists. This lack of information must have a downward effect on our findings. Other than most MSAs on our list, a number of small-town Islamic centers as well as a few neighborhood mosques are responsible for this deficiency in our report. Besides, it is almost certain that some Muslim individuals as well as households might not have appeared in the mailing lists of these institutions. Moreover, a large number of Muslim prison inmates could not be included in this research. We suspect also that we must have undercounted the number of MSAs, thus grossly underestimating the Muslim student population on college campuses.

Lastly, a large number of Muslims belonging to sects other than the dominant Sunni also escaped notice, for a great many of them rarely participate in Sunni institutions. According to the latest estimate, the Shia Muslim community in the United States is composed of 157,238 households (Hussein 2002). If their average household size is also around 5 individuals, then their total number may be in the neighborhood of 786,000. Thus, the total size of the Muslim population in the United States must be exceeding our estimate by a wide margin.

Other than these two sects of Islam in the United States, there are many who claim to be Muslims although they may not be recognized as such by the two dominant Islamic sects. For instance, the Ahmedies, an offshoot from the Sunni sect, and the Aghakhanis, from the Shia, are considered to be beyond the outer fringes of Islam, although they claim to be Muslims. Likewise, in this report we could not include the followers of the Nation of Islam led by Louis Farrakhan, who declared his adherence to the mainstream (presumably Sunni) Islam soon after this project was initiated. Thus, it seems that our findings as to the number of Muslims in the United States are closer to the estimation by Bagby and associates (2001) than to that by Smith (2001).

NOTE

This paper was made possible also by a partial grants from Islamic Studies Institute at East West University.

REFERENCES

Alam, Mahmoud. 1968. "Muslim Organizations in America." Paper presented at the Sixth Annual 1968 Convention of Muslim Students Association of U.S. and Canada, Green Lakes, Wisconsin.

Austin, Allen D. 1984. *African Muslims in Ante-Bellum America: A Source Book.* New York: Garland.

Bagby, Ihsan, Paul M. Perl, and Bryan T. Froehle. 2001. *The Mosque in America: A National Portrait.* Washington, D.C.: Council for American-Islamic Relations.

Ba-Yunus, Ilyas, 1997. "Muslims of Illinois: A Demographic Report." *East West Review* (Summer), Special Supplement.

Ba-Yunus, Ilyas, and M. Moin Siddiqui. 1998. *A Report on Muslim Population in the United States of America.* New York: Center for American Muslim Research and Information.

Bouvier, Leon F., and Robert W. Gardner. 1986. "Immigration to the U.S.: The Unfinished Story." *Population Bulletin* 41, no. 4 (November).

Davidson, Basil. 1959. *Lost Cities of Africa.* Boston: Little, Brown.

The Economist. 2002. "A Year of Living Nervously." September 17, pp. 29–30.

Ghayur, Arif. 1981. "Muslims in the United States: Settlers and Visitors." *Annals of the American Academy of Social and Political Sciences* 454 (March).

Goldman, Ari. 1991. "Portrait of Religion in U.S. Holds Dozens of Surprises." *New York Times,* April 10.

Haddad, Yvonne. 1986. "Muslims in America." *Muslim World* 76, no. 2.

Haley, Alex. 1976. *Roots.* New York: Doubleday.

Hassett, Kelly. 2002. "E. Utica Becomes a Heaven for Bosnians." *Observer-Dispatch.*

Herberg, Will. 1955. *Protestant-Catholic-Jew.* Garden City, N.Y.: Doubleday.

Hussein, Adil S. 2002. Shia Muslims in America. Annual report of the Shia Institute. Toronto: Shia Institute.

Isbister, John. 1996. *Immigration Debate.* West Hartford, Conn.: Kumarian.

Kosmin, Barry. 1989. *Research Report: The National Survey of Religious Identifications.* New York: City University of New York Graduate School and University Center.

Mehdi, Beverlee T. 1978. *The Arabs in America, 1492–1977.* New York: Oceana.

Newland, Kathleen. 1979. *International Migration: The Search for Work.* Washington, D.C: Worldwatch Institute.

Nyang, Sulayman S. 1999. *Islam in the United States of America.* Chicago: ABC International Group.

Oatling, Richard N. 1988. "Americans Facing toward Mecca." *Time,* March 23.

Park, Robert E. 1980. "Human Migration and the Marginal Man." *American Journal of Sociology* 33: 881–93.

Phillip, Thomas. 1980. "Muslims." In *The Harvard Encyclopedia of American Ethnic Groups,* ed. Stephen Rhornstorm. Cambridge, Mass.: Harvard University Press.

Poston, Larry. 1992. *Islamic Dawah in the West.* New York: Pantheon.

Quick, Abdullah H. 1996. *Deeper Roots of Muslims in the Americas and the Caribbean from before Columbus to the Present.* Boston: Taha.

Rumbaut, R. 1994. "Origins and Destinies: Immigration to the United States since WW II." *Sociological Forum* 9, no. 4.

Sertima, Ivan Van. 1976. *They Came before Columbus.* New York: Random House.

Smith, Tom W. 2001. "Estimating the Muslim Population in the United States." Unpublished report. Chicago: National Opinion Research Center, University of Chicago.

Stone, Carol. 1991. "Estimate of Muslims Living in America." In *Muslims in America,* ed. Yvonne Haddad. New York: Oxford University Press.

Weeks, John R. 1989. *Population: An Introduction to Concepts and Issues.* 4th ed. Belmont, Calif.: Wadsworth.

Weeks, John R., and M. Moin Siddiqui. 1993. *The Muslim Population of the United States: A Pilot Project.* San Diego, Calif.: International Population Center, San Diego State University.

Wiener, Lee. 1922. *Africa and the Discovery of America.* Philadelphia: Innes.

12

The Mosque and the American Public Square

Ihsan Bagby

This chapter explores the relationship of American mosques to the American public square by studying the attitudes and activities of mosques related to community involvement. For our purposes, *community involvement* refers to social services, especially to those outside the mosque, and *outreach* to local faith groups, schools, and media. The essential question underlying the issue of the mosque's relationship to the public square is whether the mosques of America are following a path of isolation from and resistance to the dominant American culture or a path of involvement and accommodation. The logical correlation is that if mosques are willing to be involved in their local community, they are more likely to follow a strategy of engagement and accommodation and not a strategy of isolation and resistance. In the aftermath of 9/11 and in light of the faith-based initiative, which seeks the involvement of religious groups in government-sponsored social services, the direction of mosques is a significant concern.

This question can be framed within the sociological discussion of church–sect typology. Beginning with Max Weber (1946) and his student Ernst Troeltsch (1931), sociologists have described a type of religious group that resists integration into the social order and opts for establishing a separate subculture; this group is defined as a *sect*. Another type of religious group embraces the dominant culture and accommodates the society's cultural norms into their religious experience; this group is termed a *church* (Dynes 1955; Johnson 1963; O'Dea 1966). Stark and Bainbridge (1985) depict the church–sect typology as a continuum, and the operational variable is the degree of tension between the religious group and the dominant culture (i.e., tension caused by the acceptance or rejection on the part of both entities). The theory postulates that the greater the tension, the greater the sectarian nature of the group; the lesser the tension, the lesser the sectarian behavior of the group. High-tension religious groups build the highest walls around their community, medium-tension groups maintain visible but modest barriers, and low-tension groups have few demarcated boundaries.

Immigrant religious groups, such as the Catholics in the 1800s, often experience tension with the dominant society, and as a result they exhibit "sectarian" characteristics. The Catholics in that period, confronting a self-confident Anglo, Protestant culture, resisted "Americanization" and opted to establish their own separate schools (Stark and Bainbridge 1985:65; Leckie 1970; Linkh 1975). Many Christian fundamentalist and evangelical groups experience tension with the dominant society and exhibit sectarian behavior, as evidenced by their reluctance to be polluted by the "world" and the low priority they give to community involvement (Hunter 1983:68; Ammerman 1987). Involvement outside the religious group, therefore, is not a general characteristic of a high-tension group—a group that rejects its social environment.

How high are the barriers between the mosque and the dominant society? Where are the mosques on the church–sect continuum? This chapter is not intended to answer these questions fully, but by focusing on the mosque's level of community involvement, it can give some indications of what the answers might be. The extent of mosque involvement in the public square gives a clear indication of whether mosques are seeking a sectarian existence of isolation or a greater church existence of acceptance and engagement in the dominant culture.

The data used in this chapter are taken from *The Mosque in America: A National Portrait* (Bagby, Perl, and Froehle 2001), a comprehensive study of mosques based on telephone interviews with 416 mosque leaders, who were randomly sampled from a list of 1,209 mosques. The Mosque in America study, conducted in 2000, was part of FACT (Faith Communities Today) (2001), a wider study of all religious congregations coordinated by the Hartford Seminary. Comments by interviewees during the interviews and comments from follow-up interviews with nine mosque leaders, which were conducted after 9/11, were also used in this chapter.

The clear picture that emerges from the data is that mosque leaders in the United States accept almost unanimously the idea that Muslims should be involved in American society. It is also clear that mosques are actively involved in providing community services and participating in outreach activities, especially African American mosques and to a lesser extent immigrant mosques. In fact, the overall rate of mosque involvement is similar to other religious congregations in the United States as determined in the FACT study. Mosque programming in social services and outreach, however, are in their initial stages of development, as reflected in their limited scope and lack of institutional infrastructure.

ATTITUDES OF MOSQUE LEADERS TOWARD INVOLVEMENT

The willingness of mosques to be involved in the American public square is demonstrated decisively in the attitudes of mosque leaders. Mosque leaders were asked whether they agreed or disagreed with the statement "Muslims should be involved in America institutions." Their responses are presented in table 12.1.

The virtually unanimous view (96 percent) is that mosque leaders want to see Muslims involved in American society—they do not envision a community isolated from the American society. Javeed Akhter, a Muslim leader in Chicago, expresses this vision when he writes:

> They must resist the understandable tendency towards self imposed isolation and avoid a retreat into the mosques and community centers. Moreover, if they isolate themselves, they will merely succeed in creating their own ghetto. They cannot ignore the problems around them, hoping to remain immune to them. Muslims must remember the Quranic injunctions to be a people of knowledge, compassion and patience, striving for positive change in the communities in which they live. (Husain, Woods, and, Akhter, 1996:81)

Based on their comments, mosque leaders describe involvement in American institutions in terms of the following types of activities: (1) social services and community activism, which might include antidrug programs, anticrime programs, feeding the hungry, and so forth; and (2) involvement with the media, churches, and educational institutions in order to improve the image of Islam.

The motivation of mosque leaders to advocate community involvement springs from a deep religious impulse founded in the Quranic ideals of doing good deeds (2:82), cooperating with others in righteousness (5:3), commanding good and forbidding evil (3:110), protecting the weak (107:2), feeding the hungry (76:8–9), expressing kindness to the needy (4:36), and standing up for justice (4:135). Other motivations include the command of God to invite others to Islam (41:33–34) and the immediate need of improving the image of Muslims and protecting the rights of Muslims.

Table 12.1.   Responses to the Statement "Muslims Should Be Involved in American Institutions"

Response	Percentage*
Strongly agree	77
Somewhat agree	19
Somewhat disagree	2
Strongly disagree	2

*"Don't know" excluded from the percentages.

Over three-fourths (77 percent) of mosque leaders "strongly agree" that Muslims should be involved. One leader explained, "Community involvement is a high priority for us. The majority of people want it. We have to show [to] our neighbors our community to improve the picture of Muslims. We want to get involved in areas that affect our [general] community the most like education, drugs, abortion, gambling. We want to cooperate with others." An African American leader reflected, "How can you have a *masjid* [neighborhood mosque] and have drugs and prostitution around it? That's a contradiction. You see churches padlocked and all kinds of things going on around it. Muslims have to purify their neighborhood."

Those who "somewhat agree" explain their answer most often in terms of priorities. They agree that community involvement is good but do not feel that it should be a high priority. A leader lamented, "Our masjid is totally consumed in running this school, and we don't have the energy for anything else."

Those few leaders who "somewhat" or "strongly disagree" either believe that this should not be the priority agenda for Muslims or feel that involvement in public affairs entails entanglements with the government or interfaith work. Working with the government or other faith groups, for these leaders, is suspect, if not outright prohibited. One leader commented on the situation in his mosque, "There is some question among our board members on the [Islamic] legality of giving money to the [non-Muslim] homeless when there are Muslims here who are suffering and Muslims in Muslim countries who are in even greater need." Another leader remarked, "We just don't believe in interfaith. There's nothing to do but tell them to be Muslim."

A number of variables will be used to analyze responses. One of the most important variables is ethnicity (see table 12.2). Mosques in the United States are mainly dominated by one of three ethnic groups: African American, South Asian, and Arab. The large presence of African American Muslims means that the Muslim view of America is not purely an immigrant

Table 12.2. Mosques Grouped According to Dominant Ethnic Groups

Ethnic Group	Percentage
South Asian	28
African American	27
Arab	15
Mixed evenly South Asian and Arab	16
All other combinations	14

Note: Dominant groups are calculated as follows: 35–39 percent of participants in one group and all other groups less than 20 percent; 40–49 percent of one group and all others less than 30 percent; 50–59 percent of one group and all others less than 40 percent; any group over 55 percent. Mixed groups are calculated as two groups with at least 30 percent of participants each.

view. The differences in opinions between the immigrant and African American leaders are distinct, and because mosque leaders are not completely isolated in their ethnic enclaves, the impact and influence of these differences are felt throughout the Muslim community.

In terms of ethnicity, Arab majority mosques support the idea of community involvement more than any other ethnic groups—90 percent of Arab mosques compared to 80 percent for South Asian and 73 percent for African American (table 12.3). Arab mosques are clearly more outward looking than other mosques.

Looking more closely at African American mosques, a marked difference appears between Muslim American Society (MAS) mosques and historically Sunni African American mosques (HSAAMs). The MAS follows the leadership of Imam W. Deen Mohammed, who became leader of the Nation of Islam in 1975 and transformed it into a mainstream Islamic organization. Imam Mohammed has come to champion patriotism, interfaith dialogue, and working within the system. The HSAAMs are defined as mosques that do not belong to MAS—most of them never were a part of the Nation of Islam. These mosques are a fractured group of mosques that have historically turned away from the syncretism as found in the Nation of Islam and sought a more authentic, normative form of Islam. The HSAAMs have been greatly influenced by the black militancy of the 1960s, and many of them are distrustful of the state, government, and politics. Many of them take the view that the U.S. government and the entire U.S political system are the oppressors and are hostile to Blacks and Muslims. Involvement in government, from their point of view, has won little for poor people and has changed little of the plight of African American people.

A remarkable 93 percent of the Muslim American Society (MAS) mosques strongly agree that Muslims should be involved, compared to 49 percent of HSAAMs (table 12.4). Among HSAAMs, 11 percent of mosque leaders strongly disagree with community involvement. The study, however, also shows that HSAAMs are as involved as MAS mosques in antidrug, prison, and feed-the-

Table 12.3.   Percentage of Mosque Leaders Agreeing/Disagreeing with the Statement "Muslims Should Be Involved in American Institutions," by Predominant Ethnicity

	Ethnicity of Mosque				
Involvement	African American	South Asian	Arab	South Asian and Arab	All Others
Strongly agree	73	80	90	76	68
Somewhat agree	19	18	10	21	30
Somewhat disagree	3	1	0	1.5	2
Strongly disagree	5	1	0	1.5	0

Note: N = 408; statistically significant at the .015 level.

Table 12.4.   Percentage Agreeing/Disagreeing with the Statement "Muslims Should Be Involved"

	Muslim American Society	Historically Sunni African American Mosques
Strongly agree	93	49
Somewhat agree	6	36
Disagree (strongly or somewhat)	1	15

Note: N = 121; statistically significant at the .000 level.

poor programs and other activities of this type. One can conclude that the reluctance of a few HSAAMs toward community involvement is aimed primarily at activities such as interfaith and government-sponsored programs.

The Mosque in America statistics indicate that the more a mosque strongly agrees that the United States is immoral and hostile to Islam, the greater the likelihood that the mosque will be reluctant to approve community involvement. The general logic is that the greater the negative view of America, the greater the tension and consequently the higher the wall around the mosque. Virtually all of the mosque leaders who disagree with the idea of involvement in American society also strongly agree that the United States is immoral and hostile to Islam (table 12.5). Nevertheless, it must be pointed out that the percentage of mosque leaders who disagree with involvement is small and that the majority (60 percent) of mosque leaders who strongly agree that America is immoral still strongly believe that Muslims should be involved.

Another variable used in analyzing responses attempts to measure the level of conservatism/traditionalism in mosque leaders (table 12.6). Three categories are delineated: (1) those who follow the basic texts of Islam (Quran and *hadith,* which refers to the sayings and actions of the Prophet) but are willing to use a contextual interpretation—this group includes a wide spectrum of leaders, some of whom are fairly liberal and the majority of whom stick closely to the classical consensus of the great scholars;

Table 12.5.   Percentage Agreeing/Disagreeing with the Statement "Muslims Should Be Involved in American Institutions," by Agreement with "America Is Immoral"

	Strongly Agree	Somewhat Agree	Somewhat Disagree	Strongly Disagree
Strongly agree	60	85	84	75
Somewhat agree	28	15	15	25
Disagree (somewhat or strongly)	12	0	1	0

Note: N = 397; statistically significant at the .000 level.

Table 12.6. Percentage Giving Each Response to "In Trying to Make Islamic Decisions, Which of the Following Do You Believe Is the Most Proper Approach?"

Response	Percentage
Refer directly to the Quran and Sunnah and follow an interpretation that takes into account its purposes and modern circumstances	71
Refer directly to the Quran and Sunnah and follow a literal interpretation	21
Follow the well-established views of a particular madhab	6
None of the above	2

(2) those mosque leaders who follow a literal interpretation of the Quran and hadith without reference necessarily to the classical legal schools—this group includes those leaders who follow the conservative interpretation of salafi thought, which is found largely in the Persian Gulf region; (3) those who follow one of the classical legal schools (*madhabs*)—they would be considered traditionalists.

Mosques that follow a literalist or madhabi (traditional legal school) interpretation of Islam are less likely to strongly agree that Muslims should be involved (table 12.7). It is interesting to note that, as with the HSAAM mosques, although the more conservative mosques have a greater likelihood of opposing the idea of involvement, in reality they are involved in community service projects to the same extent as other mosques. The problem is again interfaith and government-linked programs. Some Muslim leaders in this group feel very strongly that involvement in the American system is tantamount to supporting disbelief (*kufr*) and therefore prohibited. A flyer entitled "Register to Vote . . . Register to Commit Haram!" and distributed by Hizb al-Tahrir expresses this view:

> Whether it is in the Muslim World or the West, the systems implemented upon the people now are Kufr systems based in beliefs other that Islam. It is beyond argument that the constitution of the USA and the laws and systems emanating from it which are being implemented here are not Islamic. The rulers have no other role except to implement these man-made laws, i.e. the rulings of kufr. In no uncertain terms Allah forbids that in Quran. ("Register" 1999)

Table 12.7. Percentage Agreeing/Disagreeing with the Statement "Muslims Should Be Involved," by Islamic Approach

	Contextual	Literal	Madhab
Involvement			
Strongly agree	85	61	50
Somewhat agree	13	31	46
Disagree (strongly or somewhat)	2	8	4

Note: N = 398; statistically significant at the .000 level.

The positive attitudes toward community involvement are reflected in actual mosque programs. A strong correlation exists between mosque leaders who agree with community involvement and the level of actual mosque activity in the areas of community service and outreach.

In summary, mosque leaders are nearly unanimous in their belief that Muslims should be involved in community service and outreach. The acceptance of involvement is often expressed as an obligation of the Islamic faith—as a command of God. Commitment to the idea of involvement in American society, however, is lessened by a view that involvement is not a priority for the Muslim community at this time. Only a small number of mosque leaders reject the idea of community involvement. Primarily these mosque leaders come from groups that are African American (HSAAM), who strongly feel that America is immoral, and who take a more conservative interpretation of Islam. Even this small number of mosque leaders, however, does not reject all forms of involvement, because their mosques are active in community service activities. Their opposition, therefore, is most likely linked to their rejection of involvement in interfaith and the government-sponsored programs.

COMMUNITY SERVICES

Mosques, like religious congregations throughout the United States, are involved in providing services to their members and the general community. In the Mosque in America study, mosque leaders were presented with a list of possible services and asked whether their mosque provided or cooperated in providing within the past twelve months any of these services. In the FACT study, leaders of all religious congregations were asked a similar question. Table 12.8 gives the responses of mosque leaders and the congregational leaders from the FACT study.

Clearly, mosques in the Untied States are actively engaged in providing social services. Mosques are more than simply a place for worship, as is the case of most mosques in Muslim countries. Mosques in America function more as congregations that attempt to address social and economic needs.

Social assistance forms a major portion of mosque services. Virtually all mosques (90 percent) are involved in giving money to the needy, no matter the ethnicity, mosque location, and mosque size. Undoubtedly, mosque involvement in giving cash assistance is due to the Islamic requirement of *zakah,* a mandatory charity that is given to the poor. Almost every mosque has a box for zakah at the entrance of the mosque, and the poor regularly approach mosques for help. Poor Muslims are largely recipients of these funds, but a larger portion of the funds, in immigrant mosques in particular, goes abroad to Muslim relief projects. Almost in every mosque, a very

Table 12.8. Community Services Provided by Mosques and Other Congregations

Service	Mosques Directly Provided Service	All Congregations Directly Provided Service	Mosques Cooperated in Providing	All Congregations Cooperated in Providing	Total of Mosques* That Provided Service
Cash assistance	84%	65%	9%	22%	90%
Counseling	74%	25%	3%	15%	77%
Prison program	60%	20%	6%	11%	66%
Food	55%	42%	14%	44%	68%
Clothes	53%	27%	11%	29%	63%
Tutoring	28%	15%	5%	9%	33%
Social advocacy (antidrug/anticrime)	18%	13%	14%	12%	32%
Child care	16%	17%	4%	6%	19%
Substance abuse	12%	12%	11%	15%	22%

*Services provided directly by the mosque and/or indirectly by cooperation with another group.

small portion of the funds goes to non-Muslims who happen to come by the mosque or ask for help through a Muslim acquaintance.

About two-thirds of mosques are involved in distributing food and clothing to the poor. Mosques located in towns and small mosques have fewer food and clothing programs. Mosques located in suburbs and city neighborhoods (not inner-city neighborhoods) and large mosques have more such programs. Ethnicity here is not a factor. These two services—food and clothing—are often organized in mosques in response to an overseas crisis, such as the crises in Bosnia, Kosovo, and Palestine. Few mosques have a regular functioning food bank or thrift shop. More frequently, mosques might occasionally collect food and clothes to be stored until there is a need for them. Again, these services are aimed primarily at needy Muslims, but at times non-Muslims do benefit, especially in the few mosques that have functioning food banks and thrift shops. Many mosques simply cooperate with other organizations (44 percent of mosques did so in clothes and 29 percent in food) by collecting clothes and food and then donating them to the Salvation Army or similar organizations.

Counseling, especially marital counseling, is a regular duty (burden, many imams would say) of mosque leaders—over three-fourths of mosques do some form of counseling. Counseling services are offered at a higher rate in mosques that are African American, large, and suburban or urban, but not inner-city. However, few if any non-Muslims receive counseling through these services. A handful of mosques, such as the Milwaukee Dawah Center, are associated with a Muslim-run family service office, which offers a wide range of social services to community people.

Other social services are less frequently offered—one-third of mosques provide some form of tutoring, and only about one-fifth provide child care. African American mosques have the highest rate of involvement in tutoring (47 percent), while Arab mosques are most involved in day care (30 percent). City mosques, whether located in the inner city or an urban neighborhood, are more involved in tutoring than mosques located in suburbs or towns, but inner-city mosques have the highest rate (26 percent) of child care programs. These two programs include more non-Muslims than other programs. Tutoring is often established in conjunction with a local community program or with the mosque's Islamic school, and non-Muslim students also benefit. Child care programs, although largely Muslim, attract many non-Muslims.

Community activism is a significant part of a mosque's community services. A remarkable two-thirds of all mosques have a prison visitation program. Almost one-third have participated in social advocacy programs such as antidrug or anticrime programs. More than one-fifth are involved in substance abuse programs. By far, African American mosques are more involved in all three of these services than the mosques of other ethnic groups. Many African American mosques, located in urban environments, have a strong record of involvement in efforts to rid their immediate neighborhood of crime and drugs. The well-publicized program of Masjid al-Taqwa in cleaning up the drugs in its Brooklyn neighborhood and the little-publicized effort to end drug trafficking around the small mosque in southeast Raleigh, North Carolina, are examples of numerous programs in which mosques are involved. As noted in the earlier quote of the African American leader, African American Muslims have a strong feeling that the environment around the mosque should be free of crime and drugs.

Mosque size is not related to the rate of involvement in these programs; in fact, smaller mosques, many of them African American, do slightly better than larger mosques in this area. Except for prison programs, urban-based mosques are more involved than mosques in suburbs or towns. These programs in particular impact the wider society outside the mosque and bring Muslims into cooperation with community and governmental institutions.

In comparison to other religious congregations, predominantly Christian, mosques are not lacking in providing community services. Major differences exist in prison services—60 percent of mosques are directly involved in prison programs in comparison to 20 percent of other congregations. Also, mosques are more involved than other congregations in directly providing cash assistance and counseling services. Other congregations are more likely than mosques to cooperate with other agencies or organizations in providing these services. As Muslim social service institutions develop, mosques will undoubtedly follow the practice of allowing other non-Mosque-based groups to provide social services.

Table 12.9.   Number of People Served through Social Service Programs of Religious Congregations

Number Served	Mosques	Other Congregations
0–49	48%	58%
50–99	13%	14%
100–349	25%	21%
350+	14%	7%

Mosques also compare well with other congregations when one looks at the figures for the total number of persons served through these social service activities (see table 12.9).

The focus of this chapter, however, is the involvement of mosques in the American society, so the relevant issue is not so much the social services offered by the mosque but the extent that these services are available to the general American community. One way to judge this is to measure the number of non-Muslims served by mosque activities. The Mosque in America study shows that mosques serve many more Muslims than non-Muslims in their social service activities (table 12.10). The median number of Muslims served is forty-five, and the median number of non-Muslims served is three, which is 6 percent of all persons served. The average number of Muslims served is 203, and the average number of non-Muslims is 35, which is 17 percent of all persons served. Almost half (43 percent) of mosques do not serve any non-Muslims, and only 18 percent serve more than 25 non-Muslims. Clearly, few mosques are oriented to providing services outside the Muslim community.

Another means of gauging the orientation of mosques toward service to non-Muslims is to calculate the percentage of non-Muslims served by each mosque (table 12.11). In other words, what percentage of the total number of people served by the mosque is non-Muslim? The logic is that the percentage of non-Muslims served gives an indication of the mosque's openness to involvement in the general community and the extent to which its services are accessible to non-Muslims.

Table 12.10.   Number of Non-Muslims Served through Mosque Social Service Programs

Number	Percentage of Mosques That Serves This Amount
0	43
1–10	27
11–25	12
26+	18

Table 12.11.   Percentage of Non-Muslims Served through Mosque Social Service Programs

No non-Muslims served	44
1%–49% non-Muslims served	39
50%+ non-Muslims served	16

These figures demonstrate again that a relatively small number of mosques (16 percent) offer services that are oriented equally to Muslims and non-Muslims. The most significant factor associated with services to non-Muslims is ethnicity (table 12.12).

Over one-third (34 percent) of African American mosques serve people of which at least 50 percent are non-Muslims, while only 10 percent of immigrant mosques serve at least 50 percent non-Muslims. All African American mosques do well in this category: although slightly more MAS mosques (38 percent) serve at least 50 percent non-Muslims, the difference between HSAAM mosques (30 percent) is not statistically significant. Clearly, African American Muslims, being converts to Islam, are more open to serving non-Muslims. Many of these African American mosques view their Islamic mission as helping fellow African Americans who are economically disadvantaged.

Mosque location also is correlated with service to non-Muslims (table 12.13). Over one-fourth (28 percent) of inner-city mosques serve 50 percent non-Muslims as opposed to 5 percent for suburbs.

Table 12.12.   Percentage of Non-Muslims Served by Mosque Ethnicity

	African American Mosques	Immigrant Mosques
No non-Muslims served	18	55
1%–49% non-Muslims served	48	36
50%+ non-Muslims served	34	9

Note: N = 413; statistically significant at the .000 level.

Table 12.13.   Percentage of Non-Muslims Served and Mosque Location

	Town or Rural	Suburb City	Downtown or Neighborhood	Inner City
No non-Muslims served	60	59	35	36
1%–49% non-Muslims served	27.5	36	49	36
50%+ non-Muslims served	12.5	5	16	28

Note: N = 372; statistically significant at the .000 level.

Since more social services and community activism are needed in urban areas, urban mosques are better motivated to provide these services. The suburbs are less directly confronted with the typical social problems and therefore are less organized to help non-Muslims. Suburban churches that are socially active often sponsor or cooperate with other social agencies that provide services, largely in an urban setting. For Muslims, such social agencies or programs do not exist in substantial numbers; therefore, suburban mosques cannot easily find means of involvement. Taking into consideration that a large percentage of suburban mosques (84 percent) strongly agree that Muslims should be involved in American society, the challenge for suburban mosques is whether they will develop the motivation and means to support urban social service projects.

Whether a mosque leader's conservatism or literalism in applying Islamic law affects service to non-Muslims is not clearly answered by the Mosque in America study. A mosque leader's literal or contextual approach to interpreting Islam is not correlated with service to non-Muslims. In fact, more mosques that follow a literal, more conservative approach serve a larger percentage of non-Muslims than the mosques that follow a more contextual approach. Based on this finding, one could argue that the Islamic impulse to do good deeds and help the needy regardless of their religion is not seen as incompatible with a more conservative approach to Islam. However, a correlation does exist between service to non-Muslims and whether a mosque allows women to serve on its governing board: 60 percent of mosques that do not allow women on their board do not provide any services to non-Muslims, compared to 38 percent of mosques that do allow women on their board. Table 12.14 gives an indication that strictness, at least when it comes to women, does affect the likelihood of a mosque being involved with the outside community.

Mosque size and the educational level of the imam and the congregation are not correlated with a higher percentage of service to non-Muslims. Larger mosques and higher levels of Islamic education of Imams are also not associated with more programs for non-Muslims. If anything, the trend is just the opposite: many smaller mosques and less educated imams rank

Table 12.14.   Percentage Non-Muslims Served and Whether Women Are Allowed on Governing Board

	Are women allowed on governing board?	
	Yes	*No*
No non-Muslims served	38%	60%
1%–49% non-Muslims served	43%	29%
50%+ non-Muslims served	19%	11%

Note: N = 362; statistically significant at the .000 level.

higher in service to non-Muslims. This phenomenon undoubtedly is due to the fact that African American mosques overall are smaller, and their imams have fewer Islamic degrees.

Another prism for viewing mosque involvement in community services is to look at the number of services a mosque offers (table 12.15). A scale of community service was devised, consisting of seven items: (1) participated in an interfaith social service program; (2) served at least some non-Muslims, which would exclude mosques that served no non-Muslims; (3) provided directly or cooperated in providing anticrime programs; (4) provided directly or cooperated in providing prison programs; (5) provided directly or cooperated in providing substance abuse programs; (6) provided directly or cooperated in providing tutoring programs; and (7) provided directly or cooperated in providing child care services. A mosque that provided at least five of these services would be considered a mosque with high involvement in community services; a mosque that provided two to four of these services would be considered moderately involved; and a mosque that provided no to one service would be considered a mosque with low community service involvement. Table 12.15 shows that almost one-fourth (23 percent) of all mosques have a high involvement in community services. Over one-third (36 percent) have a low involvement, and 41 percent have a moderate involvement.

The strongest correlation with high community involvement is ethnicity of the mosque (table 12.16). Almost half (48 percent) of African American mosques rank high in community service involvement, compared to immigrant mosques, of which only 13 percent are ranked high.

Among the African American mosques, MAS mosques score the highest: 56 percent of MAS mosques are ranked high in community service involvement, as opposed to 36 percent for HSAAM mosques (table 12.17).

Table 12.15.   Community Service Involvement Scale

High (5–7 services)	23%
Moderate (2–4 services)	41%
Low (0–1 service)	36%

Table 12.16. Community Service Involvement Scale by Ethnicity

	African American Mosques	Immigrant Mosques
High (5–7 services)	48%	13%
Moderate (2–4 services)	44%	40%
Low (0–1 service)	8%	47%

Note: N = 400; statistically significant at the .000 level.

Table 12.17.   Community Service Involvement Scale by African American Mosques

	MAS Mosques	HSAAM Mosques
High (5–7 services)	56%	36%
Moderate (2–4 services)	41%	51%
Low (0–1 service)	3%	13%

Note: N = 119; statistically significant at the .027 level.

As might be expected, mosque location is positively correlated to high levels of community involvement (table 12.18). Urban mosques are more involved in community services than mosques in suburbs or towns.

The mosque's sense of vitality, purpose, excitement about the mosque's future, and commitment to social justice are all correlated with community service involvement. The Mosque in America study asked questions about the mosque's sense of vitality in respect to faith, a clear sense of mission and purpose, excitement about the mosque's future, and the commitment of the mosque to social justice (table 12.19). Mosques that scored high on these questions had a greater likelihood to score high on community service involvement. This indicates that mosque leaders view community service involvement as being linked to these four variables.

As in the case of service to non-Muslims, any particular Islamic orientation does not apparently affect community service involvement. Mosques with literal or contextual interpretations have a similar rate of community involvement. However, participation of women on the governing board is correlated with community involvement: mosques in which women are allowed to serve on the board rank higher in community service involvement.

Mosques that have a high level of activity in other areas such as religious programs, political activities, and outreach are more likely to have a high level of community service involvement (table 12.20). Activist mosques are usually active in all areas of mosque endeavors.

Mosque congregational size, income, and paid staff are correlated with high levels of community service involvement, but only if African American mosques are not included in the statistical analysis. The logical assumption would be that the greater the human and financial resources of a mosque, the greater likelihood of community service involvement. However, African American mosques rank high in community service involvement even

Table 12.18.   High Community Service Involvement by Mosque Location

Town	11%
Suburb	16%
City neighborhood	28%
Inner city	29%

Table 12.19.   High Community Service Involvement by Various Variables

High community service by mosque vitality	
High vitality	26%
Moderate vitality	21%
Low vitality	0%
High community service by clear purpose of mosque	
High purpose	31%
Moderate purpose	17%
Low purpose	0%
High community service by excitement about the mosque's future	
High excitement	29%
Moderate excitement	18%
Low excitement	0%
High community service by commitment to social justice	
High commitment	37%
Moderate commitment	21%
Low commitment	0%

though their mosques tend to have small congregations, low income, and no paid staff. Undoubtedly, resources do not limit African American mosques, because of their extraordinary commitment to pursuing social justice and serving the needs of the disadvantaged. When immigrant mosques are viewed alone, higher human and financial resources are correlated with high community involvement: the larger the number of attendees at the Juma (Friday) prayer, the greater the likelihood of high community service involvement (table 12.21). The study also shows that the larger the paid staff, the higher the community service involvement (table 12.22); and the higher the mosque income, the higher the community service involvement (table 12.23).

Judging from these last three tables, a clear conclusion is that as mosques grow in size, staff, and income, community services will more likely increase. Because mosques are growing, the logical prediction is that involvement in community services will expand.

Table 12.20.   Mosques with High Community Service Involvement by Other Areas of Masjid Activities

	High-Level Activity	Moderate-Level Activity	Low-Level Activity
Religious programs	35%	16%	15%
Outreach programs	33%	15%	4%
Political activities	45%	23%	10%

Table 12.21. High Community Service Involvement by Juma Prayer Attendance (Immigrant Mosques Only)

	Juma Attendance			
	4–100	101–200	201–500	501 +
High involvement	7%	2%	16%	31%

Table 12.22. High Community Service Involvement by Full-Time Paid Staff (Immigrant Mosques Only)

	Full-Time Paid Staff		
	0 Paid Staff	1	2 or More
High involvement	7%	10%	28%

Table 12.23. High Community Service Involvement by Mosque Annual Income (Immigrant Mosques Only)

	Mosque Annual Income			
	0–$9,999	$10,000–$39,999	$40,000–$99,999	$100,000 +
High involvement	2%	8%	17%	21%

OUTREACH ACTIVITIES

Another area for mosque community involvement is outreach. The Mosque in America study asked whether the mosque participated within the past twelve months in the following activities: (1) visiting a school or church to present Islam, (2) writing or calling the media, or (3) participating in an interfaith dialogue or program (table 12.24). Participation in such activities indicates a mosque's interest and willingness to become involved with American institutions such as schools, churches, and media in order to make clear the message of Islam.

The figures in table 12.24 demonstrate that mosques have a good record in outreach activities. In comparison to all religious congregations of the FACT study, only 6 percent of all congregations were involved in any interfaith programs.

Table 12.24. Percentage of Mosques Involved in Outreach Activities

Visit school or church	71
Write or call media	70
Participate in interfaith dialogue	65

The motivation of mosque leaders for outreach activities includes the strong Islamic impulse to invite others to Islam as well as the perceived need of combating the negative image of Islam in the United States. One mosque leader commented, "We must go out and explain our religion. If we don't, we shouldn't complain about all the misinformation and distortion of Islam that we see." Few mosque leaders would disagree: 92 percent of all mosque leaders report that their mosque stresses the importance of *dawah* (invitation to Islam) to non-Muslims.

It is clear from the comments of mosque leaders that few mosques take the initiative in arranging outreach activities. Mosque participation in these activities is largely a response to invitations from a church, school, media, or interfaith group. Because Islam has become an issue in public discourse, especially since 9/11, mosque leaders are frequently invited to speak on Islam, appear in the media, or participate in interfaith activities. Mosques are obviously responding to these opportunities. Some mosques have committees, but in most, the imam or a few designated persons take the responsibility for participating in outreach activities. Larger mosques often host church or school groups and also receive more attention from the media for photo opportunities and comment on current events. The question of allowing non-Muslim groups in the mosque area is an issue many mosques have discussed. Most mosques have decided to open their doors to non-Muslims.

The ethnicity of the mosque, just as in the case of community services, has an effect on certain outreach activities (table 12.25). African American mosques are more likely to be involved in visits to schools/churches and interfaith programs, but not in writing or calling the media. Within African American mosques, there is a sharp difference between MAS and HSAAM mosques in certain activities (table 12.26).

Table 12.25. Participation in Specific Outreach Activities by Ethnicity

	African American Mosques	Immigrant Mosques
Visit school or church	81%	67%
Write or call media	69%	70%
Participate in interfaith dialogue	78%	60%

Table 12.26. Participation in Specific Outreach Activities by African American Mosques

	MAS Mosques	HSAAM Mosques
Visit school or church	86%	74%
Write or call media	81%	57%
Participate in interfaith dialogue	93%	59%

MAS mosques are extremely active in outreach. Imam W. Deen Mohamed has stressed to his followers the need for involvement in this arena of activity—an arena in which he himself is actively involved. HSAAMs visit schools/churches at a higher rate than immigrant mosques, participate in interfaith work at a similar rate as immigrant mosques, and write/call the media at a much lower rate. Most probably, immigrant mosques participate at higher rates in writing/calling the media because the media views the larger immigrant mosques as a source for comments on international issues such as Palestine, as opposed to the African American mosques, which might be perceived to be unconnected to overseas issues.

To better analyze the data, a scale of outreach activities was devised, consisting of the three activities: visiting a school/church, writing/calling the media, and participating in an interfaith activity. A high level of outreach activity for a mosque is defined as engaging in all three activities; a moderate level is engaging in two activities; and a low level is no activity or one activity (table 12.27).

African American mosques are more engaged in outreach activities than immigrant mosques (table 12.28). Of the African American mosques, MAS mosques are the most involved, undoubtedly due to the emphasis that Imam W. Deen Mohamed places on such activities.

The Islamic approach to interpreting texts is correlated with outreach activities (table 12.29). Mosque leaders who take a contextual approach are more likely to be involved in outreach activities; and those who take a literalist and madhabi approach are less likely.

Whether women are allowed to serve on the governing board of the mosque is also correlated with a mosque's outreach activities: more than two-thirds (67 percent) of the mosques that allow women to sit on their

Table 12.27. Outreach Scale

High (3 activities)	56%
Moderate (2 activities)	21%
Low (0–1 activity)	23%

Table 12.28.   Outreach Scale by Ethnicity

	All African American Mosques	MAS Mosques	HSAAM Mosques	Immigrant Mosques
High level of outreach (3)	70%	86%	50%	51%
Moderate level (2)	17%	7%	30%	22%
Low level (0–1)	13%	7%	20%	27%

Note: Comparing African American and immigrant mosques: $N = 412$; statistically significant at the .001 level. Comparing MAS and HSAAM: $N = 123$; statistically significant at the .000 level.

Table 12.29.   Outreach Scale by Islamic Approach

	Contextual Approach	Literal Approach	Madhabi Approach
High level of outreach (3)	62%	43%	37.5%
Moderate level (2)	19%	26%	25%
Low level (0–1)	19%	31%	37.5%

Note: N = 401; statistically significant at the .004 level.

boards have a high level of outreach activities, in comparison to 31 percent of the mosques that do not allow women on their boards.

Every type of outreach activity is affected by the Islamic approach: literalists and madhabis participate less in every activity than the contextualists (table 12.30). The greatest difference is in interfaith dialogue: 51 percent of literalist/madhabis mosques participate in an interfaith dialogue, in comparison to 71 percent of contextualist. The objections to interfaith include the arguments: interfaith dialogues promote the idea that all religions are one; interfaith dialogues force the Muslim participant to compromise by acknowledging the legitimacy of other faiths; dialogues are used for the political purposes of other religious groups; dialogues are useless because the only goal for a Muslim is to present the truth, not to dialogue about it. Conservatism affects the degree of a mosque's involvement in outreach activities as opposed to community service activities where conservatism has no effect.

Attitudes of mosque leaders toward the United States are correlated to some extent with mosque performance in the area of outreach. Mosques whose leaders strongly disagree with the statement that "American society is hostile to Islam" have a higher outreach index than mosques whose leaders strongly agree with that statement (table 12.31). A strong feeling that America is hostile to Islam apparently leads to greater isolationism and alienation from American society and a reluctance to become involved.

Two important variables that are not correlated to outreach activities are mosque location and mosque vitality. In terms of mosque location, mosques in towns and suburbs are slightly more likely to be involved in outreach activities than urban mosques. Surprisingly, a mosque's sense of

Table 12.30.   Various Outreach Activities by Islamic Approach (percentage of mosques that conducted the activity)

	Contextual Approach	Literal Approach	Madhabi Approach
Visit school/church	75%	63%	50%
Write/call media	74%	61%	50%
Participate in interfaith dialogue	71%	51%	54%

Table 12.31. High Level of Outreach Activities by Statement "American Society Is Hostile to Islam"

	Strongly Agree	Somewhat Agree	Somewhat Disagree	Strongly Disagree
High outreach activities (3)	33%	59%	59%	74%
Moderate (2)	26%	21%	20%	14%
Low (0–1)	41%	20%	21%	12%

Note: N = 403; statistically significant at the .001 level.

vitality and sense of mission and purpose are not associated with a high level of outreach activities. Vitality and purpose, however, were correlated with community service involvement. A possible explanation is that, overall, mosques are not giving outreach activities a high priority in their agenda as opposed to social services. This means that mosques that do have a high sense of vitality and purpose do not devote a lot of energy to outreach activities; therefore, the source of their vitality and purpose is not found in outreach activities.

Mosque size and paid staff are correlated with outreach activities, but only when immigrant mosques are considered and when African American mosques are excluded from the statistical analysis. African American mosques, as with community service, accomplish high levels of outreach activities in spite of not having a large congregation or a paid imam or any other paid staff. Smaller immigrant mosques do quite well in engaging in outreach activities, but the larger mosques with Juma attendance over five hundred (table 12.32) and wealthier mosques with an annual income over $100,000 do the best in outreach activities (table 12.33).

Table 12.32. High Outreach Activities by Juma Prayer Attendance (Immigrant Mosques Only)

	Juma Attendance			
	4–100	101–200	201–500	501 +
High outreach	40%	58%	48%	74%

Table 12.33. High Outreach Activities by Mosque Annual Income (Immigrant Mosques Only)

	Mosque Annual Income			
	0–$9,999	$10,000–$39,999	$40,000–$99,999	$100,000 +
High outreach	35%	39%	51%	73%

A high level of outreach activities in immigrant mosques is not affected, however, by having a paid imam or paid staff. In the case of community service, paid staff is correlated to a higher level of activity. Apparently salaried imams and staff are not involved in outreach activities, and therefore having a paid imam or staff does not give an advantage over mosques without any paid staff. Volunteers largely do outreach activities. Almost all paid imams in this country were trained overseas and are recent arrivals to the United States. Their training does not prepare them to conduct outreach activities, and their newness to America means that they do not know the society and the language well enough to feel comfortable to be involved in outreach activities. Most of these imams were brought to the United States to serve in the traditional roles of imams, which entails leading the prayers and conducting educational programs in the mosque—not doing outreach activities.

CONCLUSION

The vast majority of mosques in the United States have not opted for the isolationist model—there is virtually unanimity among mosque leaders that Muslims should be involved in their local communities. Mosque leaders do not want to see their mosques as sectarian strongholds where Muslims are holed up against the dominant culture. Mosque leaders explain their commitment to community involvement as a fulfillment of their religious duties and as a means of explaining Islam and demonstrating the beautiful face of Islam. Mosque leaders interviewed after 9/11 (the Mosque in America study was conducted before 9/11) have clearly indicated that 9/11 has accentuated to them the absolute necessity for involvement in order to combat the negative images of Islam and protect the Muslim community from attacks and violations of their civil rights. In the minds of many mosque leaders, isolation from American society has been shown to be a dangerous option, because it leaves the mosque vulnerable in crisis situations. Mosque leaders have, therefore, been impelled to become more involved. Three of the mosque leaders, who were part of the follow-up interviews, had actually changed their views about involvement—from an uneasy, reluctant view of involvement to a firm endorsement of involvement.

The few mosque leaders (approximately 4 percent) in the Mosque in America study who do not favor the idea of involvement and are less engaged in outreach activities (mosque community services are not affected) are found primarily among three groups: (1) African American mosque leaders, especially among historically Sunni African American mosques (HSAAMs), who do not trust the government and other religious groups; (2) mosque leaders, who strongly feel that America is immoral and hostile to Islam; and (3) conservative or traditional leaders, who question the Islamic validity of participating in a disbelieving society. Even among these groups, however, only a minority does not support involvement. A very small minority of mosque leaders, therefore, prefer a high-tension relationship between themselves and the public square.

Mosques display their willingness to be involved through their community services and outreach activities. The record, however, is uneven. African American mosques, especially the MAS mosques that follow the leadership of Imam W. Deen Mohammed, are the most active in community involvement and most vocal in support of involvement. In fact, ethnicity is the most significant variable in analyzing the performance of mosques. African American mosques, unlike most immigrant mosques, are extremely committed to the ideal of involvement in American society in order to root out the ills that have plagued African American people. In this regard, MAS mosques are the closest to the "church" type of all the segments of the mosque communities.

In terms of outreach, immigrant mosques and African American mosques perform the same; in terms of community service, however, there are marked differences. Immigrant mosques are engaged in community service, but overall their social services are aimed at Muslims, and as a result they serve few non-Muslims. Thus, while immigrant mosque leaders endorse virtually unanimously community involvement, few immigrant mosques are actually seriously involved in their local communities.

Although desirous of moving past the existing barriers and into the general community, the reality is that most immigrant mosques still live a largely sectarian existence. Like the Catholic Church in the 1800s, it will take time for the immigrant mosque community to feel comfortable in the American public square, and concomitantly it will take time for the dominant culture to accept the uniqueness of the Muslim mosque. However, the situation could change dramatically, if African American mosques, which have few financial resources but a firm commitment to community involvement, develop cooperative relations with the immigrant community, which has much greater resources but little experience. The combination of commitment and resources could catapult the mosques in the United States to a much more significant role in the public square.

Immigrant mosques that do rank high in community involvement are those with large congregations (five hundred and above for Friday attendance), relatively large annual incomes ($100,000 and above), and paid staff. In these mosques, however, salaried imams, who are in almost all cases trained overseas for the traditional role of imam as simply prayer leader, contribute little to community involvement, because they are not trained for such activities. If mosques continue to grow as might be expected based on the Mosque in America study—73 percent of all mosques experienced at least a 5 percent growth in the past five years—the increase of mosque attendance, income, and paid staff should translate into further increase in the quality and quantity of community involvement. In addition, the longer that overseas-trained imams stay in the Untied States and become comfortable with the society and language, and the more that imams are trained here, the greater the likelihood that they will play a dynamic role in increasing the mosque's community involvement. The future of mosque involvement in American society, therefore, appears extremely bright.

REFERENCES

Ammerman, Nancy Tatom. 1987. *Bible Believers: Fundamentalism in the Modern World.* New Brunswick, N.J.: Rutgers University Press.

Bagby, I., P. Perl, and B. Froehle. 2001. *The Mosque in America: A National Portrait.* Washington, D.C.: Council on American-Islamic Relations.

Dynes, Russell R. 1955. "Church–Sect Typology and Socio-Economic Status." *American Sociological Review* 20: 555–60.

Dudley, Carl S., and David A. Roozen. 2001. *Faith Communities Today: A Report on Religion in the United States Today.* Hartford, Conn.: Hartford Seminary.

Husain, Asad, John Woods, and Javeed Akhter. 1996. *Muslims in America: Opportunities and Challenges.* Chicago: International Strategy and Policy Institute.

Hunter, James Davison. 1983. *American Evangelicalism: Conservative Religion and the Quandary of Modernity.* New Brunswick, N.J.: Rutgers University Press.

Johnson, Benton. 1963. "On Church and Sect." *American Sociological Review* 28: 539–49.

Leckie, Robert. 1970. *American and Catholic.* Garden City, N.Y.: Doubleday.

Linkh, Richard M. 1975. *American Catholicism and European Immigrants (1900–1924).* New York: Center for Migrations Studies.

O'Dea, Thomas F. 1966. *The Sociology of Religion.* Englewood Cliffs, N.J.: Prentice Hall.

"Register to Vote . . . Register to Commit Haram!" [1999]. Walnut, Calif.: Khalifornia.

Stark, Rodney, and William Sims Bainbridge. 1985. *The Future of Religion: Secularization, Revival and Cult Formation.* Berkeley: University of California Press.

Troeltsch, Ernst. 1931. *The Social Teaching of Christian Churches.* New York: Macmillan.

Weber, Max. 1946. *From Max Weber: Essays in Sociology.* Ed. and trans. Hans Gerth and C. Wright Mills. New York: Galaxy.

13

Governance in Muslim Community Organizations

Iqbal J. Unus

THE GROWING COMMUNITY

The Muslim community in the United States has grown in number and in strength in response to each catastrophic event it has faced over the centuries. It began with the few who ventured to the New World on their own initiative as traders and navigators, perhaps as early as the seventh century, and others who sailed with Christopher Columbus. It continued with centuries of involuntary migration from West Africa, via the slave trade, that separated hundreds of thousands of Muslims from their religion and culture and subjected them to inhumane oppression. Furthermore, the Muslim community in the United States developed through waves of immigrants, mostly as laborers in American factories or on American farms, in search of the promise of a better life after the economic and political devastation of their homelands during World Wars I and II.

In this same period, waves of American citizens, many of them disenfranchised and disadvantaged but somewhat conscious of their Islamic roots, sought self-identity and dignity through pseudo-Islamic and nationalistic movements in an America burdened with racism, intolerance, and ignorance. Despite the fact that both "indigenous" and "immigrant" Muslims were scattered widely in the land, and there was only restricted early contact between them, Islam resurged and replanted its roots in American soil. Over time, both groups established several houses of worship and community organizations that offered service and support to their members.

The resurgence of Islam as a religion in the United States became more publicly evident as Muslims began to come into their own in the early 1960s and 1970s. The watershed event of the 1960s was the establishment of the Muslim Students Association (MSA) of the United States and Canada by foreign and immigrant Muslim students. The watershed event of the 1970s was the proclamation by Imam Warith Deen Muhammad, which brought the Nation of Islam into the fold of mainstream Islam. Later, Imam Muhammad nominally disbanded what became the "mainstream" American Muslim Mission and adopted the role of a teacher and role model for American Muslims. This event spurred the emergence of a more integrated Muslim community in North America, with both indigenous and immigrant Muslims coming closer together in houses of worship and local community activism.

Thence, every decade has brought forth its own challenge. In the 1980s, the Iranian revolution brought Islam into focus and made it a subject of interest among Americans. In the 1990s, the Gulf War made Islam a household name, almost synonymous with CNN. In 2001 the destruction of the World Trade Center in New York has spurred such curiosity about Islam that bookstores have found it difficult to keep related books in stock. As each event phased in, Muslims first braced themselves for the inevitable and unwarranted backlash, and then found within themselves new strength and pride in their own identity. More significant, as each catastrophic event unfolded, a multitude of persons of other faiths or no faith found the end of their spiritual search by accepting Islam. Today, besieged and berated, the Muslim community is on the verge of becoming the second largest faith group in the United States. Over 1,600 Muslim community organizations (MCOs) and Islamic centers dot the landscape from east to west and north to south. Several thousand small and large Muslim businesses serve all types of customers; more than 150 Islamic schools operate on full-time basis; and dozens of professional, educational, and service organizations, as well as advocacy groups, offer Muslims the promise of a brighter future.[1]

Historically speaking, at the local level, MCOs were set up among largely immigrant communities to act as a "line of cultural defense" in response to social incidents, such as the death of someone in the community and the subsequent need for a grave plot. Sometimes it was the realization of the lack of availability of Islamic education that called for setting up a weekend school, primarily focused on keeping children from breaking away from the Muslim community.

Syrian and Lebanese Muslim immigrants who settled in the U.S. Midwest led the establishment of the International Muslim Society, later renamed Federation of Islamic Associations of the United States and Canada (FIA), on June 28, 1952.[2] The FIA sought to establish a national organization that could bring together local Muslim organizations in North America; offer education in areas of spiritual, social, and cultural development within the framework of Islamic principles; and take initiatives in promoting better understanding between Muslims and the larger society. Even though the FIA's early success was restricted to organizing annual conferences, new leadership gradually emerged from among American-born and American-educated Arab Muslims, resulting in an increased sense of identity and community among American Muslims.

In the early 1960s, Muslim students coming to the United States from abroad had increased in number, and several Muslim student associations were organized on university campuses. Active student leaders from these local organizations soon recognized that a student organization was needed at the national level to coordinate activities and further their services and outreach. This led to the establishment of the MSA in January 1963. The MSA uniquely represented the diversity and internationalization of Islam. Islam was seen as an ideology, a way of life, and a mission. The organization was not considered simply as a way to serve the community but as a means to create an ideal community and serve Islam. A large number of local community organizations of today owe their emergence to students graduating from college campuses and from campus-based organizations. College students who settled down in communities to raise families provided the incentive and energy to organize groups of Muslims in their areas to provide for the fulfillment of worship and communal needs. This phenomenon was augmented by other college students who mobilized community groups out of their zeal for planting roots of Islamic presence in American soil. Many of these groups found their national home in the Islamic Society of North America, which grew out of a maturing MSA as the 1980s began.

During this period, another stream of Islamic consciousness, winding its way through a number of short-lived experiences, had found its direction in the establishment of Darul Islam.[3] This movement sought to provide services to the community through various departments, called ministries, of defense, finance, education, external affairs, social services, and so forth. With a rapidly growing membership, overwhelmingly among African Americans, Darul Islam became the most prominent indigenous Sunni organization in America in the 1960s. However, its community base split after a scholar/activist arrived from Pakistan, and many members deserted Darul Islam to follow him instead. On the other end of the ideological spectrum in the 1960s came the Ansarullah organization. It stressed communal living, trying to accommodate in one package black nationalism, radicalism, and Islam. The Islamic Party came on the scene in 1972, but its success in the United States was short-lived.

Earlier, Elijah Poole had developed the so-called Lost-Found Nation of Islam in the Wilderness of North America into a hierarchic structure with strongly centralized leadership, anchored by an ideology based on God-given dignity and self-worth of the African American people. The founding of this movement in Georgia in 1930 had been preceded and perhaps influenced by the establishment of the pseudo-Islamic Moorish Science Temple by Noble Drew Ali in New Jersey in 1913 (which declined over the next two decades). As the last quarter of the twentieth century neared its midpoint, Elijah Poole's nationwide movement, then changed and known as the American Muslim Mission under the leadership of Warith Deen Muhammad, effectively dissolved itself in 1985, urging its local community members to join the general Muslim community.

This brief narration of Islamic growth in the United States is intended to be neither comprehensive nor complete. It is only intended to touch on the diverse facets of the Islamic experience in this country. Many of these varied historical experiences remained quite isolated from one another. Nonetheless, they form the background of present-day MCOs. Some of these experiences were oriented to a consultative form of governance, while others were rooted in charismatic and situational leadership. In either case, decidedly enthusiastic and sometimes chaotic activism often took the center stage. The search for stability in leadership and governance in MCOs continues to be an ongoing venture.

THE NATURE OF MCOs

MCOs are part of what is generally referred to as the "voluntary sector" or "civil society." They are defined by an institutional identity and structure. They are independent of any public governmental unit, and they control their own affairs. They do not return any profit to their members or managers and are largely dependent on their ability to attract voluntary contributions of time and money. As religiously motivated and oriented organizations, MCOs form a subset of the broader sector of voluntary and philanthropic activity in American society.

The process of founding, developing, enhancing, and maintaining local MCOs is slow at best and chaotic at worst. The process is initially challenged by apathy among those who may eventually become stakeholders as members and beneficiaries. It is also hampered by mistrust of the initiators who may seem to be too hasty or ambitious. Yet, as the process unfolds, prospective stakeholders begin to exert their influence, as individuals and as groups, and extract what they come to expect as their rights. A balance is eventually struck, and the organization embarks on its way in an environment of respect, loyalty, and service.

MCOs are generally the result of individual entrepreneurial initiatives. Some individuals sense needs related to the growing presence of Muslims in their locality and join together with other interested individuals to form a group in an attempt to fulfill these needs. The initial and primary needs tend to be collective worship, socialization of children, and preservation of cultural identity. These needs grow into establishing relationships with others and then becoming involved in social and political life of the community at large. In this process, a formal organizational structure begins to take shape, and necessary steps are taken to establish a legal and civic presence for the emerging group.

Another pathway to the establishment of MCOs is as branches, chapters or affiliates of national organizations that already exist, such as the Islamic Society of North America, the Islamic Circle of North America, or the American Society of Muslims. More common to college campuses than to other communities, this pathway is chosen by local social entrepreneurs with the encouragement or direct help of national organizations.

Other MCOs have grown out of a commitment to do social good by a founder or founders. Sometimes, a social service project has drawn committed volunteers who then feel the need to institutionalize their project by establishing a community organization.

TYPES OF MCOs

For the purpose of understanding the nature of MCOs, it is appropriate to group them into at least four major categories (though only organizations of the first type are the subject of the present study). These categories are worship and community, welfare and relief, research and professions, advocacy and issue-oriented.

Most MCOs belong to the first category, worship and community life. They may be called by a number of different names, such as Islamic Association of Northern Texas, All Dulles Area Muslim Society, Indianapolis Muslim Community Association, or Mississippi Muslim Association. They operate and are based at institutions that may also be called by a number of different names, such as Masjid al Fajr, Muslim Community Center, or Islamic Center of Richmond. Often, the parent organization and the institution it operates are the same, and one name serves both. In any case, these organizations and institutions derive their membership from the local community in their neighborhood, and their daily program is centered around Friday prayers and other obligatory congregational services. They place much emphasis on children and adult education as an investment toward developing the community. Lately, such MCOs have directed much effort and resources to reaching out to people of other faiths. In the process, they have shed their insular nature in favor of an openness that would have been considered uncharacteristic not long ago.

Welfare and relief organizations may be associated with a community organization or may be independently active within a community, such as Islamic Relief Worldwide. While they solicit funds from the community for their projects, they are generally not membership organizations with an elected leadership. Their programs focus on relieving hardship among distressed people around the world. So far, only a few direct their resources and efforts to needs within America.

Research institutions and professional bodies may be also affiliated with local or national organizations or be independent, such as the Association of Muslim Social Scientists. These institutions are relatively more isolated from the community and attract members or fellows with specialized interests. In recent years, there has been an increase in the number of think tank–type of organizations addressing issues that have broad implications for the Muslim community in North America, such as the Center for the Study of Islam and Democracy. These institutions are not founded or operated around the general concerns that are characteristic of local community organizations.

Advocacy and issue-oriented organizations at the local community level are more likely than not affiliated to national organizations with dedicated leadership committed to a well-defined and focused agenda. The Council for American-Islamic Relations, the American Muslim Council, and American Muslims for Jerusalem are such organizations. They depend on local community support but do not normally engage in local community activity, even though at times they may champion grassroots issues.

GOVERNANCE AND MCOs

Regardless of how MCOs come into being, they have begun to place good governance at the top of their concerns today. It is an agenda item at board meetings as well as general assembly gatherings. As membership grows, activities increase, and financial resources are stretched to their limits, members and leaders look for better ways to run the organization. Accountability becomes more of a challenge, which then leads to the question, Who does what and how? This leads to a discussion of the structure of the organization and how and whether its various components interact, or do not interact, with one another, which in turn bring into play the principles and practice of governance in the operational documents of these organizations. Thus, these questions and the desire to better organize lead to one important solution: good governance.

Why is the study of governance so important for MCOs in North America? For one, the quality and strength of these organizations are directly related to good governance. Good governance can ensure the most effective and efficient use of financial and human resources, which are always in short supply. Good governance can also ensure involvement of all sectors of the widely cosmopolitan membership of the Muslim community, thus promoting the cohesiveness and communion necessary for concerted action. No characteristic of MCOs is more critical than unity of purpose within local, regional, and national Muslim communities, and no factor can encourage and enhance that unity of purpose more than good governance. Good governance is generally the most important item on the agenda of any community organization that seeks to make a wider and more lasting impact on the civic scene than has been the lot of the Muslim community thus far.

GOVERNANCE IN PRACTICE

The *American Heritage Dictionary* defines *governance* as the "act, process, or power of governing." *Webster's Revised Unabridged Dictionary* defines it as the "exercise of authority." Other definitions include "to control actions or behavior," "to make and administer public policy," and "to direct and control . . . either by established laws or by arbitrary will."

The principal instruments of governance for nonprofit organizations are the articles of incorporation, equivalent to a charter authorizing the organization to function as such, and the bylaws. *Merriam-Webster* defines a *bylaw* as "a rule adopted by an organization chiefly for the government of its members and the regulation of its affairs." Other definitions include "a law or rule governing the internal affairs of an organization" and "a secondary law."

The governing and operational documents of most MCOs are similar to those of nonprofit organizations in general. These include the articles of incorporation, referred to as the constitution by some organizations, and the bylaws. Some organizations have a constitution that is separate, but not much different in content, from the articles that they are required to submit to the state for incorporation purposes. The bylaws, in either case, detail the provisions of the articles or constitution and determine more clearly how the organization operates.

Successful operation of a community organization, however, depends on more than the mere existence of governing documents. The principal forces that drive the organization toward success are respect for the governing documents and transparency in their implementation. Ignoring the articles or the constitution can lead to unfavorable consequences brought about by the state. More important, ignoring or misinterpreting them or the bylaws can lead to a breakdown in trust between the leaders of the MCO and members and supporters. This is indeed a more serious consequence, because at the end of the day, community organizations are groups of people who have voluntarily joined hands in a spirit of mutual trust. Without that trust, there is little to hold them together. Thus, when community organizations allege loyalty to their governing documents but do not actually operate in compliance with them, they are likely to suffer from internal squabbles, lack of commitment, and gross ineffectiveness.

The institutionally effective way to strengthen an MCO, and indeed the entire community, is to upgrade its capacity to govern itself. At a minimum, this implies that elected leaders and executive staff must be accountable to the general membership or its representatives, decision making must include effective participation by those so charged, and a system of evaluation and control must prevent possible misuse or misbehavior with regard to human and financial resources.

Governance in MCOs is also related to the mind-set and the cultural ethos of Muslims in the community. Muslims have migrated either from societies that have lived under many decades, and sometimes centuries, of foreign rule, or have "migrated" from a different religious worldview. In either case, there is no specific living tradition of Islamically motivated self-rule to fall back on and to form the bedrock for organizational behavior. Therefore, in preparation for a discussion of governance in MCOs, one needs to review basic ideas that define the Islamic perception of the political process that informs governance in a Muslim society.

THE ISLAMIC POLITICAL PROCESS

The primary role of a Muslim state, as a political institution in a Muslim society, is the fulfillment of the goals of Shariah distilled from the teachings of the Quran and the Sunnah. The primary characteristic of a Muslim state is its ability to realize this role, regardless of the form of its organizational structure. While this is an extensive subject, we will refer here to only two of the major concepts that underlie the ability of a Muslim state to realize its role: *ummah* and *Shura*.

The concept of *ummah* as a community of believers is the central concept in Muslim political thought.[4] This concept functions as a symbol of cohesion as well as a source of cohesiveness. The Quran uses the term *ummah* in a general sense as equivalent to words that refer to nations, tribes, religions, and groups. The Constitution of Medina, written under the guidance of Prophet Muhammad (pbuh), used the concept of ummah to refer to a confederated community of Muslims, Jews, and others, as well as an alliance for defense. In this sense, individuals in the ummah are not tied to one another on the basis of race or blood relation but on the basis of their faith in the One God.

More specifically, the Muslim ummah is a community of believers whom the Quran describes as the best ummah and one that follows a middle path. A *hadith* (teaching) of the Prophet (pbuh) describes it as a single body with parts that strengthen each other. This solidarity of the ummah overrides all other concerns and aspects of collective and organizational life, including political authority. Thus, while it may be desirable but not necessarily possible to maintain political unity, the ummah continues to exist in the minds and hearts of Muslims regardless. Among Sunni Muslims, the ummah is considered as the only successor of the Prophet (pbuh), with *ijma* (consensus of the knowledgeable) being the vehicle for codifying the Will of God into Shariah law.

The Islamic political process requires that "political institutions are structured in a way that makes them best suited to the promotion of the underlying central values" and "any form of government where authority of *shari'ah* is supreme is the required Islamic state."[5] According to this view, acceptable political norms or practices, not conformity, are the basis of legitimate governance. As a result, many Islamic political entities can exist as part of the ummah, and many different forms of governance are acceptable so long as they respect basic principles. Thus, "the minimal requirement for an Islamic state was . . . rule according to *Shari'ah*."[6]

The mantle of leadership in the Muslim polity is conferred by the community through a process of nomination and confirmation. While nomination may be entrusted to a select group, each member of the community has equal weight in the confirmation process. The leader and the led then enter into a compact through an oath of allegiance to the office and the community. While the methods of election may have varied historically among the Khulafah (Rightly Guided Successors of the Prophet), the basic tenet of transfer of governing authority through free elections remains true.

Both concepts—ummah and shura—are central to the organizational structure of MCOs. Effective governance in MCOs hinges on membership and participation based on the commonality of faith and values, not on ethnic or linguistic affiliations. Effective governance also depends on the willingness of members and leaders to engage in mutual consultation in making decisions and electing leaders. All MCOs in the sample incorporate these basic concepts in their bylaws to one degree or another.

Effective governance in MCOs also depends on how leadership is practiced. While this is not the place to discuss the complex subject of leadership, it is appropriate to refer to the Quranic advice to Prophet Ibrahim (pbuh) about leadership succession and to the articulation of his own responsibilities by the first Kahlifah Sayiddina Abu Bakr (RA). These two items point out the underlying principles of leadership in the Islamic framework as relevant to our discussion about MCOs.

The Quran clarifies the question of leadership succession through the example of the Prophet Ibrahim (pbuh).

When his Lord put Ibrahim to test in certain things and he fulfilled all of them, He said, "I am going to make you the leader of mankind." Ibrahim asked, "Does this apply to my descendants also?" He replied, "My promise does not apply to the transgressors." (Al-Baqarah [2]:124)

Allah SWT (the Most Glorious and Most High) offered leadership to Ibrahim (pbuh) only after he had passed certain tests, asserting that leadership is based on qualifications and has to be earned. Leadership must be earned again by the leader's progeny if they qualify for it. Thus, there is no place in Islam for passing on leadership to one's chosen successors, related by kinship or any other relationship, without a due process of testing and qualification. Each circumstance demands a new process of nomination, qualification, and election of the leader.

On the occasion of his installation as the first *khalifah,* Abu Bakr (RA) stated his policy in a sermon, as follows:

> O People! Even though, I am not the best of you, I have been given the responsibility of ruling you. I will consider the weakest among you strong until I claim for them whatever is their due. And the strongest of you I will consider weak until I have taken from them whatever is due from them. O People! I am the follower [of the Prophet], not an innovator. So, if I do well, assist me! And if I deviate, straighten me out! And reckon with yourself before you are taken to reckoning! No people ever abandoned jihad in the way of Allah except that Allah afflicted them with disgrace! And never did an obscenity appear among people except that Allah caused disaster to spread among them! Then obey me as long as I obey Allah! But if I disobey Allah or His Prophet, you owe me no obedience! I really prefer that another of you should have been given (and thus spared me) this responsibility! And if you expect to assume the same role as the Prophet in relation to Wahy [revelation], I cannot do that. I am only human, so make allowance for me. (Kanz al 'Ummal III 130–135)[7]

This sermon lays down some basic principles of leadership and governance in Islamic practice. Among many other significant points, the sermon emphasizes that leadership is conferred by others based on qualification and not simply assumed by someone based on some advantage, that the just rights of all people must be secured, that followers and leaders must work together, that leaders must hold themselves accountable to followers, and that leadership is a delegated task, with Allah (SWT) as the real Sovereign. When translated into the parlance of MCO bylaws, the sermon advocates a governance model that calls for popular elections with nominations open to all qualified members, fair grievance procedures to ward off dissension or misuse of authority, "participative" bylaws to practice shura and cooperation among all sectors of membership, and checks and balances among decision-making units to ensure accountability to themselves, their members, and the Muslim public.

THE HISTORICAL PRACTICE OF ISLAMIC GOVERNANCE

American MCOs often operate comprehensive community centers with facilities and services ranging from prayer rooms to weekend schools and sports fields. Whether they are called *masajids,* Islamic centers, or community centers, they are generally registered under relevant laws of the states in which they operate and are characterized by governing mechanisms typical of not-for-profit organizations founded for charitable purposes.

Even though MCOs are registered as religious organizations, they differ considerably from other religious organizations such as church organizations. The primary differences in the structure, governance, and leadership of church organizations and MCOs arise from the absence of religious hierarchy in Islam. While many MCOs are affiliated with organizations operating at the national level, they are not part of any ecclesiastical chain of command, as are churches normally. In developing local leadership and in shaping local policies, MCOs are independent except when they willingly enter into collaborative or cooperative endeavors with their local, regional, or national counterparts or partners. In essence, an MCO is a voluntary organization of members who determine how it should be governed and nonmembers who are generally welcome to its services without having a say or even an interest in its governance.

Just as a "back-home" mentality has influenced the Muslim perspective in other walks of life in America, many MCOs have sought to transplant ideas and structures from the cultures of their members' origin to the American environment, usually with very restricted success. However, some MCOs have seriously examined the historical roots of leadership and governance in Islamic experience. They have sought harmony between the Islamic experience and the legal and cultural ethos of contemporary social environment. I have briefly discussed earlier the theoretical characteristics of Islamically oriented governance. Historically speaking, the practice of an Islamic form of governance and administration has been characterized by three essential elements:

- The Islamic system has willingly assimilated foreign ideas and institutions that it encountered as it spread beyond its origins, as long as such institutions and their modus operandi did not come into conflict with basic Islamic values.
- God-consciousness and the resulting moral ethos have underpinned administrative and governance behavior of leaders and functionaries at all levels under the guidance of the Prophet and the Rightly-Guided Caliphs. This has led to a strong sense of accountability—what we would consider equivalent to a system of checks and balances in contemporary parlance.
- Consensus and independent reasoning (*ijma* and *ijtihad*) that springs from human experience have enriched decision making, as long as such decisions were beneficial to the people and promoted the goals of Shariah, avoiding any situation that contradicted direct commandments of the Quran and the sunnah. This judicious use of consensus

and independent reasoning, based on knowledge and wisdom, has allowed Muslims to develop systems more in tune with the needs of the time and place than would be the case otherwise. "Knowledge," the Prophet has reportedly said, "is the lost camel of a Muslim. He takes it wherever he finds it."

EFFECTIVE BOARDS

The business of governance is to steer, guide, direct, control, and influence actions that ensure that the organization carries out purposes for which it was established in a responsible and accountable fashion. As opposed to the private sector, which exists to produce a profit for the owner, and the public sector, which exists to serve the public good, the nonprofit (or voluntary) sector exists to serve a social purpose or cause directed by scientific, educational, religious, or charitable considerations.

A board of directors or trustees sets organizational direction by defining the organization's vision, mission, and values. The organization's mission deals with the reason for the organization's existence and is a concise expression of what the organization wants to be and for whom. Its vision is a verbal picture of the organization's desired future and is an expression of where it wants to go. Its values are personified in the organization's code of ethics.

The board sets major goals and defines strategies to get there. It assesses the organization's strengths and takes advantage of opportunities that may present themselves. It ensures that resources, such as funds, expertise, information, leadership, and time, are available to turn the organization's vision into reality.

The board provides supervision over all aspects of governance and administration and is accountable to the members for so doing. For example, financial supervision includes making a realistic financial plan for income and revenues, for cash flow and reserves, for internal controls and audits, and for compliance with the approved budget. The board also manages risk to the organization by acting to safeguard the organization's mission and guard against loss of financial, human, and "goodwill" resources.

The board monitors the implementation and evaluation of plans by checking that they are implemented as intended, that results are commensurate with the expenditure of resources, and that the donor's intent is respected if they use designated funds. The board also provides legal supervision over political campaigning and lobbying activities, Internal Revenue Service requirements, civil rights laws, immigration laws, safety issues, and payroll and other tax considerations. If the board does not exercise its fiduciary regulation, it may be liable in a court of law.

The board generally appoints and evaluates the chief executive officer, whether called a director or an imam, who in turn is accountable to the board (since the board personifies the organization). The board also assesses itself as to how it is performing by determining whether it is effective in making decisions, communicates with internal and external stakeholders, exerts itself to accomplish results as planned, and operates in compliance with the budget.

Individual members of the board are goodwill representatives of the organization but carry no special authority or power unless the board delegates it to them. They agree to carry out responsibilities and are authorized to make decisions as a board in full.

The board is legally protected if it carries out its three principal duties: care, loyalty, and obedience. Duty of Care means that the board stays informed, asks questions, reads materials, and participates in deliberations. Duty of Loyalty means that the board is faithful to the organization, is committed to its welfare, does not derive personal gain or gain for the benefit of someone related, and discloses any potential conflict of interest. Duty of Obedience means that the board is faithful to the mission of the organization.

The role of the chief executive—whether he or she is administrator, manager, executive director, general secretary, or imam—in the governance of the organization is to share with the board the mutually defined responsibility for organizational leadership. The board neither micromanages nor is detached from the chief executive. While the board has the ultimate power, the chief executive has immediate power to act, is accountable to the board, usually has more information than the board has, and exercises greater day-to-day influence.

A well-functioning board that operates effectively and efficiently has the required information, knowledge, and skills. It is reasonably sized, generally between five and seven members. It is composed of members who represent the community, possess useful talent, and demonstrate commitment to the job. In the interest of maintaining stability, and continuity, the board seeks balance in its decisions, fresh insight into situations, new energy and skills, and ongoing connections with stakeholders. Finally, it has a set of clearly defined roles and responsibilities.

To ensure an effective decision-making process, board meetings are carefully planned and structured. In order that meetings are efficiently conducted and time is well spent, members have an agenda and background material, work through committees, and have access to relevant information and knowledge. They exercise teamwork and communication skills, and they meet periodically as required—four to six times a year may be typical. Such boards effectively serve the public good with authority and accountability, while seeking the pleasure of Allah.

In its essence, nonprofit law requires that a nonprofit organization function in the best interest of its members, in the effective pursuit of its declared purposes, and in compliance with the legal statutes that govern organizations of its kind. Members of the board of directors or trustees have a fiduciary obligation to ensure that the organization functions in that manner. This becomes even more important for individual board members who must establish new dynamics when they come on board to replace retiring members.

One of the most important duties of the board is to ensure that tax returns and annual reports are prepared properly and filed on time. As a corollary, the board is also responsible for making sure that the organization's activities do not violate the organization's tax-exempt status. This calls for a periodic review of all activities by competent lawyers advising the organization. The organization's board must also determine which staff member or elected leaders may speak for the organization, and which of them may be authorized to legally bind the organization in any contracts.

THE STUDY

A report issued in May 2001, based on a study of mosques in America, has noted the accelerated growth of institutions of Islamic worship and community life during the last third of the twentieth century. According to this report, fully 62 percent of all mosques, about 1,600 according to some estimates, were established in the 1980s and 1990s.[8] During the last few years, the number of participants has increased at over three-fourth of all mosques, with suburban mosques registering larger increases. Besides regular prayers, most mosques are involved in outreach activities for peoples of other faiths, assistance to the needy, and children's education. The report also notes that leadership in these mosques does not appear to be highly formalized or bureaucratic. A majority of these institutions are led by volunteers, while decision-making authority rests with a board of directors or an executive committee. Generally, women are allowed to serve on boards. The picture that emerges from this report is one of a growing Muslim presence in America seeking its moorings in emerging institutions that anchor its worship and community life.

The present study focuses on MCOs functioning at the local level in Muslim communities across the United States. Starting with somewhat simpler organizational structures in the 1960s and 1970s, these organizations have evolved into their present organizational shapes over time. While early community organizations were driven more by individual initiative, charismatic leadership, or even adventurism, today's MCOs have become more structured, membership driven, and service oriented. Much of this transformation has to do with the changing legal landscape for volunteer organizations in general. Nonprofit law today demands greater transparency in making decisions, increased accountability in managing funds, and an enhanced focus on the declared mission of the organization. Furthermore, in communities with a major presence of Muslims who have migrated from around the world, governance styles have become influenced by the more open and egalitarian ethos of American society. In communities with a significant presence of Muslims who have reverted to Islam, the end of de jure segregation as a result of civil rights struggles of earlier decades has diminished the motivation to insulate the community from the outside. Both phenomena have led to nearly the same result: that of MCOs becoming somewhat more functional elements of the mainstream volunteer sector and worship communities that constitute the mosaic of American civil society.

This study is based on operational documents in place at MCOs, as opposed to how the provisions of such documents are perceived or implemented by members and leaders of these organizations. This is an important distinction because compliance with written bylaws is not a strength of many an MCO, just as it is an issue with many other organizations in the volunteer sector. Furthermore, not all MCOs have the benefit of professional legal advice when crafting their bylaws. Often, bylaws are written by well-intentioned community leaders who may focus more on warding off problems they see in the immediate future at the expense of a long-term view. They may not be fully cognizant of the dynamics of institutional decision-making processes essential to the robustness of their organizations.

It is important to note that this brief study is only the starting point of a fuller study of the organizational structure of MCOs. A more in-depth study will be expected to yield a better understanding of policy formation and decision making in MCOs. Such understanding will motivate realignment of the organizational structure to institute better processes in governance and subsequently help MCOs function more effectively in fulfilling their mission in the Muslim community at large. Enough anecdotal evidence is available to suggest that there is much room for improvement, but no data have been established yet in this respect. A great deal of work needs to be done in order to identify the underlying ideological currents and informal mechanisms that supplement and either strengthen or weaken the formal structures and processes documented in bylaws. The diversity of Muslims as to their ethnic, cultural, and experiential backgrounds gives their MCOs a unique character that may not be normally encountered in a study of nonprofit organizations in the faith-based volunteer sector.

This study began with the collection of bylaws from a variety of organizations. Bylaws of eighty-two MCOs were obtained. Of these, sixty-two bylaws were selected, studied, and analyzed for this study. They constitute the study sample referred to elsewhere in this chapter. While it does provide a broad understanding of issues involved in governance of MCOs, this study is only a first attempt and makes no claim of being a comprehensive research effort. Since there is no known published study on this subject, the only claim that I make is that of pioneering an effort that must be pursued by scholars and students of Islam and Muslims in America to understand how Muslims govern themselves in this segment of the American faith-based volunteer sector.

Increasingly, MCOs are reaching out both to the noninvolved parts of the Muslim community as well as to communities of other faiths, with enhanced volunteerism and greater confidence in their own capacity to do so. Almost as a matter of necessity, they have begun to appreciate the role of good governance in turning restricted resources into impressive results.

As would be expected, bylaws included in this study exhibited much variety in structure and presentation, from the very brief and simple to the very detailed and complex. All bylaws were reviewed, and selected items of information were identified and tabulated. The tabulated data were analyzed for frequency of identified parameters that reflect the characteristics of governance. These items included information about each organization's name, location, membership requirements, governing body size and election, general election and appointment procedures, quorum requirements, dismissal provisions, voting procedures, and miscellaneous information. Selected information was arranged, grouped as required, and charted as appropriate. As expected, MCOs exhibited a wide spread in the values of some parameters and conformity in the values of others.

The final examination of the data was restricted to the following elements of governance: (1) whether there is one level or two levels of governance; (2) what the size of the higher governing body is; (3) what its quorum requirements are; (4) how the lower level of governance (executive committee, in most cases) is elected; (5) what the nature of the organization's membership is; (6) what the restrictions on membership are; and (7) what the voting qualifications are. The study did not examine additional elements of governance such as meeting procedures and responsibilities of officers.

GOVERNING BODY LEVELS

Boards of trustees or directors, and executive committees, form the bulwark of the governance structure of most MCOs. In some cases, the board performs policymaking and oversight functions, while the executive committee, with members from within or outside the boards, carries out executive responsibilities. In other cases, only one body is responsible for both aspects of governance. It makes policy and executes it, while the oversight function is performed by the general assembly of all members meeting periodically. Among MCOs in the sample under study, there are many variations of the relationship between these two bodies, how either of them is formed, and how either functions.

Of all MCOs in this sample, less than one-half (45 percent) are governed by one governing body. In some cases, this governing body is titled the board of directors or trustees; in other cases, it is called the executive committee. In either case, it is responsible for policymaking, for general supervision, as well as for the operation of the organization's programs and services. More than one-half of all organizations (55 percent) have a second level of governance, generally in the form of an executive committee, which basically runs the organization and reports to the first level of governance, which is the board of directors or trustees (see figure 13.1). Two levels of governance are generally motivated by a desire to protect the organization from sudden changes in leadership, to check misuse of authority, or to accommodate representation of community interests. Generally, the first objective is achieved by staggered elections of officers and board members, the second objective is achieved by instituting a chain of approval, and the third objective is achieved by including ex officio members in the governing body.

Most MCOs emphasize Islamic conduct as essential to qualify for board membership, but not all specify that qualification in the bylaws. However, one MCO that does state qualifications also requires that a nominee not be "an active position seeker." The same MCO requires its election process to "request three members to volunteer themselves to be present during all executive committee meetings and assist the committee. They shall not take part in decision making."

The role of the imam is a source of much discussion and contention in

One-Level and Two-Level Governance

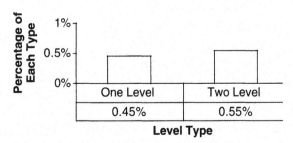

Figure 13.1

many MCOs. In a few cases, the imam is an institution in himself. In other cases, he is a functionary subject to the institutional decision-making process. In yet other cases, he is a partner in governance as well as an adviser. The first, but minority, view of the imam's role is exemplified by one MCO's bylaws, which state that "[t]he imam's position is a permanent position. He will be elected only once (for life) by the General Body (the Ummah) in an open election immediately after the Juma prayers." (The parentheses in this quote exist in the original document.) The imam is accepted in this case as a leader free from accountability to the congregation, a concept at odds with the practice modeled by Sayyidina Abu Bakr when he said in his first sermon after his election, "So, if I do well, assist me! And if I deviate, straighten me out! . . . Then obey me as long as I obey Allah! But if I disobey Allah or His Prophet, you owe me no obedience!"

Typical of a different perspective on the role of the imam is the provision in another MCO's bylaws that define its governing body as consisting of "seven voting members and the imam. The imam shall be a non-voting member." It defines the imam's responsibilities as providing "spiritual leadership and guidance in matters of fiqh. Details of his duties will be included in his contractual agreement." In another MCO, the imam is a voting member of the executive committee in which decisions "shall be conducted by Mutual Consultation (Shura)." This MCO requires that the imam "shall implement" the Quran and the Sunnah and "provide spiritual guidance and leadership." The role of the imam in other MCOs falls all along the spectrum of views between imam as an institution and imam as a staff person.

An overall review of the governing board's responsibilities leads to the general inference that, by and large, MCOs use a consultative process to make decisions. This inference is in agreement with the earlier cited study on mosques in America, which concludes that a "consultative council" makes decisions in 59 percent of all mosques, an imam has authority to make or influence decisions in 28 percent of mosques, whereas other leaders are the final decision makers in the remaining 13 percent of mosques.[9]

SIZE OF BOARD

The size of the higher MCO governing body varies between three and nine members. In some cases, this body is called the board of trustees or directors; in other cases it is called the executive board or executive committee. In only 9 percent of the cases, its size is ten members or greater. There is no case of a governing board smaller than three members. Many states require a board to be composed of three or more members. Within the major group of three to nine members, a slightly higher number of governing bodies have a size of six to nine members. These data indicate that seven members may be considered to be the typical size of the highest governing body of an MCO (see figure 13.2).

Since the board is a deliberative and consultative body, size does impact how effectively it functions. A smaller board may make decisions more quickly than a larger board. On the other hand, a larger board may bring into discussion more points of view from members representing more perspectives on the issue at hand. Thus, decisions of a larger board are likely to be better thought out and more acceptable to a greater number of stakeholders affected by such decisions. The process of decision making may take longer in larger boards, but that disadvantage has less to do with size than with procedures. If a larger board works through standing and functional committees and regulates discussion through rules of order, it can make decisions as efficiently as a smaller board.

To think through an issue, brainstorm about it, and ferret out all possible pros and cons of a prospective decision, a board with only three members seems rather small. If the chair decides to hold out till the end, one member could be weighing against only one other. A five-member board offers a better opportunity for debate and discussion, if all members are present. However, a seven-member board, even in the absence of two members and with quorum established by a simple majority, has enough members to present diverse points of view to make a reasoned decision. A seven-member board also offers the opportunity to have various groups of members-stakeholders represented at the highest policymaking level in their organization. Thus, the finding that the governing board of a typical MCO has about seven members is encouraging.

Besides their size, MCO boards exhibit a few other interesting features. In a rather unusual case for American MCOs, one MCO specifies, "The President of the Corporation must be indigenous of the Western Hemisphere."

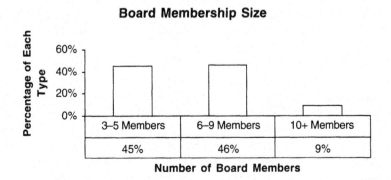

Board Membership Size

Number of Board Members		
3–5 Members	6–9 Members	10+ Members
45%	46%	9%

Figure 13.2

This president, who is the chief executive officer of the corporation and oversees the board, "may veto any resolution set forth by the Board." This is rather unusual for MCOs. However, "The Executive Board may override any veto with a two-thirds (2/3) vote." Veto provisions are found in only a few other MCOs. Another MCO places no limits on the term of board members, who "shall hold office as long as the member is in good health, living a sound Muslim life and performing well within the capacity of a Board member." They should, "preferably, be married adults, preferably with children in their care." Conditions for membership in this MCO are "attending regular meetings, functioning within guidelines of what is required by our faith, and having honorable reputations."

GOVERNING BODY ELECTIONS

In the case of two-level governance, a board of directors or trustees is assisted by an executive committee. The relation between the board and the executive committee depends on how the executive committee is elected and what role it plays in governance.

Two main types of executive committees emerge from this study. The first type of executive committee is composed simply of officers of the organization acting as a committee of the board, even if they are not designated as such in the bylaws. The second type of executive committee is a committee of officers and additional members who are generally chairpersons of major committees of the organization. Either type of executive committee may be elected by the general assembly of members, by the board of directors, or by a combination of the two. The executive committee may function independently of the board, with reporting procedures defined in the bylaws, or may function simply as a committee of the board under the latter's direction.

In the vast majority of MCOs that have both a board of directors and an executive committee (62 percent of all MCOs), officers and members of the executive committee are elected independently by the general assembly of members eligible to vote (figure 13.3). In about one-quarter of cases (24 percent), officers or members of the executive committee are elected by the board of directors or trustees. A few MCOs (6 percent) have procedures that result in a combination of the board and third parties (such as affiliating national organizations) electing their executive committees. Executive committees in the remaining MCOs (8 percent) are made up of a combination of elected and appointed members, including officers and committee chairs, who are elected by the general assembly or the board or appointed by the board. Such executive committees may also include imams, who may also be elected or appointed.

Executive Committee Elections

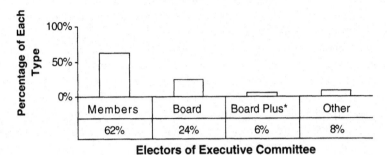

*The Board Plus column identifies the electors as members of the board plus national affiliating bodies.

Figure 13.3

QUORUM REQUIREMENTS

There is no significant variation among MCOs with respect to requirements for establishing a quorum for meetings of their governing bodies or the general assembly (figure 13.4). In almost 80 percent of cases, the presence of a simple majority of membership is sufficient to establish a quorum in a meeting of a governing body such as the board of directors or the executive committee. The remaining 20 percent of the MCOs require a higher percentage of membership, up to 80 percent in one case, to be present to establish a quorum in these bodies. With a typical board of seven members, four members must be present to conduct official business. However, an increasing number of boards are using electronic mail communication

Quorum Requirement for Board Meetings

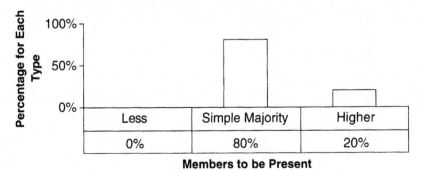

Figure 13.4

to discuss and decide issues that cannot wait for the next meeting. Electronic mail is more economical than telephone conference calls in terms of cost and time involved, and it also automatically creates a written record of motions, discussion, and votes cast.

To establish a quorum in a meeting of the general assembly, almost one-half of all MCOs require the presence of one-third of eligible members (figure 13.5). Those requiring a greater number or a smaller number are split equally among the remaining one-half of all MCOs, with each case applicable to a quarter of all MCOs. The highest quorum requirement is two-thirds; the lowest is one-tenth. These quorum requirements seem to conform fairly to normal practice in nonprofit organizations. In case of not meeting quorum requirements in the first instance, normal procedure allows a second meeting without the need for a quorum. However, most MCOs consider achieving a quorum in a general assembly meeting a test of their viability as an organization that deserves the trust of its members.

Description of quorum requirements in MCO bylaws vary from basic statements to ones with additional conditions. One MCO places fairly strict conditions on how a quorum may be established, requiring "at least four of the five members of the Governing Body" to be present and "One of them has to be the President or the Vice President." An interesting variation on quorum requirements, which emphasizes the role and responsibility of a governing body, is the provision of an MCO that "[o]ne-third of the total number of members, including two-thirds of the executive committee, shall constitute quorum to have a meeting of the General Assembly."

Quorum requirements do not generally attract the attention of directors, trustees, or officers until major contentious issues are being debated in the board or the general assembly. However, being mindful of the quorum in all deliberations, including those via the telephone or electronic mail, is the

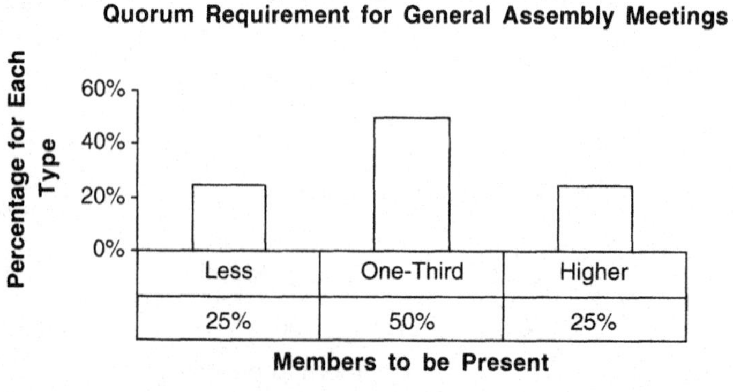

Figure 13.5

hallmark of good decision making. It is also a preventive measure against future legal and ethical problems.

NATURE OF MEMBERSHIP

MCOs face a unique challenge in forging membership policies and offering membership services. Due to the nature of its mission, an MCO and its facilities are open to all Muslims, especially for ritual worship. The worship facilities attract not only those who are committed to the organization but many more who are merely interested in using the facilities. When MCOs pursue aggressive membership development, they may attract a large number of members who expect services without making any commitment to the organization. As a result, many MCOs have put in place certain qualifications for membership, which vary in degree from one MCO to another.

These conditions and qualifications of membership are treated in MCO bylaws in a variety of ways, sometimes quite complex and confusing. In some cases, this is achieved by referring to a preamble to the articles of incorporation or the constitution, which defines the nature of the organization. Most preambles are simple statements of faith, while a few are quite elaborate with appropriate Quranic references. All of this is indicative of the perceived need to protect the organization by restricting membership to those who may have the best interest of the organization at heart. In addition, either to maintain the purity of their organization or to preempt any attempt by unwelcome individuals or groups, many MCOs attempt to define within their bylaws who they accept as a Muslim for the purpose of membership. One MCO delegates this responsibility by stating, "Any person who claims to be Muslim and belongs to a faith which is not recognized as such by Rabitat al-Alam al-Islami (Muslim World League) is not eligible for membership." However, MCO bylaws are usually silent on how a restrictive provision may be implemented or defended if challenged.

Other examples of membership conditions and qualifications are as follows:

- "All Muslims . . . in good standing within the Muslim community . . . are eligible for membership." In this case, the provision of "good standing" is subject to interpretation by the executive committee. Furthermore, in this particular case, members of the board of trustees are also selected on the basis of "commanding the respect of the community." Since board members can be replaced by three-fourth of the general assembly, how to interpret "commanding the respect" can be quite contentious. This MCO also allows the board to dissolve the executive committee if they "have violated the principles of the Quran,

Sunnah, or [its] constitution," giving rather broad uncontestable discretion to a three-member board.

- Members will "have the belief of Ahl-al Sunnah, fulfill all Islamic obligations, not commit any Big Sins (Kaba'er), and abide by this constitution." The constitution further states that its general assembly will consist of "all concerned members," leaving undefined who "concerned" members might be.

- Active members, who must receive the "endorsement of one of the members and two executive committee members . . . will be asked to come to the prayer frequently."

- An active member should "commit himself to follow the Qur'an and the Sunnah" and "actively participate in the activities" of the organization. In this case, the only difference between an active member and an associate member, who is not allowed to vote, is that the "Associate Membership is for those who are absolutely unable to actively participate due to extensive travel, work schedule, or long distance." Even with these concessions, "An Associate Member shall not be eligible to vote in the elections . . . if he has been absent . . . for more than six months."

- An interesting distinction between regular and voting members is spelled out in one MCO bylaw in the following way: Regular members are "Muslims who attend and support . . . regularly but who are not interested in the process of its organization." Voting members "shall be regular members who participate in the process of organization and are registered as voters."

- Most MCOs restrict membership to those who live in their geographic jurisdiction, but at least one MCO allows the right to vote and be nominated to the governing body to a person who is either "a resident or *employed* in an area within the jurisdiction" of the organization (italics added).

- A common example of membership restricted mainly by residency requirements is an MCO in which "Active Membership" is open to "all Muslims having at least permanent U.S. residency and six months residency in the State." This MCO defines Muslims as those "who believe in Qur'an and Sunnah," in contrast to many other cases in which more restrictive definitions apply for the purpose of membership.

- A member can be "conditionally suspended" for violating Islamic practices when such acts can be "defined as major sins by the Shar'iah." Such a member can be considered for reinstatement after the member "has guided himself to the right conduct."

- Membership can be revoked if the "[m]ember has knowingly given false information on his/her membership application."

- Occasionally, a different kind of restriction applies to participation by women in the MCO's business. The executive committee of an MCO "is a body of six brothers." This MCO has a "Women's Affairs Committee" for which "election shall be by female members . . . only." The Women's Affairs Committee "in consultation with the Executive Committee, shall appoint a brother to act as a liaison between them. Direct communication . . . can occur when the need arises for it." However, another MCO requires that the "nominee for Women's Affairs Coordinator," who acts as a "liaison between the Executive Committee and women members of the Association," shall be "a female member."

- Several MCOs have established arbitration procedures to constrain disputes from spilling over into the legal domain. Such procedures generally call for a panel to review a case and reach a binding decision. A few MCOs actually make acceptance of an arbitration procedure a formal requirement for approval of a membership application.

As is obvious from these examples, the nature of membership varies from one MCO to another. To analyze this variation, as well as to assess the involvement of their local community, we have grouped MCOs into three broad categories of membership: open, restricted, and closed.

In the case of open membership, bylaws do not stipulate any specific conditions of membership. Organizations with open membership are open to all Muslims as defined in the essentials of Islamic belief. It is expected that a prospective member believes in and practices Islam, but no questions are asked as a condition of membership. The bylaws do not indicate whether the applicant's claim should be verified and whether such verification is enforceable.

In the case of restricted membership, bylaws may specify certain constraints as a condition of membership. Such constraints include demonstrated practice of Islam and regular participation in the organization's activities. Organizations with restricted membership may also require prospective members to meet other criteria and restrictions. An example of such restrictions is that "only brothers" may be members, or only "those who come to the mosque frequently" may become members. In most cases, however, members are subjected to such additional restrictions only when voting.

In the case of closed membership, the MCO has no provision of accepting members from the general Muslim public. Closed membership means that for all practical purposes membership is by invitation only.

Among selected organizations, in the sample of sixty-two organizations under review, whose bylaws clearly stated requirements for membership, a little over one-half (52 percent) may be classified as organizations with membership open to all Muslims. A little less than one-half (47 percent) of all organizations can be said to offer only restricted membership, requiring applicants to believe in and practice Islam and demanding active participation in the organizations. Closed membership is a rare occurrence, with less than 2 percent of organizations adopting that practice (figure 13.6).

It is important to state that these categories are being used only for the purpose of getting a general sense of how MCOs view membership involvement. Additional factors must be considered to truly designate an MCO to be open, restricted, or closed as a membership-based organization. In general, it is obvious that a person intending to become a member of an MCO will be Muslim and believe in, and practice, Islam. However, MCOs that have written these requirements into their bylaws face the possibility, when challenged, of having actually to examine whether a member does believe and does practice Islam to the satisfaction of the MCO. Whether such MCOs offer open or restricted membership will then depend on whether they accept or reject members who do not meet their standards of belief and practice.

Openness is the general trend in membership qualifications in MCOs across the United States, even though anecdotally one hears complaints of restrictions and limitations placed on community members joining their local organizations. Generally, MCOs want more members to increase revenues and to enhance the potential for regular income. They achieve the security and stability of their organizations by establishing criteria that would favor the election of caring leaders with demonstrated experience and commitment to the organization.

RESTRICTING FACTORS

As noted earlier, almost one-half of all MCOs in the sample require additional qualifications for regular active membership. These qualifications covered a wide spectrum of conditions, from being a U.S. resident to believing in Islam. In considering whether membership was restricted or

Membership Types by Conditions and Qualifications

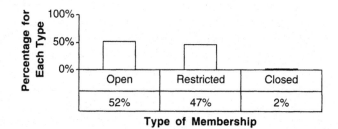

Figure 13.6

open, we examined requirements in the bylaws related to age, dues, agreement with views of the organization, participation in the organization's activities, and local residency. Five factors qualified for inclusion in this study of restricted membership versus open membership. The most common restrictive factors in order of frequency (from lowest to highest) are residence in the United States, participation in the organization, practice of Islam, belief in Islam, and references (figure 13.7).

Of those MCOs that place restrictions on membership, only about one-sixth (15.2 percent) report restricting membership to residents of the United States. Twice as many of them (30.3 percent) place restriction on membership based on references provided by current members and subsequent approval by a governing unit. About one-fourth (24.2 percent) of them allow membership only to those who participate in the organization's activities. A little less than one-third (30.3 percent) of them grant membership only to those who profess belief in Islam, and almost an equal number (27.3 percent) place restrictions based on the prospective members' practice of Islam.

Review of these restrictive factors indicates that the variation in qualifications and procedures for membership among MCOs are quite striking. The openness of one MCO in the Midwest that allows all Muslims to become members, whether they pay membership fees or not, is contrasted with the restrictions of another in the Rocky Mountain states that gives election rights only to "brothers who come frequently" to the mosque. Another MCO is open to all Muslims, but only members "observing Five Pillars" are allowed to vote. Another MCO in the Midwest uses a gradual approach, initially allowing all Muslims to become members. Then, members who pay dues become associate members. Associate members, who have a tenure of one year and are approved by the executive committee, become active members entitled to vote and hold office in the society. Nonetheless, the general trend is to open up as much as possible with increasingly more stringent qualifications required for voting in elections or being elected to

Figure 13.7

offices. While in some cases such restrictions originate in the founders' desire to control the affairs of the organization, in most cases restrictive bylaws are based on the perceived need to protect the community's interests. This is a critical concern in communities with sizable real estate and other assets, and those in which bylaws and policies grant somewhat unchecked authority to an organization's leaders.

While it is common to terminate membership of board members who do not attend a number of board meetings, one MCO demands active participation by the organization's members also. For example: "All members are required to attend 2 out of 3 meetings. All excuses for absence must be approved by the executive committee in advance, or their membership will be terminated."

VOTING QUALIFICATIONS

Many organizations restrict members from voting for a certain period of time. Among MCOs whose bylaws stipulate such a restriction for the exercise of voting rights by members in good standing, this period varies from six months to three years.

For example, among organizations that place specific limitations on voting privileges, a little over one-half (55 percent) will not allow members to vote until after three months or six months of membership (figure 13.8). Members in a little over one-quarter of all organizations (27 percent) will have to wait for a full year before they can vote, whereas two years will be the waiting period in a little over one-sixth (18 percent) of all organizations with specific waiting periods in their bylaws.

An interesting restriction on voting privileges comes from an MCO that re-

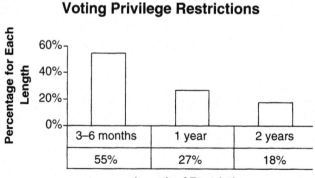

Voting Privilege Restrictions

	3–6 months	1 year	2 years
	55%	27%	18%

Length of Restriction

Figure 13.8

quires that amendments approved by its governing body be "submitted to the General Body (the Ummah) after the Juma prayer (Friday prayer) for final approval." (Parentheses are included in the original text.) The requirement that elections and amendments be put to vote immediately after Friday prayers is perhaps meant to reinforce the idea that "Active Members" are those who fulfill their Islamic obligation to offer Friday prayers. However, this condition all but disenfranchises those who have to rush back after the prayer or pray at other mosques due to their work schedule or location.

MEMBERSHIP AGE

There is very limited variation in age requirements for membership among those organizations whose bylaws do specify an age for membership. Only about 25 percent of the MCOs in the survey sample state a specific age to qualify for membership. A few others use general terms, such as *puberty* and *adult*, to set age limits for memberships. Organizations stating a specific age are divided almost equally between those requiring members to be eighteen years of age and those that allow sixteen-year-olds to become members. At least one MCO allows fifteen-year-olds to become members. A few MCOs have a formal youth membership, but by and large most MCOs have organized separate youth groups that cater to young adults between the ages of twelve and eighteen.

LEADERSHIP AND MCOs

The MCO is the focal point of the community for those who frequent it as well as for those to whom it is only a symbol of their identity. The quality of its governance reflects the quality of the community it serves as well as its place in the life of the community. For this reason, it is important to examine the prevailing practice of leadership in MCOs, assess its weaknesses, and offer solutions. Such an examination is a suitable subject for a future study; here a few comments will suffice.

In most cases, an MCO is the primary institution in the community where people come together only on the basis of their Islamic identity. They expect it to function on that basis, as distinguished from the basis on which they function in the world outside the MCO. Often, this dichotomy makes them see the principles and practice of governance to be different in their two worlds. As such, leaders and followers in the MCO are unable to exercise effective leadership and followership, even if they do so in their respective stations in life on the outside.

To remove this dichotomy, it is important that a Muslim perspective on leadership and governance, encompassing contemporary concepts within an Islamic worldview, be presented and applied in an effective way. The Islamic worldview being a comprehensive one, all that is truly good in contemporary leadership must be Islamic in its essence. What is needed is to discover the Islamic roots of contemporary leadership and governance concepts, and to develop a Muslim perspective that can enhance the quality of governance in the MCO as an institution in North America.

One of the most critical aspects of governance, and one that should distinguish MCOs from other similar organizations, is ethical conduct. The issue of ethics is deceptively simple on the surface, but quite complex in its application to conflict and divergence within an MCO and its community. Ethics is also an important issue with respect to legal and moral requirements of operating an organization in good standing in the society at large. While many MCOs have some kind of rules for resolving differences, very few have written guidelines for ethical conduct. This omission springs primarily from the simplistic notion that everyone will behave with the proper Islamic etiquette. Furthermore, the inability to include all cases of conflict and dissension in their bylaws discourages MCOs from including any ethical guidelines at all. A solution lies in adopting a separate "charter of ethical conduct" that can be referred to in the bylaws and can be updated by a designated committee as circumstances require. Ethical behavior by leaders as well as followers enhances trust, which in turn increases the level of commitment to one another, strengthens the identity of the community, and promotes members' loyalty to their MCO.

The "dominant leader" syndrome is a chronic problem of MCOs. While beneficial and even necessary in restricted situations in early stages of organizational development, this phenomenon saps energy and stunts the growth of MCOs. Oftentimes mechanisms for participation are weak and become weaker in the face of a leader who sometimes seeks and sometimes attracts dependency. The MCO then fails to motivate and inspire involvement by volunteers and community members who do not see a meaningful role for themselves. A major part of the dominant leader phenomenon is simply the inability of the leader to delegate. By failing to delegate effectively, the dominant leader encourages an organizational culture in which initiative is frowned upon and decay sets in. For an organization to function properly, leaders must act as mentors to a second tier of leadership by involving these individuals in decision making through purposeful delegation.[10]

One effective way to make a needs assessment with regard to leadership in an MCO is to conduct periodic governance audits. A governance audit involves examining the constitution, bylaws, policies, procedures, standing orders, board minutes, and other written and unwritten documents that determine how an organization is functioning. Once the audit is completed, the findings can be evaluated in comparison with generally accepted standards for successful organizations. Based on this evaluation, recommendations can be made to make improvements so that performance is significantly enhanced. In a few cases, such an audit can be conducted off-site by mail or phone, but in most cases auditors should visit the MCO being audited to get a sense of its organizational culture.

By and large, there is considerable room for improvement in how MCOs in North America are led, managed, and governed. When we consider the traditional role of an MCO and add to it the expanded role it must play in the contemporary environment, better performance becomes more crucial. The key to enhanced performance lies in enabling MCO volunteer leadership as well as its staff to upgrade their skills and capacity to lead through structured professional development and training programs.

CONCLUSION

Recent events have altered the landscape of the nonprofit charitable sector in America by directing regulatory attention to the governance of Muslim charities. The U.S. Department of the Treasury issued its antiterrorist financing guidelines in 2002 that cover voluntary best practices for U.S.-based charities.[11] The guidelines call for organizations such as MCOs to maintain an adequate governing structure. For one thing, such organizations should adopt and follow articles of incorporation and bylaws that lay down their basic goals and purposes, and define their governing board's composition, election procedures, and responsibilities. The bylaws should spell out financial reporting and accountability procedures. According to these guidelines, the governing board should meet regularly and exercise effective oversight on the organization's operation. It should establish and follow a conflict of interest policy. It should maintain a record of all its decisions and make them available to the public. The guidelines place much emphasis on transparency, requiring that names and identifying information of board members and employees as well as their financial dealings with the organization be made public. The Treasury Department's documents also establish detailed guidelines for the solicitation and distribution of funds and for accountability in financial practice.

This study initiates an effort that is much needed and quite timely. Yet this is a very limited study that points to the need for detailed research and analysis in this area. For example, in studying the characteristics of MCOs, future work should differentiate between MCOs based on various factors such as geographic location, membership size, annual budget, and so forth.

The conclusion that emerges from the study of this sample of MCOs is encouraging to the extent that MCOs do operate within the broad guidelines that would apply to nonprofit organizations in the voluntary sector in the United States. They should be able to meet the Treasury Department guidelines in principle and in practice as long as they are in compliance with their own bylaws and other governing documents. Governance audits are an effective way to ensure continued compliance.

This study finds that some broad general observations can be made regarding various aspects of governance in MCOs, given that they vary considerably from one another in the details. For example, one can say the following about a "typical" MCO:

- A "typical" MCO has a first-level governing "policy" board of seven members. This policy board meets periodically, with a simple majority as a quorum, to (1) set the general direction; (2) create plans, policies, and procedures; (3) supervise financial statements and budgets; (4) manage real estate and other assets of the MCO; and (5) oversee the affairs of the MCO with assistance from, and delegation to, a second-level "working" board and staff. A general assembly of all voting members elects officers of the organization as well as additional members, all of whom together constitute the working board, commonly called the executive committee. This working board (1) administers the affairs of the MCO with assistance from, and delegation to, designated volunteer committees and staff; and (2) represents the organization to its stakeholders.
- Less typical, although present among MCOs, is a "policy/working" board that sets the general direction, creates plans and policies, oversees finances, directly administers the organization, provides volunteer services with the help of other volunteers and staff, and represents the organization to its stakeholders.
- In addition, a "typical" MCO has an open membership policy for all Muslims, with voting privileges afforded to all members after six months of membership. Members can amend their MCO's bylaws with an affirmative vote of two-thirds in a meeting with a simple majority of members constituting a quorum.

Since almost all MCOs are registered with the states in which they operate, state statutes governing nonprofit organizations are in effect when the MCO's bylaws are silent. Most MCOs are registered with the IRS as charitable organizations under the Internal Revenue Code 501(c)3 or are members of a group registered under that code. In either case, their bylaws must and do include purposes consistent with that designation.

NOTES

1. Ihsan Bagby, *The Mosque in America: A National Portrait* (Washington, D.C.: Council of American-Islamic Relations, 1999).

2. Yvonne Haddad, "A Century of Islam," Islamic Affairs Program, Middle East Institute, Washington, D.C., 1986.

3. Sulayman S. Nyang, *Islam in the United States of America* (Chicago: ABC International Group, 1999), 145.

4. Khalid I. Jindan, *The Islamic Theory of Government According to Ibn Taymiyyah* (Washington, D.C.: Georgetown University Press, 1979), 134.

5. Jindan, *The Islamic Theory of Government*, 117.

6. John L. Esposito, *Religion, Politics, and Society* (Syracuse, N.Y.: Syracuse University Press, 1998), 31.

7. Hisham Altalib, *Training Guide for Islamic Workers* (Herndon, Va.: International Institute of Islamic Thought, 1996), 59.

8. Ihsan Bagby, *The Mosque in America* (Washington, D.C.: Council of American-Islamic Relations, 1999).

9. Bagby, *The Mosque in America*.

10. Rafik I. Beekun and Jamal Badawi, *Leadership: An Islamic Perspective* (Beltsville, Md.: Amana, 1993), 93.

11. U.S. Department of the Treasury, "Anti-Terrorist Financing Guidelines: Voluntary Best Practices for U.S.-Based Charities," 1999.

Index

About the Contributors

Mumtaz Ahmad is president of South Asian Muslim Studies Association, editor of *Studies in Contemporary Islam*, and professor of political science at Hampton University.

Taha Jabir Al-Alwani is president of the Graduate School of Islamic and Social Sciences, Leesburg, Virginia and also president of the Fiqh Council of North America.

Zafar Ishaq Ansari is director of the Islamic Research Institute, Islamabad, Pakistan and editor of *Islamic Studies*

Ilyas Ba-Yunus is professor of sociology at State University of New York at Cortland.

Ihsan Bagby is associate professor of Islamic studies at the University of Kentucky and author of *The Mosque in America: A National Portrait* (2001).

Aminah Beverly McCloud is professor of religious studies at DePaul University and author of *African American Islam* (1995).

Zahid H. Bukhari is director of Project MAPS: Muslims in American Public Square and fellow of the Center the Center for Muslim-Christian Understanding at Georgetown University.

Sylviane A. Diouf is a researcher at the Schomburg Center for Research in Black Culture and author of *Servants of Allah African Muslims Enslaved in Americas:* (1998).

John L. Esposito is university professor and founding director of the Center for Muslim-Christian Understanding: History and International Affairs, at the Edmund Walsh School of Foreign Service at Georgetown University.

Sherman A. Jackson is associate professor of Islamic studies at University of Michigan.

Omar Khalidi is an independent scholar at the Aga Khan Program for Islamic Architecture at MIT.

Kassim Kone is assistant professor of anthropology at State University of New York at Cortland.

Ali A. Mazrui is director of the Institute of Global Cultural Studies and Albert Schweitzer Professor in the Humanities, SUNY at Binghamton, New York. He is also Albert Luthuli Professor-at-Large, University of Jos, Jos, Nigeria, and Andrew D. White Professor-at-Large Emeritus and Senior Scholar in Africana Studies at Cornell University.

M. A. Muqtedar Khan is director of international studies at Adrian College and author of *American Muslims: Bridging Faith and Freedom* (2003).

Mohammed Nimer is principal investigator for the American Muslim Databank Project at the Council on American-Islamic Relations, (CAIR), and author of *The North American Muslim Resource Guide* (2002).

Sulayman S. Nyang is co-director of Project MAPS: Muslims in American Public Square, author of *Islam in the United States* (1999), and professor of political science at Howard University, Washington, D.C.

Jane I. Smith is professor of Islamic Studies at the Duncan Black Macdonald Center for the Study of Islam and Christian/Muslim Relations, co-editor of *Muslim World,* and author of *Islam in America* (1999).

Iqbal J. Unus is director of The Fairfax Institute, a division of the International Institute of Islamic Thought, and a former secretary general of the Islamic Society of North America. He has taught a course on Muslim presence in North America at the Graduate School of Islamic and Social Sciences.